AF479278

Competition Policy and Development in Asia

Also by the Asian Development Bank

Monetary and Financial Integration in East Asia (Volumes 1 and 2)

Poverty, Growth and Institutions in Developing Asia

Managing FDI in a Globalizing Economy: Asian Experiences

Early Warning Systems for Financial Crises: Applications to East Asia

Competition Policy and Development in Asia

Edited by

Douglas H. Brooks
Asian Development Bank

and

Simon J. Evenett
University of St. Gallen

First published 2005 by
PALGRAVE MACMILLAN
Houndmills, Basingstoke, Hampshire RG21 6XS and
175 Fifth Avenue, New York, N. Y. 10010
Companies and representatives throughout the world

PALGRAVE MACMILLAN is the global academic imprint of the Palgrave Macmillan division of St. Martin's Press, LLC and of Palgrave Macmillan Ltd. Macmillan® is a registered trademark in the United States, United Kingdom and other countries. Palgrave is a registered trademark in the European Union and other countries.

ISBN–13: 978–1–4039–9632–9
ISBN–10: 1–4039–9632–6

This book is printed on paper suitable for recycling and made from fully managed and sustained forest sources.

A catalogue record for this book is available from the British Library.
A catalogue record for this book is available from the Library of Congress.

10   9   8   7   6   5   4   3   2   1
14   13   12   11   10   09   08   07   06   05

Printed and bound in Great Britain by
Antony Rowe Ltd, Chippenham and Eastbourne

Contents

Tables

Figures and appendixes

Currencies

End of year exchange rates: Local currency per US dollar[a]

Country	Currency	Abbreviation	1990	1995	2000	2004
People's Republic of China	yuan	CNY	5.2	8.3	8.3	8.3
India	rupee	Rs	18.1	35.2	46.8	43.6
Republic of Korea	won	W	716.4	774.7	1,264.5	1,035.1
Malaysia	ringgit	RM	2.7	2.5	3.8	3.8
Thailand	baht	B	25.3	25.2	43.3	39.1
Viet Nam	dong	D	8,125.0	11,015.0	14,514.0	15,773.0

a   Unless stated otherwise, all dollar values in this book refer to US dollars.

Source: International Monetary Fund, *International Financial Statistics*, accessed May 2005; Datastream, accessed May 2005.

Preface

In 2001, the Asian Development Bank (ADB) approved a technical assistance grant to support a study of emerging trade and integration issues facing developing Asia. Among the issues identified by the study were foreign direct investment (FDI) and competition policy, and their contribution to the development process. Six country studies were prepared on each topic. The volume on FDI was published in June 2004.

This volume is the second output of the research project. The six country studies on competition policy are preceded by a discussion of competition issues, the relationship of competition policy with international trade and investment policies, and its interaction with industrial policies. The final chapter provides a comparative synthesis of the country studies. The aim of this volume is to call attention to the importance of interfirm rivalry as a critical input to the achievement of countries' development objectives.

The country studies cover the People's Republic of China (PRC), India, the Republic of Korea (Korea), Malaysia, Thailand, and Viet Nam. These developing Asian economies were selected for the diversity of their income levels and experience with competition policy, including competition law. Professor Simon Evenett of the University of St. Gallen, Switzerland, provided the overall direction and international perspective. Local researchers with extensive competition policy experience carried out the country studies—Ping Lin for the PRC, S. Chakravarthy for India, Seung-wha Chang and Youngjin Jung for Korea, Cassey Lee for Malaysia, Deunden Nikomborirak for Thailand, and Vu Quoc Huy for Viet Nam. ADB staff, government officials, and staff of multilateral development banks participated in the study's mid-term and finalization conferences in

Manila in May and July 2004. In particular, useful comments were received from Ying Qian for the study on the PRC, John Weiss for India, Erlinda Medalla for Malaysia, Douglas Brooks for Korea, Rughvir (Shyam) Khemani for Thailand, and Kenneth Danger for Viet Nam. Valuable input was also provided by Zhang Chenyang of the PRC, Nguyen Viet Hung of Viet Nam, Shaikh Khurshid Alam of Bangladesh, Senileba Waqainabete of the Fiji Islands, Faisal Hasan Basri of Indonesia, Rustam Duspayev of Kazakhstan, Jib Raj Koirala of Nepal, and Muhammad Arshad Parwaiz of Pakistan.

Douglas Brooks of the ADB's Economics and Research Department designed, supervised, and coordinated the various activities of the project. He was competently assisted by Lea Sumulong and Ma. Susan Torres. Jean-Pierre Verbiest gave useful counsel throughout project implementation. Beth Thomson skillfully handled the copy editing of the book with grace, persistence, and patience. Lynette Mallery provided valuable advice on the overall production of the book.

The views and opinions expressed in this volume are those of the authors and do not necessarily reflect those of the ADB or its Board of Directors.

Ifzal Ali
Chief Economist, Asian Development Bank
May 2005

Foreword

Economic theory suggests that competitive forces work best in the presence of free and open markets. This is because free and open markets allow firms to enter and exit industries without restraint. Under these conditions, new and efficient firms are able to enter the market, while old and inefficient firms are able to upgrade or exit. Competition thus creates a conducive environment for businesses to enter and grow while inducing existing firms to continually improve and perform better.

Competition policy is new in many developing countries, as it generally follows changes in the political and economic environment. In the past two decades, many developing countries have adopted market-based reforms and have begun to reduce the extent of government intervention. But the full benefits of an open market economy cannot be realized unless competition restrictions are removed.

Trade, investment, and industrial policies are generally used to promote national development objectives. In so doing, however, competition is often compromised. Imposing high import tariffs to protect domestic import-substituting industries limits competition. Disallowing foreign investors from venturing into sectors reserved for local investors restricts competition. Promoting national champions by granting special privileges tilts the playing field and distorts competition. In these cases, trade, investment, and industrial policies are all intended to contribute to the achievement of the country's development goals, but may have unintended consequences that keep a tight rein on competition. Governments throughout the region have thus been striving to find the right balance of trade, investment, industrial, and competition policies that will maximize the benefits for development.

In today's globalizing world, the development policies of one country will often affect the interests of another country. As a result, some countries favor the establishment of multilateral rules on competition. During the First Ministerial Meeting of the World Trade Organization (WTO) in Singapore in 1996, members established a working group to examine the relationship between trade and competition. Almost a decade later, no agreement has been reached to hold multilateral negotiations in this area. Nevertheless, competition policy is important in its own right. Regardless of whether multilateral rules on competition are ever negotiated under the auspices of the WTO, each country should strive to develop and implement its own competition policy.

Asia is home to countries in varying stages of competition policy development. It is for this reason that the Asian Development Bank (ADB) embarked on this study to analyze country experiences in the search for policy recommendations to help its developing member countries (DMCs) adopt and implement competition policy as an input to the development process. The study is the second volume to come out of a larger research project called 'Regional Integration and Trade: Emerging Policy Issues for Selected DMCs.' It looks at the experiences of six Asian countries and analyzes how the choice of development policies affects the state of competition in each country and how competition contributes to development. The considerable variation in policies and experiences across the countries provides a rich source of information from which lessons and information on best practice can be drawn. The first volume, which dealt with foreign direct investment, was published in June 2004.

This volume is intended for policy-makers and development practitioners, with a view to helping them maximize the benefits of competition policy. It is also intended for scholars of economic development, so that its findings may inform the ongoing development debate. Finally, it is meant to guide ADB operations as regards the importance of competition policy, its contribution to the development process, and its interaction with other policies.

Haruhiko Kuroda
President, Asian Development Bank
May 2005

Contributors

Douglas H. Brooks, Asian Development Bank, Manila, Philippines

S. Chakravarthy, Hyderabad, India

Seung Wha Chang, Seoul National University, Seoul, Republic of Korea

Simon J. Evenett, University of St. Gallen, St. Gallen, Switzerland

Youngjin Jung, Woo, Yoon, Kang, Jeong & Han, Seoul, Republic of Korea

Cassey Lee, University of Malaya, Kuala Lumpur, Malaysia

Ping Lin, Lingnan University, Hong Kong, China

Deunden Nikomborirak, Thailand Development Research Institute, Bangkok, Thailand

Vu Quoc Huy, Ha Noi National Economics University and Institute of Economics, Ha Noi, Viet Nam

1

What is the relationship between competition law and policy and economic development?

Simon J. Evenett

1 INTRODUCTION

What possible contributions to economic development can the appropriate enforcement of competition law make? What harm could result from such enforcement? These two questions are uppermost in the minds of many policy-makers, analysts, and scholars as they debate the merits of introducing and then implementing national competition laws. Now that, according to some counts, nearly 100 nations—many of which are in the Asia-Pacific—have adopted competition laws, one might have thought this debate had been won by the advocates of such legislation. However, both supporters and opponents are well aware that the effects of competition law can be neutralized or offset well after the enactment of legislation, by denying the relevant enforcement agency the resources, the freedom, and the political support to complete its assigned functions. Therefore, the debates over the merits of competition law continue and the objective of this chapter is to state and evaluate the many ways in which fostering interfirm rivalry can alter different aspects of national economic performance. A number of competing perspectives are discussed in section 3 of this chapter. First, however, the technical nature of the debate over competition law requires clarification of the meaning of a number of important terms used in the existing literature. The pay-off from this is to highlight the important difference between competition law and competition policy, two terms that are frequently confused in policy debates. The next section of this chapter is devoted to such matters and sets the stage for the substantive discussion that follows.

2   THE RELATIONSHIP BETWEEN COMPETITION LAW AND COMPETITION POLICY

Before specifying the means and ends of competition law and competition policy, I introduce some key terms that recur throughout the existing literature on the role of competition law and economic development.

Objectives, instruments, and efficiency

First, it will be useful to distinguish between the *final* and *intermediate objectives* of a state policy.[1] The former relate to the ultimate goal that the policy is intended to achieve and not to some proximate goal. The latter can be some goal, perhaps even an important goal, that must be accomplished before the final objective can be attained. For example, as will be discussed at greater length later, some scholars believe that the ultimate goal of competition policy is to further economic development, and that this can be accomplished through faster economic growth (among other means). The same scholars take the view that raising investment outlays by firms stimulates economic growth and that, using the terminology introduced above, increasing investment expenditures is an intermediate objective of competition policy.[2] Nothing prevents a state policy from having multiple final or intermediate objectives.

The *objectives* of policy are to be further distinguished from the *instruments* that a government has at its disposal to secure those objectives. These instruments include measures that a state, court, or their delegated representatives are empowered to take.

The concept of *efficiency* is widely used in discussing the objectives of competition law and policy and will be used extensively throughout this chapter. Voluntary economic exchange, by definition, involves a purchaser paying an amount for a good that is equal to or less than the most the purchaser would be willing to pay for that item. The difference between the amount actually paid and the most that a customer would be willing to pay is known as the *consumer surplus* of the transaction. Producers, on the other hand, will supply a good if the price they receive from selling it equals or exceeds their incremental costs, and this difference is called the *producer surplus* of the transaction. Adding across all transactions, the individual consumer and producer surpluses yield the sum of the total producer and consumer surpluses of a given market outcome or outcomes. Economists then define a market outcome to be *efficient* if there is no other way to organize the exchanges in the same market so as to increase the sum of the total producer surplus and the total consumer surplus.

The concept of efficiency has both static and dynamic aspects. *Static efficiency* refers to the maximization of the benefits of voluntary exchange at a given point in time, that is, maximizing the sum of producer and consumer surpluses in a given market *at a point in time. Dynamic efficiency* refers to the maximization of the sum of such surpluses *over time* or *over a specific time horizon.* The latter takes account, in particular, of the impact of technical progress, innovation, and investments of various types.[3]

When describing the concept of efficiency, some have found it useful to take another tack and distinguish between four different types of efficiency. Kolasky and Dick (2002), for example, differentiate between allocative efficiency, productive efficiency, transactional efficiency, and dynamic efficiency. In their taxonomy, the first three efficiencies are essentially static in nature. Allocative efficiency is described by them as follows:

> At the most general level, a market is said to achieve 'allocative efficiency' when market processes lead society's resources to be allocated to their highest value use among all competing uses. In the context of market exchanges between consumers and producers, the allocative efficiency principle can be restated more specifically to say that the value of a product in the hands of consumers is equalized 'at the margin' to the value of the resources that were used to produce that product (Kolasky and Dick 2002: 49).

Kolasky and Dick (2002: 51–2) then go on to specify the concept of productive efficiency:

> Production is said to be efficient when all goods are produced at minimum possible total cost. An equivalent way of phrasing the productive efficiency criterion is to say that there is no possible rearrangement or alternative organization of resources (such as labor, raw materials, and machinery) that would increase the output of one product without necessarily forcing a reduction in output for at least one other product. This restatement highlights the principle that firms' choices involve explicit trade-offs between competing demands for scarce resources.

Transactional efficiency is another type of efficiency described by Kolasky and Dick. They note that

> market participants design business practices, contracts, and organizational forms to minimize transaction costs and, in particular, to mitigate information costs and reduce their exposure to opportunistic behavior or [so-called] 'hold-ups' (Kolasky and Dick 2002: 58).

Business practices may differ in the magnitude of the costs that parties must incur in order to transact with one another, and therefore some practices may be more 'efficient' than others in this regard.

Dynamic efficiency is described by Kolasky and Dick (2002: 56) in similar terms:

> Whereas allocative and productive efficiency can be viewed as static criteria—holding society's technological know-how constant—a more dynamic view of efficiency examines the conditions under which technological know-how and the set of feasible products optimally can be expanded over time through means such as learning-by-doing, research and development, and entrepreneurial creativity.

The evolving objectives of competition law and policy

Over the past 100 or so years, there has been an evolution in the importance given to the different objectives of competition policy. The goal of the following paragraphs is to describe that evolution and to discuss the view that developing countries have objectives for their competition policies that are different from those of industrialized economies. The goal here is *not* to assess the merits of the various stated objectives of competition policy,[4] and the fact that any objective is discussed below should not be taken as an endorsement of that objective.

Initially, protecting market processes and rights to engage in commerce were accorded a high priority in national competition policies, as the following quotation from a joint World Bank and Organisation for Economic Co-operation and Development (OECD) study points out:

> While many objectives have been ascribed to competition policy during the past hundred years, certain major themes stand out. The most common of these objectives cited is the maintenance of the competitive process or of free competition, or the protection or promotion of effective competition. These are seen as synonymous with striking down or preventing unreasonable restraints on competition. Associated objectives are freedom to trade, freedom of choice, and access to markets. In some countries, such as Germany, freedom of individual action is viewed as the economic equivalent of a more democratic constitutional system. In France emphasis is placed on competition policy as a means of securing economic freedom, that is, freedom of competition (World Bank and OECD 1997: 2).

This quotation suggests that protecting economic freedom and competitive processes as well as fairness have historically been seen as objectives of competition policy in many countries. In a similar vein, the new competition law of India refers, in its preamble, to the objectives of preventing practices that may have adverse effects on competition, promoting and sustaining competition in markets, protecting the interests of consumers, and ensuring freedom of trade carried on by other participants in markets in India.[5]

Only after competition laws were enacted did a school of thought develop that justified certain competition laws on the grounds that they resulted in improvements in economic efficiency. In fact, the logic of static analyses of efficiency in markets often went hand in hand with the rhetoric of 'protecting the competitive process' as well as a focus on consumer welfare. Posner, for example, was to argue in his seminal treatise on US antitrust law that the 'fundamental objective' of such law is 'the protection of competition and efficiency' (Posner 1976: 226). This perspective gained considerable currency and accounts for the central role that static economic efficiency still plays in many accounts of competition law and policy.

More recently, a wide range of opinion has stressed the importance of dynamic efficiency as a legitimate and compelling objective of competition policy. For example, Singh (2002) argues that competition policy in developing economies should support the overall development path of an economy. He points to 'the need to emphasise dynamic rather than static efficiency as the main purpose of competition policy' (Singh 2002: 22).

In a related vein, Audretsch, Baumol, and Burke (2001), Baker (1999), Baumol (2001), and Posner (2001a) make the point that the nature of technologies or consumer preferences in certain industries and/or the fast pace of innovation in some industries call for a reassessment of the weight given to static efficiency as an objective of competition policy. Consistent with this view, in many jurisdictions with active competition regimes the promotion of innovation or dynamic efficiency gains has become an important goal of competition policy, and the application of competition law explicitly takes account of this objective. For this reason, it is misleading to suggest that competition policy as it is currently practiced in major jurisdictions attaches little or no importance to considerations of dynamic efficiency. For the moment, however, it suffices to note that scholars of market processes in developing and industrial nations increasingly point to the importance of dynamic efficiency considerations as an appropriate objective of competition policy, and that concerns about dynamic efficiency are not the sole preserve of either wealthier or poorer economies.

As well, it should be noted that many states have explicitly introduced other objectives into their national competition laws. For example, Chapter 1, article 2 of the Competition Act of 1998 in South Africa states that:

> The purpose of the act is to promote and maintain competition in the Republic of South Africa in order
>
> (a) to promote the efficiency, adaptability and development of the economy;

(b) to provide consumers with competitive prices and product choices;
(c) to promote employment and advance the social and economic welfare of South Africans;
(d) to expand opportunities for South African participation in world markets and recognise the role of foreign competition in the Republic;
(e) to ensure that small and medium-sized enterprises have an equitable opportunity to participate in the economy; and
(f) to promote a greater spread of ownership, in particular to increase the ownership stakes of historically disadvantaged persons.

This multiplicity of goals reflects the fact that:

> A fundamental principle of competition policy and law in South Africa thus is the need to balance economic efficiency with socio-economic equity and development.[6]

This example demonstrates that competition law need not be directed toward a single objective, as is often alleged.

The instruments of competition policy and of competition law

Turning now to the instruments of competition policy, it is important to recognize that such policy is concerned *both* with private anticompetitive practices and with government measures or instruments that affect the state of competition in markets. For example, trade barriers, barriers to foreign direct investment (FDI), and licensing requirements (among other things) can influence the extent of competitive pressures in markets and so are appropriate concerns of competition policy.

In some jurisdictions, the anticompetitive effects of government measures more generally are addressed through the instrument of competition advocacy activities. In a report to the International Competition Network, its Advocacy Working Group defined this instrument as follows:

> Competition advocacy refers to those activities conducted by the competition authority related to the promotion of a competitive environment for economic activities by means of non-enforcement mechanisms, mainly through its relationship with other governmental agencies and by increasing public awareness of the benefits of competition (ICN 2002: i).

The potential contribution of competition advocacy activities to national economic performance has been discussed extensively by the International Competition Network, the OECD, and the World Trade Organization (WTO) Working Group on the Interaction between Trade and Competition Policy. Specific examples of competition advocacy

> include public education activities, studies and research undertaken to document the need for market-opening measures, formal appearances before leg-

islative committees or other government bodies in public proceedings, or 'behind-the-scenes' lobbying within government (Anderson and Jenny 2002: 7).

It is noteworthy that the first function that the new competition enforcement agency in India was allowed to perform was competition advocacy. The targets of this advocacy have included sectoral regulators and national and subnational (state) government agencies and ministries.

Notwithstanding the importance attached to competition advocacy, another instrument—namely competition law and its enforcement—is at the centre of competition policy in many countries. Audretsch, Baumol, and Burke (2001: 614) describe competition law as follows:

> Competition (or antitrust) law lays down the rules for competitive rivalry. It comprises a set of directives that constrain the strategies available to firms.

Hoekman and Holmes (1999: 877) add more specificity by defining national competition law

> as the set of rules and disciplines maintained by governments relating either to agreements between firms that restrict competition or to the abuse of a dominant position (including attempts to create a dominant position through mergers).

UNCTAD (2002) provides a list of actions by firms that may fall within the purview of competition law. Although there is no agreed list of the elements of competition law, the following five figure prominently in most accounts of such laws:

1 Measures relating to agreements between firms in the same market to restrain competition. These measures can include provisions banning cartels as well as provisions allowing cartels under certain circumstances.
2 Measures relating to attempts by a large incumbent firm to independently exercise market power (sometimes referred to as abuse of a dominant position).
3 Measures relating to firms that, acting collectively but in the absence of an explicit agreement among them, attempt to exercise market power. These measures are sometimes referred to as measures against collective dominance.
4 Measures relating to attempts by a firm or firms to drive one or more of their rivals out of a market. Laws prohibiting predatory pricing are an example of such measures.
5 Measures relating to collaboration between firms for the purposes of research, development, testing, marketing, and distribution of products.

This list of five instruments is not supposed to be exhaustive, nor is it meant to suggest that each element is given the same weight or referred to in the same terms in each country with a functioning competition law.

With these foregoing remarks in mind, it is worth stressing that the following four state interventions fall *outside* the remit of competition law:

1   consumer protection laws, such as those relating to faulty products, warranties, and misleading advertising;
2   unfair trade laws, such as antidumping laws, laws on countervailing duties, and measures to protect national industries from surges in imports;
3   government policies on the registration of new businesses and on the taxation and corporate governance oversight of existing businesses; and
4   trade policies and policies on FDI more generally (note, however, that policies on mergers and acquisitions (M&As) fall within the scope of competition law).

Moreover, in those jurisdictions with competition laws, not all of the firms or sectors in the respective economies are subject to the disciplines of the competition legislation. The nature and extent of exemptions to national competition laws varies markedly across nations. Firms that engage in anticompetitive practices at the behest of the government are often exempt from competition law. In addition, many competition laws include provisions that allow the government or an independent agency to grant exemptions to firms or sectors after the competition law has been enacted.

The above discussion—which may seem laborious to those very familiar with competition law and policy—is important given the widespread misconceptions about the nature and scope of competition law. Competition law is far more narrowly prescribed than many observers think. Confusion often arises when competition law is conflated with competition policy; the former is one of the many instruments of the latter.

This section has described in some detail the elements and scope of competition law. It has shown that the objectives of competition law are not restricted to static efficiency and in many cases extend to include considerations of dynamic efficiency. Moreover, competition law is only a subset of a nation's competition policies and should not be confused with a number of other policies that can affect the intensity of competition in a nation's markets.

3   COMPETITION, THE ENFORCEMENT OF COMPETITION LAW, AND ECONOMIC DEVELOPMENT

The goal of this section is to describe the major conceptual linkages between the implementation of competition law and the factors thought to influence dynamic economic efficiency. To establish a point of departure, recall that in a competitive market, in the absence of government interventions, asymmetries of information, impediments to the entry and exit of firms, and anticompetitive practices by firms, prices and quantities will settle to levels that generate economically efficient outcomes at a given point of time; that is, they will attain static efficiency. In this situation, the prices that consumers pay for a good will equal the incremental (or marginal) costs of the firm that produced the last unit of the good. Cartelization and collusion by firms, which raise prices above incremental costs, will result in a market outcome where the sum of producer and consumer surpluses falls below the level attained with static efficiency. Consequently, measures to enforce competition laws that encourage firms to compete (or discourage or prevent firms from resisting rivalry) will improve the allocation of resources, by making market outcomes move toward the statically efficient outcome.

In general, therefore, tensions are unlikely to arise between the appropriate enforcement of competition laws and the attainment of efficiency in a static sense.[7] But does the enforcement of competition law and interfirm rivalry impede the attainment of *dynamic* efficiencies, and thereby the *long-term* performance of economies? This question is the focus of the next two subsections of this chapter.

Trade-offs between competition law enforcement and dynamic efficiency and long-term economic performance

This subsection describes and evaluates four arguments identified in the relevant literature and policy discourse concerning how the application of competition law might compromise dynamic efficiency and long-term economic performance. It is important to appreciate that the objective here is to accurately characterize—and then assess—a number of viewpoints that have received attention in discussions among policy-makers and civil society, as well as in academia, on national and international competition policy matters. For this reason, some of the perspectives presented here do not necessarily represent what might be thought of as mainstream academic opinion.

Missing markets and institutions

The basis for the first such argument is the realization that, unlike industrial countries, in many cases developing economies do not have well-functioning factor markets—such as stock exchanges and bond markets—and often have not been able to create institutions that support the operation of markets such as bankruptcy codes, efficient contract enforcement, and the like (Laffont 1998). These 'missing markets' and 'missing institutions' are said to alter the optimal degree of competition in an economy and therefore have implications for the vigor and manner with which competition law is enforced. It is also argued that these considerations are especially important when dynamic efficiency drives policy-making. Singh (2002: 19) explains the logic underlying this argument:

> In order to raise the living standards of their people over time, developing economies need high rates of investment to achieve fast rates of growth of productivity. High rates of investment in turn normally require reasonable, if not high, rates of profits in order to maintain the private sector's propensity to invest. This consideration leads to the view that there may be at times too much competition rather than too little. Competition would be too much if it leads to price wars, sharp falls in profits, all of which are likely to diminish the corporate desire to invest.

Implicit in this perspective is the assumption that firms in developing economies have to raise funds internally and not through borrowing from banks or other financial intermediaries. If such borrowing is not possible, then an attenuation of competitive pressures is said to enable firms to raise prices and secure funds for investment.[8] Tilton (1996: 3) is explicit about the effects of policies that reduce competition among firms in the following remark:

> To the degree that these policies raise prices, they channel resources from consumers towards targeted industries.

Singh (2002) also argues that reducing rivalry involves more than maintaining prices set by firms. Excess capacity must also be attended to because, in his view, it can trigger price wars. Governments would therefore have to take an active role in managing investment decisions by firms in high-growth or targeted industries (Singh 2002: 19). In sum, this argument calls into question whether a maximal degree of competition is optimal and suggests that increasing economic growth requires a mix of cooperation and competition by firms.

A slightly different variant of this argument has been advanced by Amsden and Singh (1994a) in their analysis of the optimal degree of competition and dynamic efficiency in Japan and the Republic of Korea. They observe that:

> In general, whether competition was promoted or restricted [in Japan]
> depended on the industry and its life cycle: in young industries, during the
> developmental phase, the government discouraged competition; when the
> industries became technologically mature, competition was allowed to flour-
> ish. Later, when industries are in competitive decline, the government again
> discourages competition and attempts to bring about an orderly rationalisation
> of the industry (Amsden and Singh 1994a: 945).[9]

Although the authors do not provide an explicit explanation for these
claims, two arguments that are consistent with the thrust of Singh (2002)
might be developed (without endorsement!) along the following lines. In
the case of young or nascent industries, firms may need to finance growth,
and reducing rivalry will result in higher prices that, in turn, can generate
the internal funds to attain this goal. The argument for constraining competition in declining industries might proceed as follows. If firms have soft
budget constraints or face little threat from bankruptcy proceedings, then
declining industries may experience perennial price wars and few exits
from the industry. Such price wars will result in firms building up losses
and debts year after year. These ever-growing debts may end up compromising the solvency of the principal financial backers of the firms—possibly the state itself or banks—which could in turn have serious
macroeconomic consequences. This outcome may be prevented if the state
discourages firms from engaging in price wars while firms and the government take steps to bring productive capacity into line with falling demand.

One way to assess these arguments is to identify the intermediate
objectives of competition policy that are being alluded to. In Singh's first
formulation, the intermediate objective was to increase investment outlays.[10] The question therefore arises as to whether restricting rivalry is the
least costly means to obtain this intermediate objective, a claim that is not
demonstrated in Singh's analysis. As Tilton acknowledges, reducing
rivalry has the effect of increasing prices paid by customers. In contrast,
an investment subsidy or tax credit that stimulated investment by the same
amount as that achieved by reducing rivalry would not have the same
direct *and* adverse effect on customers' welfare. Admittedly, the investment subsidy or tax credit would have implications for the government's
budget. Another alternative could be to channel investment funds through
the nation's banking system. Arguably, Singh, Tilton, and others have
failed to demonstrate that these alternative policy measures are inferior to
restricting rivalry through cartelization or other anticompetitive practices.

Large firm size is necessary to compete on global markets

A second possible trade-off between competition law and dynamic efficiency is said to occur when firms need to attain a certain size in order to

compete effectively on world markets. Some argue that in order to reach the appropriate size, state action is called for, essentially to create or foster so-called 'national champions.' These state actions may include forced M&As (when a state instructs two or more firms to form a single commercial entity) and state-encouraged M&As by private firms (which can result from adopting merger review regulations that place few constraints on mergers by firms, or that overlook the consequences of a proposed merger or acquisition that are unrelated to competitiveness). Furthermore, there is an issue as to what should be the appropriate competition law enforcement regime for national champions after their formation. The following discussion clarifies why size might be important for a firm's competitiveness and then discusses some of the implications of the potential relationship between enforcement of competition law, firm size, and dynamic efficiency.

In principle, firm size is said to be important for corporate 'competitiveness' for the following reasons:

1   Firms benefit from economies of scale (where larger production runs are associated with lower average costs of production).
2   Firms need to attain a certain minimum scale to successfully innovate or imitate, or to raise funds on capital markets.
3   Learning-by-doing is faster in larger firms.

When firms do have pronounced economies of scale, then it is possible to construct arguments, on efficiency grounds, that enforcing competition law so as to maximize rivalry between firms is not necessarily a good idea. The following representative argument by Lau (1996: 59) is couched in efficiency terms:

> ... the government has to take into account the existence of increasing returns to scale which render the usual market allocation inefficient. For example, if the size of the market will support it, it is better to have one minimum-efficient-scale plant than to build two sub-minimum-efficient-scale plants. This is where the government can and should intervene to prevent potentially inefficient and possibly ruinous competition.

These arguments still resonate with certain policy-makers and scholars. Some point to the desirability of subordinating competition law to the goal of creating national champions, or 'national leaders' to quote the term used in Amsden's influential account of the rise of non-western economies (Amsden 2001). Referring to the latter as 'the rest,'[11] she argues:

> After floundering for a century, 'the rest' succeeded in creating professionally managed, large scale, national firms (Amsden 2001: 190).

This was accomplished in the following manner:

> National leaders in 'the rest,' private or public, all shared one characteristic: *they tended to be a product of government promotion* (Amsden 2001: 193).[12]

Such promotion could include inducements to firms to merge, forced takeovers, and the like.

Another important feature of policies employed to create national champions is that they can involve discrimination against foreign firms; that is, these policies have ramifications for international commerce. Such discrimination can be de jure, for example when foreign firms are simply banned from buying or merging with domestic firms in certain sectors. Alternatively, a foreign firm's proposal to buy or to merge with a domestic firm may be reviewed under a different and potentially more stringent procedure than when two domestic firms decide to form a single combination. The discrimination could also be de facto, for example when merger review procedures are implemented in such a way that proposed combinations involving domestic firms are treated differently from those involving at least one foreign firm.

For the present purposes, the issue is not whether governments should or should not promote national champions. Nor is it whether mergers or acquisitions actually attain the efficiencies and cost reductions that are envisaged, a matter that has been debated extensively in the industrial organization literature. Rather, the question is whether, in order to promote champions, governments need or are well advised to relax the enforcement of competition law. Critics point to at least three arguments in this regard. First, to the extent that the domestic and international markets for a given product are integrated (which is likely to occur when barriers to importation of the product are low or nonexistent), then properly executed merger policy is unlikely to challenge the creation of national champions in the first place. This is because prevailing or potential competition from abroad is likely to prevent the merged firm from raising prices and harming domestic consumer welfare. There are circumstances, therefore, where there is no tension between the objectives of competition law and the desire to form national champions. Moreover, in an era of falling trade and investment barriers, the relevance of this argument is growing. It is also worth noting that in relatively integrated markets, policy-makers should be aware that the creation of national champions will, at best, result in lower costs (through greater scale and so on) rather than stronger market power. The impact of such champions on national export performance will, therefore, be through selling larger quantities rather than through improving the terms of trade (raising export prices).

The second argument is that funding overseas expansion through the domestic profits 'earned' from gouging high prices from domestic consumers is only one source of such finance. If the gains from overseas expansion are so clearly evident to national policy-makers and to the managers and owners of putative national champions, then they should be clear to potential investors too.[13] Relatedly, why should governments sacrifice domestic consumers' welfare (through lax enforcement of competition law) when investors can finance the overseas expansion of national firms?

The third critique builds on longstanding research by Michael Porter and others finding that export performance is fostered by greater rivalry between domestic firms. Sheltering domestic firms from competition, through a relaxation of the application of national competition law or some other means, is therefore harmful to promoting national export performance. In sum, there are compelling conceptual and evidential reasons to question whether national competition law should be sacrificed at the altar of promoting national champions. These reasons are logically distinct from those that evaluate the merits of promoting national champions in the first place.

Market power fosters innovation

The first two perspectives described above purport to show that government measures to restrain rivalry can, in certain circumstances, enhance dynamic efficiency. In contrast, the third perspective purports to show that governments need not intervene to promote rivalry—that is, by attacking market power—in markets where innovation is the principal source of competition between firms and there are no barriers to entry by new firms. This third perspective is of much older vintage than the first two. Schumpeter in his classic book *Capitalism, Socialism, and Democracy* contrasted his view of the dynamics of a capitalist economy—which he referred to as 'plausible capitalism'—with the

> essentially static conception emphasized in the contemporary neoclassical economic analyses, both at the time he wrote and (with only modest amendments) fifty years later (Scherer 1992: 1,416–17).[14]

Schumpeter argued that the following types of innovations (or 'technological progress' as he put it) drove economic growth: new consumer goods, improved production methods and means of transportation, new markets, and new forms of firm structure and industrial organization. Innovation, however, is an endogenous outcome and is itself driven by entrepreneurs seeking higher profits. According to this view, the riskiness of innovation is such that entrepreneurs are more inclined to invest in innovation when

> firms could deploy an array of restrictive practices to protect their investments (Scherer 1992: 1,417).

Thus,

> Schumpeter went beyond economists' long-accepted view that the expectation of a monopoly position (e.g. through patent protection on inventions) was necessary to make the venture worthwhile. Monopoly power already held also supported investments in technological progress. Here, Schumpeter argued, both economists and trust-busters had their priorities wrong (Scherer 1992: 1,418).

In Schumpeter's own words:

> What we have got to accept is that [the large-scale establishment or unit of control] has come to be the most powerful engine … of progress and in particular of the long-run expansion of output not only in spite of, but to a considerable extent through, this strategy which looks so restrictive. … In this respect, perfect competition is not only impossible but inferior, and has no title to being set up as a model of ideal efficiency (Schumpeter 1942: 106).

Schumpeter argued, further, that innovation resulted in a continual process by which new products simultaneously undermined the position of even entrenched incumbent firms (the so-called process of 'creative destruction'). He crystallized the differences between his thesis and the neoclassical conception of competition and its emphasis on static efficiency as follows:

> But in capitalist reality as distinguished from its textbook picture, it is not [price] competition which counts but the competition from the new commodity, the new technology, the new source of supply, the new type of organization … competition which commands a decisive cost or quality advantage and which strikes not at the margins of profits and the outputs of existing firms but at their foundations and their very lives. This kind of competition is as much more effective than the other as a bombardment is in comparison with forcing a door, and so much more important that it becomes a matter of comparative indifference whether competition in the ordinary sense functions more or less promptly; the powerful lever that in the long run expands output and brings down prices is in any case made of other stuff (Schumpeter 1942: 84–5).

As these quotations demonstrate, although Schumpeter presented an alternative conception of the dynamics of market economies—and criticized orthodox analyses for their characterization of market processes—he did not depart from the orthodox prescription that fierce competition between firms is the motor for economic advance. Hence, Schumpeter's theory is not a rejection of competition as the basis of innovation, economic progress, and growth but an alternative vision of how competition occurs.

The implications of Schumpeter's analysis for competition policy can be summarized as follows: state measures that seek to arbitrarily reduce concentration levels or to reduce the profitability of innovative firms should be avoided, since this will diminish the incentives of both incumbent and potential firms to invest in potentially profitable innovations and related activities in the first place.[15] Rather, according to this perspective, attention should focus on addressing barriers that reduce the profitability or likelihood of entry by new firms into an industry.[16] As will be seen below (pp. 22–3), to an important extent the enforcement of competition law in jurisdictions with active competition regimes has already adapted itself to these insights, by de-emphasizing the control of market concentration per se and placing more emphasis on entry conditions and other factors that affect the incentives for innovation in markets.

It is worth noting, in this connection, that extensive empirical research has confirmed that barriers to entry are substantially higher in developing economies than in industrial nations (Djankov et al. 2002; De Soto 2001). If reforms cannot be introduced to effectively lower these barriers— perhaps because in some situations poor governance practices cannot be eliminated in any realistic timeframe—then dynamic efficiency may actually be best served by competition laws that prevent incumbent firms from setting too high prices over the longer term. Moreover, to the extent that the enforcement of competition law prevents or discourages incumbent firms from taking steps to foreclose entry by potential rivals, then such enforcement will strengthen the incentives of the latter firms to invest in innovation. This is because these potential competitors will place a lower probability on their eventual entry into a market being impeded and so will have greater confidence that their investments in innovation will bear commercial fruit. In summary, preserving the ability of innovative firms to enter a market—one of the sources of long-term economic performance in the Schumpeterian world—may well be contingent on the appropriate enforcement of competition law.

Network externalities

A fourth source of potential tension between competition policy, rivalry, and the realization of dynamic efficiency relates to the existence of atypical production cost or consumer preference structures in certain economic sectors. A possible example of this would be the existence of a natural monopoly—that is, a situation where, due to overwhelming economies of scale, a market is most efficiently served by a single supplier. Another example that has received much attention in recent literature and policy debates relates to industries where so-called network externalities are pervasive.[17] In the presence of such externalities, the maximum amount that consumers are willing to pay for a good or service depends, in part, on the number of other consumers who also purchase the item in question. Admittedly, much of the discussion of network externalities takes place within the context of markets where firms have advanced technologies, such as the market for computer software. (In the latter market consumers effectively place a premium on programs that create files which can be opened and, in principle, amended by many other persons.) However, it should not be forgotten that many communication and infrastructure services that are important for economic development exhibit network externalities. Such services include telephones, railways, and so on (Laffont and Tirole 2000).

Although the analysis of market outcomes in the presence of such externalities can be complex, one theme that does emerge from much of the literature is that there are instances where consumers will prefer that a smaller number of goods (and possibly a single good) be available in the marketplace. If a small number of firms each supplies a different product to a large number of consumers, then the externalities generated for consumers (which result from the fact that each product they consume is consumed by many others) may well exceed any adverse impact on prices that may follow from a high degree of market concentration. Put simply, there may be instances in which consumers may prefer concentrated market outcomes with a small number of firms because of the network externalities that large output levels can create.

Moreover, in such industries, firms may adopt pricing strategies that deliberately take into account the impact of the current number of customers on the desirability of their product to potential customers in the future. The latter may only be willing to buy the product once the number of existing customers exceeds a critical level, in which case firms will have an incentive to keep prices lower at present than in the absence of network externalities. Therefore, network externalities benefit current consumers both directly and through the stronger than usual disincentives to firms to raise prices. Both theoretical and empirical analyses of industries with network externalities have shown that firms often adopt complex pricing strategies which typically involve substantial price discrimination across customers.

It is worth emphasizing that the above arguments *can* provide an efficiency-based rationale for not taking steps to maximize rivalry between firms in particular (limited) circumstances. Put another way, in *certain sectors* with *observable* and *identifiable* technological characteristics, maximizing rivalry among firms may harm the interests of both consumers and producers. Nonetheless, this does not imply that there is no role for competition law in these markets; rather, it means that competition law must be applied in ways that take account of the technological characteristics of such markets—as indeed competition authorities increasingly do.[18] Indeed, recent contributions highlight the importance of (appropriately tailored) competition rules in network industries, due precisely to concerns over the market power that can be created or entrenched through network effects (see, for example, Church and Ware 1998). As well, since network externalities are not found in every sector of the economy, this fourth perspective provides at most a sector-specific and not a general counterargument to the contention that enhanced rivalry promotes dynamic efficiency.

To summarize the findings of this subsection, although all four perspectives outlined above imply that dynamic efficiency may not be best served by consistently maximizing the number of competitors in markets, they differ in other important respects. The fourth perspective is sector-specific in nature, whereas the first three perspectives may be of more general application. Of the three perspectives with general application, only the first two call for state measures to constrain competition. With regard to the third perspective, in a smoothly running Schumpeterian world where there are no significant state-orchestrated barriers to entry, it might be argued that there is no need for competition law enforcement to promote rivalry. Yet, once one allows for the possibility that private firms can create barriers to entry or foreclose entry to a market by new firms, then improving dynamic economic performance may well require the appropriate enforcement of competition laws.

The four perspectives also differ sharply in the assumptions they embody as to the appropriate *intermediate* objectives of competition law, if any. Increasing private sector investment is the intermediate objective associated with the first perspective (recall the writings of Singh), whereas export competitiveness could motivate the second perspective. Even if one accepts the intermediate objectives of each perspective as legitimate, one is entitled to ask whether constraining competition is the policy response that most effectively meets these objectives. For example, what is the empirical and theoretical support for the contention in a developing country setting that restraining competition to bolster investment is *more effective and less costly* than offering firms an investment subsidy or tax credit, or taking measures that encourage banks to lend to firms? Unfortunately, this line of questioning has not received the attention it deserves in the existing literature.

Complementarities between interfirm rivalry, competition law, and economic development

Proponents of the view that rivalry between firms can improve national economic performance over time have pointed to a wide range of circumstances under which competition contributes to innovation, productivity, and growth. The five perspectives described below highlight the important contribution that the appropriate enforcement of competition law can make to development.

First, greater competition between firms is said to encourage managers and capitalists to focus on improving their enterprise's performance so as to maximize profits or at least stave off the threat of bankruptcy, takeover, or some other loss of control. One of the United States' leading jurists in the early twentieth century, Judge Learned Hand, once observed that:

> Possession of unchallenged economic power deadens initiative, discourages thrift and depresses energy ... Immunity from competition is a narcotic and rivalry a stimulant to industrial progress.[19]

The propensity of firms to attain the minimum level of costs for a given level of output, and the circumstances in which they are most likely to do so, has been debated extensively by economists (see, for example, the differing views in Leibenstein 1966, Stigler 1976, and Leibenstein 1978). One interesting feature of this debate is the finding that more intense competition in product markets tends to intensify the pressure on firms to lower costs (see, for example, Primeaux 1977 and Leibenstein 1978). Consistent with this view, in a major survey of the impact of regulatory reform across a wide spectrum of American industries, Winston (1998) found that introducing competition into previously regulated industries significantly strengthened the efficiency of firms and improved economic performance over time.

The view that interfirm rivalry provides incentives for efficiency-enhancing restructuring also finds considerable support in the empirical literature on enterprise reform in Eastern Europe and among the members of the Commonwealth of Independent States (CIS). Fortunately, a detailed survey of the literature on the determinants of the pace of restructuring in transition economies has recently been published (Djankov and Murrell 2002). This survey includes a critical discussion of 54 analyses of the impact of product market competition on the rate of firm restructuring;

what is especially appealing is that it uses objective measures to assess the quality of the research papers being reviewed. Djankov and Murrell (2002: 43) find that:

> The analyses indicate that product market competition has been a major force behind improvements in enterprise productivity in transition economies as a whole ...

They also note that their

> results are upheld in a survey of over 3,300 enterprises in 25 transition economies (Carlin et al. 2001) that shows strong positive effects of the reduction in market concentration on firm efficiency (Djankov and Murrell 2002: 44).

Another striking finding of the Djankov and Murrell survey is that, in contrast to authors' findings with respect to the importance of competition in domestic markets, competition from imports is a far less robust determinant of beneficial restructuring. Djankov and Murrell (2002: 44) state that:

> The findings on the effect of import competition deserve special attention. In the CIS, import competition has a large negative effect in economic terms, although this effect is statistically not robust. In Eastern Europe, import competition has a positive effect in economic terms, but the results of individual studies are mixed, consistent with the literature on developing economies.

This suggests that measures to promote rivalry among domestic firms tend to have a more consistent effect on restructuring—and on dynamic economic performance—than trade liberalization. Therefore, according to this perspective, it would be imprudent to rely solely on lowering trade barriers to discipline entrenched market power and provide sharp incentives to firms to keep costs under control.

A *second* source of complementarity between competition law enforcement and long-term economic performance is provided by the longstanding contention that the intended benefits of trade reform may not be realized without active enforcement of competition law. The concern here is that reductions in official trade barriers will be replaced by anti-competitive private practices, the latter counteracting the price-reducing effects of trade reforms. To the extent that reductions in the prices of imported machinery and other capital equipment bolster investment and enhance dynamic economic performance, then reductions in trade barriers on these durable goods may not translate into higher growth without measures to discipline private anticompetitive practices. The enforcement of competition law therefore increases the effectiveness of cuts in trade barriers on growth-enhancing imports.

The general point that the objectives of trade reform can be frustrated by anticompetitive practices was made with considerable force in a contribution by Argentina to the WTO's Working Group on the Interaction between Trade and Competition Policy in 1998. The contents of this contribution are summarized as follows:

> In a recent contribution to the Group (document W/63), Argentina has set out the results of 18 empirical case studies which, in its view, illustrate the importance of an effective national competition policy, even in the context of external market liberalization. The presumption underlying these studies is that, in general, when a country implements far-reaching trade liberalization, domestic prices will tend toward import parity levels. The competition agency of Argentina had, nonetheless, identified several situations where this response had not been forthcoming, due to the existence of anti-competitive practices of enterprises. Factors that tended to facilitate or underlie such anti-competitive practices included high market concentration levels, inelastic demand (reflecting a lack of substitutes), the prior existence of a cartel, and control by a dominant enterprise of scarce facilities that were necessary for imports to occur. Based on these findings, the representative of Argentina concluded that effective national competition policies are vital to ensure that the process of adjustment to external liberalization and resulting benefits for efficient economic development are not circumvented by anti-competitive practices (WTO 1998: 13).

A *third* source of complementarity between competition law and dynamic economic performance involves FDI. In particular, the appropriate enforcement of competition law both enhances the attractiveness of an economy as a location for foreign investment and is important to maximize the benefits that flow from such investment.[20] A synthesis paper on the relationship between competition policy, trade policy, and development reported on the following pertinent discussions in the WTO's Working Group on the Interaction between Trade and Competition Policy:

> The point has been made in various oral and written contributions to the Group that the implementation of a transparent and effective competition policy can be an important factor both in enhancing the attractiveness of an economy to foreign investment, and in maximizing the benefits of such investment. More specifically, these contributions have suggested that competition policy can enhance the attractiveness of an economy for foreign investment by providing a transparent and principles-based mechanism for the resolution of disputes involving such investment that is consistent with international norms that are widely-accepted internationally. This increases investor confidence and therefore the propensity to invest. Vigorous competition in markets, reinforced by competition policy, also helps to maximize the benefits of such investment to host countries, by encouraging participating firms to construct state-of-the-art production facilities, to transfer up-to-date technology into host countries and to undertake appropriate training programmes, and by preventing the exploitation of consumers (WTO 1998: 8).

It is also argued in the People's Republic of China and India country studies in this book that the failure to effectively enforce competition law against certain foreign firms has reduced the benefits accruing from certain foreign direct investments.

A *fourth* set of complementarities arises from the substantial body of research into the effects of greater competition in the product market on the incentives for firms to innovate. Comprehensive surveys of the latter can be found in Ahn (2002), American Bar Association (2002), and Anderson and Gallini (1998). Leading economic researchers have explored three distinct channels through which competition in product markets stimulates innovation. Ahn (2002: 7) summarizes these as follows:

> – Darwinian effect: Intensified product competition could force managers to speed up the adoption of new technologies in order to avoid a loss of control … due to bankruptcy (Aghion et al., 1999). More generally, firms should innovate to survive under competitive pressure (cf. Porter, 1990).
> – Neck-and-neck competition: In a simple model of 'creative destruction' the incumbent firms unlike new entrants have no incentive to innovate. Under a more gradualist technological progress assumption with incumbents engaged in step-by-step innovative activities competition could increase innovation. It is because more intensive product market competition between firms … will increase each firm's incentive to acquire or increase its technological lead over its rivals.
> – Mobility effect: In the learning-by-doing model of endogenous growth, the steady state rate of growth may be increased if skilled workers become more adaptable in switching to newer production lines … In this case, more competition between new and old product lines will induce skilled workers to switch from old to new lines more rapidly (Aghion and Howitt, 1996).

Ahn (2002: 5) offers the following summary of the evidence:[21]

> Competition has pervasive and long-lasting effects on firm performance by affecting economic actors' incentive structure[s], by encouraging their innovative activities, and by selecting more efficient ones from less efficient ones over time.

By contrast:

> The claim that market concentration is conducive to innovation does not appear to be supported by recent empirical findings … On the whole, however, there is little empirical support for the view that large firm size or high concentration is strongly associated with higher levels of innovative activity (Ahn 2002: 5).

A *fifth* channel through which competition law enforcement can contribute to dynamic economic performance is highlighted in the mushrooming literature on 'innovation markets,' a term introduced by Gilbert and Sunshine (1995). This literature emphasizes that innovation itself is a result of market interactions and that even firms that are not currently competing with each other in actual (existing) product markets may be competitors in markets for future innovations. Furthermore, competition in such markets (and hence the incentive for innovation) can be undermined by mergers or other (potentially) anticompetitive practices.

This perspective has become sufficiently influential that, in the United States, the federal agencies responsible for conducting merger reviews have explicitly incorporated concerns about innovation markets into published enforcement guidelines dealing with matters such as intellectual property licensing issues[22] and have sought to block corporate mergers on the basis of the threat they would pose to incentives for innovation (Gilbert and Tom 2001). Although some analysts (Gallini and Trebilcock 1998) have argued that the more conventional theory of 'potential competition' already encompasses the principal insights stressed by the conception of innovation markets, at a minimum the latter further illustrates the scope for anticompetitive practices to undermine the incentives for innovation, and hence the positive contribution that competition policy can make to long-run economic performance. Moreover, this argument qualifies the Schumpeterian view that unfettered firms will maximize the degree of innovation of new products and processes. The literature on innovation markets reminds us that some firms have the incentive and the means to stall innovations by others.

This subsection has highlighted five ways in which interfirm rivalry, which can be bolstered by the appropriate enforcement of competition law, has positive pay-offs for economic development. Those pay-offs are not confined to lower prices, but include greater innovation and more opportunities for private sector development in emerging markets.

4 CONCLUDING REMARKS

After stating the various ends and means of competition law and competition policy, this chapter has evaluated the principal arguments concerning the relationship between interfirm rivalry, competition law, and economic development. The following four arguments were advanced to question whether unfettered rivalry between firms promotes development:

1 Missing markets, especially financial markets, imply that investments can only be financed out of retained profits, which are eroded by unfettered competition between firms.
2 Firms need to achieve a certain size to compete effectively on world markets or to withstand competition from imports. This view has clear

implications for the conduct of reviews of proposed M&As, especially in those sectors where so-called national champions currently, or might in the future, operate.

3   Governments need not intervene to promote rivalry in markets where innovation is the principal source of competition. In such markets, current monopoly profits act as a spur to innovation and the creation of new products and processes.

4   Maximizing rivalry leads to inefficient outcomes in national monopolies and in some network industries.

The following five arguments contend that promoting rivalry between firms enhances dynamic economic performance:

1   Greater competition between firms sharpens incentives to cut costs and improve productivity.

2   The benefits from trade reform, deregulation, and privatization will not be realized without the potential for active and effective enforcement of competition law.

3   The appropriate enforcement of competition law adds transparency to a nation's commercial landscape, which in turn attracts FDI.

4   Greater competition in product markets stimulates both product and process innovations.

5   Rivalry in the market for future innovations can be protected by the active and appropriate enforcement of M&A laws to prevent, for example, one firm taking over another firm that has a potentially strong, but not as yet fully developed, range of rival products.

The conceptual and evidential material presented in this chapter strongly suggests that innovation, productivity improvements, and other forms of long-term economic performance are likely to be promoted rather than impeded by interfirm rivalry, and therefore by the enforcement of competition laws that promote such rivalry. Nonetheless, it is also apparent from the literature that specific situations—principally relating to the technologies available to firms in an industry—can be identified where the maximization of either the number of competitors in a market or the degree of competition between firms may lead to inefficient outcomes. It should be stressed that according to the thinking of leading scholars in the field of industrial organization (for example, Carlton and Perloff 1994), such situations do not call for the wholesale rejection of competition law as a tool of economic governance, but rather for the appropriate tailoring of the application of competition law to take account of relevant technological and other considerations.

NOTES

1   Alternative accounts of the objectives of competition law and policy can be found in Graham and Richardson (1997: 8–13) and in American Bar Association (2003: sections III and IV in particular).

2   It is not the purpose of the current discussion to assess the validity of these claims; that matter will be taken up later.

3   It should also be noted in this regard that a link between dynamic efficiency and commonly used and observable measures of long-term economic performance, such as economic growth, is often implied—if rarely stated—in the existing literature on the role of competition policy in economic development. This is in spite of the fact that, strictly speaking, the definitions of dynamic efficiency and variables such as economic growth are different.

4   There is a fairly rigorous debate on this subject; see, for example, the references in note 1 of this chapter.

5   India, Competition Act, 2002 (No. 12 of 2003), available at <http://dca.nic.in/competition_act2002.pdf>.

6   Taken from the introduction, web page of the South African Competition Commission, at <http://www.compcom.co.za/aboutus/aboutus_intro.asp?level=1&desc=7>.

7   This statement assumes that the approach taken to the enforcement of competition law gives due regard to technological and other considerations (such as the importance of scale economies) that may arise in particular sectors.

8   Of relevance to this argument is the evidence presented in Glen, Lee, and Singh (2001, 2002) that implies that the profits earned by firms in developing countries tend to fall faster than those earned by firms in industrialized economies. If this finding is correct, and firms in developing countries are indeed unable to raise funds from banks or from stockmarkets, then market forces would effectively be undermining the capacity of profitable firms to invest.

9   Amsden and Singh (1994a) cite Okimoto (1990) in support of this claim.

10   Whether the increased investment outlays are actually used productively or as intended is another important matter, but one that is beyond the remit of this issues paper.

11   Amsden's use of this term is not meant to be derogatory. She wishes to juxtapose 'the West' and 'the Rest.'

12   Italics are in the original quotation.

13   One way of putting this is to ask, 'What is the informational advantage of the government in this respect?'

14   Scherer (1992) is cited extensively in this discussion because his article contains a balanced account both of Schumpeter's thinking about the operation of market processes and of the research programs that were spawned by his seminal contributions.

15   This raises the empirical question of whether industries with more concentrated sellers tend to have more innovative firms. Scherer (1992) recounts the

twists and turns in the empirical literature and summarizes the findings of what he believes is the best research paper on the subject: Geroski (1990). Scherer (1992: 1,424) described the results of the latter study of the propensity to innovate by British firms as follows:

> … innovation was found to be less vigorous in more concentrated industries. Thus, the results did not support the 1942 Schumpeterian conjectures.

16   For related discussion, see Audretsch, Baumol, and Burke (2001: 619).

17   See White (2001) for an accessible economic analysis of such externalities and the implications for regulatory and competition policy.

18   A review of the websites of the Antitrust Division of the US Department of Justice (http://www.usdoj.gov/atr/), the Bureau of Competition of the US Federal Trade Commission (http://www.ftc.gov/ftc/antitrust.htm), the European Commission's Directorate-General for Competition (http://europa.eu. int/comm/competition/index_en.html), and the Canadian Competition Bureau (http://strategis.ic.gc.ca/SSG/ct01250e.html), to name just a few of the enforcement agencies in the industrialized world, reveals that such efficiency-based arguments figure extensively in the analyses undertaken and decisions made by enforcement officials, particularly though by no means exclusively in merger enforcement.

19   United States v. Aluminum Co. of America,148 F.2d 416, 427 (2d Cir. 1945).

20   Such an argument is developed, for example, in UNCTAD (1997) and the references contained therein.

21   See Table 1.1 and section IV.1 of Ahn (2002).

22   See, for example, the intellectual property guidelines published by the US Department of Justice and Federal Trade Commission in 1995, especially section 3.2.2.

2

Competition policy, international trade, and foreign direct investment

Douglas H. Brooks

1   INTRODUCTION

Competition plays a central role in the process of globalization. Competition is also a spur to better economic policy, to the extent that the option of 'exit' for investors exerts a policy discipline on governments, while greater entry of market participants is likely to raise the levels of employment, consumer choice, and, consequently, political awareness among society.

As globalization proceeds, attention has increasingly turned to the cross-border implications of anticompetitive practices. At the international level, entry into markets in a foreign country requires access either by trade or by the establishment of an affiliate in the foreign country with national treatment in order to compete on equal terms with domestic producers there. Consequently, the interaction of competition policy with international trade and investment policies is becoming increasingly important.

Cross-border trade in developing Asia has grown rapidly in recent decades. Global exports of goods and services rose by an annual average of 5.8 percent in real terms and 10.3 percent in nominal terms from 1970 to 2004. Exports increased from 11.6 percent of output in 1970 to more than 27.2 percent in 2004. Within developing Asia, South Asia has more or less followed the world trend, while East Asia has seen increasing exports relative to output, surpassing the world average in 1979. Southeast Asia has also consistently achieved a higher export to GDP ratio than South Asia since 1970.

Meanwhile, foreign direct investment (FDI) outflows have risen tremendously since the early 1990s relative to world output and exports

*Figure 2.1   Indices of world exports, FDI outflows, and GDP
              (1990 = 100)*

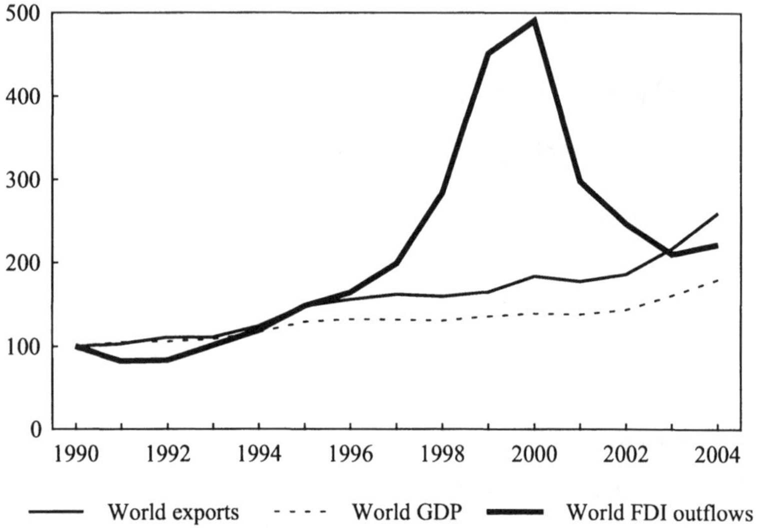

Source: Exports and GDP: World Economic Outlook database, accessed April 2005; FDI outflows: UNCTAD database, accessed September 2004.

(Figure 2.1). World FDI outflows increased almost five times between 1990 and 2000 before falling in 2001, while world exports and output grew at a more modest pace between 1990 and 2004.

From only $53.7 billion in 1980, annual global FDI outflows reached $1.2 trillion in 2000. After that, however, the weaker global economy considerably reduced outflows, which dropped by 39 percent in 2001, a further 17 percent in 2002, and 15 percent in 2003, before picking up by 6 percent in 2004. The upsurge in FDI in the 1980s and 1990s substantially changed the international economic landscape. This expansion in FDI was strongest during 1985–90, when many host countries began to relax regulations in order to attract FDI, and during 1995–2000, when many mergers and acquisitions (M&As) followed in the wake of privatization programs in Latin America and the 1997–98 Asian economic crisis. Thus, developing Asian economies

received increasingly larger shares of world FDI inflows beginning in the 1990s, but the Asian economic crisis temporarily reversed this trend. FDI flows soon recovered, particularly in the wake of M&As after the crisis. M&As in developing Asia rose more than 128 times by value between 1987 and 2001, from only \$256.1 million to \$32.9 billion. In descending order of size, Hong Kong, China; Republic of Korea (Korea); Philippines; Singapore; and PRC were the top five recipients of M&A flows between 1997 and 2001. This has made East Asia the top subregional recipient in developing Asia, followed by Southeast Asia ...

All subregions in Asia experienced a sharp increase in the average ratio of FDI inflows to gross fixed capital formation during the 1990s, with South Asia seeing a fivefold increase, although from a low base ... FDI inflows to developing Asia grew from only \$694 million in 1970 to a huge \$138.6 billion in 2000, before declining to \$90.1 billion in 2002, representing an average growth rate of 15.2 percent per year (ADB 2004: 215–16).

Such massive capital inflows bring potential benefits, and competition policy can facilitate the realization of benefits for the domestic economy from integrating into international trade and investment patterns. Barriers to trade and FDI influence the extent of competitive pressures in both domestic and international markets. As Lloyd (2001: 81) has stated:

> Policies relating to the liberalization of international trade, reduction in restrictions on foreign direct investment, privatization, deregulation and the protection of intellectual property rights are all relevant to the promotion of competition in markets.

The complementarity of competition and competition policy with industrial, trade, and FDI policies highlights the need for active competition advocacy. Too often the advocacy functions of competition authorities are neglected at the expense of enforcement of competition law, only to create the need for even greater enforcement as other legislation is enacted without consideration of the implications for competition.

2   TRADE LIBERALIZATION AND COMPETITION

Economic theory suggests that trade liberalization will usually increase national welfare in the context of a competitive domestic market. The mutual liberalization of trade facilitates the entry of domestic producers into external markets, bringing them export opportunities that allow them to increase output and reduce costs by achieving economies of scale. In addition, because more firms are active in export markets, competition among them is likely to be harsher, forcing producers to increase production efficiency, adopt more effective marketing and distribution techniques, and impose stricter quality control measures. As a result, domestic as well as foreign consumers will benefit from lower-priced and higher-quality products.

Similarly, greater access by foreign producers to domestic markets spurs efficiency improvements among domestic firms and broadens the range of choices of final products available to domestic consumers and of intermediate goods available to domestic firms. Greater competition may give rise to thick market effects, which arise when increased volumes of trade in a particular market increase the efficiency with which the market operates. A number of mechanisms related to competition give rise to thick market effects, including improved matching of buyers and sellers, reduced monopoly or monopsony power, and a finer division of labor as suppliers specialize to fill niche markets. In labor markets, workers and firms are better able to match their specific skills and needs the thicker the market. Greater scale also reduces the chance that excess supply of or demand for specific skills will arise (Burgess and Venables 2004).

In some cases, however, domestic producers may be unable to effect the efficiency improvements necessary in the more competitive environment. Often driven by ostensibly nationalist sentiment, governments may adopt restrictive trade practices to protect domestic industries from competition from external sources. Import tariffs are perhaps the most common instrument that developing country governments use. But when consumer interests or international commitments prevail, some governments reduce import tariffs, exposing local producers of tradable goods and services to greater competition and thereby increasing pressure to raise productivity and lower costs.

However, removal of import tariffs alone is usually not enough to keep competition at an optimal level in all economic sectors. In addition, while trade barriers have generally been reduced in many countries, they still exist. Non-tariff forms, such as contingent protection and antidumping regulations, have sometimes been adopted to replace tariffs that have been removed following international negotiations.

For small, open economies, trade liberalization may induce a market structure that encourages competition and attenuates monopolistic behavior. But when the domestic market is not competitive, the intended benefits of trade reform may not be realized without application of competition policy. When official trade barriers are reduced, they may be replaced by private anticompetitive practices that counter and dominate the price-reducing effects of trade reform. For example, lower import tariffs may merely result in higher profit margins for monopolistic (or oligopolistic) importers, instead of the benefits reaching consumers and the broader economy. To the extent that falls in the prices of imported capital equipment bolster investment and enhance dynamic economic performance, measures to discipline private anticompetitive practices may be necessary for the reductions in these trade barriers to translate into higher growth. In such cases, the enforcement of competition law can reinforce the effectiveness of cuts in trade barriers in raising the contribution to growth of imported capital goods.

It should be stressed that while international pressure from trade can help, competition from imports is less effective than domestic competition in ensuring restructuring in domestic markets that will benefit domestic consumers. Measures to promote rivalry among domestic firms tend to have more consistent effects on restructuring—and on dynamic economic performance—than does trade liberalization. Therefore, again, trade liberalization should be complemented by competition policy. It may not be enough to rely solely on the lowering of trade barriers to discipline anticompetitive practices and provide strong incentives for firms to keep costs low (OECD 2003a).

With increasingly open economies, some large producers may attempt to protect their markets through such anticompetitive acts as forming cartels, abusing a dominant position, or infringing intellectual property rights (IPRs). Local suppliers may also develop exclusive arrangements with local retailers to effectively shut out imports from the domestic market. Instead of nurturing competition, trade liberalization can sometimes result in an increase in anticompetitive practices. This may happen, for example, when international cartels take advantage of trade liberalization to expand their markets or when domestic and foreign firms collude to set prices or market shares. When this occurs, the full potential benefits of trade liberalization will not accrue to consumers, since government trade barriers are simply replaced with private anticompetitive barriers. An effective competition policy would ensure that such anticompetitive practices could be challenged and stopped if proven to violate the existing competition law. In this case, an effective competition policy would allow trade liberalization to deliver its full benefits to domestic purchasers.

Thus, while an open trade policy is supportive of competition policy objectives in principle, it is not necessarily a guarantee of competition in practice. Both government policies and private practices may still pose a threat to competition, particularly if they give rise to restraints and distortions in trade and in market signals. All trade policies should therefore be formulated in such a way that they comply with competition principles. An effective competition policy that ensures that trade policies fall within these contours is in the interests of both consumers and free trade (Government of India 2000).

Trade liberalization can both help and hinder the development of anticompetitive practices. The country studies in subsequent chapters highlight cases where reforms have led to foreign firms undermining domestic anticompetitive practices, lowering prices toward costs, and having a beneficial effect on productivity, efficiency, and choice. However, without the threat of sanctions being imposed under competition law, external suppliers and their domestic rivals would be tempted to replace lower government-imposed trade barriers with their own agreements to keep prices high. The very lowering of trade barriers in Asian economies has also sometimes enabled foreign firms to engage more profitably in anticompetitive acts. Competition law and its effective enforcement thus play an important role in maximizing the realized benefits of trade liberalization.

In the six countries studied in this volume, a range of both internal and external factors has influenced the interaction of competition policy with international trade and investment policies. These factors include a recognition that outward-oriented economies generally grow more quickly than closed economies, and that it is still possible to achieve a wide variety of national objectives in the context of an open economy where competition is promoted. Competitive trade and investment liberalizations—to keep an economy at least as open as its rivals—have been another factor. Foreign pressure, including the requirement to join international agencies, has often contributed, as in the case of the Republic of Korea (Korea), where external pressure as a result of the Asian financial crisis played a key role. Conversely, the dissolution of an international benefactor (the former Soviet Union) was a major factor leading to the onset of reform in Viet Nam.

Promotion of competition, through its effects on trade, can also play an important role in the recovery of crisis-hit economies. When consumer demand is slack, government budgets are tight, and investment has fallen due to reduced confidence, exports play a critical role in stimulating recovery. Crucial to the competitiveness of exports is productivity enhancement resulting from the efficiency gains of competition. The 1997–98 financial crisis also served as a reminder that although restrictions on competition may at first appear compatible with an open trade and FDI regime, mounting tensions may remain hidden. This reinforces the precautionary value of considering competition concerns when formulating trade and investment policies.

Openness to the international economy varies significantly among the six countries studied in this volume. All have become more open to trade in recent decades, as indicated by both trade reforms and rising export to GDP ratios. This ratio has increased by 50 percent or more in all of the countries since 1990. Malaysia and Thailand are among a select group of developing economies that were classified as 'always open' by Sachs and Warner (1995). Both exhibit very high trade shares, low average tariffs, modest interindustry tariff dispersion, and limited non-tariff barriers.

Korea also now has a fairly low average tariff rate. Notwithstanding recent reforms, the People's Republic of China (PRC), India, and Viet Nam still have relatively high tariff and non-tariff barriers. Again, the more protected an economy is, the more limited is competition, likely reducing the degree of allocative efficiency.

Among the six countries, Korea's trade and investment regime has been the most unusual. From the early 1960s until the late 1990s, it achieved very rapid export-led growth in the context of very restrictive policies toward imports (except those required as inputs for manufactured exports) and toward FDI. Its industrial policy resulted in great achievements, but at a relatively high cost. In addition to tariff reform and a reduced incidence of non-tariff barriers, Korea's reforms in the 1990s included a reduction in subsidies as well as customs simplification. Much of the liberalization was driven by a desire to join the General Agreement on Tariffs and Trade/World Trade Organization (WTO) and the Organisation for Economic Co-operation and Development (OECD), and by the imperative to implement reforms following the 1997–98 crisis. Partly as a result, the country has now become an active advocate for the benefits of competition policy and hosts the OECD's Regional Competition Centre for Asia.

Viet Nam's re-engagement with the international economy is more recent. Consequently, its official trade regime remains opaque and poorly documented, as is typical of a late reformer. Only quite recently was a formal tariff schedule released. Viet Nam still retains very high levels of protection (several hundred percent) for its automotive, sugar, and garment industries, limiting competition in those sectors. Much of the remaining protection is firm-specific in nature and tailored to the needs of inefficient state-owned enterprises (SOEs). Viet Nam aspires to WTO membership in the near future. This may constitute a strong incentive for it to continue with and broaden the reform process, increasing the role of competition and competition policy.

Notwithstanding their diversity, almost all developing Asian economies have adopted progressively more open policies toward international competition during the past decade or two, and this trend seems set to continue. This more open posture has been demonstrated, among other measures, in the adoption of more liberal trade and FDI regimes. This process has had profound implications for the promotion and enforcement of competition. The resulting changes have been so rapid in some cases that the policy and institutional framework in which they occur has been unable to keep pace.

3   TRADE-RELATED PROVISIONS IN COMPETITION LAW

For many countries, export cartels are outside the scope of competition law. Export cartels can be competition restricting, but are nevertheless exempted from competition law because they do not affect competition in the domestic market. In India, for example, an exception to the provisions on anticompetitive agreements protects the right of any person to export goods or services from India. One justification for the exemption of export cartels is that countries do not wish to deter export efforts for fear of reducing their trade or current account balances. Countries allowing export cartels argue that they help to realize cost-reducing and output-enhancing efficiencies (OECD 2003b). However, the exemption of export cartels goes against the idea of free competition, as the circumstances relating to a soda ash cartel operating in India make clear (Chapter 5). Consequently, other countries' competition laws explicitly or implicitly exempt export cartels.

In India, the new Competition Act also has extraterritorial reach. The jurisdiction of the competition authority extends to restrictive trade practices of enterprises outside India that have the effect of preventing, distorting, or restricting competition in India, or that give rise to restrictive trade practices there. However, the Supreme Court of India ruled that the Monopolies and Restrictive Trade Practices Commission could obtain jurisdiction only after goods had been imported and a restrictive trade practice was found to have taken place.

Korea's competition law likewise claims extraterritorial jurisdiction. In 2002 the Korea Fair Trade Commission (KFTC) applied Korean antitrust law extraterritorially, for the first time, to six foreign manufacturers of graphite electrodes and imposed fines on the manufacturers for price fixing (Chapter 6). The following year the KFTC concluded a large-scale investigation into an alleged international cartel by six foreign vitamin manufacturers, again levying fines. It also introduced a system of notification for foreign-to-foreign M&As. Attempts such as these to regulate behavior outside the domestic jurisdiction reflect a growing concern about the economic impact of such extraterritorial anticompetitive behavior on domestic markets.

This illustrates that as markets integrate, international anticompetitive practices—especially those associated with abuse of a dominant position and international cartels—are receiving more attention in Asian policy circles. Although Asian enforcement experience against foreign anticompetitive practices has been mixed, such enforcement would not have been possible in the first place without competition laws, which have both formed a prerequisite for enforcement and provided the basis for nurturing international cooperation to tackle such practices.

At the international level, in 1980 the United Nations General Assembly adopted a 'Set of Multilaterally Agreed Equitable Principles and Rules for the Control of Restrictive Business Practices' (the 'UN Set'). In 1995, the Osaka Action Agenda of the Asia-Pacific Economic Cooperation (APEC) forum included competition policy as one of 15 policy areas to be developed by member countries, noting that

> APEC economies will enhance the competitive environment in the Asia-Pacific region by introducing or maintaining effective and adequate competition policy and/or laws and associated enforcement policies, ensuring the transparency of the above and promoting cooperation among the APEC economies, thereby maximizing, inter alia, the efficient operation of markets, competition among producers and consumer benefits (APEC 1995).

This was reinforced by a collective action plan as well as individual action plans in the area of competition policy and, in 1999, by the APEC Principles to Enhance Competition and Regulatory Reform.

In July 2004, the General Council of the WTO decided that only one of the four so-called Singapore issues (trade facilitation, but not competition policy, investment, or government procurement) would be included in the Doha Round of negotiations, because developing countries needed more capacity building and institution building in these areas first. However, given the importance of competition in ensuring economic efficiency in both its static and dynamic aspects, competition policy remains of considerable interest to developing countries in both the domestic and international contexts. Indeed, in the context of multilateral negotiations, as the head of the UK's Office of Fair Trading has noted:

> developed country protectionism ... is bad not only for developing country producers and consumers everywhere but also for developed country credibility in global negotiations to remove trade barriers. What is needed is more globalization, not less (Vickers 2003: 8).

4   FOREIGN DIRECT INVESTMENT AND COMPETITION

Another area where competition law can enhance dynamic efficiency is in its interaction with FDI. In particular, appropriate enforcement of competition law both enhances the attractiveness of an economy as a location for foreign investment and is important to maximize the benefits that flow from such investment.

If both labor and capital are fully employed before and after an international capital flow, the total and average returns to capital increase, and total and average returns to labor decrease, in the source country, changing the distribution of income among factors of production. While the source country gains as a whole, income is redistributed from labor to capital. Meanwhile, in the recipient country, income is redistributed from capital to labor, as total and average returns to capital decrease and total and average returns to labor increase. The result is potentially a win–win situation for both countries. However, competition authorities need to be aware that income redistribution also changes the incentives for competition.

Capital inflows do not always increase welfare in the host country. For example, when capital flows to an industry in which an existing firm has monopoly power in the world market, an increase in output from the new competition lowers the price of the exportable, thus reducing the terms of trade and lowering welfare in the host country. Also, the benefits from foreign investment are usually assessed under the assumption that host countries can absorb a large inflow of capital without a large decline in its rate of return. But if capital grows much faster than the productivity of labor, its productivity will fall, which might reduce its rate of return.

Under full employment, a capital inflow that reduces the relative scarcity of capital and raises the productivity of labor in the host country can raise real wages across the board and reduce income disparity within the host country. However, the question of distribution also arises with respect to the competition for gains between foreign capital and host country factors. Traditionally, foreign investment was geared toward primary commodity exports. In some cases this led to capacity expansion, productivity growth, declining prices of exportable commodities, and deterioration in the host country's terms of trade, possibly leading to welfare losses. In addition, there were (and are) generally few spillovers to the rest of the host economy from primary commodity production. The resulting view was that the gains from capital inflows favor the source economy more than the host economy. This has been superseded by a more favorable view as FDI flows have increasingly moved into sectors with greater benefits for host economies.

Overall, FDI inflows can contribute significantly to competition and development. But while most developing countries have already opened their doors to foreign investors, governments are well aware that there is no guarantee that the potential benefits of FDI will automatically accrue to the host economies.[1] This is partly because FDI does not always result in a more competitive market structure and can result in anticompetitive practices. FDI in the form of cross-border M&A activity in particular may lead to concentration and market dominance in some industries. Since such activity often merely results in an increase in the stake of foreign investors in existing domestic firms, it may not increase the number of market players. In such an event, the dominant firm could have price-setting abilities and would likely enjoy higher profit margins. In some cases, large multinational enterprises (MNEs) can even eliminate competition by crowding out domestic producers. As an integral part of global value chains, MNEs have a built-in advantage (for example, economies of scale and scope) over their local competitors.

Alternatively, affiliates of different MNEs can set up competing businesses in a developing host country. If the parent MNEs in the home country or countries then merge their operations, the affiliates in the host country are likely eventually to merge as well, possibly creating a firm with market power. It could even be the case that the merger eliminates competition in the host country while not doing so in the MNEs' home country.

Just as with trade reform, FDI liberalization in Asia has both undermined and created anticompetitive practices. Because foreign investors often come with better technologies and management practices, assessing the advantages and disadvantages of cross-border M&As requires careful evaluation of the efficiency effects as well as of any potential price-increasing effects. In some cases, FDI has been driven by changes in competition policy or regulations in source countries. For example, deregulation, privatization, and financial sector liberalization have spurred a surge in cross-border M&As.

Competition concerns should therefore influence the nature of FDI liberalization, and vice versa. A typical relevant provision in competition laws is the ban on any merger, acquisition, or takeover that would give the newly merged firm a dominant position in the market, or that would prevent potential competitors from gaining access to a market. To complicate matters, avoiding these consequences entails the adoption of effective competition policy in both the home and host countries, arguing for international coordination of competition policies.

As trade and investment policies have been liberalized, the old 'tariff factory' model of FDI has given way to a new concentration of FDI in areas that generate greater exports. This is sometimes characterized as a switch from 'rent-seeking' to 'efficiency-seeking' FDI. This transformation has profound implications for competition in host countries and for their management of FDI. The contemporary challenge for developing countries is to develop a new approach to managing FDI and its effects on domestic industrial structures.

As foreign investors search for the location that will provide the highest returns on their investment, they may be drawn to countries with abundant natural resources but low-quality institutions. Weak and inefficient institutions, including those that would allow anticompetitive practices, allow the extraction of natural resources at a pace faster than the maximum allowable for sustainable development. In the same context, the market access and attraction of a location for foreign trade and investment depends on its infrastructure, and in particular on the quality of the internal and external transport and communications links that serve it.

In a globalizing world, competition for FDI is rarely any longer about economic rents, but instead focuses on the establishment of an enabling, business-friendly commercial environment, consistent with national development objectives. In this context, a useful paradigm is the so-called 'three Is': incentives, institutions, and infrastructure. That is, as economies open up, these three factors are key determinants not only of the overall rate of economic growth, but also of the magnitude and productivity of capital flows and of the rate at which potential benefits from competition are realized (Hill 2004).

The growing evidence that foreign investment can make a significant contribution to domestic development has increased the proliferation of incentives to attract FDI. Government action at the national level can enhance FDI prospects by significantly reducing uncertainty, asymmetric information (and related search costs), and other transaction costs faced by foreign investors (especially the amount of time and number of steps involved in acquiring approval).

Tax breaks and subsidies are also common, but generally influence investment location decisions only at the margin. More important to most potential investors are the size and expected growth rate of the market that could be served, long-term macroeconomic and political stability, the supply of skilled or trainable workers, and modern transportation and communications infrastructure. Only once these criteria have been satisfied are typical financial incentives likely to influence the investor's choice of suitable sites. Of greater importance for competition, such financial incentives usually create distortions and inefficiencies (Brooks, Fan, and Sumulong 2004).

Such schemes distort the relative costs for other sectors and investment projects that are not targeted for incentives. They thereby typically discriminate against smaller and domestic investors, as well as against areas of comparative advantage that are not recognized as such by policymakers. Over time, these actions can also contribute to the development of a governance system that lacks transparency and accountability.

Too often, policies ostensibly designed to maximize the net benefits of FDI for recipient economies have inhibited competition by encouraging the construction of subscale manufacturing plants. These frequently result from mandatory joint ventures that are not allowed to source inputs freely and that contribute little to the technological, social, or economic development of the country. Arrangements between foreign investors and host country authorities that block other new entrants to the industry or that restrict alternative low-cost sources of supply are also common, but are generally not in the best interests of the host country. Counteracting the competition-limiting impact, the host country can capture part of the rents from scale economies through a licensing fee or an increase in factor prices in the export sector, when foreign firms bid up factor costs above the level sustained by the small domestic export industry.

The potential benefits to the host economy are greatest when international companies can exploit economies of scale both locally and globally, and are continually driven to update their technologies and managerial practices in order to remain competitive. Incentives for foreign investors and benefits for the host economy are less when the investments are directed toward serving small and protected domestic markets. Competition policy can therefore strengthen the benefits associated with FDI for the host economy.

Similarly, investors will invest more of the latest proprietary technology and procedures when they feel that they have the greatest control over protection of the proprietary content and greatest freedom in its use. Restrictions such as forced sharing of technology through mandatory joint ventures, local content, or other performance criteria reduce the investor's incentives to apply the most modern techniques and technologies, hindering integration into the global sourcing network of the parent company. In this manner, they also constrain competition. Subsidiaries have been found to receive greater resources than partially licensed or partially owned or independent firms, with lower transaction costs involved in technology transfer. Thus, multinational investment is found to be superior to direct licensing of technology to independent firms. Technology transfer and interchange of managers and technicians between parent and subsidiary firms have been found to be significantly higher for wholly owned subsidiaries than for joint venture partnerships or licensees (Ramachandran 1993).

Import-substituting industries that benefit from infant industry protection have rarely grown to become globally competitive. The hopes that some countries once held that domestic content and joint venture requirements for foreign investors would stimulate domestic supply chains have faded. In fact, empirical evidence has accumulated in the last two decades to show that the reverse is actually more likely. FDI facilitates unconstrained integration into international supply chains, allowing host economies to both increase the efficiency of existing activities and enter into new economic activities. Wholly owned affiliates of foreign firms will compete to source from wherever they find most advantageous. This helps domestic suppliers to compete, as they achieve economies of scale and become integrated into global supply chains, often under the direct supervision of the foreign-owned buyers. Foreign buyers have increasingly helped local suppliers export first to sister plants and later to independent purchasers in order to lower the suppliers' costs of production through economies of scale, thereby promoting contract manufacturing as an implicit new infant industry development strategy. Externalities in the adoption of production, quality control, and managerial processes (including export coaching) frequently spread vertically within the invested sector and eventually to other sectors of the host economy (Moran 2002).[2]

Generally, MNEs are attracted to locations with competition policies already in place. This is because the existence of a competition policy indicates some commitment by the government to ensure a level playing field among investors, whether domestic or foreign. Thus, government policy on FDI must be consistent with the objectives of competition policy in order to gain the full benefits of FDI. For example, governments should avoid trying to attract foreign investors by granting anticompetitive concessions, such as monopoly rights to particular markets or industries, because that increases the chance that the overall long-run impact on the economy will be negative.

In recent years all of the six countries studied in this volume have generally been open to FDI. This has been true in Malaysia and Thailand for longer than in the other countries. Relaxing foreign participation requirements can generally be expected to contribute to an increase in competition in the domestic economy, but this has not always resulted in increased competition in the domestic markets. This is because other government regulations and policies have created barriers to the development of free competition. In the PRC and Viet Nam, for example, local content requirements are used to encourage backward linkages. This provides a constraint on foreign-invested firms trying to obtain their inputs from the best possible source, compelling them to use local suppliers instead. Thus, even with FDI liberalization, other regulations can effectively limit the potential expansion of rivalry, and increased competition is not guaranteed.

In India, Korea, and Malaysia, protection of small-scale firms prevents entry by large firms in certain sectors and industries. As a result, some service industries, such as retailing, have remained uncompetitive in spite of FDI liberalization. In Korea, larger retail stores need approval by the local government advisory board, but these boards generally have strong connections with existing retailers who lobby against the big retailers. In Malaysia, as noted in Chapter 7, more stringent conditions were initially imposed on foreign-owned hypermarkets in an effort to protect small local retail stores. Eventually a five-year ban on the establishment of new foreign-owned hypermarkets was enforced, perpetuating inefficiencies in the domestic retail industry.

In every country, competition enforcement and advocacy play an important role. Effectively enforced competition law discourages detrimental FDI without placing an inordinate burden on efficiency-enhancing foreign investment. However, poorly or arbitrarily enforced competition law can deter overseas investors. Moreover, there is a role for competition advocacy to ensure that the inducements offered and requirements placed on foreign investors in an effort to attract or control FDI do not seriously distort competition. In the resulting competitive environment without distortions, FDI can contribute substantially to growth and development.

The evidence concerning the effects of FDI on competition, concentration, and profitability in the six economies studied in this volume is mixed, as it is in the general literature. A priori, FDI entry might be expected to lower concentration simply because a new entrant means more producers. In the longer term, concentration could rise if the foreign firms were able to drive out local competitors or if they located in oligopolistic industries (as they often do, to exploit firm-specific advantages). In addition, the host country's trade policy matters: MNEs are more likely to be attracted to countries with outward-oriented regimes to be able to fully exploit vertically integrated international production processes. Thus, if their primary motivation is export orientation, as it normally is, competition issues may largely be irrelevant.

Moreover, in open economies, high concentration levels per se are not necessarily a problem—certainly not in tradable goods sectors, where industry is exposed to foreign competition. Of course, even in the most open economies, there are public policy concerns about activities that may be characterized as natural monopolies, or that are essentially non-traded. However, there is typically much less discussion or concern about monopolies in an open economy than in countries with more interventionist regimes.

In reality, much of the analysis of concentration, including the effects of FDI, focuses on a commercial environment featuring state-sanctioned monopolies combined with restrictive trade barriers. In other words, the 'competition problem' has more to do with the removal of government privileges, barriers to entry, and protection from imports. In the PRC and

Viet Nam, SOEs continue to receive special assistance from government, some of it in the form of restrictions on competition. Where these SOEs form joint ventures with foreign firms, MNE entry may then appear to be a cause of increased concentration, whereas in fact the main problem lies with the regulatory regime.

Similar general comments apply to Korea and India, although their SOE sectors have historically been smaller. The promotion of *chaebol* (conglomerates) in Korea resulted in high levels of concentration and an underdeveloped small and medium-sized enterprise sector. India's interventionist industrial planning regime also stifled competition. For this reason also, studies of the effects of FDI in the pre-reform period provide little indication of likely effects in the post-reform era.

The extent of competition is best measured by 'contestability,' as illustrated in Thailand. After its recent FDI liberalization, concentration fell significantly in the banking industry, but may have risen in the retail sector as large international companies pushed out small traders. However, although there may have been some adverse social consequences in the retail sector, competitive pressures from new entrants appear to have lowered retail margins.

5   DYNAMIC CONSIDERATIONS

A major challenge for policy-makers is to keep up with a rapidly changing international commercial environment. In the case of competition, as with FDI, for an economy to reap the full benefits, the quality of incentives, institutions, and infrastructure matters. In transition economies, the first round of reforms has typically focused on macroeconomic stabilization and partial trade liberalization, while other, microeconomic, components essential for competition typically lag.

During economic transition or reform, the benefits of an open market economy cannot be fully realized unless restrictions on competition are removed. This has been reflected recently in India (where competition policy has been revised and expanded), Viet Nam (where a new competition policy was adopted in late 2004), and the PRC (which has firm plans to develop and implement a new competition policy).

Globalization can create waves of increases in competition. Initial foreign investments by MNEs create demand for local suppliers and improve their productivity, product range, and quality. Large numbers of local firms enter to supply components or assembly services to the foreign-invested firms, increasing competition among suppliers. This growth of component and other intermediate goods supply and increase in productivity in turn create a forward linkage effect to the final goods producers, subsequently drawing in even more foreign and domestically owned firms, boosting competition further. There subsequently follows a second round (and further rounds) of backward linkages, with local firms eventually displacing the original multinational entrants in some cases (Hobday 1995).

The dynamic spread of spillover effects across sectors depends in part on the diversity of the environment, with innovation being stimulated by opportune interactions occurring in a large and diverse urban area. Knowledge spillovers may also take place within narrowly defined sectors, as production information is transmitted from firm to firm. Positive dependence of productivity on employment levels in the same city and industry has been found for a number of countries, including Indonesia (Henderson and Kuncoro 1996) and Korea (Henderson, Lee, and Lee 2001). Note that the acquisition and the spread of knowledge are important in selling as well as in production (Roberts and Tybout 1997).

As emphasized above, freedom of entry and exit is a crucial condition for maximizing the efficiency benefits of competitive markets and for generating the resulting lower production costs that can boost the competitiveness of the country's exporters in foreign markets. However, the industrial structure most efficient for static resource allocation is not necessarily the most efficient for dynamic efficiency. Some temporary market power after a new invention or innovation is introduced may be necessary to provide firms with the incentive to undertake such inventions or innovations. This will require consistency and coherence among industrial, trade, investment, competition, and intellectual property regimes.

An area of notable tension between competition concerns and incentives for invention and innovation that will contribute to long-term development is thus IPRs. Protection of IPRs also plays an important role in attracting advanced technology production processes through FDI. Weak intellectual property protection deters foreign investors in technology-intensive sectors that rely heavily on IPRs, and encourages investors to undertake projects focusing on distribution rather than local production (Smarzynska 2002).

The importance of IPRs in influencing potentially beneficial temporary deviations from competition arises in international as well as domestic contexts. The appropriate international IPR policy takes account of one's competitors' policies and may involve a role for game theory in policy formulation:

> A country's optimal patent policy is found by equating the sum of the extra deadweight loss that results from strengthening the IPR protection granted to

domestic firms and the extra consumer surplus loss that results from expanding the fraction of goods that are subject to monopoly pricing with the benefits that flow from providing greater incentives for innovation to firms worldwide. A country's optimal IPR protection depends on the policies set by its trading partner, because the strength of foreign patent rights affects the responsiveness of global innovation to a change in a country's own patent policies (Grossman and Lai 2004).

While this argues for international coordination of competition policies, the need for a multilateral agreement in the WTO context remains contentious.

6   CONCLUSIONS

Countries with different initial conditions of competition and at different stages of reform or integration with global trade and investment flows may follow different paths to reaping the gains from competition. However, the globalizing economic environment imposes a form of discipline on domestic economic activity, creating pressure to promote the sort of efficiency improvements that competition can bring.

Two factors have been important. The first has been the more or less simultaneous liberalization of both trade and FDI regimes. The second has been technological advances in transport costs and production technologies. The rise of the 'global factory' has been made possible by substantial reductions in international transport costs and by disaggregated, transborder production processes, particularly in MNE-intensive industries such as electronics and automobiles. In the most successful cases of these industrial clusters, production operations constitute a seamless web in which national boundaries virtually disappear. Consequently, boundaries between domestic competition and international competition have become less meaningful.

The trend toward greater openness and globalization is likely to continue, with competition playing a key role in enhancing the international competitiveness of a country's firms. In turn, growing firms will contribute to the country's growth and employment. In this context, participating in international organizations such as the WTO or OECD is an effective way to bring the pressures of international competition to bear on domestic markets. Most measures to protect domestic industries or firms create barriers to entry and can lead to high concentration in affected sectors. At the subnational level, local protectionism can lead to market fragmentation and low regional specialization.

Opening markets is not enough by itself for countries to begin reaping the benefits of competition. Firms will still face incentives to engage in anticompetitive practices. Thus, the intended benefits of trade reform may not be realized without active enforcement of competition law. The Korean case illustrates that trade liberalization does not automatically lead to greater competition in the domestic market, and that the best outcomes are achieved when liberalization is accompanied by measures to increase competition. It highlights the importance of having confidence in the benefits of competition from an early stage of economic growth and of incorporating competition policy into the broader economic policy framework.

With regional and global integration accelerating, the pressures of international competition and their context have become increasingly palpable. However, as we have seen, competition policy is important in its own right for domestic reasons, and does not have to be considered jointly with the rest of the Doha Round's Singapore issues. Regardless of whether multilateral rules on competition policy are negotiated under the WTO, each country should strive to develop and implement its own competition policy.

The general conclusion is that competition confers net benefits on an economy. Productivity rises, choice expands, and some (generally the bulk) of the increased benefits are appropriated by domestic consumers and factors of production. These benefits appear to be especially important in connecting the country to the global economy and ensuring the international competitiveness of its firms as the country develops. At the same time, the discipline of participating in a globalizing economy reinforces the importance of competition and of competition policy.

NOTES

*   The author is grateful to the other authors in this volume and staff at the Asian Development Bank for helpful comments and much useful information, and to Lea R. Sumulong for assistance in preparing this chapter.

1   For a more complete discussion of FDI in developing Asia, see Brooks and Hill (2004).

2   However, the affiliates of foreign investors generally try to avoid horizontal technology transfers that may increase the level of competition they face.

3

Would enforcing competition law compromise industrial policy objectives?

Simon J. Evenett

1 INTRODUCTION

One recurring concern in the debate over the efficacy of enacting competition laws in developing countries is that their enforcement may compromise important industrial policy goals and associated measures. This concern has been raised in regional fora and in multilateral organizations such as the World Trade Organization (WTO), where officials have considered the pros and cons of including competition provisions in international trade agreements. However, the concern is broader, and often national debates over the merits of adopting a competition law touch on the implications for the operation of national industrial policies. In fact, as the chapters in this book on the People's Republic of China (PRC), Malaysia, and Viet Nam attest, the apparent primacy given to industrial policy has substantially colored recent debates on whether to adopt a competition law. Given the recent upturn in interest in industrial policy in Europe and Latin America,[1] and the considerable dissatisfaction with the Washington Consensus elsewhere in the developing world, the discussion in this chapter will also be of interest to scholars and policy-makers outside of East Asia. In Europe, none other than the European Commissioner for Enterprise and Industry was reported in January 2005 as calling for a re-evaluation of the way in which prospective mergers and acquisitions are reviewed (a form of competition law enforcement) so as to bolster international competitiveness, a traditional industrial policy goal.

This chapter is devoted to examining the extent to which active industrial policy-making in East Asia has necessitated government measures to curb interfirm rivalry. So as to fix ideas, the leading notions (definitions is too strong a word) of industrial policy are described and their relationship to competition law and its enforcement discussed. Then post-war evidence on the extent to which the intensity of interfirm rivalry has been modulated as part of national industrial and development strategy is discussed, drawing on leading analyses of four fast-growing East Asian economies: Japan, the Republic of Korea (Korea), Taipei,China, and the PRC. This account also sheds light on the prevalence and effectiveness of attempts to modulate competition in these economies and, therefore, on the extent to which industrial policy objectives would have been compromised by the effective enforcement of competition law. In addition, five ways in which competition law can be drafted or implemented so as to carve out space for industrial policy concerns are identified on the basis of actual national experience. This last section is important, for if readers are not persuaded by the post-war evidence presented here, they can be assured that countries can find ways—and have found ways—to reconcile the implementation of competition law with the goals of industrial policy.

A few words of warning are appropriate before readers progress further. Understanding the relationships between interfirm rivalry, competition law, and industrial policy is not straightforward. This is not because of any inherent difficulty in understanding the causal links at work, but rather because three factors have muddled thinking on this important subject. The first is that, despite the voluminous literature on industrial policy, there is remarkably little agreement on what it is (a point that will become abundantly clear in the next section). Agreement on the relationships between any other subject and industrial policy is therefore hard to establish when the latter is 'defined' in so many different ways, generating the impression of much controversy. In contrast to this lack of definitional clarity is the almost religious[2] belief that many writers have in the efficacy or inefficacy of industrial policy. All of this makes for a discussion dominated by more heat than light. In this chapter, I do not need to take a stand on whether or not industrial policy works. Rather I focus on the narrower question of whether the implementation of competition law compromises the effectiveness of industrial policy, as conceived by a number of leading authors.

The second hurdle facing readers interested in the links between competition law and industrial policy is that much of the (admittedly scarce) writing on this subject actually refers to the broader question of the relationship between interfirm rivalry and industrial policy. It should be remembered that properly executed competition law is only one way to bolster interfirm rivalry (see Chapter 1). Therefore, seeing a positive contribution for competition law does not imply an endorsement of every means to promote interfirm rivalry, including, potentially, trade reforms and liberalized investment regimes.

Given the imprecise and diverse definitions of industrial policy and the confusion of measures to promote interfirm rivalry in general with competition law in particular, a writer in this field runs the serious risk of inadvertently mischaracterizing the arguments in existing scholarship. (Indeed, in some cases there is a risk of summarizing an argument in such a way as to make it more coherent than the original formulation!) To give readers the best possible opportunity to judge competing arguments and perspectives, I have quoted generously from the leading contributions on industrial policy and East Asian development *that make some reference to the role played by interfirm rivalry or measures to promote or retard competition between firms*. As I hope will become clear, when one describes precisely what various scholars have said, the range of opinion actually narrows markedly. Moreover, some long-held views have been undermined by recent empirical analyses. In short, there is a pay-off to going beyond appeals to first principles and paradigms to examine what was actually argued and what evidence has been advanced. As far as the question addressed in this chapter is concerned, I would argue that the approach taken here has no peer in the existing literature on interfirm rivalry, industrial policy, and East Asian economic development. This approach also has a policy-relevant pay-off, namely that there are clearly identifiable circumstances under which effectively enforced competition law can be a useful—if not essential—complement to national industrial policy. The question should therefore *not* be whether the former compromises the latter, but whether in the future the latter can be pursued effectively without the former.

2   CHARACTERIZING INDUSTRIAL POLICY

The characterization of industrial policy in the extant literature is considerably less precise than in the case of competition law,[3] and this alone is no doubt a source of considerable confusion in discussions on development policy. Given that no single accepted definition of industrial policy exists, a number of different perspectives are described in detail below.

A recurring theme is that an objective of industrial policy in developing economies is to facilitate a 'structural transformation' of their economies. Singh (2002: 22) puts it this way:

> … the crucial importance of industrial policy is to achieve structural changes required for development.

Likewise, in their survey of developing countries' industrial policies, Dervis and Page (1984: 436) argue:

> In the period following the Second World War, structural change in favour of industry was viewed as a necessary pre-requisite for modernisation and growth in most, if not all, developing economies. The primary objective of their industrial policy was to speed up the process of industrialization in order to achieve levels of industrial development that were comparable with those in Europe and North America.

Pugel (1984: 421) in his analysis of post-war Japanese industrial policy strikes a similar note:

> Japan's industrial policy in general aims at achieving real economic growth by encouraging shifts in resources to more productive uses, both shifts within firms and industries and shifts in the relative sizes of different industries.

The final objective of industrial policy appears to be faster national economic growth and development; the intermediate objective is to expand the output of those sectors with high value-added or the potential for considerable growth in value-added. It is worth emphasizing that not every industry need—on the definitions above—be identified as having high value-added or offering prospects for fast growth. Furthermore, nothing in principle prevents a non-industrial sector—such as a service or an agricultural sector—from being so identified.

Some scholars are unsatisfied with the available definitions of industrial policy and have detected other objectives for industrial policy. For example, Bora, Lloyd, and Pangestu (1999: 1–2) argue as follows:

> It should be pointed out at the outset that the term 'industrial policy' is not a well-defined one. It is ill-defined in relation to its objectives, the industries that are covered and the instruments that are used. The World Bank (1993)[4] has provided a working definition of industrial policy as 'government efforts to alter industrial structure to promote productivity based growth.' This definition is useful since it focuses on the objective of economy-wide factor productivity growth rather than on merely changing the structure of outputs.
>
> With regard to objectives, many developing countries have in mind the potential for long-run productivity growth improvements. However, in most cases industrial policy is pursued with multiple objectives, increasing short-term employment, increased output, better income distribution and enhancing technological capacity. There are often also, rightly or wrongly, non-economic objectives of national pride and prestige, as well as the perceived need to promote 'strategic' domestic industries.
>
> These objectives are further confused to the extent that many developing economies have taken the view that ownership of assets matters. There is a concern that foreign ownership may not always fit in well with broader development objectives, including enhancing domestic capabilities. In some cases, foreign ownership could crowd out domestic firms. Thus, even if the World Bank definition is adopted ... the fact remains that developing countries have raised concerns about the source of growth.

In sum, then, there appears to be a multiplicity of objectives of industrial policies employed by developing economies.

There is no accepted set of instruments that is considered part of industrial policy. Several characterizations of this set can be found in the literature. In his path-breaking and heterodox analysis of East Asian industrialization, Wade (1990) differentiates between functional and sectoral policy instruments. The latter he defines as follows:

> A sectoral industrial policy aims to direct resources into selected industries so as to give producers in those industries a competitive advantage (Wade 1990: 13).[5]

In contrast, functional policy instruments affect economy-wide factors (such as the supply of engineers or the price of energy) or, in principle, alter in the same manner firms' or investors' incentives irrespective of the industry or sector in which they operate. An example of a functional instrument of industrial policy would be an economy-wide investment subsidy or tax credit.

Tilton (1996) identifies two types of industrial policy instrument in his analysis of post-war Japanese economic performance. The first instrument is described below:

> The principal way industrial policy functions here is by allocating resources to favoured sectors. It can do so through policies that directly provide resources to industries, such as tax breaks, loans, subsidies, and import protection. More important, however, have been policies to reduce competition between firms … Industrial policy may also support industry by providing or helping to circulate information about market or technological opportunities (Tilton 1996: 2–3).

He goes on to add:

> A second form of industrial policy, strategic trade policy, seeks to appropriate the benefits of strategic industrial sectors by promoting them at home and helping them gain a larger share of world markets (Tilton 1996: 3).[6]

For the purposes of this chapter, Tilton's characterization of industrial policy is important because it highlights how some competition policy and trade policy instruments are also seen by some as industrial policy instruments.

Pangestu (2002: 150–51) presents perhaps the most exhaustive categorization of the instruments of industrial policy:

> In practice, countries have used a wide range of instruments in the name of industrial policy. These can be categorized as external, product, and factor market interventions.
>
> *External market interventions* involve protecting domestic industries from imports, using instruments such as import tariffs, quotas, licensing, and local content programs, as well as export promotion measures to assist industries to

catch up and break into new markets. Common export promotion instruments are export subsidies, export promotion zones, and subsidized credit (sometimes tied to export targets).

Product market interventions to promote competition in domestic markets include competition policy (to ensure fair competition between domestic players as well as for foreign players) and domestic market entry regulations.

Factor market interventions include policies such as performance requirements and restrictions on foreign direct investment (FDI) designed to influence the operations of foreign affiliates so that the host country realizes a net benefit from FDI. Factor market interventions in the capital market and the financial sector are aimed at correcting financial market imperfections, promoting infant industries, and protecting or phasing out declining industries. These measures include setting up development finance institutions, providing direct capital subsidies to selected industrial enterprises, furnishing capital subsidies and capital assistance to declining or mature industries, and providing priority access to credit (often at subsidized rates) by requiring financial institutions to lend to particular sectors or types of companies. Intervention in the labor market may have efficiency and equity objectives. The former have to do with human resource development through education and training; the latter include minimum wage requirements and social safety net schemes.

Pangestu's characterization of the instruments of industrial policy is of interest for a number of reasons. First, her characterization highlights how the enforcement of competition law is *one* of the large number of policy instruments associated with industrial policy.[7] This is important because it implies that the preponderance of industrial policy instruments fall outside the domain of competition law. Second, Pangestu presumes that the goal of competition law here is to promote rivalry, and not to restrain it as Tilton suggested. This is the first hint here of divergent views as to the contribution of rivalry between firms to economic development. Third, the very fact that Pangestu feels the need to list so many policy instruments so as to accurately characterize the term 'industrial policy' suggests that the latter term is so wide-ranging as to be of little more than descriptive value.

3   THE POST-WAR EXPERIENCE OF FOUR EAST ASIAN ECONOMIES

The goal of this section is not to describe or summarize *current* policies in East Asia, nor is it to dwell on the broader and voluminous literature on the factors responsible for the region's economic fortunes. Rather, it is to assess the *post-war* relationship between competition policy and industrial policy in the national development strategies of selected East Asian economies that have been the subject of scholarly contributions relevant to this subject. The discussion focuses in particular on the extent of governmental competition policy-related measures to stimulate or retard inter-firm rivalry, and their contribution to firm, industrial, and national economic performance. Only the literature that speaks directly to this matter is described at any length below; consequently, the reader may not see reference to some leading studies of East Asian development that do not place particular emphasis on the role of competition policy in the region's economic performance.[8] This section looks, in particular, at the experience of four economies: Japan, Korea, Taipei,China, and the PRC.

Japan

Amsden and Singh (1994a) have analyzed Japan's use of competition policy instruments during the high economic growth period of 1953–70, an era that some have argued is particularly relevant to developing economies today.[9] They observe that the legacy of the antitrust laws imposed by the US occupation authorities in the post-World War II period was short-lived. Increasingly, the Japanese government prioritized the achievement of national development goals over competition and is said to have managed competition pragmatically in key domestic industries. Institutionally, it is argued, this was reflected at the time by the dominance of Japan's Ministry of International Trade and Industry (MITI) over the Japanese Fair Trade Commission. In fact, in order to promote investment and stimulate increases in productivity, MITI encouraged the formation of cartels and mergers in a variety of industries, particularly during the 1950s and 1960s. Most of MITI's policies during the high-growth years were characterized by a bias against competition, implemented through the agency's use of 'administrative guidance' to firms and industry associations. Furthermore, as noted earlier, government guidance to a domestic industry was carefully tailored to the stage of the lifecycle that the industry was in.

On this view, competition policy in Japan was implemented with dynamic considerations in mind, with MITI orchestrating collusion and competition so as to best serve the goals of external competitiveness, factor accumulation, and technological progress. Amsden and Singh (1994a: 45) quote approvingly the following characterization of MITI's methods by Yamamura (1988: 176):

> What MITI did was to 'guide' the firms to invest in such a way that each large firm in a market expanded its productive capacity roughly in proportion to its current market share—no firm was to make an investment so large that it would destabilize the market. The policy was effective in encouraging competition for the market share (thus preserving the essential competitiveness of the industrial markets), while reducing the risk of losses due to excessive invest-

ment. Thus it promoted the aggressive expansion of capacity necessary to increase productive efficiency in output.

More generally the 'Japanese model,' as the country's state-led industrialization effort is usually referred to, comprised a much larger set of policies than those relating directly to competition. Porter, Sakakibara, and Takeuchi (2000: 22) state that the 12 main building blocks of this model are activist central government with a stable bureaucracy; the targeting of priority industries to enhance economic growth; aggressive promotion of exports; extensive 'guidance,' approval requirements, and regulations; selective protection of the home market; restrictions on foreign direct investment (FDI); lax antitrust enforcement; government-led industry restructuring; official sanctioning of cartels; highly regulated financial markets and limited corporate governance; government-sponsored cooperative research and development projects; and sound macroeconomic policies.

Those who view such government intervention as having played a crucial role in Japanese post-war development tend to argue that

> the Japanese were the first to recognise that international competitive advantage could be deliberately created by government not just to nurture a few infant industries to supply the domestic market but to push broad sets of industries toward areas of growth and technological change in the world economy (Wade 1990: 25).

The combination of protection and restrictions on domestic competition assured high levels of domestic profits, which, it is said, translated into high rates of investment and strengthened incentives to upgrade technology, so enabling Japanese firms to compete successfully in foreign markets. Moreover, Amsden and Singh (1994a: 946) identify

> the emphasis on exports and on maintaining oligopolistic rivalry—instead of concentrating resources and subsidies on a single 'national champion' as the key factor distinguishing Japanese policies from those of other dirigiste countries.

Furthermore, concentration ratios in Japan's major industries fell over time. Amsden and Singh (1994a: 947) contend that

> in contrast to the conventional paradigm in economic development ... which proposes that competition leads to economic growth, the Japanese experience suggests reverse causality; that it was growth which stimulated competition, at least in the sense of reducing industrial concentration, rather than the other way round.

The view that restricting rivalry promoted Japanese economic development is not universally shared. It is not a matter of challenging the argument that the Japanese authorities attempted to limit rivalry, but rather of questioning the effectiveness of such state initiatives. As noted earlier, Porter, Sakakibara, and Takeuchi (2000) identified lax antitrust enforcement, government-led restructuring (often through state-inspired mergers between private firms), and official sanctioning of cartels as elements of Japan's industrial policy. Given this record of state intervention, the authors asked whether the application of these state measures actually discriminated between Japan's competitively successful and unsuccessful industries. Porter and his co-authors formed a sample of 20 internationally competitive sectors and another sample of seven uncompetitive sectors, and then examined in detail the nature, timing, and extent of government interventions in those sectors. Thus, the focus was not just on the successful sectors. Furthermore, this approach enabled the contribution of competition policy to be assessed alongside other government initiatives in the same industry.[10]

Porter, Sakakibara, and Takeuchi (2000: 29) summarize their findings as follows:

> In this broad sample of competitive industries, we found that the government model was almost entirely absent. ... There were no major subsidies and little or no intervention in competition. We found only one partial exception, sewing machines, an older industry that was targeted in the early years after World War II to meet domestic demand for clothing and provide employment. Yet even here, Japan today is competitive not in household but in industrial sewing machines, where targeting and the other practices were largely absent. The Japanese government model, then, does not explain Japan's competitive successes.

This is not to say that *all* forms of Japanese government intervention were ineffective in promoting the internationally competitive industries. Porter, Sakakibara, and Takeuchi (2000: 29) go on to argue that:

> Looking deeper at the internationally competitive industries, we found that the government was indeed involved, but in various unexpected roles. Through a slew of initiatives, government stimulated early demand for new products, helping to foster the competitiveness of some industries.[11]

Moreover:

> To these government policies that encouraged competitive success, three other cross-cutting Japanese government practices can be added: policies to encourage patient capital, a universal and rigorous basic education system, and a supply of engineering graduates from universities. Although not figuring prominently in the traditional model, those practices are important in the success cases (Porter, Sakakibara, and Takeuchi 2000: 31).

They conclude:

Overall, then, ... government did play a variety of roles in the successful Japanese industries. However, these roles were very different from what is closely associated with Japan, and they were not the Japanese policies that have been the most widely emulated. Not only was there little of the intervention in competition associated with the received government model; in some successful industries, such as automobiles, the industry actually spurned government's efforts to suppress competition (Porter, Sakakibara, and Takeuchi 2000: 31).

Turning to their analysis of unsuccessful Japanese industries, Porter, Sakakibara, and Takeuchi (2000: 33) argue that

the policies widely believed to explain Japan's success were far more prevalent in the nation's failures ...

One such policy was the state-sponsored formation of cartels, whose purported goals included preventing 'destructive competition' and fostering cooperation and collective action. Porter, Sakakibara, and Takeuchi (2000: 36–9) document the formation of such cartels, showing that in 1965 just under 250 were active. They go on to examine whether these industries became competitive because of such cartels or in spite of them. On the basis of case studies of several industries in which cartels operated, they argue that

cartels are rarely found in competitive industries. In the relatively few competitive industries in which cartels were formed, they were not strong enough to significantly limit rivalry because of the industry's structure. Conversely, cartels were common in uncompetitive industries. Legalized cartels, then, were not a source of competitiveness, they actually contributed to uncompetitiveness (Porter, Sakakibara, and Takeuchi 2000: 39).

Noland and Pack (2003) also discuss the effectiveness of the tolerance of anticompetitive practices in Japan and their potential contribution to the country's post-war economic growth. They argue:

Another possible channel of industrial policy was the tolerance of anti-competitive behavior by private firms, explicitly by the sanctioning of 'recession' or 'rationalization' cartels, or implicitly through the lax or absent enforcement of competition policies. While there is considerable evidence that anti-competitive behavior, typically facilitated by government regulation, has impeded the access of foreign goods and investment to the Japanese market, the scope for using such practices as industrial promotion policy is less clear: the most obvious examples are related to declining natural resource sectors such as soda ash or the construction industry and appear to be driven by narrow parochial political concerns and not forward-looking strategic policies (Noland and Pack 2003: 32).

Moreover, Noland and Pack (2003: 36) observe in a discussion of the potential contribution of informal administrative guidance to Japanese economic performance that:

The one study that attempted to model the impact of administrative guidance (Weinstein 1995) found that administrative encouragement of cartels had only a minor impact on prices, margins, and sectoral resource allocation during the period 1957–88. Sakakibara and Porter (2001), who examine the impact of the tolerance of cartels on domestic competition and international trade performance, interpret their results (cartels are negatively associated with domestic competition which, in turn, is positively associated with international competitiveness) as undercutting what they perceive as the conventional wisdom that sectorally targeted policy has promoted Japanese competitiveness.

In the light of these findings, it would be misleading to argue that there is an intellectual consensus behind the proposition that limiting rivalry promoted Japanese economic development.

Republic of Korea

To the extent that accounts of Korean economic development focus on government measures to alter interfirm rivalry, the case has been made that steps were taken to promote the development of large firms that could compete on international markets while at the same time encouraging fierce competition between these firms. That is, these measures are thought to have secured the benefits of large firm size without the costs associated with diminished competition. The paragraphs below describe this argument and discuss why—in the eyes of some—this argument has fallen out of favor in recent years.

Rodrik (1995: 2,946–7) succinctly summarizes the thesis of one of the leading authorities on Korean economic development since World War II, Alice Amsden:

> Amsden (1989) describes in detail the Korean government's use of trade protection, selective credit subsidies, export targets (for individual firms), public ownership of banking sector, export subsidies, and price controls—all deployed single-mindedly in the service of acquisition of technological capabilities and of building industries that will eventually compete in world markets. She argues that government policy was successful not because it got prices right, but indeed because it got them purposefully wrong. However, a key element of the strategy, Amsden argues, was that in exchange for government subsidies and trade protection the government also set stringent performance standards. Firms were penalized when they performed poorly, as when they became subject to 'rationalization' (government-mandated mergers and capacity reduction) in the wake of over-extension. They were rewarded when they fulfilled government objectives, as when they were awarded subsidized credit for fulfilling export targets. Such discipline kept the system free of the rent-seeking that has contaminated incentive regimes in other settings ...

The implications of this apparent mix of policies is described further by Amsden and Singh (1994a: 948), who contend that:

> The Korean government both contributed to the rise of big business, through its licensing and subsidised credit policies (it owned or controlled virtually all financial institutions), and went out of its way to ensure that big business did not collude, by allocating subsidies only in exchange for strict performance standards.

High and growing concentration ratios were thought to be the result of these policies. Smith (2000) reports a trend of growing market power by Korea's large, privately owned business conglomerates (*chaebol*) from 1970 to the mid-1980s. From 1977 to 1994, the 30 largest *chaebol* controlled between 32 and 40 percent of total national output. Total sales by the top five business groups as a percentage of national income in 1994 was 49 percent (Smith 2000: 114). Amsden (1989) shows that in 1982, out of 2,260 commodities, only about 18 percent, or 30 percent of all shipments, were produced under competitive conditions. With such facts in mind, Smith (2000: 12) argues that:

> The end result has been an industrial structure different from that which the market would have produced. The actions of the Korean state have also been complemented by large, diversified business groups which occupied a dominant position in the economy. Their size and level of diversification meant they were less subject to the discipline of the market than to the discipline of managerial hierarchies.

In his recent overview of Korean industrial policy, Lall (2004: 19) makes the following telling points:

> One of the pillars of Korean strategy, and one that marks it off from the other Tigers (but mirrors Japan), was the deliberate creation of large private conglomerates, the *chaebol*. The *chaebol* were handpicked from successful exporters and were given various subsidies and privileges, including the restriction of [multinational enterprise] entry, in return for furthering a strategy of setting up capital and technology-intensive activities geared to export markets ... This was a costly and high-risk strategy. The risks were contained by the strict discipline imposed by the government: export performance, vigorous domestic competition and deliberate interventions to rationalise the industrial structure.

Others have argued, however, that the costs of creating such a cadre of large firms could not be so readily contained. It has been said that the *chaebol* used their market power at home to frustrate entry by rivals, to raise prices and slow the pace of technological change,[12] and to resist the enactment and enforcement of competition laws that could have put a stop to their activities. These points were made with some force in a submission by the government of Korea to the WTO's Working Group on the Interaction between Trade and Competition Policy in 2001. The submission notes that:

The Korean government first tried to introduce competition law in 1963, but its efforts were not successful. The government's concern was mainly focused on stabilizing prices of monopolies and oligopolies and preventing cornering and hoarding practices. There were some efforts of course to introduce competition law, but it never passed the National Assembly due to lack of perception of its importance and heavy lobbying from the corporate sector (WTO 2001: 3).

Moreover:

Korea's experience demonstrates that it is better to introduce a competition regime at the initial stage of economic growth, when monopolies have not yet gained political and economic power. Despite their merits of achieving economy of scale, large monopolies, if left unchecked, are very likely to engage in excessive facility investments, cause price hikes resulting from their inefficient operations, and hinder opportunities for new entrants. This eventually necessitates the introduction and enforcement of competition policy to remove anti-competitive elements in the market under the political and social pressure stemming from the rising public discontent against the unbalanced distribution of wealth (WTO 2001: 3).

In addition:

Korea had to pay dearly for its failure to reconcile industrial policy with competition in the domestic economy from the initial stage of economic development. In many ways, the 1997 financial debacle and the ongoing malaise experienced by *chaebol* are linked to the absence of a competitive domestic economic environment during the past decades. Building on lessons learned the hard way, the Korean government is currently making strenuous efforts to establish a pro-competitive market structure, although it is encountering various problems in the process as vested interests in the status quo are showing more resilience than expected. The nurturing of monopolies or oligopolies through industrial policy has created these vested interests and, after decades of expansion and dominance over the economy, their necessary conversions exact a heavy toll on the economy. The Korean experience points to the importance of having faith in the benefits of competition from the early stage of economic growth and of incorporating competition policy based on the market function of autonomous adjustment into the basic framework of economic policy (WTO 2001: 3).

For policy-makers convinced of the need for industrial policies to groom internationally competitive firms or 'national champions,' one implication of the Korean experience is that mitigating the adverse domestic side effects of such a policy will require measures, such as the enforcement of competition law, that stimulate or ensure rivalry between these firms. In fact, the Korean experience turns the question posed in the title of this chapter on its head by arguing that industrial policy is *less* likely to deliver optimal results without the active enforcement of competition law.

Taipei,China

The role of government intervention in the economy of Taipei,China is generally regarded as having been on a smaller scale than in Korea, with a greater role ascribed to market forces. Rodrik (1995: 2,946–7) summarizes the findings of one leading analyst of development in Taipei,China as follows:

> Wade (1990) does not deny that there were elements of the free-market (i.e. Hong Kong) recipe in the Taiwanese strategy, but he qualifies the picture significantly. He calls Taiwan a [regulated] market economy, characterized by: (i) high levels of investment; (ii) more investment in certain key industries than would have resulted in the absence of ... intervention; and (iii) exposure of many industries to international competition. He documents the pervasiveness of incentives and controls on private firms through import restrictions, entry requirements, domestic content requirements, fiscal investment incentives, and concessional credit. He argues that Taiwan has consistently acted in anticipation of comparative advantage in such sectors as cotton textiles, plastics, basic metals, shipbuilding, automobiles, and industrial electronics ...

With reference to official measures that are related to competition law, there is some evidence of selective measures aimed at industrial reorganization. Wade (1990: 186) argues that:

> Industrial reorganization programs—to promote mergers, encourage greater specialization between firms in the same industry, and promote modernization of equipment—have been attempted only selectively. Most of the time the government has encouraged and supported an industry's own efforts at greater specialization and modernization, but has not tried to compel them; and it has been distinctly ambivalent about promoting mergers.

Having said that, Wade (1990: 186–7) goes on to argue that:

> Occasionally, however, the government has taken the initiative in promoting mergers when vital sectors are in trouble. In one such case the government virtually ordered the four polyvinyl chloride (PVC) producers to merge ... Another example is the merger of five of Taiwan's major synthetic fiber producers in 1977.

It would seem that only rarely were policies toward mergers implemented with certain industrial policy goals in mind, and then only in declining industries. Wade (1990: 187) also notes that mergers were forced on unwilling partners only very infrequently. Government intervention was more prevalent in encouraging long-term relationships between buyers and sellers, which, in principle, could have had implications for the enforcement of laws on vertical restraints. However, after describing some initiatives to this effect, Wade (1990: 187) argues that

> with long-term subcontracting relations being unfamiliar in Taiwan, the results have so far been meagre.

Interestingly, Wade's account does not point to official toleration or encouragement of cartels in the manufacturing sector of Taipei,China. (The authorities did, however, fix the price of certain agricultural products; see Wade 1990: 302). None of this is to suggest that the authorities did not try to influence the degree of competition between firms. (Indeed, Wade documents how entry into markets and access to investment funds were actively regulated by official bodies.) Rather, Wade's account demonstrates that the measures typically associated with relaxed enforcement of competition law (tolerance of cartels, enforced mergers, sympathetic assessments of proposed mergers, and vertical restraints) were used rarely if at all, and that, when they were used, they were largely ineffective.[13]

People's Republic of China

Over the last two decades, the role that interfirm rivalry has played in advancing development in the PRC has differed from that in Japan, Korea, and Taipei,China. Unlike the latter economies, the PRC started out as a centrally planned socialist economy and has subsequently managed its transition toward a socialist market economy (Wang 2002). Throughout this transition, the rate of economic growth in the PRC has regularly exceeded 7–8 percent per annum and tens of millions of people have been lifted out of poverty, especially in the coastal regions. Although much has been written about the development of the PRC's economy,[14] very few researchers have focused *specifically* on the role that interfirm rivalry has played in promoting or detracting from the PRC's development.

Although this transition has been accomplished without the full range of competition laws, it would be a mistake to suppose that national measures did not deliberately attempt to influence the degree of interfirm rivalry. In fact, according to Jiang (2002a), it is possible to identify three such phases, differentiated by the effects that industrial policies were intended to have on competition. Jiang (2002a: 49) argues that:

> From the perspective of market competition, China's industrial policies have undergone three stages of development: (1) from the late 1970s to the mid-1980s, the industrial policies promoted competition; (2) from the mid-1980s, the industrial policies limited competition; and (3) since the mid-1990s, industrial policies have promoted and limited competition in concert.

During the first phase the government saw value in injecting some competition into the prevailing economic system, a point that Jiang (2002a: 49) makes in the following paragraph:

> During the economic restructuring in China in the late 1970s, the Chinese government became keenly aware of the drawbacks of central planning and thus

began to encourage enterprises to compete with each other to increase output, improve efficiency, develop new products, and increase employee salaries. To effectuate this new emphasis of Chinese industrial policies on competition, the government employed three new policy measures: (1) the encouragement of new enterprises; (2) the encouragement of competition among existing enterprises; and (3) the relaxation of price controls.

In the refrigerator manufacturing industry, the effect of these policies was to reduce the four-firm concentration ratio from 74.5 percent in 1982 to 29.0 percent in 1988. During the same period, total output rose 75 times to 7.576 million units per annum (Jiang 2002a: 57).

The growing competition faced by state-owned enterprises (SOEs) caused them increasing difficulties. In the PRC this takes on an additional dimension as SOEs are not only large employers but also providers of social and other welfare services. Concerns that increased rivalry was undermining the viability of these enterprises led the government from the mid-1980s to the mid-1990s to adopt measures that restricted competition between firms (Jiang 2002a: 58). These included measures to restrain the establishment of new small and medium-sized enterprises (principally through regulations on construction), measures to restrain competition between rural enterprises and SOEs, and requirements that only designated enterprises could produce certain products.

For example, Jiang (2002a: 60) reports that during this period the Ministry of Light Industry decided that only five firms would be allowed to produce refrigerators. The medium to long-term effectiveness of such measures has, however, been called into question. Jiang (2002a: 62) remarks that:

> This restrictive policy ultimately worked for only one or two years. With domestic demand snowballing and the refrigerator industry remaining lucrative, local governments and enterprises scrambled to build new refrigerator manufacturing firms by bypassing the restrictions of the central government's industrial policy under various pretexts. Throughout 1987 and 1988 [two and three years after the initial measures were announced], refrigerator production in China reached an all-time high with the addition of an additional 180 refrigerator factories.

Industrial policies since the mid-1990s are said to have had a mixed effect on the degree of interfirm rivalry. On the one hand, domestic consumers and investors were dissatisfied with the prevailing mix of quality and prices in concentrated industries. Jiang (2002a: 64) offers the following account of the decision to promote competition:

> During the mid-1990s, pressure from three groups prompted the central government to deal with the issue of competition in these monopolistic industries.

First, domestic consumers resented the poor quality and unreasonable fees of these industries and demanded improvements in the industries' efficiency and services. Second, new investors wanting to enter these industries began to pressure the central government to address these industries' long-standing monopolies and high profit levels. Third, with China's recent accession to the WTO, China will have to give in to long-standing external pressure to open its service markets. This pressure originally convinced both the central government and the monopolistic industries that they would be unable to compete with transnational companies from foreign countries once China entered into the WTO if they did not break up the monopolies and improve efficiency through competition. As a result, in the past five years, Chinese industries that several large state-owned enterprises formally dominated have reoriented themselves to prepare for foreign competition.

On the other hand, the continuing erosion in the viability of SOEs in the mid to late 1990s—with its attendant consequences for unemployment, labor unrest, and social welfare—is said to have persuaded some PRC policy-makers of the need to moderate competition in certain sectors (Jiang 2002a). Typically, they did so by reducing production capacity in an affected sector. In particular:

> The government focused on closing down five types of small non-state enterprises: coal mines, steel rolling plants, cement factories, refineries, and glass-producing firms. The shutdowns in 1999 accounted for 10%–15% of the production capacity in each of these respective industries. The government believed that the closure of these small enterprises would solve the problem of overproduction and alleviate the pressure of competition on the state-owned enterprises (Jiang 2002a: 65).

It should be recognized, however, that these policy measures may have been motivated by other concerns, not least the inability of smaller non-state enterprises to meet the social and financial obligations borne by other firms.

Yet the extent of rivalry that the government appears to have decided is best for its own development is increasing, according to Jiang (2002a). He contends that, since the mid-1990s:

> Chinese industrial policies widely carried out to support industries in short supply and restrict industries in overproduction have seen their domains dwindling steadily over the last few years. In contrast, antimonopolistic industrial policies are becoming inextricably intertwined with government policies (Jiang 2002a: 65).

In sum, then, as far as competition in domestic markets is concerned, the PRC's industrial policies have shifted toward encouraging interfirm rivalry. This has been accomplished without compromising another stated government goal, that of building a cadre of large firms able to withstand competition on world markets.[15] Moreover, to the extent that enhancing competition in domestic markets is a prerequisite for performing well on global markets, industrial policies toward rivalry in domestic markets may well have underpinned the exporting prowess of this select group of firms.

4   RESOLVING THE PERCEIVED CONFLICT BETWEEN COMPETITION LAW AND INDUSTRIAL POLICY

Even if one is persuaded that there has been no general post-war tendency to subordinate interfirm rivalry to the goals of industrial policy, specific situations may arise that give policy-makers cause for concern. Moreover, there may be a variety of economic, political, and social reasons why governments will sometimes wish to shield particular activities or sectors from the application of competition law, or pursue goals or initiatives that may be in conflict with the objectives of such a law. Consequently, this section is devoted to describing five means by which potential tensions between competition law and industrial or other policy objectives have traditionally been managed in economies having active competition regimes, including industrialized and developing economies. The fact that these five means exist further reinforces the argument that competition laws can be introduced in developing countries that have active industrial policies.

First and foremost, it should be emphasized that measures taken by governments in their capacities as sovereign states, even where they tend to restrict competition in markets, are not actionable under many national competition laws. For this reason, most of the traditional instruments of industrial policy—such as tariffs, subsidies, training programs, public ownership, and concessionary financing for exports—are most unlikely to be challengeable under competition law. Even regulations or policy directives that deliberately restrict entry to markets or otherwise limit competition (for example, state-mandated mergers) are unlikely to raise concerns under competition law, so long as they are implemented pursuant to valid governmental authority and otherwise meet the tests or requirements that may apply under national laws (WTO 1997).

A second way in which the potential tensions between competition law and the attainment of developmental objectives are managed in many countries is through the explicit incorporation of these objectives in national competition laws. For example, as has already been pointed out in Chapter 1, the Competition Act of 1998 in South Africa includes a multiplicity of objectives. Opinion is divided as to the merits of introducing wider social goals into competition law, and there appears to be a general trend toward focusing on economic efficiency or consumer welfare as the principal goal of competition policy. The following quotation from a submission by the Republic of Ireland to the Third OECD Global Forum on Competition (OECD 2003c: 3) is representative of this point of view:

> Policy makers may seek to use competition policy to further other (broader) policy objectives such as industrial policy, regional development or 'the public interest,' as for example in a public interest test for mergers. There are two reasons why it is best not to use competition policy as a wider policy instrument. First, broadly specified policy objectives can be ambiguous and as such are subject to 'capture' or 'hijack' by the politically strongest private interests, usually those of producers or workers. Thus de jure public interest objectives may de facto serve private interests. Secondly, non-competition policy mechanisms are generally superior for achieving non-competition policy objectives. To elaborate, restricting competition in an attempt to achieve a broader policy objective will have inevitable anti-competition side effects ...

Nonetheless, it is beyond dispute that other goals have frequently been referred to and have served to guide the application of national competition laws in industrialized as well as developing countries.

A third point to be made is that, even where developmental or similar goals are not explicitly written into competition laws, officials can and increasingly do take into account dynamic as well as static efficiency considerations in the application of these laws. Indeed, given that the goal of improving long-term economic performance is one of the often-stated objectives of industrial policy, it is worthwhile pointing out that in a growing number of jurisdictions, the actual application of competition law has deliberately been adapted to take dynamic factors into account. This shift toward greater openness to dynamic efficiency considerations has, in most cases, not required an overhaul of competition legislation; rather, it has been achieved through the progressive adaptation of guidelines and the techniques used in case analysis. This trend has been evident since at least the mid-1990s and, in some cases, before then (WTO 1997; see Anderson and Khosla 1995 for a survey of developments in various industrialized countries).

As one illustration of efforts to adapt the application of national competition laws to facilitate and promote the achievement of efficiency gains, in the United States successive versions of the antitrust agencies' merger guidelines over the past two decades have placed progressively greater emphasis on these matters (US Department of Justice and Federal Trade Commission 1997). The concept of 'innovation markets' was developed for the specific purpose of ensuring that competition law enforcement in the United States is well adapted to promote rather than impede the realization of dynamic efficiency gains. This concept recognizes that:

(i) competition is a key underpinning of innovation; and (ii) anticompetitive mergers or other interfirm arrangements can undermine the incentives for innovation in certain cases (Gilbert and Sunshine 1995). Such concerns have been the basis for a number of decisions by the US competition agencies to block certain mergers (Gilbert and Tom 2001).

The growing propensity to enforce competition law with considerations of innovation and dynamic efficiency in mind is highlighted in a recent analysis of the evolution of US antitrust policy in the 1990s by Litan and Shapiro (2001). They point out that

> the 1990s covered a period during which new technologies had a marked impact on a range of markets, with the Internet and information technology leading the way. Increasingly, the fruits of competition are seen in the form of new technologies which lead to new and improved products. At the same time, intellectual property rights, in the form of patents, copyrights, and trade secrets, increasingly have become a key source of competition advantage for firms controlling such rights. How natural, then, that antitrust authorities have paid more attention to 'innovation competition' and intellectual property rights (Litan and Shapiro 2001: 3).

Similarly, after carefully reviewing the enforcement record of US agencies since 1990, Gilbert and Tom (2001: 3) conclude that

> innovation is not quite 'King' in antitrust authorities, although its role has become increasingly important and has been decisive in several merger and non-merger enforcement actions that have potentially very significant impacts for consumer welfare.

A fourth way in which the potential tensions between competition law and the attainment of industrial policy objectives can be managed is to allow for exemptions, exceptions, and exclusions from competition law. Almost all jurisdictions with competition statutes have some exemptions and exclusions. The rationale for exemptions from national competition laws has been clearly articulated by Allan Fels, the former chairman of the Australian Competition and Consumer Commission:

> A competition regime needs to operate in conjunction with other government policies. Inevitably, conflict between policies will arise and it will therefore be necessary to determine priorities based on an assessment of national interests. For this reason, a mechanism is needed to provide for exceptions from the general application of a competition regime (Fels 2001: 3–4).

A fifth option would be to allow a governmental body to overrule a decision made by the competition enforcement agency on the grounds that national development priorities would be compromised. This governmental body could be the national cabinet, the head of government, or a minister. Although some nations' competition laws, for example Germany's, provide for such overrides in certain well-defined circumstances, the clear trend is toward eliminating such overrides and strengthening the independence of the agencies that enforce competition law (WTO 1997).

In concluding this section, it is worth noting that each of these five means of reconciling industrial policy measures or its objectives with the implementation of competition law has pros and cons. The fact that an institutional arrangement is feasible does not make it desirable. For example, the last option could substantially undermine the effective independence of the competition agency and essentially politicize competition law enforcement. When policy-makers conceive of a tension between industrial policy and competition law, care will have to be taken to identify which of the five options outlined above (and potentially others) best attains the industrial policy objective while compromising the goals of competition law the least.

5　CONCLUDING REMARKS

This chapter has a very specific purpose, namely, on the basis of the development experience of four East Asian economies, to assess whether measures to retard competition (or interfirm rivalry) were an important complement to the implementation of national industrial policy. This assessment is very important given the fear articulated by some that the implementation of competition law in particular, and the fostering of interfirm rivalry in general, will undermine national industrial policies. In the light of the muddled existing literature, it is also important to state what this chapter is *not* about. This chapter does not present a general assessment of the effects of industrial policies in East Asia, and indeed I do not take a position here on the efficacy of such policies. Even with this chapter's narrower focus, a number of findings emerge from the foregoing discussion of the extant literature.

First, in the PRC and Japan the state occasionally took measures to constrain competition, and in both cases, scholars have in recent years presented evidence that questions the effectiveness of such measures. Second, the Korean experience was instructive in highlighting the need for effective enforcement of competition law to counter the adverse domestic consequences of policies to create national champions. This point is accepted by authors from very different schools of thought. Third, the special problems faced by transition economies were highlighted in the account of the PRC's reforms since the late 1970s. Concerns about employment loss and social dislocation have, it is argued, led to some measures to constrain competition. Yet, the frequency with which such measures are employed seems to have been declining.

Overall, any claim that measures constraining rivalry were a central component of development policies, and certainly the view that such measures were effective, is increasingly at odds with the conclusions of more recent empirical research into East Asian development. Recent research on the effectiveness of cartelization in Japan seriously calls into question whether the success of Japan's internationally competitive industries depended on state-sponsored or state-tolerated price fixing and similar practices. Korean and PRC experience seems to suggest that policies to create large national firms ought to be complemented by measures to ensure continued rivalry in domestic markets. In sum, this recent literature adds further credibility to the view that the active and appropriate enforcement of competition law in these four East Asian economies would have reinforced rather than compromised their national industrial policies and overall development strategies.

The policy recommendations of this chapter are of especial interest at a time when industrial policy advocates appear to be making something of a resurgence in the Asia-Pacific and elsewhere. Many such advocates argue that national firms need to be sheltered—or given 'breathing room'—through the use of tariff barriers or restrictive policies toward FDI. These measures surely reduce the degree of rivalry faced by domestic firms from abroad. However, this is an argument for reducing one type of interfirm rivalry—not an argument for reducing every type of interfirm rivalry. Competition law addresses, among other matters, the corporate practices that restrict interfirm rivalry within a nation's borders. Determining whether to reduce rivalry from abroad and determining whether to reduce rivalry between domestic firms are logically distinct choices that require the use of different policy instruments. Therefore, an advocate of industrial policy could be a keen supporter of measures to bolster competition between domestic firms while simultaneously seeking to shelter them from foreign competition. Indeed, one of the lessons of this chapter's review of the relevant East Asian development experience is that industrial policy of the 'sheltering' type tends to work better when intense rivalry between domestic firms spurs them to improve productivity and performance—a finding that calls for strong competition law enforcement to complement certain national industrial policies.

NOTES

1　See Melo (2001), Rodriguez-Clare (2004), and Rodrik (2004).

2　I use this word quite deliberately.

3　Competition law is defined in Chapter 1 of this volume.

4　Here Bora, Lloyd, and Pangestu are referring to the World Bank's well-known study titled *The East Asian Miracle*.

5　Noland and Pack (2003: 10) define selective industrial policies in a similar manner to Wade's definition of sectoral policies:

> We define selective intervention or industrial policy briefly as an effort by a government to alter the sectoral structure of production towards sectors it believes offer greater prospects for accelerated growth than would be generated by a typical process of industrial evolution according to static comparative advantage.

This observation is of interest as Noland and Pack present an orthodox or neo-classical perspective on East Asian development that reaches very different conclusions from those of Wade.

6　Strategic trade policy involves the setting of national trade policies—such as tariffs—so as to enable a domestic sector to reap greater economies of scale from the protected home market or to enable the sector to expand output and lower costs through so-called learning-by-doing effects. Both of these result in lower production costs, enabling a nation's exporters, in principle, to expand foreign sales. In addition to expanding the output of the domestic industry, proponents of strategic trade policy note that it can result in profits being effectively 'shifted' from foreign firms to domestic firms.

7　Noland and Pack (2003: 10) offer a similarly extensive list of policy interventions as constituting part of industrial policy, arguing that:

> Credit directed at specific sectors at below-market interest rates for long-term and working capital, sectorally differentiated profit taxes, subsidized electricity rates, research and development subsidies, control of the entry and exit of firms, export targets, and highly differentiated tariffs and non-tariff barriers are all forms of industrial policy.

8　Much of the recent literature on East Asian development is summarized in World Bank (2003a).

9　Singh (1999: 10) later remarked that:

> The evolution of Japanese competition policy in the 1970s and 1980s is interesting but not as relevant to developing countries as the competition policy practised by Japan between 1950 and 1973. This is because, at the beginning of the period, Japan was very much like a developing country with low levels of industrialisation and economic development.

10　Porter, Sakakibara, and Takeuchi's summary tables of the nature of government interventions in the 27 sectors are available from the author upon request.

11　Porter, Sakakibara, and Takeuchi (2000) then describe such initiatives in the fax machine and robotics sectors.

12   Noland and Pack (2003: 44), for example, report the following:

> Park and Kwon (1995) conclude that during the heavy and chemical industry drive, the establishment of oligopolistic positions by the *chaebol* restricted technological change.

13   In their account of the industrial policy of Taipei,China, Noland and Pack (2003) do not mention state measures to reduce rivalry between domestic firms. Reducing competition from abroad, principally through the trade regime, was one of the three pillars of the country's industrial policy according to these authors. The other two pillars were directed credit and the creation of state enterprises to undertake economic activity when private sector entrepreneurship was not forthcoming (Noland and Pack 2003: 52–3).

14   See, for example, Lardy (1998), Naughton (1995), Nolan (2001), Perkins (2001), Steinfeld (1998), and World Bank (2003a).

15   During the 1990s, Nolan (2001) contends, the perceived need to develop a number of large enterprises as the PRC's means of competing in international markets grew even stronger. Nolan (2001: 18) describes the creation of these enterprises as follows:

> In the 1990s a 'national team' of 120 large enterprise groups was selected by the State Council in two batches, in 1991 and 1997 respectively. These enterprises were predominantly in those sectors considered to be of 'strategic importance,' including electricity generation (8), coal mining (3), automobiles (6), electronics (10), iron and steel (8), machinery (14), chemicals (7), construction materials (5), transport (5), aerospace (6) and pharmaceuticals (5).

As a result, by the late 1990s, Nolan (2001: 20) contends that

> the 120 enterprise groups chosen by the State Council were invariably leaders in their industries. The six trial groups in electricity generation and supply, for example, produced over half of China's electricity. The eight metallurgy groups produced 40 per cent of the nation's iron and steel and the six approved vehicle makers manufactured 57 per cent of China's vehicle output. The three civilian airlines controlled over 55 per cent of the domestic market. The groups were based upon large-scale enterprises which were the 'core members of the group' with the 'capability to act as investment centres' ... In 1997 the 120 groups accounted for one-third of total output value of the whole state-owned sector, they accounted for over 50 per cent of total profits, paid 25 per cent of taxes and made over 25 per cent of all sales. Of the 120 groups less than ten were loss-makers at the end of 1995.

4

People's Republic of China

Ping Lin

1   INTRODUCTION

In its now two-decade-long transition from a centrally planned to a market economy, the People's Republic of China (PRC) has made remarkable progress in introducing competition to its industries. It recognized that it was essential to build an effective competition policy system so as to create a level playing field for all business enterprises. During this transitional period, industrial policies and inward foreign direct investment (FDI) played a crucial role both in transforming industry and in facilitating the development of competition policy. This chapter reviews the competition policy framework in the PRC with emphasis on its interactions with industrial and FDI policies.

I review existing competition law in the PRC in section 2, focusing in particular on the 1993 Anti Unfair Competition Law, which deals with unfair methods of competition as well as restrictive behavior on the part of public utilities and administrative monopolies, and the 1998 Price Law, which prohibits price fixing, price discrimination, and predatory pricing. I also review the draft antimonopoly law, which has gone through many revisions since the early 1990s and which is likely to be legislated soon. Section 2 also provides information on law enforcement together with detailed case studies illustrating the current status of competition law enforcement, and public awareness, in the PRC.

Since the start of economic reform and the introduction of an open door policy in 1978, the PRC has vigorously promoted industrial policies. The government strongly believed that, by guiding resource allocation with a 'visible hand,' it could establish industries that were capable of competing in international markets while at the same time avoiding the fluctuations that accompany the free play of market forces. During the 1990s, the PRC actively pursued a strategy of building up giant conglomerates and national champions, following the example of the Republic of Korea (Korea). Although the Asian financial crisis led the government to reconsider this strategy, industrial policies remain the guiding force in many economic policies. Section 3 of this chapter examines the interactions between industrial policies and competition policy in the PRC.

Local protectionism is another major obstacle to competition policy development in the PRC. For historical reasons, local governments have had a strong incentive to protect local enterprises from competition from other regions. This has contributed to the duplication of investments and to excess capacity in some industries, and thus the PRC's observed low degree of industrial concentration. Section 4 focuses on the role of regional protectionism in attracting FDI. It gives an example of a car tariff war between Shanghai city and Hubei province to illustrate the prevalence of regional protectionism and its effects on competition and FDI allocation.

Section 5 examines the effects of inward FDI on competition, in particular through two contrasting case studies of acquisitions of domestic brands by multinational enterprises (MNEs). Whereas Unilever and Procter & Gamble have reportedly adopted a 'brand-killing' strategy in relation to the brands they acquired from their local joint venture partners, L'Oréal appears to be committed to the two leading skincare brands it acquired in late 2003 and early 2004. This section also discusses the country's first merger and acquisition (M&A) notification system, set up in 2003 in response to the increase in FDI-related M&As.

In sections 6 and 7 of the chapter I provide some observations on competition and poverty reduction, and offer some concluding remarks.

2   COMPETITION LAW IN THE PEOPLE'S REPUBLIC OF CHINA

The PRC did not have a competition policy until the late 1970s when it started the transition process from a centrally planned to a market economy. Under the traditional central planning system, competition had no role to play either in theory or in practice, and therefore there was no need whatsoever for a competition policy.

In the early 1980s, the PRC moved toward a more decentralized economy. The government permitted the development of a private sector and introduced competition into economic life. There was then a need to set up rules to govern competition. Currently the main competition laws and regulations in the PRC are the 1980 Provisional Regulations Concerning Development and Protection of the Socialist Competition Mechanism, the 1993 Anti Unfair Competition Law, and the 1998 Price Law. The PRC began drafting a comprehensive antimonopoly law in the early 1990s, but this has not yet been legislated.

The objective of competition policy in the PRC is described in article 1 of the 1993 Anti Unfair Competition Law as being to

> safeguard healthy development of the socialist market economy, encourage and protect fair competition, stop acts of unfair competition and to defend the lawful rights and interests of operators and consumers.

The 1980 regulations

The first government document related to competition in the PRC—the Provisional Regulations Concerning Development and Protection of the Socialist Competition Mechanism—was issued by the State Council on 17 October 1980. It stipulates that

> in economic activities, with the exception of products managed exclusively by state-designated departments and organizations, monopolization or sole proprietary management of other products is not allowed (article 3).

The contents of the regulations are brief and the regulations were never properly enforced. Nevertheless, even at this early stage of competition policy development, it is apparent that the State Council recognized the need to curb administrative monopolies and regional protectionism. Article 6 states that

> competition must be introduced by breaking down regional blockades and departmental barriers. No locality or department is allowed to block the market. No locality or department should impose any ban on the entry of goods made in other places. Localities should ensure that raw material can be transferred out according to state plans and must not create any blockade. Departments in charge of industry, transport, finance and trade must revise any part or parts of their existing regulations and systems which impede competition so as to facilitate competition.

The 1993 Anti Unfair Competition Law

The 1993 Anti Unfair Competition Law, which took effect on 1 December 1993, was the PRC's first competition law.[1] Its goals were to protect competition and prevent unfair trade practices. The promulgation and implementation of this law represented a significant step toward the establishment of a competition policy in the PRC.

The law proscribed trademark counterfeiting (article 5); restrictions on the use of related products imposed by public enterprises and other legal monopolies (article 6); abuse of administrative power or restraints on free trade among regions by government agencies or their associates (article 7); bribery in business transactions (article 8); deceptive advertising (article 9); obtaining, disclosing, or using trade secrets without the consent of the owner (article 10); predatory pricing (article 11); tied sales (article 12); deceptive sales tactics such as prize draws (article 13); uttering and disseminating false information that would hurt the reputation of a competitor (article 14); and bid rigging (article 15). The prohibited acts can be classified into the following three categories.

1   *Deceptive advertising and other business activities involving dishonesty (articles 8, 9, 13, and 14).* Article 8 prohibits bribery in business transactions, especially in the form of kickbacks whereby buyers of commodities are rewarded, in money or materials, in transactions that do not appear in the company books. Article 9 prohibits false or misleading advertising. It extends the liability for false advertising to advertising agencies that are or should be aware of a seller's misrepresentation. Article 13 limits the use of prize draws as a marketing strategy. To be legal, a draw must be conducted honestly and the value of the prize must not exceed CNY5,000. Article 14 outlaws the utterance and dissemination of information intended to injure the reputation of a competitor.

2   *Protection of intellectual property rights and trade secrets (articles 5 and 10).* Article 5 offers protection against trademark infringement. It prohibits not only the forgery of trademarks and certificates of quality and origin, but also the use of similar brand identification—brand names, packaging, or designs—that would be likely to confuse the consumer. A fine of 100–300 percent of the value of the illegal gains may be imposed for breaches of the law. Criminal sanctions may also be imposed in accordance with the PRC Trademark Law. Article 10 protects trade secrets, defined as technical and operational information that is not known to the public, that is capable of bringing economic benefits to the owners of the rights, that has practical applicability, and that the owners of the rights have taken measures to keep secret. The law imposes a fine of CNY10,000–200,000 on those who obtain such secrets illegally, or who know or should know that a trade secret was obtained illegally but nevertheless agree to distribute such knowledge to a third party.

3   *Antitrust provisions (articles 6, 7, 11, 12, and 15).* Five of the 11 acts prohibited by the Anti Unfair Competition Law can be classified as

antitrust provisions. Article 6 states that 'Public utility enterprises or other business operators that have a legal monopolistic status shall not force others to buy the goods or services of their designated business operators in order to exclude other operators from competing fairly.' Violations may incur fines of CNY50,000–200,000, as well as confiscation of 100–300 percent of the illegally acquired revenue (article 23).

Article 7 addresses the behavior of government officials who coerce customers into buying products from their designated suppliers, stating that 'A local government and its subordinate departments shall not abuse their administrative power to force others to buy the goods of the operators designated by them so as to restrict the lawful business activities of other operators.' It also prohibits blockades of regional competition: 'A local government and its subordinate departments shall not abuse their administrative power to restrict the entry of goods from other parts of the country into the local market or the flow of local goods to markets in other parts of the country.'

Article 11 prohibits predatory pricing. It prevents operators from selling products at below cost in order to drive out competitors—while not spelling out what 'cost' actually means. Article 11 excepts a number of practices from its provisions: the sale of fresh products; the disposal of products whose period of validity is about to expire, or of overstocked products; seasonal reductions in prices; and the sale of products at reduced prices to pay off a debt, or due to a change in product lines or the closure of the business.

Article 12 provides that, in selling a product, a business operator shall not make a tied sale against the wishes of the buyer, or attach any other unreasonable conditions.

Article 15 prohibits collusion in the tendering process (bid rigging).[2] Violators can be fined CNY10,000–200,000 depending on the seriousness of the offense (article 27).

The 1993 Anti Unfair Competition Law provides for criminal penalties only in the cases of trademark infringement (article 21) and bribery (article 22). Even the hard-core collusive behavior of bid rigging does not attract a criminal penalty under the 1993 law, although it does under the Public Tendering Law of the People's Republic of China, which took effect in January 2000.

The State Administration for Industry and Commerce (SAIC) is the administrative body responsible for enforcing the 1993 Anti Unfair Competition Law.[3] It has branches throughout the country at the provincial, city, and county levels, and had over 61,000 staff nationwide in 2002. All

SAIC branches have investigative power. They can issue warnings and take corrective measures, including imposing fines and suspending business licenses.

SAIC is under the State Council and has a long tradition of protecting market order even under the traditional central planning system. The Fair Trade Bureau created within SAIC in 1994 has three divisions, responsible for preventing unfair trade practices, investigating monopolies, and consumer protection. SAIC's other duties include administration of business licenses, registration of trademarks, and enforcement of related laws such as the Trademark Law and the Advertising Law.

Table 4.1 contains information on SAIC's enforcement activities during 1995–2002. Although the majority of the cases listed in the table involve trademark infringements or trade secrets, SAIC has also been active in combating antitrust violations. In 1995 SAIC handled 194 antitrust cases. The figure has continued to rise since then, reaching as high as 2,208 in 2001 and 1,547 in 2002. A large number of these cases involved public utilities, with bid rigging constituting another main component. The sharp rise in the number of such cases in recent years reflects the increased attention SAIC has paid to fighting the abuse of administrative power and restrictive practices by public utilities. In 2001, it launched a nationwide campaign specifically to counter such practices. In 2002, the State Council launched its own campaign to break down sectoral monopolies and regional blockades, and combat other anticompetitive acts (Wang 2001). As a consequence, the number of administrative monopoly cases rose substantially in 2000 and reached a record high of 137 cases in 2001. The number of cases involving public utilities increased from 432 in 1999 to 785 in 2000, then more than doubled to 1,614 in 2001 before declining to 1,089 in 2002. Other types of antitrust violations have experienced a similar pattern, except for predatory pricing, which accounts for 30–40 cases per year.[4]

During the decade since the introduction of the 1993 Anti Unfair Competition Law, SAIC has issued over 70 administrative explanations to local SAIC branches giving specific guidance on law enforcement. In the area of international cooperation, it has established cooperative relationships with over 20 competition agencies from other countries (Gan 2003). In addition, it has conducted various competition advocacy activities to raise public awareness of competition policy. The State Council promoted SAIC from vice-ministerial to ministerial level in 2001, further strengthening its authority and position.

While the enforcement record of SAIC is impressive, one point worth noting is that most of the cases it has dealt with have involved administra-

Table 4.1   PRC: *Competition cases handled by SAIC, 1995–2002 (no.)*

Type of case	1995	1996	1997	1998	1999	2000	2001	2002
Consumer protection/business dishonesty	709	2,160	2,441	1,756	2,651	4,260	6,841	8,490
Infringement of trademark/trade secret	4,361	8,856	9,296	9,698	11,011	14,525	15,575	18,454
Antitrust violations	194	264	261	281	603	1,154	2,208	1,547
Abuse of administrative power	22	38	13	10	10	56	137	88
Restrictions by public utilities	55	102	94	131	432	785	1,614	1,089
Predatory pricing	10	59	32	19	26	39	31	43
Tied sales	91	42	85	44	84	64	110	139
Bid rigging	16	23	37	77	51	210	316	188
Removing/concealing/destroying illegal assets	24	108	46	35	43	21	29	29
Other cases	–	–	2,847	2,876	3,891	6,093	10,718	12,331
Total number of cases	5,288	11,388	14,891	14,646	18,199	26,053	35,371	40,851
Total amount of illegal gains (CNY million)	419.1	738.2	843.9	648.1	1,230.0	1,906.1	3,358.9	3,080
Value of confiscations & fines (CNY million)	36.8	85.4	107.8	195.0	144.7	269.2	472.1	499.5
No. of cases transferred to judicial system	35	104	5	n.a.	n.a.	n.a.	n.a.	11

n.a. = not available.

Source: SAIC.

tive measures, with only a tiny percentage turned over to the judicial system. This indicates the heavy reliance of competition law enforcement on administrative channels.[5]

In addition to the national Anti Unfair Competition Law, many provinces and major cities have their own laws and regulations designed to counter unfair competition.[6] For example, price fixing was first prohibited by Guangdong province under implementing regulations on unfair competition. Beijing enacted an Anti Unfair Competition Law in 1994, shortly after the promulgation of the national law. To date, over 20 provinces and cities in the PRC have enacted similar laws and regulations, some of them simply detailed guidelines for implementing the national law (Kong 2001: 15). Sectoral regulations such as the 2000 Telecommunications Ordinance of the People's Republic of China also incorporate competition-related provisions.

The 1998 Price Law

Five years after the promulgation of the Anti Unfair Competition Law, the government enacted another important piece of competition legislation, the 1998 Price Law. The main objective of this law, which came into effect on 1 May 1998, is to fight price fixing and predatory pricing. Article 14 declares the following practices to be unfair and illegal: conspiracies aimed at controlling market prices that result in damage to other operators and/or consumers; predatory pricing; and price discrimination.[7] The penalty for violating the provisions of the 1998 Price Law can be as high as five times the illegal gains. In extremely serious cases, business licenses can be suspended. However, no criminal penalties can be imposed.

The Price Law is a good complement to the Anti Unfair Competition Law in that it specifically outlaws price cartels, which the 1993 law did not do. It also makes up for the failure of the 1993 law to provide a definition for 'cost' in its predatory pricing provisions: the Price Law defines 'cost' as referring to production and operational costs (article 8). A provision on discrimination against particular business operations is designed to prevent monopolies from using a price squeeze strategy to drive competitors out of related markets. The 1993 law contains similar provisions on discrimination against particular business operations.[8]

Responsibility for enforcing the Price Law rests with the State Development and Reform Commission (SDRC) and its price administration agencies at the provincial, city, and county levels. This enforcement system was very inexpensive to set up as the SDRC and its local branches were already in place; it was this body that had been responsible for setting the prices of virtually all commodities during the central planning era.[9] Although detailed data on the SDRC's law enforcement record are not available, it is clear that it has not been as busy as SAIC, partly due to the differences in the nature of the violations covered by the two laws. The SDRC has, however, been tested by some price-fixing cases that have drawn national attention, such as a cartel in color television sets (Box 4.1). Enforcement activity by local SDRC branches has also been reported. For example, in July 2000 the Beijing Price Bureau successfully broke an agreement among nine licensed travel agencies in Beijing to collectively set minimum prices on package trips to several Southeast Asian destinations.[10]

An important lesson that can be drawn from the case of the color television cartel is that the government needs to do more to raise public awareness of the Price Law. The TV manufacturers involved in the price cartel initially did not realize that their agreement was illegal, and even a high-ranking official in the Ministry of Information Industry was not aware that they had violated the Price Law. Other firms have been similarly caught out.[11] Better competition advocacy would certainly improve the effectiveness of competition law in the PRC.

Moreover, the occurrence of price wars and subsequent closure of some firms does not necessarily mean that competition is excessive or vicious. On the contrary, it may be an indication of a market system that is functioning well and of improvements in efficiency as less-efficient players are driven out of the market. One does of course also need to be aware of the danger of predatory behavior. But in any case, it should be the law, rather than self-regulation on the part of the players, that deals with any instances of anticompetitive conduct.

The draft antimonopoly law

The PRC's existing competition laws focus primarily on unfair competition. They do not deal with monopolization, abuse of a dominant position, or M&As. In 1994, the government announced its intention to promulgate an antimonopoly law to supplement the provisions of the Anti Unfair Competition Law. The drafting group formed in May 1994 consisted of officials from the State Economic and Trade Commission and SAIC. The antimonopoly law they prepared has been revised several times, based on the suggestions of scholars from international organizations such as the Organisation for Economic Co-operation and Development (OECD), the World Bank, the United Nations Conference on Trade and Development,

---

Box 4.1 A case study of a color television cartel

The television industry underwent six price wars during the period 1996–2000, with several leading manufacturers experiencing losses in 2000 (Lee and Chan 2002). On 9 June 2000, at a summit held in Shenzhen, the top managers of nine TV manufacturers agreed to form an alliance to address the problems in the industry.

The nine manufacturers who took part in the summit were Konka, Skyworth, TCL, Rova, Hisense, Xoceco, Jinxing, Panda, and Westlake, who together account for more than 80 percent of the domestic color TV market. The PRC's leading manufacturer, Changhong, did not participate. The agreement reached at the summit covered three areas: research and development (R&D) cooperation in developing new products and a digital technology standard for the industry; joint efforts to promote exports to other countries; and the setting of minimum prices for TVs sold domestically.

The third element is clearly a price cartel agreement. The manufacturers jointly announced that the retail prices of 21-inch, 25-inch, 29-inch, and 34-inch color television sets would henceforth be at least CNY1,050 ($127 at the current official rate of CNY8.27/$1), CNY1,700 ($206), CNY2,600 ($310), and CNY4,200 ($500) respectively. *Beijing Youth Daily* reported that the alliance also planned to cut production for the domestic market by 15–20 percent. This would amount to a reduction of about two million television sets (*China Daily*, 25 June 2000, 11 August 2000). According to the manufacturers, the prescribed minimum was so low that any TV sold at a lower price would have to be of very poor quality.

It appears that the TV manufacturers were not aware that their collective action would violate the 1998 Price Law. The managers of some of the companies openly defended their decision, saying that collective action was needed to end the losses caused by the price wars in the industry. The State Development and Planning Commission (SDPC)—which is now the SDRC—had to make it publicly clear that their acts were indeed a breach

---

and Asia-Pacific Economic Cooperation, and from countries such as Germany, the United States, Japan, Korea, and Australia.

The most recent version of the law that is publicly accessible was drafted in 2002. It has eight chapters containing 58 articles. The chapters cover price fixing, predatory pricing, price discrimination, refusal to deal, tied sales, exclusive dealing, resale price maintenance, M&As, administrative monopolies, the establishment of a competition authority, legal liability, and so on, accompanied by both civil and criminal remedies. (A detailed table of contents for the draft law is given in Appendix A4.1.) The

of the law. An SDPC official criticized the alliance as a monopoly in disguised form, and said that the SDPC would investigate the case intensively.[12] But Konka for one fought back, saying that the price floor set by the alliance was sufficient only to cover production costs. The company's executive vice-president, Liang Rong, pointed out that the cost of producing a television set included such things as materials, labor, overheads, taxes, after-sales services, and employee training fees, as well as the company's spending on R&D. 'Sales under the floor price, or production costs, should be regarded as unfair competition,' he said (*China Daily*, 25 June 2000).

A high-ranking official in the Ministry of Information Industry, which supervises the sector, seemed to take the industry's side; on the same day that the summit was held, he stated that the formation of such an alliance was a sign of the maturing of the color TV sector, indicating the 'healthy development of the industry via self-protection, self-discipline, and voluntary cooperation.'[13] But on 3 August 2000, after meeting with the nine producers, the SDPC and the Ministry of Information Industry jointly declared that while there was nothing wrong with the manufacturers discussing long-term issues affecting the industry as a whole, setting minimum prices nevertheless violated the 1998 Price Law.[14]

No formal action has been taken against the manufacturers, perhaps because of the internal problems that quickly developed within the alliance. Only a day after its establishment, the Nanjing-based company, Panda, reportedly priced one of its models at CNY600 ($72.30), lower than the floor price set by the alliance. According to An and Yang (2002), the alliance had agreed to impose a fine of CNY500,000 on any manufacturer that violated the agreement, but this rule was never implemented. Supermarket statistics also indicate the failure of the agreement: there was an actual increase in the number of color TV sets sold after the alliance declared it would limit production and raise prices (*China Daily*, 25 June 2000).

latest draft of the antimonopoly law was submitted to the State Council's Legislative Affairs Office in March 2004 and has been placed on the legislative agenda of the current National People's Congress (which ends in 2007).

The coverage of the draft law is quite comprehensive and generally in line with international standards.[15] However, one major area, namely the provisions on legal liability, has aroused debate. Chapter 7 of the draft law spells out the maximum penalties for violations of the law: CNY5 million for price fixing, CNY10 million for abuse of a dominant market position and for non-compliance with merger control decisions, and so on. However, it fails to specify the basis for imposing a specific penalty for any given violation. Is the penalty supposed to be equal to the illegal gains? Can multiple damages be imposed? Economic principles tell us that for laws to have a deterrent effect, the penalty needs to be greater than the illegal gains from the violation (because the probability of detecting a violation is less than 1).[16] Unlike the 1993 Anti Unfair Competition Law and 1998 Price Law, which both allow multiple damages and thus are consistent with the economic principles for an optimal penalty, the draft anti-monopoly law has yet to explicitly incorporate the notion of a deterrent effect.[17]

A distinct feature of the PRC's draft antimonopoly law is that it deals explicitly with administrative monopolies. Chapter 5 identifies five types of administrative monopoly: forced transactions, regional blockades, sector and industry monopolies, forced joint activities that restrict competition, and regional and sectoral regulations that limit competition. Administrative monopolies are rooted in the traditional central planning system and will continue to be extremely difficult to tackle.

The two types of administrative monopoly that are most prevalent in the PRC are regional blockades (discussed in more detail in section 4) and sectoral monopolies. One illustration of the latter is found in the telecommunications industry as documented by Sheng and Zhang (2000). Telecommunications services were provided by one giant monopoly, the Ministry of Posts and Telecommunications, until the early 1990s. In 1994, China Unicom, a new service provider jointly established by the Ministry of Electronics, Ministry of Electricity, and Ministry of Railroads, entered the telecommunications markets with the authorization of the State Council. The industry thus became a duopoly between China Unicom and the dominant incumbent, which was also the industry regulator.

According to Sheng and Zhang (2000), the Ministry of Posts and Telecommunications adopted several anticompetitive practices shortly after the entry of China Unicom in order to defend its monopoly position. The new entrant was required to apply to the ministry for permission to operate in any of the PRC's many geographic markets. By delaying consideration of its applications, the ministry could ensure that China Unicom's newly developed infrastructure could not be put to use for some time. The ministry also set up administrative barriers, and charged unreasonable interconnection rates for access to its network. It made it difficult for the new entrant to obtain critical resources such as telephone numbers, airwave frequencies, and satellite channels, occasionally disconnected services to China Unicom's customers, and employed other restrictive business practices such as predatory pricing and cross-subsidization.

3   LINKAGES BETWEEN COMPETITION POLICY AND INDUSTRIAL POLICY

Since the start of its open door policy in the late 1970s, the PRC has persistently pursued targeted industrial policies. Industrial policy objectives are embedded in the country's FDI, science and technology, education, land use, and taxation policies. According to Jiang (2002a: 49), the central government issued more than 80 comprehensive industrial policies between 1978 and 1997, pertaining to virtually every government department and every industry. She divided these industrial policies into four categories: policies designed to reform the industrial landscape; those containing interventionist measures; policies that supported particular industries and enterprises; and those that restricted certain industries and enterprises.[18]

Jiang (2002a) identified three stages of policy development.[19] During the first stage, from the late 1970s to the mid-1980s, the PRC's industrial policies promoted competition, by encouraging the entry of new firms (particularly in non-state sectors), by introducing competition among existing enterprises, and by relaxing price controls. In the second stage, from the mid-1980s to the mid-1990s, the country's industrial policies limited competition. They restrained the establishment of new small and medium-sized enterprises, restricted competition between rural and state-owned enterprises (SOEs), and provided preferential treatment to large SOEs. In the third stage, which began in the mid-1990s, industrial policies have both promoted and limited competition: they have been used to promote competition in monopolistic industries, but they have also been used to rescue SOEs that were facing difficulties.

Jiang's characterizations of the effects of industrial policies on competition are fairly sensible. Until the mid-1990s, the PRC's policy-makers regarded industrial policies as the cure for virtually every economic problem and as the key to long-term economic development. Whenever a shortage or surplus occurred in the marketplace, or competition was judged to be 'excessive' (as seen by price wars or a large number of loss-making enterprises), the public expected the government to step in and correct the situation with 'proper' industrial policies.

During the early stage of economic reform (late 1970s to mid-1980s), a primary goal of the government was to improve the performance of enterprises by introducing competition—relaxing price controls, removing entry barriers, and so on. On the whole these measures worked well, significantly boosting enterprise performance. However, during that period—and indeed until the mid-1990s—the market mechanism was regarded as supplementary to central planning. As competition intensified in the domestic industry, the government was faced with new problems such as the duplication of investments and the crowding out of large SOEs by small-scale, mostly non-state-owned, new entrants. To combat these 'problems,' the government introduced new industrial policies. The second stage in Jiang's analysis thus corresponds roughly to a correction period for industry. After a period of consolidation, during which order was restored and industrial activity slowed, a new round of stimulatory industrial policies was launched.

In October 1992, at the 14th Congress of the Chinese Communist Party, the PRC decided to replace its traditional approach in which the market was supplementary to central planning with one aimed at establishing a socialist market economy. Gradually the market mechanism has been recognized as an alternative, and possibly much better, means to overcome economic problems. Nowadays, the most competitive industries in the PRC, such as home appliances and textiles, are those that experienced the most turmoil and excessive competition during the past two decades.

Nevertheless, industrial policies continue to play a very important role. In particular, the promotion of large-scale enterprises remains an important part of central government policy. Influenced by the approach of Korea, the PRC regarded the establishment of large conglomerates as the best way for domestic enterprises to obtain economies of scale and compete with MNEs both domestically and in international markets. It also saw M&As as an effective vehicle to absorb and transform loss-making SOEs.[20] In 1991 and again in 1997, the State Council selected a 'national team' of 120 large enterprise groups, primarily from industries considered to be of strategic importance, to receive special treatment from the government.[21] To enhance their competitiveness, these 'national champions' were granted tariff protection, special rights to engage in international trade, access to foreign technology, 'easy loans' from state-owned banks, and other preferential treatment.[22]

Although the Asian financial crisis, and its effects on Korea in particular, led the PRC to reconsider its original approach, establishing large domestic enterprises has remained a top priority for the government. Not surprisingly, many of the large-scale M&As that have taken place in recent years have been government managed. For example, in a government-ordered merger in 2002, the Civil Aviation Administration of China forced nine domestic airlines under its direct control to form three super groups: China National Aviation and China Southwest became subsidiaries of Air China; Yunnan Airlines and China Northwest became subsidiaries of China Eastern; and China Northern and Xinjiang Airlines became subsidiaries of China Southern. Because the mergers were carried out through administrative transfers, the super groups obtained the assets of the regional carriers for free.

In another example, under its 10th five-year plan for the auto industry (2000–05), the government decided to encourage 100 small automobile manufacturers to merge with the three giants: First Automotive Works Corporation, Dongfeng Automobile Company, and Shanghai Automobile Group. In 2002, First Automotive Works bought a majority stake in Tianjin Xiali Ltd in the largest M&A transaction in domestic auto-manufacturing history. This acquisition was more market oriented than the airline transactions in that First Automotive Works actually purchased 51 percent of Tianjin Xiali's stock (Global M&A Research Center 2003: 393–7).

Industrial policy and the delay in enacting antimonopoly legislation

As mentioned earlier, the PRC began drafting an antimonopoly law in the early 1990s. While there are many reasons for the long delay in enacting this legislation, the pursuit of industrial policy has been one factor holding back the effort to set up a comprehensive competition law.

Views on the need to introduce an antimonopoly law in the PRC differ. One view holds that it is too early to enact such a law because the PRC is still in the early stage of building a market system and its markets are not well developed. The issue for most industries in the PRC is not high concentration, but rather the reverse: major firms have not yet attained economies of scale, and so action against monopolies is largely irrelevant (Yang 2002). A related position held by many government officials is that the government should actually continue to encourage the formation and development of large enterprise groups and promote economies of scale so as to enhance the international competitiveness of domestic enterprises. The introduction of an antimonopoly law would work against these goals (Li and Ma 2002). Both of these views seem to equate competition policy with a bias against bigness.

Advocates of antimonopoly legislation, meanwhile, hold that the enactment of an antimonopoly law is not only consistent with, but also necessary for, enhancing the competitiveness of large enterprises, especially SOEs. According to this view, only through fair market competition where efficient firms survive and prosper and inefficient ones exit the marketplace can large domestic enterprises really grow and become competitive (Wang 2004; Kong 2001: 259). The proponents of this view believe that creating and maintaining a level playing field, as opposed to protecting domestic enterprises, benefits all firms.

A more pessimistic view holds that the most crucial issue facing the PRC today is the fight against administrative monopolies, a problem that will not be resolved by a single piece of antimonopoly legislation. The proponents of this view maintain that the administrative monopolies inherited from the traditional central planning system can only be dealt with through further economic reform and the PRC's transformation into a true market economy (Li and Ma 2002).

Promulgating an antimonopoly law is now at the top of the agenda for the National People's Congress. However, even with such a law in place, conflicts between competition policy and industrial policy are likely to occur. For example, in evaluating the competition effects of a merger, the government is likely to take into account its desire to encourage large enterprise groups and promote national champions. Also, in situations involving competition between domestic firms and foreign investors, pro-tection of domestic players may continue to carry some weight. The chal-lenge for the competition law enforcement agency will be to demonstrate that it can deal with such conflicts.[23] In the author's view, it is extremely important for the PRC to establish a truly independent enforcement agency with sole responsibility for enforcing competition law. If, instead, the task of enforcing the antimonopoly law rests on the shoulders of an existing agency that has traditionally been charged with promoting industrial pol-icy, then it will be more difficult to guarantee the full implementation of competition policy and its non-interference with industrial policy.

4   LOCAL PROTECTIONISM AND COMPETITION

Local protectionism is prevalent in the PRC. It has taken such forms as imposing taxes on commodities made in other provinces (Box 4.2), ban-ning exports to other regions of locally made raw materials that are of high quality or in short supply,[24] or even preventing law enforcement officers from dealing with local firms that counterfeit the brands of other regions (Lin 2001). With the move toward fiscal decentralization since 1978, local governments have had a strong incentive to shield local firms and protect their tax base. The desire to guarantee local employment is another eco-nomic as well as political incentive for local government officials. Throughout the 1990s, local governments competed to attract FDI, even adopting protective measures that would ensure the profitability of locally based foreign firms.

Local protectionism leads to market fragmentation and thus to low regional specialization. The eight-firm concentration ratios reported in Table 4.2 are consistent with widespread local protectionism in the PRC.

Box 4.2 A case study of protection in the local auto industry

The city of Shanghai and the province of Hubei are the PRC's two leading car manufacturing bases. In 1984 Volkswagen, the German auto manufacturer, set up a 50:50 joint venture with a consortium of domestic partners led by the Shanghai Automotive Industrial Corporation to produce Santana passenger cars in Shanghai. In 1992, Automobiles Citroën of France and Dong Feng Motor Corporation of the PRC set up the Dong Feng Citroën Automobile Company in Wuhan, the capital of Hubei, to produce and sell Fukang passenger cars.

In mid-1998, Shanghai introduced local regulations to protect its Santana sedans. The municipal government slapped extra licensing fees and sales taxes on consumers who bought cars made outside Shanghai, thereby adding some CNY80,000 ($9,600) to the already high prices of such cars.[25] This badly affected the Fukang; in the first half of 1999, Dong Feng Citroën sold only 24 cars in Shanghai whereas Shanghai Volkswagen sold 6,400 Santanas.

In swift and severe retaliation, Hubei began levying taxes on consumers who bought Santanas rather than the locally made Fukang. Taxes included irrigation construction fees (abolished long ago by the central government) and a dubious CNY70,000 ($8,400) levy to 'help loss-making SOEs overcome their difficulties.' As a result, the price of a Santana in Wuhan rose to CNY326,000 ($39,000)—nearly double its usual price of CNY172,000 ($20,700).

Both Shanghai's and Hubei's regulations on car purchases came into being despite a 1990 directive from the State Council banning such restrictions on interprovincial trade. A spokesperson for the Machinery Industry Department of Hubei claimed that the province had been forced to issue the restrictions because 'everyone else does the same.' It is indeed true that, with more than 120 car-makers nationwide, nearly every locality that boasts an auto plant applies restrictions to outside manufacturers in order to keep its own local champion afloat.

Unable to enforce regulations among competing localities, the central government decided to take the PRC's three leading car-makers under its protection and support the creation of a mainland-style auto *chaebol*. The chosen three included the two companies at the center of the Shanghai–Hubei car war—Shanghai Automotive Industrial Corporation and Dong Feng Motor Corporation—as well as First Automotive Works, which is based in Jilin province. In late January 2000, Shanghai announced that it would scrap its protective licensing fees and, from 19 January 2000, throw open its market to outside manufacturers.

Source: *Asia Times Online*, 15 January 2000.

Table 4.2   PRC: Eight-firm concentration ratios in selected manufacturing industries, 1995 and 2000 (%)

Industry	1995	2000
Food processing	5.3	7.5
Food production	9.9	13.1
Beverage production	8.6	20.4
Tobacco processing	33.0	54.0
Textiles	2.8	6.6
Garments & other fiber products	3.8	9.3
Leather, furs, & related products	2.9	n.a.
Timber & straw products	5.7	n.a.
Furniture manufacturing	5.4	n.a.
Papermaking & paper products	5.3	10.9
Printing & recorded medium products	5.1	n.a.
Educational & sporting products	8.1	n.a.
Petroleum processing & coking	44.9	82.8
Chemical materials & products	11.3	7.9
Pharmaceutical products	11.8	28.8
Chemical fibers	37.6	13.8
Rubber products	18.3	36.4
Plastic products	3.6	6.0
Non-metal mineral products	2.4	6.1
Ferrous metals	30.2	39.5
Non-ferrous metals	13.3	10.3
Metal products	4.6	9.5
Ordinary machinery	6.5	9.9
Equipment for special purposes	6.2	11.7
Transport equipment	20.9	28.9
Electrical equipment & machinery	8.8	30.8
Electronic & telecommunications equipment	14.7	23.1

n.a. = not available.

Source: China Statistics Press (1997, 2002).

Although the degree of concentration has generally increased since 1995, very few industries have a concentration ratio above 50 percent, and for most the ratio is below 20 percent.

Recent empirical studies on the effects of local protectionism on regional economies in the PRC have come up with mixed findings. Young (2000) provides anecdotal evidence of a rise in local protectionism during the reform era, especially in the 1980s, and presents statistical evidence of declining regional specialization. Naughton (1999), on the other hand, finds evidence of increasing regional specialization between 1987 and 1992. More recently, Bai et al. (2005) use more comprehensive statistical methods to find evidence of local protection of industries with a high tax-plus-profit margin and a high degree of state ownership. They also find that the degree of regional specialization has been increasing since the mid-1980s, after an earlier decrease. Nevertheless, the case study of the auto industry presented in Box 4.2 demonstrates that regional protectionism was prevalent even in the late 1990s, despite the revised trend.

The central government has long been trying to prohibit regional protectionism. This was the intention of article 6 of the State Council's Provisional Regulations Concerning Development and Protection of the Socialist Competition Mechanism, issued as early as 1980. Enforcement of these regulations over the past two decades has, however, been poor. Perhaps the passage of an antimonopoly law, especially the provisions on administrative monopolies, will allow regional barriers to trade and competition to be torn down more effectively.

Possibly even more important than external forces such as enforcement are internal incentives on the part of localities. In June 2004, nine provinces in southern PRC joined the Macao and Hong Kong, China special administrative regions to form the Pan Pearl River Delta regional trading block.[26] This was an encouraging development given that the sole goal of the agreement was to break down trade barriers and build a vast common market for the 11 member regions. The formation of this trading block was driven by increasingly intense competition between the Pearl River Delta region (consisting of Guangdong province and the Macao and Hong Kong, China special administrative regions) and the Yangtze River Delta (consisting of the city of Shanghai and the provinces of Zhengjiang and Jiangsu in eastern PRC).

5   FOREIGN DIRECT INVESTMENT AND COMPETITION

A major factor affecting the degree of competition in the PRC is the massive inflow of FDI over the past two decades. Since the PRC adopted an open door policy in the late 1970s, and particularly since 1993 when Deng Xiaoping made his famous tour of the south, inward FDI has been a driving force for increased competition in the PRC. The presence of foreign-invested companies has greatly changed the landscape of competition for almost every industry.

Table 4.3 contains information on the presence of foreign firms in various manufacturing industries. As can be seen, in 2002 foreign-invested enterprises accounted for over 30 percent of total sales in many industries. The ratio was over 50 percent in industries such as leather and fur products and cultural and sporting goods, and as high as 74 percent in electronic and telecommunications equipment. In most industries the foreign presence has increased since 1995, highlighting the trend toward increased competition from foreign firms in the domestic market.

However, entry into the PRC has been far from free for foreign investors. They are subject to numerous government regulations, including the requirement to abide by the central government's *Catalog Guiding Foreign Investment in Industry* (MOFTEC 2003). This catalog divides industries into those that are 'prohibited,' 'restricted,' 'allowed,' and 'encouraged' in terms of their openness to FDI.[27] Depending on the amount of investment, every new project involving foreign investment must be approved by either the provincial/regional government concerned or the Ministry of Foreign Trade and Economic Cooperation (MOFTEC, which became the Ministry of Commerce in 2003).

The government has also set requirements for the mode of foreign entry. Until the mid-1990s, joint ventures were the main mode of entry for FDI, driven by the PRC's desire to have local partners learn about advanced foreign technology. It was only in the late 1990s—in fact, in the lead-up to the PRC's accession to the World Trade Organization (WTO) in January 2002—that the PRC allowed wholly foreign-owned enterprises to operate in the country, and permitted foreign firms to acquire domestic firms through new FDI inflows. The government has actively used local content requirements as a means to foster the backward linkage effects of FDI, through vertical technology transfers to local suppliers, for example.

The presence of FDI has affected industrial structures in the PRC through two channels. First, increased competition from foreign companies—often equipped with superior technology and management—has driven inefficient local firms out of the market, increasing the degree of industrial concentration. Second, foreign firms have become the dominant players in important industries—automobiles, mobile phone production, chemical products such as detergents and cosmetics, and soft drinks—by merging with or acquiring leading domestic enterprises.

Table 4.3   PRC: Ratio of foreign-invested enterprise sales to industry sales, 1995–2002 (%)

Industrial sector	1995	1997	1999	2001	2002
Food processing	21.2	23.6	24.0	24.6	25.9
Food production	30.5	35.0	37.7	41.8	40.7
Beverage production	26.2	25.5	27.7	30.6	30.9
Tobacco processing	0.6	0.9	0.8	0.7	0.5
Textiles	17.9	18.7	21.3	21.8	21.7
Garments & other fiber products	50.8	44.9	49.2	46.8	45.5
Leather, furs, & related products	54.1	50.1	58.2	54.4	53.2
Timber & straw products	27.3	27.1	32.6	29.6	25.8
Furniture manufacturing	30.7	29.8	42.8	46.6	47.2
Papermaking & paper products	17.0	19.6	28.3	33.0	32.8
Printing & recorded medium products	18.3	20.8	31.1	34.6	33.8
Cultural & sporting goods	50.7	49.3	60.6	60.3	60.0
Petroleum processing & coking	1.4	4.1	5.4	9.0	9.9
Chemical materials & products	12.6	14.2	18.8	21.7	22.2
Pharmaceutical products	18.3	20.3	21.8	22.0	21.7
Chemical fibers	12.7	17.5	33.3	21.0	25.4
Rubber products	25.0	23.1	33.2	36.2	39.0
Plastic products	33.0	33.0	42.0	44.0	42.0
Non-metal mineral products	11.4	11.5	16.1	19.3	19.2
Ferrous metals	6.2	4.0	6.5	7.9	7.6
Non-ferrous metals	12.5	11.8	13.2	11.8	12.6
Metal products	26.6	30.0	35.5	36.8	37.2
Ordinary machinery	14.5	16.1	20.7	22.6	24.0
Special purpose equipment	9.0	10.5	14.4	18.9	20.2
Transport equipment	25.2	22.8	29.6	31.5	32.6
Electrical equipment & machinery	24.2	27.2	32.2	33.8	33.6
Electronic & telecommunications equipment	60.8	62.5	69.5	73.8	73.9

Source: State Statistics Bureau (various years).

**Box 4.3 A case study of local brand
acquisitions by Unilever and P&G**

In early 2002 a bitter row erupted between Unilever, the consumer goods multinational, and Shanghai Toothpaste Factory (STF), a well-known domestic company, over a brand agreement for Zhonghua toothpaste. Zhonghua has been the best-selling toothpaste brand in the PRC for decades. In 1993, Unilever and STF signed an agreement giving Unilever the sole right to manufacture, market, and sell the Zhonghua brand in the PRC. The agreement had an unlimited term, subject to trademark renewal every 10 years. The key condition for renewal was that the total production volume in the last year of the agreement should be higher than that in the first year.

As the end of the first 10-year period approached, STF told Unilever that it wanted to end the agreement and take back the brand because it had 'suffered bad treatment at Unilever's hand'(*China Daily*, 16 January 2002). STF had already taken back another brand of toothpaste leased to Unilever—Maxam—in 2000. Unilever (China) Limited responded that, far from shelving the product, it had given it more attention than it deserved. The company claimed to have spent a considerable sum on developing the Zhonghua brand—on average 53 percent of its annual advertising and promotion budget in the oral category—and pointed out that production of the toothpaste had risen to 40,000 tons in 2002 compared with 35,000 tons in 1993. Unilever also said it had invested in new packaging for the Zhonghua brand and had launched a promotional campaign in August 2001 to boost sales (*China Daily*, 16 January 2002).

There is now a growing concern that foreign enterprises may soon dominate all of the country's industries, and that domestic firms will be driven out of business. The potentially negative consequences of foreign acquisitions for domestic brands is illustrated by the case of a leading domestic brand of toothpaste that is allegedly being 'killed off' by the foreign MNE that bought it (Box 4.3). In contrast, two acquisitions by L'Oréal of prominent brands in the skincare industry were apparently not motivated by the desire to freeze out a competing brand (Box 4.4).

Merger controls and FDI policy

Since the late 1990s, and especially since the PRC's accession to the WTO in early 2002, foreign investors have been keen to merge with or acquire domestic enterprises. In 2002, its first year as a WTO member, the PRC

> But STF disagreed. 'Unilever did not manage to push the sales higher till almost the end of the first decade. Nevertheless, we are determined to take back the Zhonghua brand. Zhonghua is a national brand name, with a long history; we must protect it,' said a top manager (*China Management Daily*, 22 November 2001). In 2003 Unilever and STF finally settled their dispute, with STF agreeing to renew the contract for the Zhonghua brand name. One of the conditions of the contract was that Unilever would give the brand a leading position among its product lines (*Southern Daily*, 22 September 2004). Some reports suggest that Unilever's compliance with this condition, and its recent national campaign to promote the brand, is part of a damage control effort to change its negative image among domestic consumers of being a 'domestic brand killer' (*Beijing Modern Commerce Daily*, 29 September 2004).[28]
>
> Another multinational, Procter & Gamble (P&G), has also been accused of 'freezing' a local brand. In 1994, P&G set up a joint venture with Beijing Second Daily Cosmetic Factory to produce and sell Panda detergent. The Beijing firm was given a 35 percent share of equity in the joint venture in return for access to its manufacturing facilities and the Panda brand name. Panda was among the three best-selling detergent brands in the PRC when the joint venture was launched, but today it is hard to find it in the shops. In September 2000, the Beijing firm bought back the brand. But by that time its position in the market had been reduced to almost nothing whereas P&G's own brand, Tide, had become a family name. In six years, production of Panda detergent had dropped from 60,000 to 4,000 tons (*China Daily*, 16 January 2002).

overtook Japan to become the most active M&A market in Asia. Foreign companies spent $13.9 billion between January and November 2002 on purchasing domestic firms, up 180 percent over the $4.9 billion spent in 2001 (US–China Business Council 2003). M&As are an important vehicle for foreign investors to gain a strategic position in the domestic market; they offer immediate access to distribution channels, customers, and domestic companies with great potential.[29]

In response to the rapid emergence of FDI-related M&As, the government set up an M&A notification/evaluation system in March 2003, the first of its kind in the country.[30] The purpose of the Interim Provisions on Mergers with and Acquisitions of Domestic Enterprises by Foreign Investors is to

> promote and regulate foreign investors' investment in the PRC and the introduction of advanced technology and management experiences from abroad,

---

Box 4.4 A case study of the acquisition of a local brand by L'Oréal

L'Oréal, one of the world's leading manufacturers of beauty products, recently reached agreement to take over two leading domestic brands in the PRC: Mininurse, which it acquired in December 2003, and Yue-Sai, which it acquired in January 2004. L'Oréal has been exploring the PRC market since the 1980s. In 1996 it set up a joint venture in Suzhou city in the eastern province of Jiangsu to produce cosmetics by Maybelline, the large American company it had purchased. L'Oréal faces stiff competition in the PRC from such well-known companies as P&G, Estee Lauder, Avon, Unilever, and Shiseido.

Mininurse is among the three leading skincare brands in the PRC. A mass-market brand based on the quality and affordability of its products, Mininurse is distributed through some 280,000 outlets found throughout the PRC. Its market share was 5 percent in 2003. The acquisition was L'Oréal's first in the PRC market, and included a manufacturing facility in Yichang city in Hubei province. Paolo Gasparrini, general manager of L'Oréal, said: 'Mininurse complements L'Oréal's brand portfolio perfectly and enables us to move more quickly into the Chinese consumer skincare market' (L'Oréal News Release, 11 December 2003). An important condition of the agreement was that the creator of Mininurse, Li Zhida, must not engage in the skincare business in the future.[31]

L'Oréal's acquisition of Mininurse was followed a month later by the acquisition of Yue-Sai Cosmetics, a company founded by TV celebrity Yue-Sai Kan. She had set up a factory in 1992 in Shenzhen to produce her

---

improve the utilization of foreign investment, rationalize allocation of resources, ensure employment, and safeguard fair competition and national economic security (article 1).

Article 3 stipulates that as a general rule M&As

shall not create excessive concentration, eliminate or hinder competition, disturb social and economic order or harm public interests.

The provisions require investors to notify MOFTEC (now the Ministry of Commerce) and SAIC if any of the following thresholds are met for an M&A directly involving a domestic enterprise (article 19):[32]

1 the business turnover of a party to the merger or acquisition in the domestic market in the current year exceeds CNY1.5 billion (approximately $182 million);

eponymous brand of cosmetics, promoted as being specifically designed for local women's skin. By 1996 Yue-Sai had become the leading brand in the PRC, with surveys showing that brand name recognition was especially high among city women (*China Daily*, 7 August 2001). Yue-Sai had 18 sales offices and over 800 outlets in 240 of the PRC's largest cities prior to the transaction. In 2000, the brand accounted for 26 percent of the color cosmetics market and 17 percent of the skincare market (*China Daily*, 30 October 2000). In 2003, Yue-Sai reported sales of almost 38 million euros ($47 million) (*China Daily*, Hong Kong edition, 28 January 2004). But the brand has faced increased competition since the mid-1990s when foreign competitors realized the PRC's market potential and launched large-scale marketing campaigns.

In 1998, Yue-Sai formed a joint venture with multinational fragrance and cosmetics firm Coty Inc. to produce up to 60 million units of cosmetics and skincare products per year in Shanghai. Yue-Sai Kan said that she hoped Coty's backing would help her brand survive even if other domestic brands were eventually overwhelmed by foreign giants (*China Daily*, 26 October 1998).

When L'Oréal purchased Yue-Sai in 2004, Gasparrini affirmed the company's intention to look after the valued brand:

> Yue-Sai, a symbolic brand for the Chinese women of today, will naturally slot into L'Oréal's portfolio ... The brand strengthens the group's leadership in make-up and facial skincare. The group's technological input will enable Yue-Sai to win new market share (L'Oréal news release, 26 January 2004).

2   the foreign investors have merged with or acquired more than 10 domestic enterprises in aggregate in the relevant industry in the PRC within one year;

3   the market share of a party to the merger or acquisition in the domestic market has reached 20 percent; or

4   the market share of a party to the merger or acquisition in the domestic market will reach 25 percent as a result of the transaction.

The 2003 provisions are the most comprehensive set of M&A regulations in the PRC to date. Although they apply to FDI-related M&As only, and fall short of international standards from a technical viewpoint, their establishment nonetheless represents a milestone in antitrust development. They are the first set of official rules ever in the PRC to adopt an antitrust approach to the regulation of M&As.[33]

Report of the State Administration for Industry and Commerce

In early June 2004, after a year-long investigation, SAIC released a report entitled *The Competition-restricting Behavior of Multinational Companies in China and Countermeasures* (SAIC 2004). This report, the first of its kind in the country, stated that some MNEs commanded obviously dominant positions in their industries and were using their advantage to curb competition. It accused several multinationals of attempting to limit competition through strategies such as predatory pricing, exclusive dealing, tied sales, and M&As. The report specifically mentioned Microsoft and Eastman Kodak, which both denied any wrongdoing.[34]

In the case of Kodak, SAIC drew attention to the agreement signed in 1998 between Kodak, the SDRC, the State Economic and Trade Commission, and MOFTEC under which Kodak undertook to invest a total of $2 billion in acquiring all of the country's domestic imaging factories, except those of Lucky Film. On its part, the government agreed not to allow the establishment of any other joint venture in the imaging sector between 1998 and 2000. In response to the SAIC report, Kodak released a statement saying that the company had never done anything to circumvent the normal processes of market competition. However, insiders say that the agreement gave Kodak three golden years to develop its market in the PRC free from foreign competition. Kodak now has over 50 percent of the market. Fujifilm, Kodak's nearest rival, had 48 percent of the market until 1998, but by 2003 its share had dropped to 15 percent as a result of Kodak's rapid progress (*China Business Weekly*, 8 June 2004).

Lu Fu, a professor at the China University of Political Science and Law, said that the report showed that the PRC urgently needed a complete set of laws on monopolistic practices and unfair competition (*China Business Weekly*, 8 June 2004). He argued that while continuing to welcome foreign investment, the PRC should learn more about the potentially negative effects of the presence of multinational giants and take steps—such as passing antimonopoly legislation and revising the 1993 Anti Unfair Competition Law—to prevent them from employing anticompetitive practices. He is not the only one to be concerned about the potential for MNEs to abuse their market power in the PRC; some scholars expressed the view, even before SAIC issued its report, that the new antimonopoly law should be used to check the monopoly power of transnational corporations (Wang 2002: 230).[35]

Given that it specifically targets MNEs and was issued by the sole enforcer of the 1993 Anti Unfair Competition Law, the SAIC report has made many multinationals in the PRC uneasy.[36] Foreign investors are deeply concerned about whether they will be treated in the same way as domestic players after an antimonopoly law is promulgated.[37] It is perhaps unfortunate that two of the country's most powerful government agencies, SAIC and MOFTEC, have each targeted foreign investors recently, and especially prior to the introduction of antimonopoly legislation—SAIC with its report and the ministry with merger regulations that apply exclusively to foreign investors. Given recent developments, it may take some time, or even some noteworthy cases, for the enforcement agency of the antimonopoly law (whoever it turns out to be) to convince the world that the PRC's competition laws do apply equally and fairly to all players.

6   COMPETITION, DEVELOPMENT, AND POVERTY

The 'economic miracle' of the past two decades has greatly raised the standard of living in the PRC. According to the World Bank, the proportion of the population living on $1 or less per day declined from 33 percent in 1990 to 16 percent in 2000. This rapid reduction in poverty is undoubtedly associated with increased economic freedom for individuals and enterprises, improved flows of trade and resources among regions, and the introduction of competition to domestic sectors.

However, the process of poverty reduction has been accompanied by some practices that have limited competition. For instance, due to limited labor mobility and restrictions on residence inherited from the central planning period, attracting outside capital has been of critical importance in developing local economies. The prevalence of regional protectionism stems directly from local governments' desire to boost their local economies and increase the living standards of residents. Like protectionism in international markets, this phenomenon can be dealt with primarily through two approaches: interregional collaboration to abolish trade barriers; and more effective implementation of existing laws prohibiting regional blockades and protectionism.

One should note, however, that public awareness of competition issues is very low in the poorer regions of the country, where law enforcement is also lacking. Business operators in poor areas may act to maximize their short-run profit at the expense of the long-term development of the local economy. Of the three bid-rigging cases SAIC reported to the OECD Global Forum on Competition in 2001, for example, two concerned school construction projects, one in Changding county in Fujian province and the other in Lichuan county in Jiangxi, one of the poorest provinces in the country (Wang 2001). It is encouraging that SAIC has been targeting this type of violation. Local government officials need to understand that competition law is enforced not just to ensure fair competition, but also as an important means to reduce poverty and promote the long-term development of local economies.

7   CONCLUSION

The PRC has made significant progress over the past decade in setting up an antitrust system. The passage of the 1993 Anti Unfair Competition Law and the 1998 Price Law, together with active law enforcement, laid a solid foundation for creating and maintaining a level playing field for competition in the PRC. The enforcement effort of SAIC is to be applauded. After a decade of deliberation and numerous revisions, it appears that the PRC is finally willing and ready to enact a comprehensive antimonopoly law.

Industrial policies have had direct and significant effects on industrial structure and the degree of competition in the PRC over the past two decades. From the late 1970s to the mid-1990s, the government vigorously pursued industrial policies. While the pursuit of such policies has cooled since the 1997 financial crisis, and especially since the PRC acceded to the WTO in 2002, industrial policies remain an important policy instrument for the government, particularly in major sectors such as airlines and automotives, as recent M&A activity illustrates. The long delay in passing an antimonopoly law is related to the government's fear that the business conglomerates it has nurtured through its targeted industrial policies may be adversely affected by such legislation.

Another major driving force in antitrust development over the past two decades has been inward FDI, which has had a huge impact on industrial structure, firm conduct, and the degree of competition in the PRC. On the one hand, FDI has contributed to market fragmentation as regional governments competed to attract foreign capital and technology, causing duplication of investments in many sectors. Local governments have even erected regional trade barriers to protect foreign-invested enterprises in their regions. On the other hand, the presence of foreign enterprises has seen less-efficient local enterprises driven out of business, leading to a rapid increase in the level of industrial concentration. Moreover, MNEs have been actively merging with or acquiring local firms, to get quick access to their distribution channels, customer base, and so on. FDI-related M&As have been particularly common since the PRC acceded to the WTO in 2002, and began to allow foreign investors to combine with domestic enterprises in early 2003.

The presence of foreign enterprises prompted the PRC to establish a merger control regime, albeit applying to FDI-related transactions only. The 2003 Interim Provisions on M&As marked a milestone in the development of an antitrust system in the PRC. One can predict that the interplay of FDI policy and competition policy, and the accompanying interaction among foreign and domestic firms, will continue to be a primary factor shaping industrial structure, firm conduct, and performance in the PRC for years to come.

With a general antimonopoly law likely to be in place within the next two years, the PRC will soon have a fairly complete set of competition laws. Law enforcement will then be the biggest challenge facing the country. One difficult task will be to tackle the administrative monopolies inherited from the old central planning system, which have proven to be extremely resilient throughout the entire economic reform era. As illustrated by the case studies in this chapter, sectoral monopolies and regional protectionism will continue to pose enforcement problems for the new competition agency.[38] With regard to regional blockades, the recent formation of the Pan Pearl River Delta alliance with the sole goal of breaking down regional trade and investment barriers is an encouraging development. There is good reason to expect that similar common markets will be formed among other regional economies as interregional competition intensifies further, and as regional governments realize the full extent of the damage caused by interregional trade wars.

Another major challenge for the PRC will be to deal with the potential conflicts between industrial policy and competition policy. Although industrial policies will become less important as the PRC fulfills its WTO obligations in the years to come, they remain deeply rooted in government regulations. The 2003 M&A provisions, for instance, take the clear stand that competition policy is secondary to industrial policy.[39] The industrial policy mentality may also influence the enforcement of competition laws in the PRC, including the antimonopoly law even if it does not explicitly incorporate industrial policy concepts. In addition, the recent SAIC report has created great concern among foreign investors. It will be interesting to see how the government balances fair competition on the one hand against protection of domestic enterprises on the other.

For all of the above reasons, it is crucial for the PRC to set up a powerful and independent competition authority. The competition authority should have the power and capability to combat administrative monopolies, and should therefore not be affiliated to any existing government ministry or agency. Ideally it would be placed directly under the State Council to guarantee that it has the real authority to challenge administrative monopolies.[40]

In addition, to ensure that competition law is enforced without interference from other government policies with potentially conflicting objectives, the competition authority should be separated from those agencies that have had responsibility for implementing the country's industrial and FDI policies in the past. There needs to be a clear recognition that having the will and intent to implement competition rules fairly and equally is a different matter from being seen to apply the rules fairly and equally. Because of such factors as asymmetric information, the competition authority's methods of dealing with given cases will never be perfectly observable to outsiders. If in addition the agency is charged with a dual role that requires it to implement potentially conflicting policies, its independence may be compromised in the public mind.[41] While it may be costly to set up a new competition agency, the PRC's policy-makers should be aware that competition laws are the fundamental rules of the game for a market economy and that the benefits of investing in institution building should not be underestimated.

Other important factors for an effective antitrust system include capacity building, competition advocacy, and development of a culture of fair competition. Overall, the PRC has much to learn from the experiences of other countries, particularly those in East Asia.[42] Perhaps the most valuable lesson concerns the importance of a truly independent competition authority. In Japan, for instance, the conflict between the Fair Trade Commission, which administrates competition policy, and the Ministry of International Trade and Industry (now the Ministry of Economy, Trade and Industry), which implements industrial policy, has impeded the enforcement of competition law (Sanekata and Wilks 1996). The PRC should fully exploit its late-mover advantage in competition policy development and should not repeat the mistakes other countries have made, particularly in institutional design.

NOTES

*   I thank Douglas Brooks, Simon Evenett, Ying Qian, Chenyang Zhang, and other participants at the competition policy workshops held by the Asian Development Bank for valuable comments and suggestions.

1   An English version of the law can be found at <www.apeccp.org.tw/doc/China.html>.

2   It is worth noting that the Anti Unfair Competition Law does not prohibit price cartels (price fixing) in general, even though almost all of the competition laws of other countries consider such cartels to be per se illegal. This omission was fixed in the 1998 Price Law.

3   The People's Courts also play a role in enforcing the law.

4   The tendency of firms to rely heavily on price competition, as opposed to non-price competition (advertising, quality, research and development, service), may account for the seemingly large number of predatory pricing cases in the PRC compared with other countries (see, for example, Xie 2001).

5   This approach is not confined to competition law; reliance on administrative channels is also common in other areas of law enforcement, such as the enforcement of intellectual property rights.

6   Two additional laws that support national competition legislation, but that are not discussed in detail in this chapter, are the Law of the People's Republic of China for Protecting Consumers' Rights and Interests, promulgated in 1993, and the Public Tendering Law of the People's Republic of China, enacted in 1999. The latter law covers bid rigging in more detail than the 1993 Anti Unfair Competition Law.

7   The law also prohibits conduct such as spreading rumors about price hikes, attracting business through deceptive pricing, and so on.

8   The Law of the People's Republic of China on International Trade, promulgated in 1994 and revised in April 2004, prohibits predatory pricing and bid rigging in the context of international trade (articles 32 and 33).

9   Exactly why a separate enforcement agency was chosen for the Price Law, rather than getting the SAIC to do the job, is unknown.

10   For instance, the agencies set a minimum charge on a one-week trip to Thailand at CNY3,900, compared with as low as CNY2,800 before the agreement was reached. See Kong (2001: 188–9) for more details.

11   On 20 January 2000, the Chinese Automobile Industry Association publicized a decision by 10 domestic automobile manufacturers not to fight a price war. However, because they did this more discretely than the color TV manufacturers, the case did not receive as much media attention (*China Daily*, 3 August 2000).

12   Under the Price Law and the Anti Unfair Competition Law, manufacturers who manipulate market prices can be fined CNY30,000–300,000 ($3,600–36,000), and any illegal income can be confiscated.

13   See 'Cooperation started among the nine domestic color TV producers' at <http://www1.people.com.cn/GB/channel3/22/20000609/97046.html> [in Chinese].

14   See Li Jialu, 'Price cutting behavior since the color TV summit' at <http://www1.people.com.cn/GB/channel3/22/20000809/180077.html> [in Chinese].

15   Jung and Hao (2003) provide a comprehensive evaluation of the draft anti-monopoly law, especially from a legal perspective.

16   See Becker (1968) and Posner (1977). The treble damage system of US antitrust law, for instance, is consistent with these basic economic principles.

17   The administrative surcharges imposed under Japan's Antimonopoly Act used to be based on the idea of 'confiscation of illegal gains.' Japan is currently planning to change this arrangement to one that imposes multiple damages. See Lin (2005) and Fair Trade Commission of Japan (2004) for further details.

18   Jiang (2002a: Table 1) provides a detailed description of the various measures included in the industrial policy framework.

19   See also Jiang (1996) for a comprehensive study of the PRC's industrial policies from the late 1970s to the mid-1990s, from both a theoretical and practical perspective.

20   In 1987, it was made clear at the 13th Congress of the Chinese Communist Party that small SOEs could be sold to collectives and individuals. In 1994, the government began to conduct mergers of large and medium-sized enterprises in 100 pilot cities.

21   These industries included electricity generation, coal mining, automobiles, electronics, iron and steel, machinery, chemicals, construction materials, transport, aerospace, and pharmaceuticals. See Nolan (2001) for a detailed study.

22   In the mid-1990s, as part of a reform of the country's innovation system, many R&D centers affiliated with ministries or other government agencies were transferred to members of the national team. The goal was to enhance their R&D capacity as well as to overcome the entrenched problem of research projects not being motivated by the actual needs of the market simply because so many R&D centers were not linked to real business entities.

23   Some scholars say that one important reason for the long delay in introducing antitrust legislation is competition among the present enforcement agencies—SAIC, the SDRC, and the Ministry of Commerce (which took over the task of drafting the antimonopoly law in 2003)—to gain the power to enforce the general antimonopoly law (Neumann and Guo 2003).

24   Watson, Findlay, and Du (1989) cite the 'wool war' and the 'silk war' of the mid-1980s as examples of local governments trying to keep raw materials within the locality in order to favor local manufacturers.

25   Because PRC auto-makers tend to be overstaffed and produce on a small scale, a few years ago the prices of domestically produced cars were two to three times higher than the world average. Large domestic manufacturers relied on import tariffs of 80–100 percent to maintain their profitability. However, import tariffs have been declining since the PRC's accession to the WTO in early 2002.

26   The nine provinces were Fujian, Jiangxi, Hunan, Guangdong, Hainan, Sichuan, Guizhou, Yunnan, and the Guangxi Zhuang Autonomous Region. The 11 regions together account for 47 percent of the economy and more than half of foreign trade.

27   The catalog has been revised several times—most recently in 2002 after the PRC entered the WTO—becoming increasingly less restrictive. According to the 2002 version, prohibited industries include certain financial services, air transportation, media, and electricity transmission.

28   In addition to Zhonghua and Maxam, Unilever acquired four other local brands in the PRC during the 1990s in the fields of detergent, tea production, and ice cream. Most have either struggled or disappeared (*Beijing Modern Commerce Daily*, 29 September 2004).

29   In 2001, for example, Emerson took over Avansys, the entire electronic wing of Huawei Technologies, a leading telecommunications supplier in the PRC,

for $750 million in cash, making it the largest M&A deal between a private domestic company and a foreign investor to date. In the banking sector, Hong Kong and Shanghai Bank spent $62 million to purchase an 8 percent stake in Shanghai Bank in January 2002, thus becoming the first foreign bank to own a stake in a state-owned domestic bank (Global M&A Research Center 2003).

30 The English version of the regulations can be found at <http://bizchina.china daily.com.cn/guide/law/law05.htm>.

31 See *China Youth Daily*, 12 December 2003. A similar condition was contained in the agreement with Yue-Sai Kan; see *Yangcheng Wuanbao* [*Yangcheng Evening Paper*], 10 February 2004.

32 A different set of thresholds applies to off-shore M&As that affect domestic markets.

33 According to private sources, the Ministry of Commerce has received and approved many merger applications from foreign investors since the regulations were issued, but has not challenged any of them.

34 *China Daily*, Hong Kong edition, 18 June 2004. Microsoft stated that the company's conduct in the PRC was in line with PRC laws and regulations (*China Daily*, 2 June 2004).

35 Other scholars are less worried about the presence of foreign companies in the PRC, arguing that the dominant market share of foreign firms as a whole, rather than of a single firm, does not necessarily imply monopoly in PRC markets (see, for example, Jiang 2002b). Also, according to SAIC data, less than 10 percent of the cases dealt with by SAIC have involved foreign firms.

36 Abbott B. 'Tad' Lipsky, a partner with Latham & Watkins LLP in Washington DC, said that 'there are going to be a lot of foreign investors losing sleep until economic and procedural rationality and proportional remedy are established as the organizing principles of Chinese antitrust' (*Global Competition Review*, 2 July 2004, <www.globalcompetitionreview.com/news/news_print. cfm?item_id=1825>).

37 An anonymous official of the National People's Congress recently said that the PRC's antimonopoly law would 'definitely treat all enterprises equally' (*China Daily*, 2 June 2004).

38 One major difficulty for SAIC in enforcing the 1993 Anti Unfair Competition Law has been interference from local governments, which on many occasions have tried to prevent its staff from investigating firms in their localities (SAIC 2002).

39 Lin (2004) argues that the incorporation of competition provisions in the 2003 M&A provisions places an additional constraint on the set of permissible mergers *within* the traditional industrial policy framework. Under the regulations, even mergers that would enhance competition are not allowed if they would violate industrial policy as stipulated in the *Catalog Guiding Foreign Investment in Industry* (MOFTEC 2003).

40 However, it has been reported that in the latest draft of the antimonopoly law, submitted to the State Council in secrecy, the article on setting up an independent competition authority directly under the State Council has been

dropped. It is not clear whether SAIC, the Ministry of Commerce, or some other agency will be responsible for enforcing the antimonopoly law (*China Daily* 29 June 2004, <www.chinadaily.com.cn/English/doc/2004-06/29/content_343701.htm>).

41   See Chen and Lin (2002) for a discussion of the informational problem associated with the dual role in the context of competition policy in Hong Kong, China's telecommunications industry.

42   For a discussion of the implications of East Asian experiences for competition policy in the PRC, see Lin (2005).

*Appendix A4.1   PRC: Table of contents of the draft antimonopoly law,
February 2002*[a]

Chapter 1   General provisions

Article 1   Objectives
Article 2   Area of application
Article 3   Monopolies
Article 4   Definition of 'business operator' and 'specific market'
Article 5   Responsibilities of government
Article 6   Enforcement organs
Article 7   Social supervision

Chapter 2   Prohibition on monopoly agreements

Article 8   Prohibition on monopoly agreements
Article 9   Application for exemption
Article 10   Submission of agreements
Article 11   Approval of agreements
Article 12   Modification or revocation of agreement approvals
Article 13   Publication of approvals

Chapter 3   Prohibition on abuse of dominant market position

Article 14   Prohibition on abuse of dominant market position
Article 15   Dominant market position
Article 16   Presumption of dominant market position
Article 17   Prohibition on setting monopolistic prices
Article 18   Prohibition on predatory pricing
Article 19   Prohibition on discriminatory treatment
Article 20   Prohibition on refusal to deal
Article 21   Prohibition on forced transactions
Article 22   Prohibition on tied sales or imposition of unreasonable transaction terms
Article 23   Prohibition on exclusive dealing
Article 24   Prohibition on resale price maintenance

Chapter 4   Control of enterprise mergers and acquisitions (concentration)

Article 25   Definition of enterprise mergers and acquisitions (concentration)
Article 26   Application for enterprise mergers and acquisitions (concentration)
Article 27   Content of applications
Article 28   Approval of applications
Article 29   Conditions for approval

---

a   Translated from the original by the author.

5

India

S. Chakravarthy

1   INTRODUCTION

This chapter addresses the competition regime in India. It traces the metamorphosis of the existing competition law, the Monopolies and Restrictive Trade Practices Act, 1969 (MRTP Act), into the new competition law passed in December 2002 and currently being phased in, the Competition Act, 2002 (Competition Act). In particular it seeks to show the influence of the new global paradigm of liberalization, privatization, and globalization on the development of the new law. During the first year of its introduction, the MRTP Act remained in force, with the new regulatory authority performing only competition advocacy functions. Once all the provisions of the new act are brought into force, the old act will be repealed.

The metamorphosis of the outgoing competition law into the new law has its rationale in the new policy paradigm of economic reform ushered in by the government in 1991 and refined since then. The pre-1991 paradigm was characterized by licensing, planning, and government control.[1] The post-1991 paradigm is grounded, rather, in liberalization, privatization, and globalization. Sections 2 and 3 of the narrative that follows outline the major features of the outgoing and incoming laws. Section 4 examines the interface between competition policy and other government policies, focusing in particular on combinations and foreign direct investment (FDI). Section 5 discusses competition in the context of pro-poor concerns. Section 6 summarizes the main arguments of the chapter.

2   THE MONOPOLIES AND RESTRICTIVE TRADE PRACTICES ACT, 1969

Development of the act until 1991

The MRTP Act drew its inspiration from the mandate enshrined in the Directive Principles of State Policy in the Constitution of India. Article 38 of the constitution mandates that the state shall strive to promote the welfare of the people by securing and protecting a social order in which justice—social, economic, and political—informs all the institutions of national life; article 39 requires the state to direct its policy toward ensuring (a) that the ownership and control of material resources of the community are so distributed as best to serve the common good, and (b) that the operation of the economic system does not result in the concentration of wealth and means of production to the common detriment.

Three inquiries and their associated reports provided the impetus for the enactment of the MRTP Act. The first was of industrial licensing procedures under the Industries (Development and Regulation) Act, 1951. The committee in charge of the inquiry concluded that the licensing system had resulted in the disproportionate growth of some business houses in India (Hazari Committee Report 1955).

The second was of the distribution and levels of income in India. In its report, the Mahalonobis Committee (1964) noted that the top 10 percent of the population was receiving as much as 40 percent of all income. It commented that the 'planned economy' model practiced by the government was leading to the emergence of big business houses, and suggested the need to collect comprehensive information on the various aspects of concentration of economic power.

The third inquiry was carried out by the Monopolies Inquiry Commission (1965). The commission studied the extent and effects of the concentration of economic power in private hands, and the prevalence of monopolistic and restrictive trade practices in important sectors of economic activity (other than agriculture). It found evidence of concentration of economic power across products and industries, noting that a few industrial houses were controlling a large number of companies and that restrictive and monopolistic trade practices were widespread. The Monopolies Inquiry Commission drafted a bill designed to prevent concentration of economic power to the common detriment, and to regulate monopolistic and restrictive trade practices prejudicial to the public interest. After being amended by a parliamentary committee, the bill became the MRTP Act, 1969. It was enforced from 1 June 1970.

The MRTP Act is regarded as the competition law of India because it defines a restrictive trade practice to mean a trade practice that may have the effect of preventing, distorting, or restricting competition in any manner. In comparison with the competition laws of many other countries, however, it has proved inadequate for fostering competition in the market and reducing anticompetitive practices in domestic and international trade.[2]

The MRTP Act was based on the premises of unrestrained interaction of competitive forces, maximum material progress through rational allocation of economic resources, availability of quality goods and services at reasonable prices, and a fair deal for consumers. An interesting feature of the statute was that it covered the production and distribution of both goods and services. Less than a decade after it came into force, the government appointed a committee to review the act and suggest changes based on the experience gained thus far. The committee observed that the act contained no provisions to protect consumers against misleading advertising and similar unfair trade practices (Sachar Report 1978). The act was amended in 1984 to bring unfair trade practices within its ambit. Two years later, parallel legislation known as the Consumer Protection Act, 1986 was also put in place to control unfair trade practices, resulting in an overlap between the MRTP Act and the Consumer Protection Act in the area of unfair trade practices.

The regulatory provisions of the MRTP Act covered three areas: concentration of economic power, competition law, and consumer protection. The concentration provisions were designed to regulate the growth of enterprises, not prevent it, and to control growth only if it were detrimental to the common good. Companies with assets of more than Rs 1 billion (about $22 million) were required to seek government approval to establish a new undertaking, expand an existing undertaking, or carry out a merger, amalgamation, or takeover, as these were believed to lead to an undesirable concentration of economic power. The act frowned on the expansion of giant undertakings and prevented them from acquiring sufficient power to put a stranglehold on markets and consumers, or hold back industrial expansion in India. The objective of the competition law and consumer protection provisions, meanwhile, was to curb monopolistic, restrictive, and unfair trade practices. The act's provisions applied to almost every area of business: production, distribution, pricing, investment, purchasing, packaging, advertising, sales promotion, and (until 1991) mergers, amalgamations, and takeovers. They sought to afford protection and support to the public by reducing the extent of monopolistic, restrictive, and unfair trade practices.

Development of the act since 1991

The most important set of amendments to the MRTP Act occurred in 1991 and reflected the government's adoption of the new paradigm of liberalization, privatization, and globalization. The reforms initiated in 1991 were on a wide scale. The industrial policy statement issued by the government of India on 24 July 1991 stated:

> The attainment of technological dynamism and international competitiveness requires that enterprises must be enabled to swiftly respond to fast changing external conditions that have become characteristic of today's industrial world. Government policy and procedures must be geared to assisting entrepreneurs in their efforts. This can be done only if the role played by the Government were to be changed from that of only exercising control to one of providing help and guidance by making essential procedures fully transparent and by eliminating delays (Industrial Policy 1991).

The principal objectives of the act under the pre-1991 paradigm had been to prevent a detrimental concentration of economic power, to control monopolies, and to prohibit monopolistic, restrictive, and unfair trade practices. Of these five, the first two were de-emphasized in the 1991 amendments to the act while the last three were re-emphasized. Under the amendments, the provisions relating to the concentration of economic power were deleted, along with entry restrictions that required investors to gain central government approval to establish a new undertaking, expand an existing undertaking, or undertake a merger, amalgamation, or takeover. Thus, the thrust of the act since 1991 has been to curb monopolistic, restrictive, and unfair trade practices with a view to preserving competition in the economy and safeguarding the interests of consumers, while size as a factor in the concentration of economic power has been given up.

Monopolistic trade practices have or are likely to have the effect of:

- maintaining the prices of goods and services at an unreasonable level by limiting, reducing, or otherwise controlling their production, supply, or distribution;
- unreasonably preventing or reducing competition in the production, supply, or distribution of goods or services;
- limiting technical development or capital investment to the common detriment, or allowing the quality of goods or services produced, supplied, or distributed in India to deteriorate;
- unreasonably increasing the cost of production of goods, or charges for the provision and maintenance of services;
- unreasonably increasing the prices at which goods and services are sold or resold, or the profits that are derived from their production, supply, or distribution; or

- preventing or reducing competition in the production, supply, or distribution of goods and services through the adoption of unfair or deceptive methods and practices.

Restrictive trade practices generally have the effect of preventing, distorting, or restricting competition. In particular, a practice that tends to obstruct the flow of capital or resources into the stream of production would be considered restrictive. Similarly, practices that impose unjustified costs or restrictions on consumers—such as the manipulation of prices, conditions of delivery, or the flow of supply—are regarded as restrictive. Common types of restrictive trade practices enumerated in the MRTP Act are refusal to deal, tied sales, full-line forcing, exclusive dealing, price discrimination, resale price maintenance, and area restrictions.

Unfair trade practices fall into the following categories under Indian law: misleading advertising and false representation; bargain sale, bait, and switch selling; offering but not providing gifts or prizes, and conducting promotional contests; non-compliance with product safety standards; hoarding or destruction of goods; and false or misleading representation of facts to disparage the goods, services, or trade of another person or business.

Applicability of the act

Originally the MRTP Act applied essentially to private sector undertakings only. However, in 1991 the government issued a notification that the act would henceforth apply to all public sector undertakings as well, thus eliminating the distinction between public sector and private sector companies in the matter of monopolistic, restrictive, and unfair trade practices. India's airlines, nationalized banks, railways, posts and telegraphs, telecommunications, and housing and urban development authorities could all expect to be held accountable if they indulged in such practices. Of course a few areas, such as defense, remained outside the ambit of the act. On the other hand, the amendment of the act to enlarge the definition of a 'service' brought the activities of a large number of building and real estate operators within the reach of the law.

The Monopolies and Restrictive Trade Practices Commission

The MRTP Act provided for a Monopolies and Restrictive Trade Practices Commission (MRTP Commission), assisted by a Director General of Investigation and Registration who carries out investigations, maintains a register of agreements, and conducts proceedings during inquiries before the commission. As well as the normal powers vested in a civil court, the commission has the power to:

- direct an errant undertaking to discontinue a trade practice and not to repeat the offense;
- pass a cease and desist order;
- grant a temporary injunction restraining an errant undertaking from continuing an allegedly unfair trade practice;
- award compensation for loss suffered or injury sustained on account of a monopolistic, restrictive, or unfair trade practice;
- direct parties to modify agreements containing restrictive clauses;
- direct parties to issue corrective advertising; and
- recommend to the central government the division of undertakings or the severance of connections between undertakings, if their current practices are prejudicial to public interest or may lead to monopolistic or restrictive trade practices.

Individual consumers, registered associations of consumers, and trade associations are able to approach the commission with a complaint. The commission can also act on complaints referred to it by the Director General of Investigation and Registration, the central government, or a state government. Finally, the law provides for *suo motu* action on the part of the commission if it possesses information or has acquired it from any other source.

3   THE COMPETITION ACT, 2002

Development of the new act

During the 30 years and more in which the MRTP Act has been in force, the Supreme Court of India has made a large number of binding rulings on the law. The MRTP Commission has also issued precedent-creating bench decisions. Eventually, the accumulation of judicial pronouncements on the inadequacy of the existing law made the redrafting of a new law inevitable. More importantly, a perusal of the MRTP Act would show that it lacks explicit definitions for, or even fails to mention, certain offending trade practices that are restrictive in character, such as abuse of dominance, cartels, bid rigging, and predatory pricing.

The dynamic context of international and domestic trade also put pressure on the Indian government to revisit its competition law provisions. When the MRTP Act was drafted in 1969, the prevailing economic and trade milieu constituted the premise for its various provisions. There has subsequently been a change in that milieu, with considerable movement toward the post-1991 paradigm of liberalization, privatization, and globalization. The need to reflect the changes taking place in the trade and economic environment therefore constituted another important reason for the decision to frame a new competition law. In this respect India was simply following the example of many other countries, such as the United Kingdom, Canada, Australia, and European Union countries, that have enacted new competition laws that are more in tune with current thinking.

In October 1999, the government appointed a High Level Committee on Competition Policy and Competition Law to advise on a modern competition law that would be in line with international developments.[3] The committee was asked to suggest a legislative framework for a new law, or appropriate amendments to the existing act. It took evidence from a wide cross-section of society, including chambers of industry and commerce, professional institutes, consumer and non-government organizations, experts, academics, and government officials. Members visited metropolitan areas and met with many of the stakeholders who were likely to be impacted by the new law. The committee also examined the 80 or so competition laws of other countries that existed at the time. In the end, however, the committee did not recommend adopting the competition law of any one country as a model, although features of certain competition laws that were considered relevant to India did give shape to its report (High Level Committee 2000).

The committee presented its competition policy report to the government in May 2000. Most of the recommendations were unanimous, but two members—including the author—attached supplementary notes advising a phased introduction of the proposed competition law and cautioning against a rigid bureaucratic structure for the associated regulatory authority, the Competition Commission of India.[4] During the widespread consultations that again took place after the competition law was drafted, it became apparent that business organizations favored a lenient competition law (with high thresholds for combinations regulation, for example) whereas consumer organizations wanted a tight competition law accompanied by severe penalties for violations.[5]

The competition law bill introduced to parliament was accompanied by a statement of objects and reasons for its enactment. The statement ran thus:

[I]n the pursuit of globalization, India has responded by opening up its economy, removing controls and resorting to liberalization. The natural corollary of this is that the Indian market should be geared to face competition from within the country and outside. The Monopolies and Restrictive Trade Practices Act 1969 has become obsolete in certain respects in the light of International Economic Developments relating more particularly to competition laws and there is a need to shift our focus from curbing monopolies to promoting competition. ... The Competition Bill ... seeks to ensure fair competition in India by prohibiting trade practices which cause appreciable adverse effect on competition in markets within India and, for this purpose, provides for the establishment of a quasi-judicial body to be called the Competition Commission of India ... which shall also undertake competition advocacy for creating awareness and imparting training on competition issues (Mittal 2003: 306).

After effecting some refinements suggested by a standing committee, parliament passed the Competition Act in December 2002.[6]

Coverage of the law

Three areas of enforcement provide the focus for most competition laws in the world today (including legislation on regulatory authorities). These are agreements among enterprises; abuse of dominance; and mergers, or, more generally, combinations among enterprises. There are, however, differences in emphasis and interpretation across countries, and over time within countries. In addition, the above-mentioned three areas are not mutually exclusive and there is considerable overlap between them. India's new Competition Act essentially has four compartments—anticompetitive agreements, abuse of dominance, combinations regulation, and competition advocacy—treated in turn below.

Anticompetitive agreements

Some of the agreements firms enter into have the potential to restrict competition. Most of the world's competition laws make a distinction between 'horizontal' and 'vertical' agreements between firms. The former are agreements between two or more competitors that occupy the same stage of the production chain and are in the same market. A particularly pernicious type of horizontal agreement is the cartel. Vertical agreements involve a purchasing or selling relationship between firms, and may be pernicious if they are between firms in a position of dominance. Most competition laws view vertical agreements more leniently than horizontal agreements because, prima facie, the latter are more likely to reduce competition than are agreements between firms in a purchaser–seller relationship.

If a *horizontal agreement* between enterprises dealing in the same product is believed to have breached competition law, the appreciable adverse effect on competition in the market will be critical to the application of the law. If the parties to the agreement are both producers or are both retailers (or wholesalers), they will be deemed to occupy the same stage of the production chain.

A specific goal of competition policy/law is to prevent economic agents from distorting the competitive process either through agreements with other companies or through unilateral action designed to exclude actual or potential competitors. The law therefore needs to control agreements among competing enterprises (horizontal agreements) on prices or other important aspects of their competitive interaction. Similarly, it must address agreements between firms at different levels of the manufacturing or distribution processes (such as vertical agreements between manufacturers and wholesalers) that are likely to harm competition, even though these are less likely to be harmful than horizontal agreements. The foremost constituent of any competition policy/law is obviously the objective to foster competition, and its obverse is the need to deal effectively with practices and conduct that subvert competition. The Competition Act therefore outlaws any agreement that may cause an 'appreciable adverse effect' on competition within India.

The Competition Act requires most agreements to be subjected to a rule-of-reason test before being declared illegal. However, certain kinds of agreements are presumed not to serve any useful or pro-competitive purpose and to have an appreciable adverse effect on competition. Lawmakers do not subject such agreements to a rule-of-reason test but place them in the per se illegal category. The Competition Act presumes that the following four types of horizontal agreements between enterprises or associations of enterprises (including cartels) engaged in the manufacture or trade of similar goods or services have an appreciable adverse effect on competition and are per se illegal:

1 agreements on prices, including all agreements that directly or indirectly fix the purchase or sale price of goods or services;
2 agreements on quantities, including agreements aimed at limiting or controlling production, supply, markets, technical development, investment, or the provision of services;
3 agreements on bids (collusive bidding or bid rigging), including tenders submitted as a result of any joint activity or agreement; and
4 agreements to share markets, the sources of production, or the provision of services by allocating geographical market areas, types of goods or services, or the number of customers in the market.

Per se illegality implies limited scope for discretion and interpretation on the part of the prosecuting and adjudicating authorities, and almost no scope for errant enterprises to rebut the presumption of illegality. Errant enterprises would, however, be able to negotiate penalties.

As noted earlier, *vertical agreements* would generally not be subjected to the rigors of competition law, except where they have the potential to distort or prevent competition. Under the Competition Act, tied sale arrangements, exclusive supply agreements, exclusive distribution agreements, refusal to deal, and resale price maintenance will be subjected to a rule-of-reason test. The act lists the following factors to be taken into account in determining whether an agreement or practice has an appreciable adverse effect on competition:

- creation of barriers to new entrants in the market;
- existing competitors driven out of the market;
- foreclosure of competition by hindering entry into the market;
- accrual of benefits to consumers;
- improvements in the production or distribution of goods or the provision of services; and
- the promotion of technical, scientific, and economic development by means of the production or distribution of goods or the provision of services.

The new Competition Act has certain exceptions built into it. The provisions relating to anticompetitive agreements will not restrict the right of any person to restrain others from infringing his or her intellectual property rights, or to impose such reasonable conditions as may be necessary for the purpose of protecting any of the rights conferred on the person under the Copyright Act, 1957; Patents Act, 1970; Trade and Merchandise Marks Act, 1958 or Trade Marks Act, 1999; Geographical Indications of Goods (Registration and Protection) Act, 1999; Designs Act, 2000; and Semi-conductor Integrated Circuits Layout–Design Act, 2000. The bundle of rights that accompanies an intellectual property right undoubtedly does have an anticompetitive character, even bordering on monopoly power. But without such protection, there would be little incentive for human creativity and innovation, the development of new technology, and the enhancement of the quality of goods and services. It should be noted, however, that the Competition Act does not permit the protection or exploitation of intellectual property rights to override all other considerations. In other words, licensing arrangements that are likely to have an adverse effect on the price, quantity, quality, or variety of goods and services will fall within the contours of competition law as long as they are not in reasonable juxtaposition with the bundle of rights that accompany intellectual property rights.

For example, a licensing arrangement may include restraints that adversely affect competition in a goods market by dividing the market among firms that would otherwise have competed using different technologies. Similarly, an arrangement that merged the research and development (R&D) activities of two of only a few entities that could plausibly engage in R&D in the relevant field might harm competition for the development of new goods and services. Exclusive licensing that give rise to anticompetitive concerns include cross-licensing by parties collectively possessing market power, grantbacks, and acquisitions of intellectual property rights.

Another exception to the provisions on anticompetitive agreements protects the right of any person to export goods or services from India. In other words, export cartels are outside the purview of competition law in India as in most other countries. Many countries regard export cartels as competition restricting, but nevertheless exempt them from competition law because they do not affect competition in the domestic market. A further justification for their exemption is that countries do not wish to shackle their export efforts for fear of disturbing their trade balance or balance of payments. Between them, Evenett, Levenstein, and Suslow (2001) and OECD (2003d) have identified 15 countries whose competition laws explicitly or implicitly exclude export cartels. Meanwhile, the proponents of export cartels argue that they are a lawful way of realizing cost-reducing and output-enhancing efficiencies (OECD 2003a). Holistically, however, exemption of export cartels does go against the concept of free competition, as the circumstances relating to a soda ash cartel operating in India make clear (Box 5.1).

Finally, the central government has the power under the Competition Act to exempt a class of enterprises, a practice, or an agreement from the application of the act, as discussed in more detail later in the chapter. Provisions relating to unfair trade practices (which find a place in the outgoing MRTP Act) do not figure in the new Competition Act. The rationale for this is that such practices are already adequately covered by the Consumer Protection Act, 1986.

Abuse of dominance

'Dominant position' is appropriately defined in Chapter II of the Competition Act as a

> position of strength, enjoyed by an enterprise, in the relevant market, in India, which enables it to (i) operate independently of competitive forces prevailing in the relevant market; or (ii) affect its competitors or consumers or the relevant market, in its favour.

This definition may appear somewhat ambiguous and capable of different interpretations by different judicial authorities. The justification for this ambiguity is that even a firm with a low market share of, say, 20 percent,

---

Box 5.1 Export cartels: The case of a soda ash cartel

In September 1996, American Natural Soda Ash Corporation (ANSAC), an export trading company comprising six American producers of soda ash, attempted to ship a consignment of soda ash to India. ANSAC is registered under the Webb–Pomerene Act, US legislation that exempts associations of American firms engaged in export trade from the country's antitrust laws so long as they do not restrain any US competitor of the association. The Alkali Manufacturers Association of India, whose members include all major Indian producers of soda ash, filed a complaint against ANSAC before the MRTP Commission alleging cartelization. The commission imposed an interim injunction on ANSAC restraining it from exporting soda ash to India as a cartel, while making it clear that the companies could continue to do so individually. Quoting from the ANSAC membership agreement, the commission held that ANSAC was prima facie a cartel. It found that ANSAC was carrying out part of its trade practices in India, giving the commission extraterritorial jurisdiction under section 14 of the MRTP Act even though the cartel itself was formed outside India (MRTP Commission 1997).

ANSAC then lodged an appeal with the Supreme Court, which eventually overturned the commission's orders. The court held that the wording of the MRTP Act did not give the commission extraterritorial powers. It stated that the commission could take action only if it could prove that an anti-competitive agreement involved an Indian party, and even then only after the goods had been imported into India (Supreme Court 2002).[7] Thus the commission could not take action against ANSAC or prevent the importation of soda ash into the country.

The verdict of the Supreme Court was announced while the new competition bill was pending in the Indian parliament. With the court's ruling in mind, the bill was amended to allow the Competition Commission of India to grant a temporary injunction restraining any party from importing goods if it could be established that such imports would contravene the substantive provisions of the law. It is hoped that the Competition Commission will be able to take effective action against export cartels outside the country under the new Competition Act.

---

with the remaining 80 percent held by a large number of competitors, may be in a position to abuse its dominance, while a firm with a 60 percent market share with the remaining 40 percent held by a competitor may not be in a position to do so because of key rivalry in the market. Specifying a threshold for dominance may either allow offenders to escape (as in the first example above) or result in unnecessary litigation (as in the second example). Hence, in a dynamic, changing economic environment, a static arithmetical figure for 'dominance' may be an aberration.

Under the new law's broad definition of dominance, the regulatory authority will have the freedom to tackle errant undertakings and encourage competitive market practices regardless of whether the market consists of small or large players. Abuse of dominance is the key concept in the Competition Act in so far as dominant enterprises are concerned. It is important to note that the new law has been designed in such a way that its provisions on this count take effect only if dominance is clearly established. It seeks to ensure that abuse of dominance can only be alleged after dominance has been clearly established. Any ambiguity on this count could endanger large but efficient firms.

Before assessing whether an undertaking is dominant, it is important to determine what the relevant market is. A relevant market has two dimensions: the product market and the geographical market. On the demand side, the relevant product market includes all substitutes that the consumer could switch to if the price of the product being investigated were to increase. On the supply side, the relevant market includes all producers who could, with their existing facilities, switch to the production of substitute goods. The geographical boundaries of the relevant market can be similarly defined. The geographic dimension involves identification of the geographical area within which competition takes place, whether local, national, or international. Some factors relevant to the geographic dimension are consumption and shipment patterns, transportation costs, the perishability of goods, and the existence of barriers to the shipment of products between adjoining geographic areas. For example, the high transportation costs of cement generally mean that the relevant geographical market is the region close to the manufacturing facility.

In general, actions that are considered anticompetitive and illegal in the context of agreements are also illegal if undertaken by a dominant firm. These would include unfair pricing and restrictions on quantities, markets, and technical development. Discriminatory behavior and any other exercise of market power leading to the prevention, restriction, or distortion of competition would obviously be included. It should be noted that there is a fine distinction between defending one's market position or market share, which is perfectly legal and legitimate and may involve a certain level of aggressive competitive behavior, and behavior that is exclusionary and anticompetitive. However, as noted above, a greater threat to competition is posed by the actions of dominant firms that are inimical to future competition. These would include predatory pricing and actions that make it difficult for potential entrants to enter the market (exclusionary or anticompetitive behavior).

Predatory pricing is one of the most pernicious forms of abuse of dominance. It is defined in Chapter II of the new Competition Act to mean

> the sale of goods or provision of services, at a price which is below the cost, as may be determined by [the regulatory authority's] regulations, of production of the goods or provision of services, with a view to reduce competition or eliminate the competitors.

As this definition suggests, predatory pricing occurs where a dominant enterprise charges low prices over a long enough period of time to drive competitors out of the market or deter others from entering it, and then raises prices to recoup its losses. The greater the diversification of the enterprise's activities in terms of products and markets, and the greater its financial resources, the greater is its ability to engage in predatory behavior.

There is a danger of confusing pro-competitive pricing with predatory behavior, however. In reality, predation is only established after the fact, that is, once the rival has left the market and the predator has acquired a monopoly position in the market. But any law to prevent predation is meaningful only if it takes effect *before* the fact, that is, before the competitor has left the market. In the case of Modern Food Industries described in Box 5.2, the MRTP Commission took due care to lay down the factors underlying predatory pricing. These may prove useful in future predatory pricing cases filed under the new Competition Act.

The Competition Act does not frown on dominance as such, but on the abuse of dominance. To attract the attention of the act, it needs to be established that a dominant enterprise is restraining competition by creating barriers to new entry or forcing existing competitors out of the market. The key issue is the extent to which such arrangements foreclose the market to manufacturers (interbrand rivalry) or retailers (intrabrand rivalry) and the extent to which these raise rivals' costs and dampen existing competition. The costs of such arrangements need to be weighed against the benefits. For example, some restraints may help to overcome the free-rider problem and allow for the exploitation of scale economies in retailing.

Under the Competition Act, dominance is determined by taking the following factors into account:

i   market share of the enterprise;
ii   size and resources of the enterprise;
iii size and importance of competitors;
iv   economic power of the enterprise, including commercial advantages over competitors;

Box 5.2 Predatory pricing: The case of Modern Food Industries

In 1996 the MRTP Commission heard a complaint of predatory pricing against Modern Food Industries, which produces bread and other bakery items (MRTP Commission 1996: 154).

Although the MRTP Act does not explicitly use the expression 'predatory pricing,' it does prohibit agreements to sell goods at prices that would have the effect of eliminating a competitor. The wording of this provision potentially limits its applicability to coordinated predation by a group of enterprises, leaving out predation by a single enterprise. However, the commission extended the provision to a single seller on the grounds that 'in fixing the prices, there is an understanding that the seller will sell the product at a particular price,' thus bringing the practice within the purview of the relevant provision of the act.

The commission observed that the essence of predatory pricing is pricing below cost with a view to eliminating a rival while making it clear that the 'mere offer of a price lower than the cost of production cannot automatically lead to an indictment of predatory pricing' and that evidence of 'malafide intent to drive competitors out of business or to eliminate competition' is required. The logic underlying the caution of the commission was that price cutting may be for genuine reasons, for example in cases of surplus inventory. Price cutting must therefore be coupled with the intent to eliminate a competitor to become an offense under the law.

The two principles enunciated in this case—evidence of pricing below cost and the intent to eliminate competition—are in conformity with international practice on predatory pricing cases. The commission used a principle resembling the well-known Areeda–Turner test to compare price to marginal cost and determine whether Modern Food Industries' prices could be considered predatory. It ruled that the offense was not established, thereby exonerating the company.

---

v   vertical integration of the enterprise, or of its sales or service network;

vi   dependence of consumers on the enterprise;

vii   monopoly or dominant position of the enterprise, whether acquired as a result of a statute or by virtue of being a government company or public sector undertaking or otherwise;

viii   entry barriers, including regulatory barriers, financial risk, the high capital cost of entry, marketing barriers, technical barriers, economies of scale, and the high cost of substitutable goods or services for consumers;

ix   countervailing buying power;

x   market structure and size of the market;

xi   social obligations and social costs;

xii   the relative advantage, by way of the contribution to economic development, of the enterprise enjoying a dominant position having or likely to have an appreciable adverse effect on competition; and

xiii   any other factor that the commission considers relevant.

Abuse of dominance having an appreciable adverse effect on competition occurs if an enterprise:

i   directly or indirectly imposes an unfair or discriminatory (a) condition on the purchase or sale of goods or services, or (b) price (including predatory price) on the purchase or sale of goods or services;

ii   limits or restricts (a) the production of goods or provision of services, or the markets for these goods and services, or (b) the technical or scientific development of goods or services to the detriment of consumers;

iii   employs practices that result in denial of market access;

iv   draws up contracts that require other parties to accept supplementary obligations that, by their nature or according to commercial usage, have no connection with the subject of such contracts; or

v   uses its dominant position in one relevant market to enter or protect another relevant market.

Combinations regulation

The provisions dealing with combinations attracted the most debate while the Competition Act was still in draft form, and therefore demand detailed treatment here. Although the act defines combinations to include mergers, amalgamations, acquisitions, and acquisitions of control, for the purposes of the discussion that follows, only merger regulation is considered.

Like agreements, mergers are typically classified into horizontal and vertical mergers. In addition, mergers between enterprises operating in different markets are called conglomerate mergers. Mergers are a legitimate means by which firms can grow, and are generally as much a part of the natural process of industrial evolution and restructuring as new entry, growth, and exit. From the point of view of competition policy, it is horizontal mergers that are the focus of attention because of their potential to reduce competition. In rare cases, where an enterprise in a dominant position makes a vertical merger with another firm in an adjacent market to further entrench its position of dominance, a vertical merger may also provide cause for concern. Conglomerate mergers would generally be beyond the purview of any law on mergers.

A merger leads to a 'bad' outcome only if it creates a dominant enterprise that subsequently abuses its dominance. To some extent, the issue is analogous to that of agreements among enterprises and also overlaps with the issue of dominance and its abuse, discussed earlier. Viewed in this way, there is probably no need for competition law to contain merger control provisions. The reason that such provisions exist in most laws is to pre-empt the potential abuse of dominance, as subsequent unbundling can be both difficult and socially costly. Thus the general principle, in keeping with the overall goal, is to challenge mergers only if they reduce or harm competition and adversely affect welfare.

The Competition Act makes it voluntary for parties to notify a proposed agreement or combination to the Mergers Bench (one of the benches of the Competition Commission of India) if the aggregate assets of the combining parties have a value in excess of Rs 10 billion ($220 million) or turnover in excess of Rs 30 billion ($660 million). In the event that either or both of the combining parties are outside India, the threshold limits are $500 million for assets and $1,500 million for turnover. If one of the merging parties belongs to a group that controls it, the threshold limits are Rs 40 billion ($880 million) in terms of assets and Rs 120 billion ($2.6 billion) in terms of turnover. If the group has assets or turnover outside India, the threshold limits are $2 billion for assets and $6 billion for turnover. The thresholds for assets and turnover are to be revised every two years on the basis of the wholesale price index or fluctuations in the exchange rate of the rupee or foreign currencies.

The Competition Act makes the notification of combinations voluntary rather than mandatory in order not to discourage FDI and the participation of major international companies in the economy, while still laying down threshold limits for combinations that would fall under its surveillance. If the parties to a combination choose not to notify the Competition Commission of India, as is their right, they may run the risk of a post-combination action by the commission if it is discovered subsequently that the combination has an appreciable adverse effect on competition. There is a rider that the Competition Commission of India shall not initiate an inquiry into a combination after the expiry of one year from the date on which the combination takes effect.

On threshold limits, the High Level Committee (2000: 46) had this to say:

> [I]t is extremely important that the law regarding mergers be very carefully framed and the provisions regarding prohibition of mergers be used very sparingly. This is particularly important at the current stage of India's corporate development. Relative to the size of major international companies, Indian firms are still small. With the opening of trade and Foreign Direct Investment,

> Indian firms need to go through a period of consolidation in order to be competitive. Any law on merger regulation must take account of this reality.
>
> The Committee, however, would like to raise a note of caution regarding the monitoring of mergers by the Competition Law Authority (Competition Commission of India/Mergers Commission). At present, very few Indian companies are of international size. In the light of continuing economic reforms, particularly the opening up of trade and foreign investment, a great deal of corporate restructuring is taking place in the country. Thus there is a need for mergers, amalgamations and takeovers as part of the growing economic process before we can be on an equal footing to compete with global giants.

The government accepted the advice of the High Level Committee and prescribed limits in such a way that only major combinations would fall within the ambit of the competition law.

The Competition Act lists the following factors to be taken into account for the purpose of determining whether a combination would be likely to have an appreciable adverse effect on competition:

i   the actual and potential level of competition through imports;
ii   the extent of barriers to entry into the market;
iii   the level of combination in the market;
iv   the degree of countervailing power in the market;
v   the likelihood that the combination would result in the parties to the combination being able to significantly and sustainably increase prices or profit margins;
vi   the extent of effective competition likely to sustain in a market;
vii   the extent to which substitutes are available in the market;
viii   the market share in the relevant market of the persons or enterprises in a combination, individually and as a combination;
ix   the likelihood that the combination would result in the removal of vigorous and effective competitors;
x   the nature and extent of vertical integration in the market;
xi   the possibility of a failing business;
xii   the nature and extent of innovation;
xiii   the relative advantage, by way of the contribution to economic development, of any combination having or likely to have an appreciable adverse effect on competition; and
xiv   whether the benefits of the combination outweigh its adverse effects.

The Mergers Bench of the Competition Commission of India has been given the task of adjudicating on mergers and weighing up their potential losses and gains. To ensure that it does not delay its scrutiny, the Competition Act requires it to issue a decision within 90 working days. If it does not do so, the merger will be deemed to have been approved.

Competition advocacy

The Competition Act extends the mandate of the Competition Commission of India beyond merely enforcing the law; under the advocacy provisions of the act, the commission will be able to participate in the formulation of the country's economic policies and in the review of laws related to competition. The provisions allow the central government to refer existing or proposed laws to the commission for an assessment of their effects on competition. The commission must respond to such a request within 60 days. The commission will therefore be assuming the role of competition advocate, acting proactively to bring about government policies that lower barriers to entry, promote deregulation and trade liberalization, and enhance competition in the marketplace.

The Competition Act seeks to bring about a direct relationship between competition advocacy and competition law enforcement. One of the main objectives of competition advocacy is to foster conditions that will lead to a more competitive market structure and business behavior, thus avoiding the need for intervention and enforcement by the Competition Commission of India.

Investigation, adjudication, and selection procedures

The new Competition Act separates the investigative wing from the adjudicative wing. At the apex of the investigative wing is the director general. He does not have *suo motu* powers of investigation and can only look into complaints received from the Competition Commission of India. The director general will be the prosecuting authority and has been vested under the law with the powers conferred on the Competition Commission of India. The director general's team of investigators will be solely responsible for making enquiries, examining documents, investigating complaints, and liaising with other investigative agencies of the government including ministries and departments. Staff must be chosen for their experience in investigation, for their integrity and outstanding ability, and for their knowledge of accountancy, management, business, public administration, international trade, law, or economics. Under the MRTP Act, investigative staff were drawn routinely from the Department of Company Affairs. The new law thus induces professionalism in the investigative wing, a step in the right direction.

Central to effective implementation and enforcement of competition policy and competition law is an effective adjudicative body. The Competition Commission of India is the adjudicating body under the Competition Act, and is vested with autonomy and administrative powers. The chairperson and members of the commission must have been—or be qualified to act as—a High Court judge, or have substantial expertise, knowledge, or experience in economics, law, international trade, business, commerce, industry, finance, accountancy, management, public affairs, or administration. In addition they must be persons of ability, integrity, and standing. Each bench of the Competition Commission of India will have a judicial member, as the benches have the power to impose prison sentences in addition to levying fines.

It cannot be overemphasized that the government should ensure that the Competition Commission of India is free from political control. The High Level Committee (2000) recommended a collegium selection process for choosing the chairperson and members of the commission. However, the Competition Act as passed by parliament left the selection procedure to the government. It will therefore need to frame appropriate selection rules that reduce the extent of political favoritism in the selection of candidates for positions on the commission.

Exemptions

The Competition Act empowers the central government, by notification, to exempt from the application of the law for such period as it deems fit: any class of enterprise if an exemption is deemed necessary for national security or in the public interest; any practice or agreement arising out of an obligation assumed by India under any treaty, agreement, or convention with another country; or any enterprise that performs a sovereign function on behalf of the central government or a state government.

Appeal and review procedures

An appeal against a decision or order of the Competition Commission of India must be lodged with the Supreme Court within 60 days. Thus, the status accorded the Competition Commission of India is very high, with only the Supreme Court having the power to overturn its orders. The commission also has the power under the law to review its own orders on application from an aggrieved party.

Extraterritorial reach

The new Competition Act has extraterritorial reach. The Competition Commission of India has the power to inquire into an agreement, abuse of dominance or combination that has an appreciable adverse affect on competition in the relevant market in India even if the agreement or combination has been entered into outside India; any party to such an agreement, abuse of dominance, or combination is outside India; or any other matter or practice or action arising out of such an agreement or dominant position or combination is outside India. These provisions are based on what is known as the 'effects doctrine,' which justifies the application of competition law to firms outside the borders of the state when their behavior has an appreciable adverse effect within the relevant market inside state borders.

Both the outgoing and incoming competition laws contain provisions that give the competition authority extraterritorial jurisdiction. The jurisdiction of the competition authority extends to restrictive trade practices employed by enterprises outside India that have the effect of preventing, distorting, or restricting competition in India, or that give rise to restrictive trade practices in India. On the provisions relating to extraterritorial jurisdiction in the MRTP Act, the Supreme Court ruled that the MRTP Commission would obtain jurisdiction only after goods had been imported and a restrictive trade practice had taken place, as discussed in Box 5.3.

Phased introduction of the act

The government decided on a calibrated introduction of the Competition Act. During the first year of implementation, the Competition Commission of India carried out competition advocacy functions only. These were intended to educate business and the public on the features of the new law and their implications. The first year was also devoted to imparting training and providing exposure to all concerned in the implementation and administration of the law, including members of parliament and legislatures. During the second year, the provisions relating to anticompetitive agreements and abuse of dominance will be brought into force. As the Competition Commission of India would then take responsibility for dealing with offenses relating to provisions of the new law, the MRTP Act would stand repealed and the MRTP Commission would be wound up. During the third year, the provisions on combinations regulation will come into force. This calibrated introduction of the Competition Act is strategically a step in the right direction, as it will allow the country to make gradual but steady progress on competition-related matters.

Enforcement

The gains sought from competition law can only be realized through effective enforcement. Weak enforcement can be worse than the absence of competition law, and often reflects factors such as inadequate funding

---

Box 5.3 Extraterritorial jurisdiction: The case of float glass

In September 1998 the All India Float Glass Manufacturers' Association (AIFGMA) filed a complaint with the MRTP Commission alleging that three Indonesian float glass manufacturers, in association with Indian importers, had resorted to restrictive and unfair trade practices, in particular by selling float glass at predatory prices. They claimed that the alleged predatory pricing of float glass would restrict, distort, and prevent competition by pricing Indian producers out of the market. The commission found in favor of AIFGMA and issued an injunction against the Indonesian companies from exporting float glass to India.

The matter then went to the Supreme Court on appeal. During the hearing of the case, the Supreme Court considered the extraterritorial jurisdiction of the MRTP Commission. While observing that 'a competition law like the MRTP Act is a mechanism to counter cross-border economic terrorism', the Supreme Court ruled that the MRTP Commission had no extraterritorial jurisdiction in the float glass case. The court said that allowing the commission to actually prevent manufacturers from importing goods would be tantamount to giving it the jurisdiction to adjudicate upon the legal validity of the provisions in other legislation relating to imports. In the opinion of the Supreme Court, the commission did not have such a jurisdiction—its jurisdiction would commence only after goods had been imported and a restrictive trade practice had subsequently taken place. To quote the Supreme Court:

> the action of an exporter to India when performed outside India would not be amenable to jurisdiction of the MRTP Commission. The MRTP Commission cannot pass an order determining the export price of an exporter to India or prohibiting him to export to India at a low or predatory price (Supreme Court 2002: 600).

This decision led to the arming of the new Competition Commission of India with the power to take action by restraining imports that contravene substantive provisions of the new law relating to anticompetitive agreements, abuse of dominance, and combinations regulation.

---

of the enforcement authority. The government should therefore provide the required infrastructure and funds to make the Competition Commission of India an effective tribunal to prevent and eliminate anticompetitive practices and play a leading role in competition advocacy.

The government began by appointing a chairperson and one member to the commission in October 2003; it has also appointed several experts who will be responsible for analyzing the cases brought to it. As mentioned, the Competition Act permits the chairperson to be from any of a number of disciplines, not just the judiciary. Despite this, the fact that the chairperson was not from the judiciary sparked a petition to the Madras High Court, and the case was then taken over by the Supreme Court for a hearing. Initially the attorney-general assured the court that until the matter was settled, the commission would perform only administrative and not judicial functions. Later, during the hearing of the petition, the government informed the Supreme Court that it intended to make certain amendments to the Competition Act and rules. In consideration of this, on 20 January 2005, the Supreme Court declined to pronounce on the matters being argued before it and disposed of the petition.

4   THE INTERFACE BETWEEN COMPETITION POLICY AND OTHER GOVERNMENT POLICIES

If the new Competition Law is to succeed in its mission of fostering competition, the government will need to make competition the driving force behind all its policies. In this section, three areas that have a bearing on the interface between government policies and competition are examined: prerequisites for competition policy; the effects of government policies on combinations; and the effects of government policies on FDI inflows. While many other topics could be considered relevant, the discussion is confined to combinations and FDI for illustrative purposes.

Prerequisites for competition policy

Trade policy, industrial policy, financial policy, privatization, deregulation, regional policy, and labor and social policy all need to be conducted in a manner compatible with the market mechanism for an economy to function as efficiently as possible. These policies need to be conducted in a complementary manner, and also need a mechanism to incorporate the competition dimension. Experience suggests that the existence and application of competition policy can usefully support other policy initiatives during the process of transition to a less regulated and more open economy, in developing countries in particular (APEC 1999). In this context, it is necessary for countries, before they lay down a competition policy or enact a competition law, to examine the existing legal milieu and executive policy decisions in order to ensure that they incorporate competition principles.

A source of tension in many countries, particularly developing ones, is the priority attached to competition policy relative to that placed on other government policies, including policies that have the support of statutes. In some areas the respective objectives of competition policy and other government policies are likely to be complementary, as in the case of initiatives directed at deregulation and the privatization of state-owned enterprises (SOEs). However, in other areas, such as trade, investment, and regional development, conflicts often arise. The extent of consistency between the government's various policy measures may support or thwart the objectives of competition policy.

If the objectives of other policies are allowed to rein in competition policy, the results may be detrimental to consumers. For instance, if the goal of promoting small businesses and maintaining employment takes precedence over the goal of attaining economic efficiency, competitors rather than competition may be protected. Although concerns such as community breakdown, fairness, equity, and pluralism—concepts that are hard to quantify or even define—have a place in government policy-making, attempts to accommodate such concerns in competition policy may result in inconsistent application and interpretation of the law. The peril is that the competitive process may be undermined if too many objectives are built into competition policy, and too many exceptions to it allowed.

The central exercise is therefore to pursue an appropriate competition policy that is not constrained by, and does not conflict with, other public policy objectives. The main issue in this exercise is the priority attached to competition policy objectives in the overall framework of government policies. Government policies that are particularly affected by the application of competition policy include industrial policy, reservations for the small-scale industrial sector, privatization and regulatory reform, trade policy, financial policy, state monopolies policy, and labor policy, all of which need to be adjusted to take competition principles into account. Indeed, competition policy can be regarded as the fourth cornerstone of the governmental economic framework, along with monetary, fiscal, and trade policies.

The following subsections contain a few thoughts on how policy-making in each of the above areas could be refined. It should be noted, however, that these suggestions should not be regarded as a panacea for the problems and ills of the Indian economy.

Industrial policy

The Industries (Development and Regulation) Act, 1951 (IDR Act) was designed to promote and regulate industrial development. It empowered the state to channel private investment through the extensive use of industrial licensing. Over the years, this gave the state comprehensive control over the direction and pattern of investment. With some exceptions, the IDR Act placed tight restrictions on entry into all industries and on the expansion of capacity. Product mix and technology were also subject to control. Geographical location and the import content of the initial investment were additional criteria for the issuing of industrial licenses. The pattern of investment thus fostered emphasized the development of heavy industry and of the capital goods sector. There was a noticeable reallocation of resources away from the production of consumer goods toward the production of machine tools and capital goods (High Level Committee 2000).

The reforms carried out in 1991 and since then have led to the abolition of industrial licensing requirements in all but six industries as the government sought to promote domestic competition, encourage entry and investment, and achieve better capacity utilization and economically viable scales of production. The sugar industry was delicensed in 1999, although it remains subject to a number of other controls. Public sector monopolies have been done away with except where security and strategic concerns remain. Many major industries are now open to private sector investment.

The Industrial Policy, 1991 liberalized the existing industrial policy regime, including FDI, foreign technology agreements, and compulsory industrial licensing. It allowed automatic approval for foreign investment in 34 industries involving an equity stake of up to 51 percent; 100 percent foreign ownership was permitted in export-oriented units. A Foreign Investment Promotion Board was established to process applications not subject to automatic approval. Several additional measures were undertaken during 1992–93 to encourage investment flows, including FDI, portfolio investment, non-resident Indian investment, and deposits and investment in global depository receipts. By 1994, subject to certain restrictions, foreign investment in the consumer goods and pharmaceutical sectors was permitted. The upper limit on foreign holdings was increased to 74 percent in 1996. These measures provided the catalyst for competition in the manufacturing and service sectors.

If competition, fair and free trade, and a market-driven environment are desirable objectives, a regulatory statute for industrial development may not be necessary at all. There should be no need for industrial undertakings to obtain a license to establish or expand a business except on such grounds as location (to avoid excessive urban concentration), environmental protection (to prevent pollution in urban areas and protect scarce resources such as timber), and public health. Subject to such safeguards and similar ones in the national interest, the IDR Act no longer seems relevant (High Level Committee 2000).

Reservations for the small-scale industrial sector

For several decades, India has encouraged and protected its small-scale industrial sector by reserving certain goods and products for manufacture by this sector. The handloom sector is similarly protected. The country has both efficient and inefficient small-scale units; some are well managed and others are not. Competition theory would dictate that the inefficient, ill-managed firms should exit from the market, but this would aggravate unemployment in a vulnerable sector. The small-scale sector is a significant generator of employment, if at considerable cost to the exchequer by way of revenue lost through the plethora of exemptions from indirect taxes available to this sector of the economy. Thus, while a policy of welfare for the small-scale sector cannot be regarded as unreasonable, it must be tempered by the knowledge that it involves heavy costs.

The reservation system has led to poor-quality output. Many small-scale and micro enterprises are suppliers of ancillary goods to organized producers. Their substandard output therefore affects the quality of finished products produced in other sectors of the economy. The small-scale sector is also characterized by a lack of skills, low capital availability, poor-quality machinery, heavy labor orientation, poor cost control, and low output.

Exempting small-scale industries from competition law is not necessarily in the interests of the sector. Protecting them from competition not only constitutes a drag on the economy, but is also a waste of scarce resources (particularly capital resources). If there is to be a national goal in this area, it should be the welfare of the efficient and well-managed small-scale sector. Exemption from competition principles will only protect the laggards.

In the meantime, the policy of preferential treatment for small-scale industries continues. Reservation policies have not undergone any major change since 1991. Although some items have been removed from the reserved category of products, the total number of reserved items remains large, at about 600. To benefit from their status as small-scale producers, firms producing these items are necessarily restricted from growing. Quota restrictions on imports of consumer goods and relatively high tariffs on other goods reserved for the small-scale sector have also protected small-scale industry from (foreign) competition. Clearly, this situation is inefficient and welfare reducing due to the higher prices that consumers have to pay (Chakravarthy 2004).

To meet its commitments to the World Trade Organization (WTO), India has already removed its quantitative restrictions and lowered tariffs. Tariffs will be reduced further over the next few years. This implies that although firms in the small-scale sector will be protected from competition from large domestic firms, they will be subject to competition from abroad. Such asymmetric exposure to competition will have an adverse effect on domestic welfare as a result of profit shifting from domestic to foreign firms.

The sector needs to be opened up to entry by large domestic firms. Although this may have some impact on income distribution, the efficiency gains that will arise from better technology, increased competition, and more efficient scales of production will lead to improved social welfare. In any case, if firms are not allowed to grow and entry is not free, the current incumbents are unlikely to survive in the face of foreign competition. In these circumstances, it is far from efficient to restrict the entry and growth of firms. Such a policy is anticonsumer and, worse, not synonymous with helping small entrepreneurs. What would be in the interests of the sector is a separate set of policies specifically designed to help new entrepreneurs to enter and small firms to grow (Abid Hussain Committee Report 1997).

In this respect, the following suggestions by the High Level Committee (2000) on how to encourage and assist efficient and well-managed small-scale units may merit consideration. First, there should be no reservation of products that are open to imports. Second, there should be a progressive reduction and ultimate elimination of reservation of products for the small-scale and handloom sector. At the same time, these enterprises should be given cheaper access to credit. More specifically, the bank credit rate should be linked to the inflation rate but made cheaper, to enable the small-scale sector to become competitive both domestically and internationally. Finally, the threshold limit for small-scale enterprises to obtain cheap credit should be raised. The existing limit is too low, and has been eroded by inflation and exchange rate fluctuations.

Privatization and regulatory reform

The post-1991 period has seen widespread regulatory reform and the privatization of many SOEs undertaken as a result of increased awareness of regulatory failure. In 1991 the government abolished public sector monopolies except where security and strategic concerns remained. Iron and steel, heavy electrical equipment, aircraft, air transport, shipbuilding, telecommunications equipment, and electric power are now open to private sector investment. These reforms had two objectives: greater autonomy for public sector enterprises and greater private sector ownership.

Although India is now in the process of formulating and implementing a second generation of economic reforms, price controls and dual pricing continue to distort the market. For instance, restrictions on sugarcane pricing, procurement, and production, the dual pricing of sugar (levy and non-levy), and restraints on sugar exports and imports allow inefficient sugar producers to continue to prevent the rise of a competitive industry (Rao 1998).

Although privatization and disinvestment in the public sector have been negligible, it continues to get preferential treatment in government procurement. Public sector firms dominate the market in a number of sectors, with significant implications for efficiency. The prices of certain important commodities—including petroleum products, fertilizers, and sugar cane—continue to be administered, distorting production and consumption decisions in these areas. Administered prices are also prevalent in sectors such as power and transport where the public sector dominates. Progress in introducing competition or effective regulation in power, transport, and communications has been far from satisfactory. Due to changes in technology, a number of these infrastructure sectors are no longer natural monopolies, and it would be possible to introduce direct competition. If private entry is allowed, there will be a need to establish effective and independent regulatory agencies.

It is therefore imperative to make further progress on liberalization, deregulation, disinvestment, and privatization, to enable consumers to reap the benefits of competition in the market. Nonetheless, a caveat needs to be added that while competition principles need to govern and inform all government policies, there should be some flexibility in competition policy to provide for the needs, aspirations, and goals of the country (Expert Group 1999). It also needs to be said that liberalization, deregulation, privatization, and other economic reforms should be designed to strengthen competition policy, and vice versa (High Level Committee 2000).

Trade policy

Trade policy includes tariffs, quotas, subsidies, antidumping actions, domestic content regulations, and export restraints. Until the 1970s, the focus of trade policy was on regulating the utilization of foreign exchange through the use of quota restrictions. This implied licensing for all categories of imports. The broad objectives of trade policy were across-the-board import substitution and the protection of domestic industry.

The two criteria for the allocation of licenses were the 'essentiality' and 'indigenous non-availability' of the proposed import. The latter criterion implied that 'if it could be shown that there was domestic production of the imports demanded, then the imports were not permitted (regardless of cost and quality considerations)' (Bhagwati and Srinivasan 1975). The actual allocation of licenses across industries and across firms within an industry was essentially ad hoc, based on bureaucratic perceptions of 'fairness' and 'equity.'

In addition to the fact that certain key raw materials were produced in the public sector, a number of commodities were subject to price and quantity controls. Industries providing important commodities such as edible oils, sugar, fertilizers, pharmaceuticals, aluminum, cement, steel, coal, and petroleum products were subject to price controls and quantity controls to a varying degree. This implied that even in sectors where there was a private sector presence, conditions and outcomes were far from competitive. A complex system of excise and corporate taxes further distorted incentives.

Early reforms saw an increase in the number of capital goods, intermediate goods, and raw materials included in the Open General License list; a reduction and rationalization of duty rates on selected capital goods, intermediate goods, and industrial raw materials; and less stringent rules in the granting of licenses for items that continued to be under discretionary control. Quantitative restrictions were gradually replaced with tariffs. Between 1971 and 1979, the rupee depreciated by 32 percent in real terms against key currencies. This trend was reversed during 1979–81 and was followed by a corrective real depreciation of 7.6 percent after which the real exchange rate stabilized. A flexible exchange rate policy since 1985 has had a positive impact on exports.

Reforms since 1991 have centered on licensing and tariff reform. The export and import (EXIM) policy of 1990–93 was replaced by the EXIM policy of 1992–97 and then by the EXIM policy of 1997–2001. Whereas the earliest EXIM policy contained a negative list of goods subject to import licensing that included almost all consumer goods, by the time the most recent policy was introduced, the list of restricted consumer goods had been pruned, the number of canalized items reduced, and the import of some restricted items liberalized by permitting their importation through freely transferable special import licenses. To meet its WTO commitments, India has done away with its quantitative restriction regime. Tariffs are also being reduced in a phased manner. Prior to 1991, India's tariffs were among the highest in the world. The government reduced the average applied tariff rate from 125 percent in 1990/91 to 35 percent in

1997/98 and to 20 percent in 2001/02, with the peak rate declining from 335 percent in 1990/91 to 40 percent in 1999/2000 and 35 percent in 2001/02. In addition, India has bound about 3,300—or nearly 70 percent—of its 4,700 tariff lines. Of these, 99 percent have been bound at rates of 40 percent or lower, with the applied rates much lower than the binding rates for most products (Mehta 2003). All non-tariff barriers have been phased out for all tradables. All these reform measures infused and enhanced competition in the market (Kumar 2003; Mehta 2003).

Trade liberalization and competition policy are complementary, and neither can fully achieve its objects without the other. Given this premise, an appropriate approach would be to adopt competition policy simultaneously with trade liberalization and other economic reforms such as privatization and deregulation. In this way, competition policy would act as a catalyst for economic reform and development based on market-oriented principles. Trade policies that do not conform to competition principles should be refashioned so that they do. All physical and fiscal barriers to domestic trade should be removed. This would mean introducing new fiscal measures such as a uniform sales tax, abolishing *octroi* duties and other state-level entry and exit taxes, and eliminating all physical controls on the movement of goods throughout the country (High Level Committee 2000).

While an open trade policy would be supportive of competition policy objectives, it is not necessarily a guarantee of competition in all circumstances. Government policies, particularly those that give rise to restraints and distortions in trade practices and the market, may be a threat to the attainment of competition objectives. All trade policies should therefore be required to comply with an established framework of competition principles. An effective competition policy that ensures that trade policies fall within these contours is in the interests of both consumers and free and fair trade (High Level Committee 2000).

Financial policy

Like other sectors, the financial sector was subject to government intervention and control for several decades. As a result, the financial system was characterized by an almost total lack of competition. With the nationalization of 14 large commercial banks in 1969, about 85 percent of the assets of the banking system came under public control. The long-term lending business had very few players. Because term lending institutions were all publicly owned, they generally acted as a consortium and had the characteristics of a lending cartel. There was virtually no competition between term lending institutions, which concentrated on medium and long-term finance, and commercial banks with their emphasis on working-capital finance.

In the equity market, the main policy impediment was the entry barrier put up by the Controller of Capital Issues, who had to approve every issue and set the issue price. A company could approach the financial markets to raise funds only after a project had been approved by the government. Thus, the number of new issues in any period was relatively small. Underpricing would have resulted in the transfer of wealth from existing to new shareholders; the former group therefore had a strong incentive to prefer rights offerings over public offerings. This hindered the widening of the investor base. In addition, public sector financial institutions, dominated by the Unit Trust of India, the insurance companies, and the domestic financial institutions, were all major players in the equity market, giving the government effective control over pricing. This dominance was compounded by the fact that there was no competition from foreign institutional investors.

A process of gradual deregulation of the financial sector began in 1988–89. Although new entry has not been substantial since then, the entry of domestic and private foreign banks is permitted. Further rationalization and mergers in this segment should help to provide more effective competition for public sector banks. With the liberalization of regulatory controls on non-bank financial companies, these now provide some competition to traditional banks. Domestic financial institutions are also conducting more conventional banking activities—in particular short-term lending—providing some competition to the conventional banking sector. Commercial banks have also increased their term lending activities, thus reducing the oligopolistic position of the domestic financial institutions (Chakravarthy 2004).

The office of the Controller of Capital Issues was abolished in 1992, leading to freer pricing of issues. Private sector mutual funds and foreign institutional investors were permitted to trade in equities, increasing competition on the buyer side of the equities market and reducing the importance of publicly owned foreign institutional investors. Competition in exchanges was introduced with the establishment of the National Stock Exchange.

State monopolies policy

State monopolies are regarded by many countries as inevitable instruments of public growth and public interest. While ideology may have played some role in spurring their growth, much of the increase can be attributed to the pragmatic response of the government and public to the prevailing milieu, which is frequently an outcome of the historical past. A view shared by many is that India's state monopolies and public enterprises have played a vital role in the development process, have engineered growth in critical core areas, and have carried out valuable social functions. Nonetheless, there is also a recognition—derived from the adverse financial results of these enterprises and their ceaseless demands for budgetary oxygen from the government treasury—that there is scope not only for reform but also for structural and operational improvements. This recognition spurred the trend toward privatization, which is one part of the more general process of liberalization and deregulation. Privatization involves not only the divestiture and sale of government assets, but also a gradual decline in the interventionist role played by government.

State monopolies have harmful effects that are antithetical to the scheme of a modern competition policy. For instance, government patronage and support for state monopolies may encourage them to abuse their dominant positions or adopt policies that are tantamount to restrictive trade practices. A common example is for them to give preference to public sector units in tenders and bids. State monopolies also suffer from administered pricing schemes, which are contrary to the spirit of competition policy.

It is widely accepted that competition is one of the keys to improving the performance of state monopolies and public enterprises. The oft-noted inefficiency of government enterprises stems from their isolation from effective competition (Aharoni 1986). While the government should reserve the right to grant statutory monopoly status to certain public enterprises in the broad national interest, it also needs to be remembered that the deregulation of statutory monopolies and privatization are likely to engender competition that would be healthy for the market and consumers.

State monopolies persist in a number of important infrastructure industries, including transport, power, and communications. In some cases limited privatization has taken place but a suitable regulatory framework is still evolving. In areas that were traditionally considered natural monopolies, one solution was to establish state-run monopolies on the assumption that these would set the right prices and maximize welfare. The other option was to have regulated private participants, where the regulator's job was to set prices that mimicked those in a competitive market and thus maximized welfare. In certain cases, changes in technology have made competition possible in areas that were hitherto considered natural monopolies. There is considerable scope for introducing regulated competition into these areas.

Rail transport in India continues to be a state monopoly, with administered prices and very limited competition from other modes of transport. In civil aviation, some competition has been allowed although restrictions on entry remain. The state-owned domestic airline continues to play a major role and is a market leader in setting prices. Most states have state-owned road transport corporations with an administered fare structure and limited competition.

With a few exceptions, the generation, transmission, and distribution of power is controlled by monopolies owned by the central and state governments. Prices are administered, costs are high, and the quality of service is generally poor and unreliable. Welfare maximization requires that competition be introduced in this sector. A prerequisite for this is the unbundling of India's monolithic SOEs and the establishment of effective and independent regulatory authorities.

Although some competition is permitted in the area of telecommunications, much more needs to be done. The only area where some competition exists is mobile telephony. Basic and long-distance telephony is virtually a state monopoly. However, the situation is still evolving, and the role and authority of the regulator as well as the status of the state-owned monopolies have still not been clearly established.

Efficiency is related more to the degree of competition than to ownership (Jones, Tandon, and Vogelsang 1990). Government policy in this regard should be to divest itself of its shares and assets in state monopolies and public enterprises and privatize them in a phased manner. This policy should be adopted for all except core sectors and areas related to national security and the sovereign functions of the state. In other words, where the government is involved in a business it has no reason to be in, it should exit through divestiture and privatization (High Level Committee 2000).

Labor policy

The Industrial Disputes Act, 1947 and connected statutes constitute the country's primary labor legislation. These statutes have evolved over a period of time, the balance generally being to protect the interests of labor. While this may appear to be the correct approach, it is also true that firms desiring to exit are sometimes prevented from doing so by provisions in the existing labor legislation. Exit barriers in the form in which they exist today—that is, the requirement to obtain prior government approval for lay-offs, retrenchments, and closures—were instituted in the mid-1970s. Considering that these restrictive provisions apply to no more than 3 percent of the working population, their retention deserves careful examination. A question often asked is why it is so critical to provide a high level of protection for a nominal 3 percent of the working population when the other 97 percent can exist without such protection. The answer may lie in the political power of the trade unions in the organized sector.

Clearly such laws have an adverse effect on employment by distorting the relative price of labor and capital. At best, they end up protecting those that are already employed rather than promoting employment. The Industrial Disputes Act and connected statutes therefore need to be amended to allow relatively easy exit. This does not mean cheap exit; because India has limited social security, the government has an obligation to ensure that retrenched workers receive reasonable exit payments (Chakravarthy 2004).

The Sick Industrial Companies (Special Provisions) Act, 1985 governs exit for medium-sized and large firms through the Board of Industrial and Financial Reconstruction. The restructuring and closure of sick firms is subject to a decision of the board, but cases referred to it often languish there for years before a final decision is reached. In the interim, sick and unviable units continue to function. The board also advises on financial restructuring—a matter that would ideally be left to market-driven financial entities—leading to the misallocation of scarce financial resources. Another problem is that the board deals with individual cases of sick firms rather than with industrial sickness as a whole. Already, legislation has been proposed to repeal the Sick Industrial Companies (Special Provisions) Act and do away with the Board of Industrial and Financial Reconstruction.

The effects of government policies on combinations[8]

The regulatory framework and trends in merger activity

Exogenous and firm-specific factors determine the level of merger activity in most cases. Exogenous factors include changes in demand and supply conditions, technology, industrial policy shifts (such as deregulation), and competitive conditions, all of which can be bracketed as the 'environment' in which enterprises operate. Firm-specific factors include economies of scale, market power, tax advantages, growth, and operating performance. All these factors constitute a trigger for mergers between enterprises.

Mergers affect competition by reducing the number of players, enhancing dominance and sometimes monopoly power, allowing the exercise of market power and dictation of prices to the detriment of consumers, and discouraging new entrants in the market. Mergers may also have countervailing advantages such as greater economies of scale, better

*Figure 5.1   India: Distribution of merger activity, 1973/74–2001/02
(no. of mergers)*

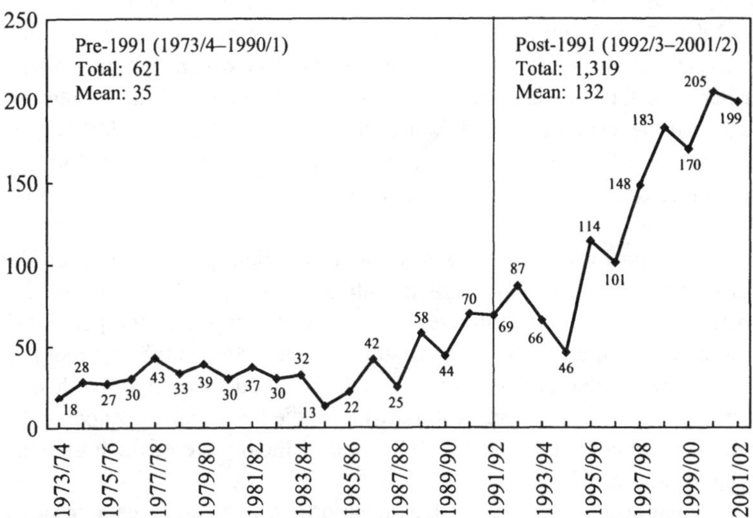

Source: Centre for Monitoring Indian Economy (various issues); Beena (1998); Basant (2000); Kumar (2000a); Agarwal (2002).

opportunities for labor, and enhanced global competitiveness. Thus mergers can be benevolent and/or malevolent. Horizontal mergers are the most likely to fall into the 'malevolent' category because of their tendency to restrict competition.

The MRTP Act contained merger control provisions until 1991, when it was amended and its merger provisions deleted. The new Competition Act contains elaborate provisions on mergers above certain threshold limits, as described in section 3 of this chapter. As the provisions in the new law have yet to be brought into force, there is at present no surveillance over mergers based on the touchstone of competition. (Mergers are, however, regulated under the Companies Act, 1956 from the perspective of the interests of shareholders and stakeholders). The spurt in mergers over the last decade or so can be attributed to the absence of merger regulation since 1991 and to changes in the executive policies of government. The distribution of merger activity over the 29-year period from 1973/74 to 2001/02 is shown in Figure 5.1.

Although the graph distinguishes only two phases of merger activity, it is in fact possible to identify four such phases: steady and largely nonfluctuating merger activity from 1973/74 to 1987/88; gradually increasing merger activity from 1987/88 to 1992/93; declining merger activity from 1992/93 to 1994/95; and sharply increasing merger activity from 1994/95 to 2001/02. The graph clearly shows the spurt in merger and acquisition (M&A) activity since 1991, a watershed year in which the government ushered in far-reaching economic reforms. The mean of the number of deals has recorded almost a four-fold increase in the post-1991 period compared to the pre-1991 period. This is a significant jump, denoting a conscious thrust by the Indian corporate sector toward consolidation since 1991.

The main form of mergers in India during both periods has been the horizontal type, as a survey of the literature shows. Beena (1998), for instance, found that a little over two-thirds of mergers in the post-1991 liberalized regime had been horizontal and that a large number of mergers were between enterprises belonging to the same business group with similar product lines. Basant (2000), who studied a sample of about 400 mergers, concluded that about 60 percent of them were of the horizontal type during the 1990s.

A note needs to be added on acquisitions, which constitute a genre of combinations. The policy and regulatory framework governing acquisitions was fine-tuned in the 1990s. Until 1990, an open offer was mandatory when acquiring a stake of 25 percent or more in a company. In 1990 this threshold was lowered to 10 percent of a company's capital. However, in the case of acquisitions by multinational enterprises (MNEs), the provisions of the Foreign Exchange Regulation Act, 1973 applied, and these imposed a general limit on foreign ownership of 40 percent. In addition, under the MRTP Act the government had the power to prevent an acquisition if it was considered that it might lead to 'concentration of economic power to the common detriment.' This power was removed by the 1991 amendments to the act. In 1992, the government established the Securities and Exchange Board of India to regulate the domestic capital market and protect investors' interests. As part of the new post-1991 paradigm, the restrictions on foreign ownership of Indian companies under the Foreign Exchange Regulation Act were abolished. In 1994 the Securities and Exchange Board of India issued guidelines for substantial acquisitions of shares and takeovers. The Takeover Code of 1994, as it is commonly known, is revised from time to time. At present it provides for the acquirer to make a public offer for a minimum of 20 percent of the target company's capital as soon as 10 percent of ownership and management control has been acquired. The liberalized policies adopted since 1991 have encouraged Indian enterprises to consider acquisitions as a means to consolidate their operations.

Exogenous factors

Exogenous factors have also had an impact on mergers. For the better part of four decades after independence in 1947, the thrust of India's political and economic philosophy was what has been described as the pre-1991 paradigm of licensing, planning, and government control. The government used licensing in particular to regulate and channel private industry. It was the instrument of choice to regulate entry into industry and control the expansion of capacity. While some deregulation of the industrial sector took place in the mid-1980s, when 25 broad categories of industries were delicensed, it was only after 1991 that the entire complexion of government control changed. All but 18 industries were delicensed in 1991 and today only six industries require a license. The list of industries reserved for the public sector has been reduced from 17 to the current level of four. The removal of restrictions on enterprises to tap capital markets has reduced entry barriers.

The post-1991 paradigm of liberalization, privatization, and globalization has led to the restructuring and consolidation of enterprises through M&As, with an increasing tendency for Indian enterprises to substitute their greenfield growth plans with takeover strategies. The relaxation and removal of restrictions under the various statutes has significantly reduced microeconomic rigidities and enhanced competition in the market (Basant 2000).

The impact of delicensing on merger activity may be seen in Table 5.1. It shows major spurts in vegetable and animal oils, electronics, electrical machinery, iron and steel, motor vehicles, metal products, organic and inorganic chemicals, textiles, and drugs and pharmaceuticals (in that order) following industry delicensing. While the impact of delicensing is conspicuous in the data, it cannot be gainsaid that enterprises' perceptions of future opportunities for profitability, conditions of demand and supply, contestable markets (easy entry, easy exit), and the extent of competition in the market have also influenced the extent of restructuring and mergers. Another important factor was the deletion of the merger control provisions in the MRTP Act in 1991.

Government legislation, in particular the Income Tax Act, 1961 and the Sick Industrial Companies (Special Provisions) Act, 1985, has been another exogenous factor affecting merger activity. Fiscal concessions are available under the Income Tax Act to encourage healthy and profitable enterprises to merge with sick ones. A healthy enterprise that merges with a distressed one is able to offset the accumulated losses and unabsorbed depreciation of the sick enterprise against profit. Fiscal concessions of this nature facilitate the rehabilitation of sick enterprises while giving healthy

Table 5.1   India: Impact of delicensing on merger activity

Industry	Year of delicensing	Total number of mergers	Mergers since delicensing	
			(no.)	(%)
Textiles	1991/92	104	52	50.0
Electrical machinery	1991/92	102	76	74.5
Drugs & pharmaceuticals	1995/96	81	40	49.4
Electronics	1991/92	79	64	81.0
Iron & steel	1991/92	49	34	69.4
Organic & inorganic chemicals	1991/92	41	22	53.7
Motor vehicles	1991/92	39	27	69.2
Metal products	1991/92	35	23	65.7
Vegetable & animal oils	1997/98	17	14	82.4
Machinery (other than transport & electrical)	1991/92	87	23	26.4
Sugar	1998/99	28	4	14.3
Jute	1991/92	16	0	0.0
Wood & wood products	1997/98	11	2	18.2
Bicycles	1991/92	3	0	0.0
Glass & glass products	1991/92	1	0	0.0

Source: Agarwal (2002).

enterprises the opportunity to recoup some of the costs of the merger. The Sick Industrial Companies (Special Provisions) Act empowers the Board of Industrial and Financial Reconstruction to organize mergers and takeovers of sick enterprises by healthy, profitable ones. Beena (1998) noted that 22 percent of all acquisitions by profitable enterprises were of enterprises that were incurring losses.

The impact of government policies—removal of the merger control provisions, delicensing, incentives for healthy enterprises to merge with or take over distressed firms—has been to enhance the number of mergers and, in particular, the number of horizontal combinations. This does not necessarily mean that competition has suffered. This will depend on whether merger activity in the post-1991 regime has led to consolidation and an increase in anticompetitive practices.

Table 5.2   India: Intraindustry and interindustry mergers,
*   1973/74–2000/01 (no.)*

	Companies
Mergers	1,810
Mergers where product category information is available for both the acquiring and target company	1,573
Intraindustry mergers	843
Interindustry mergers	730

Source: Agarwal (2002).

Consolidation

Table 5.2 shows data collected by Agarwal (2002) on mergers within and between industries from 1973/74 to 2000/01. Mergers of enterprises belonging to the same industry or business are styled horizontal and have the potential to be anticompetitive in nature. They therefore have the potential to be prejudicial to consumer interests. After disaggregating the data into the pre- and post-1991 periods, Agarwal found that more than 60 percent of the mergers that occurred in the latter period were of the intraindustry type. Intraindustry mergers clearly outnumbered interindustry mergers, particularly after 1991. The data support the conclusion that enterprises have been resorting to mergers as a means to consolidate their activities in the same business line (Agarwal 2002).

Basant (2000) has argued that the pre-1991 licensing regime resulted in overdiversification and that excessive regulation in the pre-reform period often forced enterprises within the same group to compete with each other for market share. In Basant's view, the more liberal post-1991 regime has rectified some of the anomalies of the pre-reform period. Yet, one cannot escape the conclusion that government policies have resulted in increased merger activity and also in the consolidation of enterprises. More particularly, there has been an increase in horizontal combines of an intraindustry character. This is not likely to enthuse competition purists.

The consolidation process has had adverse effects in the form of an increase in dominance leading to oligopoly or even monopoly, as the case of the current duopoly in the Indian cement industry illustrates (Box 5.4). Consolidation has pluses as well as minuses, however, and these need to be weighed against each other when determining whether a merger is

---

**Box 5.4 Industry consolidation: A case study
of acquisition in the cement industry**

In June 2003, Grasim Industries struck a deal to acquire the cement division of Larsen and Toubro, a professionally managed engineering company. Grasim is part of the family-owned Aditya Birla conglomerate, which has been strengthening its position in recent years in a range of intermediate commodities, such as aluminum and other metals, cement, and fertilizers. Grasim had an installed cement-manufacturing capacity of 14.5 million tons per annum. With the acquisition of Larsen and Toubro's cement division, it now controls almost one-quarter of the installed capacity in India, of 141 million tons per annum in 2002/03. Another combine, comprising Gujarat Ambuja Cement and Associated Cement Company (ACC), controls about 20 percent of installed capacity. Several other cement-manufacturing companies share the remaining 50 percent, but they are all small compared with the duopoly consisting of Grasim and Larsen and Toubro on the one hand and Gujarat Ambuja and ACC on the other.

Cement's bulk makes it difficult and expensive to transport over long distances. This is one of the reasons why importing cement has not been an attractive proposition for MNEs such as Lafarge, which has been seeking a capacity acquisition in India. The geographical spread of the Indian market demands that cement companies have diffused capacities in order to reduce transportation costs. Precisely for this reason, several small players have emerged. But consolidation resulting in duopoly is affecting a change in the industry: new players are being deterred from entering the market while the existing small players are being driven out. Sridhar (2003), an analyst, has described Grasim's acquisition of Larsen and Toubro's cement division and Gujarat Ambuja's combination with ACC as the 'cannibalisation of market shares that occurs when dominant companies entrench themselves as monopolies.'

---

desirable from a competition perspective (Box 5.5). The Competition Act therefore correctly requires the Competition Commission of India to consider whether the benefits of a combination outweigh its adverse consequences when determining whether or not it should be allowed.

Concentration index

The concentration index is another measure of whether M&As have led to concentration, which generally would portend trouble for competition in the market. Table 5.3 presents data on M&As by domestic and foreign-owned companies in India between April 1999 and January 2004, for 38

**Box 5.5 Costs and benefits of mergers: A case study of
the effects in India of a merger in the United States**

In 2002 Hewlett Packard (HP) acquired Compaq in the United States. Both companies are information technology giants. The effects of the combination were felt not only in the United States, but also in many other countries where the two companies had previously had an individual presence. In India, the impact was to make the combined entity the clear leader in the market for personal computers. In the fiscal year ending March 2001, the revenue of the combined entity was Rs 33 billion (about $730 million), putting it ahead of India's three largest computer companies, namely TCS (less than $700 million), Wipro, and Infosys.

In combinations of this type, there is always the potential for synergies. The biggest gain for HP in India has been the increase in its customer base. By eliminating overlapping computer product lines, it has managed to reduce costs while maintaining the same level of revenue. The economies of scale achieved by the combined entity have led to lower prices for consumers, who also benefit from being able to shop at superstores selling the gamut of products from computer systems to printers and associated services. As well as achieving product synergies, HP has been able to take advantage of Compaq's traditional strength in services and systems distribution in India, which complements its own strength in printers and scanners. By reducing its operations to a single factory, improving its logistics system, and strengthening its distribution system, HP has been able to achieve further cost savings that it can pass on to consumers.

But the combination is not entirely benevolent. The different corporate cultures of HP and Compaq have made it difficult and time consuming to streamline the two companies' structures, product lines, and processes. Consumers now have less choice, as the combination leaves only IBM and DELL as the two major US competitors in the computer and server arena. In addition, 10 percent of the combined workforce of the two companies is under threat of being laid off, thus prejudicing what one might call the public interest.[9] One could also argue, though, that a reduction in the workforce will bring about cost savings that may lead to lower prices and ultimately be in the consumer interest, and therefore that this is a benevolent factor.

industrial and six service sectors. The table also shows the Herfindahl–Hirschman concentration index for the chosen sectors. Broadly, the following conclusions emerge from Table 5.3.

First, in terms of numbers, domestic companies recorded more mergers and more acquisitions than foreign-owned companies except in six

Table 5.3　India: M&As in selected manufacturing and service sectors, April 1999–January 2004, and Herfindahl–Hirschman concentration index, 1997/98–2001/02

Industry/ service sector	Acquisitions by Indian-owned companies		Mergers with Indian-owned companies		Acquisitions by foreign-owned companies		Mergers with foreign-owned companies in India		Total	Rank	Herfindahl–Hirschman concentration index				
	(no.)	(%)	(no.)	(%)	(no.)	(%)	(no.)	(%)			1997/ 98	1998/ 99	1999/ 00	2000/ 01	2001/ 02
Manufacturing															
Drugs, pharmaceuticals	173	55.8	47	15.2	79	25.5	11	3.6	310	18	0.010	0.010	0.012	0.013	0.016
Steel	60	74.1	11	13.6	10	12.4	0	0.0	81	51	0.111	0.108	0.108	0.102	0.107
Cement	62	80.5	7	9.1	8	10.4	0	0.0	77	53	0.043	0.049	0.047	0.051	0.055
Sugar	52	88.1	6	10.2	1	1.7	0	0.0	59	68	0.003	0.002	0.003	0.004	0.005
Tea	34	61.8	12	21.8	8	14.5	1	1.8	55	72	0.062	0.086	0.068	0.081	0.082
Paper	42	77.8	5	9.3	6	11.1	1	1.9	54	75	0.010	0.009	0.011	0.014	0.016
Beer	15	35.7	2	4.8	20	47.6	5	11.9	42	92	0.152	0.092	0.074	0.117	0.103
Machine tools	14	38.9	2	5.6	18	50.0	2	5.6	36	98	0.011	0.007	0.008	0.007	0.006
Wires & cables	26	74.3	4	11.4	5	14.3	0	0.0	35	101	0.033	0.029	0.029	0.028	0.025
Dyes & pigments	9	32.1	3	10.7	15	53.6	1	3.6	28	110	0.036	0.026	0.023	0.020	0.020
Motors & generators	15	53.6	2	7.1	11	39.3	0	0.0	28	110	0.073	0.085	0.084	0.080	0.084
Paints & varnishes	9	39.1	3	13.0	8	34.8	3	13.0	23	126	0.168	0.154	0.164	0.171	0.166
Aluminum products	15	65.2	6	26.1	1	4.4	1	4.4	23	126	0.172	0.134	0.132	0.113	0.124
Vegetable oils	10	58.8	3	17.7	4	23.5	0	0.0	17	142	0.004	0.004	0.004	0.007	0.010
Chemicals machinery	7	41.2	2	11.8	7	41.2	1	5.9	17	142	0.212	0.267	0.556	0.180	0.200
Transformers	10	62.5	3	18.8	2	12.5	1	6.3	16	145	0.098	0.099	0.078	0.077	0.101
Material handling equipment	7	46.7	0	0.0	8	53.3	0	0.0	15	151	0.062	0.100	0.077	0.109	0.093
Copper/copper products	9	75.0	2	16.7	1	8.3	0	0.0	12	165	0.049	0.089	0.129	0.173	0.212

Caustic soda	7	70.0	2	20.0	1	10.0	0	0.0	10	182	0.053	0.055	0.060	0.061	0.061
Pig iron	7	70.0	1	10.0	1	10.0	1	10.0	10	182	0.103	0.095	0.097	0.077	0.081
Ferro alloys	7	70.0	1	10.0	2	20.0	0	0.0	10	182	0.080	0.067	0.050	0.051	0.059
Tractors	7	70.0	0	0.0	3	30.0	0	0.0	10	182	0.179	0.171	0.177	0.172	0.158
Granite	5	55.6	1	11.1	3	33.3	0	0.0	9	190	0.037	0.036	0.036	0.043	0.049
Storage batteries	5	55.6	1	11.1	3	33.3	0	0.0	9	190	0.302	0.410	0.448	0.391	0.360
Textile machinery	4	50.0	1	12.5	3	37.5	0	0.0	8	196	0.027	0.027	0.039	0.049	0.034
Coffee	6	85.7	1	14.3	0	0.0	0	0.0	7	201	0.030	0.030	0.021	0.014	0.017
Refractories	1	16.7	0	0.0	5	83.3	0	0.0	6	203	0.084	0.079	0.087	0.085	0.086
Valves	2	33.3	0	0	3	50.0	1	16.7	6	203	0.104	0.091	0.075	0.079	0.116
Dry cells	3	50.0	0	0.0	1	16.7	2	33.3	6	203	0.283	0.222	0.217	0.175	0.207
Vanaspati[a]	5	100.0	0	0.0	0	0.0	0	0.0	5	211	0.049	0.042	0.039	0.028	0.036
Phosphatic fertilizers	3	60.0	1	20.0	1	20.0	0	0.0	5	211	0.055	0.063	0.064	0.063	0.044
Abrasives	4	80.0	1	20.0	0	0.0	0	0.0	5	211	0.322	0.311	0.307	0.279	0.258
Sponge iron	4	80.0	0	0.0	1	20.0	0	0.0	5	211	0.179	0.171	0.151	0.139	0.153
Starch	4	100.0	0	0.0	0	0.0	0	0.0	4	221	0.069	0.074	0.080	0.084	0.076
Acetic acid	3	75.0	1	25.0	0	0.0	0	0.0	4	221	0.153	0.149	0.149	0.171	0.127
Bicycles	3	75.0	0	0.0	1	25.0	0	0.0	4	221	0.215	0.243	0.262	0.273	0.285
Carbon black	1	33.3	0	0.0	2	66.7	0	0.0	3	228	0.191	0.211	0.235	0.252	0.299
Printing machinery	2	100.0	0	0.0	0	0.0	0	0.0	2	231	0.008	0.046	0.059	0.078	0.061
Services															
Production of TV serials/films	38	60.3	5	7.9	19	30.2	1	1.6	63	62	0.144	0.107	0.114	0.078	0.083
Shipping	26	76.5	2	5.9	6	17.7	0	0.0	34	104	0.316	0.272	0.241	0.201	0.191
Housing construction	12	48.0	12	48.0	1	4.0	0	0.0	25	119	0.123	0.100	0.099	0.107	0.126
Road transport	3	30.0	5	50.0	1	10.0	1	10.0	10	182	0.117	0.090	0.079	0.073	0.082
Air transport	3	60.0	1	20.0	1	20.0	0	0.0	5	211	0.300	0.325	0.280	0.277	0.271
Courier services	4	80.0	0	0.0	1	20.0	0	0.0	5	211	0.304	0.193	0.183	0.184	0.189

a Vanaspati is a hydrogenated vegetable fat used as a butter substitute in India.
Source: Centre for Monitoring India Economy.

**Box 5.6 A case study of concentration
in the consumer goods industry**

Food and beverages, household appliances, pharmaceuticals, and personal
care products are some of the consumer goods industries in which M&A
activity involving MNEs has led to concentration. Products in these industries are highly sensitive to marketing networks and brand loyalty. To avoid
the time and expense involved in establishing new marketing networks and
building brand name awareness, MNEs often prefer to acquire domestic
firms with established marketing and distribution networks and existing
brand loyalties.

The case of Coca-Cola illustrates this mode of activity. Coca-Cola
entered (actually re-entered) the country in 1993 by acquiring Parle, the
largest player in the Indian soft drink market with several well-established
brands and a nationwide bottling and marketing network. This gave Coca-
Cola a head start over its rival Pepsi, which, despite having entered the
country five years earlier, was still struggling with a market share of only
25 percent compared to Parle's 60 percent. Pepsi later adopted the same
strategy as Coca-Cola by acquiring Duke, a smaller soft drink manufacturer, to build its market share. Today Coca-Cola and Pepsi dominate the
soft drink market in India: Coca-Cola/Parle is believed to have a 50 percent
market share while Pepsi/Duke has about 48 percent (Kumar 2000b). As a
result, most other soft drink manufacturers have fallen by the wayside. In
addition, the restructuring undertaken by Coca-Cola to rationalize its bottling operations is reported to have resulted in the loss of 100 jobs (*Economic Times*, New Delhi, 22 January 2000).

---

industries (beer, machine tools, dyes and pigments, refractories, valves,
and carbon black). Second, acquisitions outnumbered mergers. Third, for
most industrial and service sectors listed in the table, the concentration
index is low and did not change significantly between 1997/98 and
2001/02; as the table shows, the number of companies listed in each sector remains large. Thus it appears that on the whole M&As are not leading to changes in market structure. An exception is fast-moving consumer
goods industries, where M&As by foreign multinationals have led to an
increase in concentration (Boxes 5.6 and 5.7).

A broader conclusion is that in the post-1991 regime there has been
more M&A activity, more consolidation of activities in the same business
line, and little or no concentration or competition-distorting threat (except
in fast-moving consumer goods). The steep post-1991 increase in M&As

Box 5.7 A case study of market domination through M&As

Unilever has used M&As to increase its presence in India since first commencing business there in 1913. Initially it merged with several companies engaged in the soap trade. Hindustan Lever Limited, a subsidiary of Unilever, has also followed the same strategy to grow and expand its range of activities and strengthen its market presence. During the pre-1991 regime, Hindustan Lever acquired a number of small enterprises that had run into financial difficulties. These acquisitions added capacity to Hindustan Lever's activities and helped it to diversify into garments, marine products, and other business areas.

Following the 1991 liberalization, Hindustan Lever sought to restructure its diversified product portfolio and strengthen its market presence. Following the M&A route, it has added tea, ice cream, frozen food, coffee, and detergent to its kitty of products over the last 10 years. The net impact of these M&As on the market share of Hindustan Lever and its associates in different product segments is summarized in Table 5.4. In products such as ice cream, cosmetics and toiletries, synthetic detergent, dental hygiene products, and sauces, ketchups, and jams, Hindustan Lever has a dominant market share of 40–75 percent.

Table 5.4   *India: Market share of Hindustan Lever and associated companies, 1992/93–1997/98 (%)*

Segment	1992/93	1996/97	1997/98
Ice cream	0.0	68.8	74.1
Sauces, ketchups, & jams	0.0	60.0	63.5
Animal feed	n.a.	10.8	12.7
Tea	n.a.	20.7	20.5
Coffee	n.a.	5.2	5.9
Glycerin	37.4	39.6	40.9
Sodium tripoly phosphate	44.8	64.8	65.1
Diammonium phosphate	7.9	9.3	8.8
Cosmetics & toiletries	n.a.	56.3	56.5
Dental hygiene products	11.2	35.7	41.6
Soap	19.7	25.3	26.0
Synthetic detergent	33.1	47.2	46.7
Vanaspati[a]	0.9	12.6	13.9

n.a. = not available.
a   Vanaspati is a hydrogenated vegetable fat used as a butter substitute in India.
Source: EIS (1999).

compared with the pre-1991 period is attributable, among other things, to the government policy of doing away with merger surveillance and regulation after 1991. Support for this assertion is provided by Figure 5.1, which shows that the mean for M&A activity in the 10 years since 1991 is 132, whereas that for the 18 years in the pre-1991 period is only 35. That is, there has been an almost four-fold increase in M&A activity since surveillance and regulation were removed through the amendment of the MRTP Act.

The effects of government policies on foreign direct investment

The post-1991 regime

India had a very restrictive policy on FDI in the 1970s and a less restrictive one in the 1980s. The Industrial Policy, 1991 then released the shackles on FDI, with reform continuing since then (Kumar 2004). The post-1991 paradigm has influenced the volume and patterns of FDI inflows into the country, as Figure 5.2 illustrates. The figure shows steep increases in FDI from 1991 to 1997, when it reached $3.6 billion; moderate declines from 1997 to 1999; and moderate to significant increases from 1999 to 2004, when it reached $4.6 billion (based on provisional figures). Based on the 2001–02 figures of around $3.4 billion, India receives less than one-tenth of the annual inflows of the People's Republic of China, amounting to about $40 billion in recent years.

It would be incorrect to attribute the increase in India's FDI inflows solely to liberalization and economic reform in the post-1991 regime. Kumar (1998) attributes part of the increase experienced by India to the sharp expansion in global outflows during the 1990s. Thus, the post-1991 regime could be viewed as a necessary but not sufficient condition for increased flows of FDI into India. Kumar (2003) argues that India's improved macroeconomic fundamentals also help to explain the phenomenon of increased FDI to India.

While agreeing with Kumar's (1998, 2003) conclusions, it may also be appropriate to posit that the 1991 reforms injected a significant element of competition into the Indian economy. Pruning the negative list of industries requiring industrial approval, expanding the list of industries for which FDI received automatic approval, expanding the list of industries open to FDI, and liberalizing the country's local content requirements were all instrumental in promoting competitiveness, particularly in the manufacturing sector. In other words, the general perception among FDI providers that the Indian economy fostered competition in the manufac-

Figure 5.2   India: Inflows of FDI, 1991–2004 ($ billion)[a]

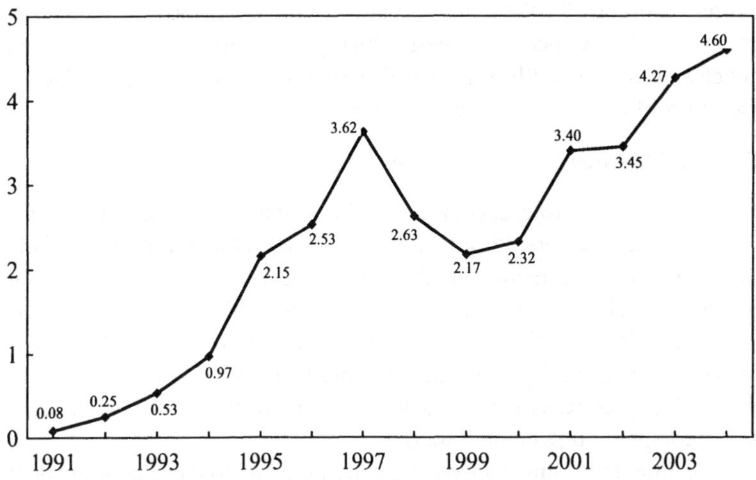

a   Figures for 2004 are provisional.
Source: UNCTAD (2004); Reserve Bank of India bulletins.

turing and service sectors, and in the market in general, could be regarded as a plausible reason for the upward direction of FDI since 1991.

Kumar (2003) suggests that FDI projects sometimes crowd out domestic investments from product or capital markets, or substitute for them, and that in some cases FDI inflows crowd in domestic investments. Nonetheless, it is the cumulative effect of government policies that influences the effect of FDI on domestic investments. The policy of the Indian government has been to approve FDI projects while imposing performance requirements that compel foreign investors to develop the country's domestic capability. A case in point was the use of performance requirements to build a domestic manufacturing capability in the automobile industry. India's now famous Maruti cars were the result of a joint venture signed between the Indian government and Suzuki Motor Corporation of Japan in 1982. The government stipulated a phased manufacturing program that would lead to an increase in local content to 75 percent within five years. To achieve this goal, Suzuki established a vendor development program under which it set up joint ventures with Indian manufacturers of auto components and provided them with new technology. Domestic investments in the sector followed, and gradually the proportion of local value-added increased. In 2000, in line with its changed post-1991 goals, the government withdrew the dividend-balancing and related export obligation conditions for the industry, policies that had helped the auto components industry become internationally competitive. An important conclusion from this illustration is that government policies do influence the effect of FDI on domestic investment.

Greenfield investment versus mergers

FDI in greenfield projects is of great value in developing the manufacturing and service sectors. Prior to 1991, most FDI inflows were in the form of greenfield investment, but the preference since then has been for M&As. As Table 5.5 shows, about 40 percent of FDI inflows during the peak period of 1997–99 took the form of M&As of existing Indian enterprises by foreign enterprises. This form of FDI does not normally enhance the stock of productive capital, generate favorable knowledge transfers, or foster competition (Kumar 2000b).

Greenfield investments have a greater potential to enhance inflows of knowledge than M&As because they are more likely to have a high content of new production, marketing, and organizational know-how. M&As, on the other hand, simply increase the stake of foreign companies in existing Indian companies and thus the inflow of knowledge into the country is somewhat limited. Similarly, greenfield investments increase the number of players in the market, and thus enhance competition, whereas M&As tend to reduce the number of players and lead to market concentration. A dimension worth noting is that investments through M&As may have an adverse effect on employment if the foreign enterprises introduce labor-saving managerial techniques that lead to a displacement of labor.

Foreign direct investment and the software industry

India witnessed phenomenal growth in the software industry during the 1990s. Over the last few years information technology software and services have been two important areas of spectacular growth. Although the software industry is reported to have grown at a compound annual rate of more than 50 percent per annum during the post-1991 period, FDI flows into this sector have not been substantial. Export revenue from software increased from $100 million in 1990 to nearly $10 billion in 2002. This success story is attributable to local enterprise, resources, and talent rather than FDI and government policies targeting software development. It is an outcome of the cumulative investments of the government over the last five decades in what are known as 'national innovation systems' (Kumar 2003). These include government investments in higher education, engi-

Table 5.5   India: Share of M&As in FDI inflows, 1997–99

Year	FDI inflows ($ million)	Value of M&As ($ million)	Share of M&As (%)
1997	3,200	1,300	40.6
1998	2,900	1,000	34.5
1999 (January–March)	1,400	500	35.7
Total	7,500	2,800	39.4

Source: Kumar (2000b).

neering, and technical disciplines; in the creation of the institutional infrastructure for science and technology; in building centers of excellence for technology development; and in the establishment of training institutes.

To sum up this subsection, the liberalization of FDI policy was a necessary but not sufficient condition for expanding FDI flows to India. Macroeconomic management exercised a strong influence on the volume of inflows and provided a positive signal that India was an attractive and favorable destination for FDI. India must continue to adopt policies that will create a stable and attractive environment for foreign investors. These policies should be geared toward increasing the potential for FDI to crowd in domestic investments. FDI should be allowed to enter areas where a local capability does not exist. Equally important is the dissemination of knowledge brought in by foreign enterprises through vertical linkages with domestic enterprises.

Summary

Competition policy and competition law complement each other. In a manner of speaking, competition law may be regarded as a subset of competition policy. Competition policy pervades a number of areas, including industrial policy, trade policy, financial policy, state monopolies policy, labor policy, and economic policy. Policy initiatives in all these areas must be inhered with an element of competition in order to create a competitive environment and a culture of competition. Competition law is merely an instrument to deal with anticompetitive practices perpetrated by market players. If the government does not pay sufficient attention to competition law, and enforcement is limited and lackadaisical, then the market itself will not be driven by competition and consumers will suffer.

This is not to imply that competition should blindly envelop all economic activities. India, like any other developing country, has many impoverished people whose needs and advancement need to be taken into account in positing a competition policy for the country. For instance, in the area of food security there should be enough flexibility to apply competition policy and enforce competition law in a limited manner given that a large section of society is dependent on government agencies for food and other essential commodities. Whatever the deficiencies of the public distribution system, it does serve a purpose and cannot be eliminated from the policy package in the name of competition. What this implies is that competition policy and law should be introduced and implemented in a phased manner, and be flexible enough to cater to the specific needs of the country.

The small-scale industrial sector is another area where a case can be made for applying competition policy flexibly so as not to destroy the livelihoods of those who depend on cottage and small industries for their survival. While one may accept the theory that inefficient firms should exit from the market, the small-scale industrial sector should be given the opportunity to improve its performance and efficiency over a transition period of, say, 7–10 years before being forced to face the challenge of competition. This recommendation may be viewed as being tantamount to a dilution of the spirit and concept of competition, but in India the consequences of unbridled competition could prove disastrous for the people and industries that depend on the umbrella of government protection.

Exceptions of this type should be made only if serious adverse effects are noticed in the domestic economy resulting from the application of competition policy and competition law. Otherwise, the enforcement of competition policy and law should be immediate and effective.

5   COMPETITION POLICY AND PRO-POOR CONCERNS

An often voiced criticism of competition policy is that it favors the interests of the well-to-do sections of society over those of the poor. In India there is a demand for economic reforms to have a 'human face,' that is, to be so fashioned as to serve the interests of the poor and not merely those of the rich.

A slightly dated example under the MRTP Act concerns small-scale manufacturers making footwear for Bata India Limited, the dominant firm in the industry, in the 1970s. The Indian manufacturers were essentially very poor cobblers and leather workers. Their agreements with Bata prohibited them from purchasing raw materials and components from parties other than those approved by the company. The agreements also stipulated that they use only the molds supplied by Bata and not sell any additional production to other parties without the company's approval. The MRTP Commission found that the conditions imposed by Bata constituted a restrictive trade practice under the MRTP Act and were prejudicial to the public interest (MRTP Commission 1975).

The government's pro-poor approach is reflected in the overall policy orientation of the new coalition government elected in May 2004. The United Democratic Alliance, led by the Congress Party, has announced a Common Minimum Programme (CMP) in which there is a reference to FDI. The CMP emphasizes that 'FDI will be encouraged and actively sought particularly in areas of infrastructure, high technology and exports and where local assets and employment are created on a significant scale.' One can presume from this that FDI will not be encouraged in the consumer durables sector, where goods cater mainly for the affluent, but may be encouraged to build infrastructure and create employment-intensive industrial and service enterprises. While CMP policies have yet to take shape, Majumder (2004), an economics commentator, had this to say about the new approach:

> The CMP's focus on confining FDI to infrastructure and other hi-tech areas would break the momentum of foreign investments. ... Globally FDI has become a competitive investment instrument. It goes where the returns are best. Global FDI destinations are not decided by the host country's social objectives, but by the potential that exists. ... At present, the global FDI market is looking at M&As and relocation of plants to reap profits in shorter timeframes. Infrastructure investment means longer gestation to reap returns.

According to the same commentator, the liberal FDI policy in manufacturing and to a lesser extent services has resulted in a new economic growth pattern:

> It stimulated both domestic investment sentiments and the market forces. The poverty ratio fell from 29 percent in 1996–97 to 18 percent in 2001–02, dispelling claims that the benefits of reform have not trickled down to the poor. With large FDI flows, the consumer durables sector, comprising automobiles, household electronics, electrical goods, computers and so on, surged ahead and one witnessed the emergence of a buyer's market.

Advances in telecommunications as a result of FDI inflows have narrowed the rural–urban divide. Exports of value-added goods have ballooned with FDI inflows; nearly $2 billion worth of automobile and auto parts were exported in 2003.

6   CONCLUSION

The chapter describes the extant MRTP Act, 1969 and the new Competition Act 2002, and lists the causal factors for the metamorphosis of the old law into the new law. One of the main factors has been the adoption of a new paradigm of liberalization, privatization, and globalization since 1991, which may be called the post-1991 paradigm. This has seen the ushering in of wide-ranging economic reforms, deregulation, and liberalization.

The birth of the new law was preceded by extensive debate among competition experts, academia, ministry officials, professional institutes, chambers of industry and commerce, and consumer organizations. The competition bill was remitted to a standing committee of parliament that made specific recommendations on the legislation. The government incorporated most of these recommendations before enacting the bill into law.

The new Competition Act is being introduced in a phased manner. Competition advocacy among business people, the public, and members of parliament will precede enforcement of the provisions relating to anti-competitive agreements, abuse of dominance, and combinations regulation. This process is now under way.

The new Competition Act explicitly defines certain practices that prejudice competition, such as cartels and predatory pricing, that are not defined in the outgoing law. Size and dominance are not by themselves regarded as anticompetitive in the new law, but abuse is.

The new law treats combinations regulation somewhat leniently, with fairly high threshold limits for assets and turnover for firms to fall within its ambit. Notification of combinations is voluntary rather than mandatory. This is because Indian enterprises are small in size compared with those in the developed world; they need to be allowed to grow in size to enable them to compete in the global market, subject of course to the caveat that the combination is not having an appreciable adverse effect on competition.

Extraterritorial reach is an important provision in the new law.

To maximize the benefits of competition policy, other areas of government policy (industrial policy, trade policy, financial policy, and so on) need to adhere to competition principles. Indeed, competition policy may be regarded as the fourth cornerstone of the economic framework along with the country's monetary, fiscal, and trade policies.

By and large, the country's post-1991 industrial and trade policies have triggered competition in the market, both in the goods and services sectors. Some countries in South and Southeast Asia are looking at the Indian experience with interest, particularly Malaysia and Singapore, which are themselves in the process of enacting competition legislation.

In the post-1991 regime, M&A activity has increased almost four-fold. This is attributable, among other things, to the government policy of doing away with merger surveillance and regulation after 1991. The large number of M&As has resulted in consolidation of businesses in the same business line. But there has been little or no concentration or competition-distorting threat, except in fast-moving consumer goods industries.

Government policies on FDI metamorphosed from being restrictive in the 1970s to being liberal in the 1980s. Since 1991 India has had a liberal FDI and trade policy regime, and has reformed its capital market and exchange controls. FDI inflows recorded steep increases from 1991 to 1997 and moderate to significant increases from 1999 to 2003. But it would not be correct to attribute the increases solely to liberalization and economic reform; India's macroeconomic fundamentals also explain the phenomenon of increased FDI. The nexus between competition policy and FDI inflows is apparent; there is a correspondence between the industrial growth rate in one year and FDI inflows in the following year. Since 1991, the service and infrastructure sectors have experienced significant FDI inflows and the share of manufacturing sector FDI has gone down. Of late, the pattern of investment shows that FDI is choosing M&As over greenfield investment, the predominant type of FDI prior to the 1991 reforms. This gives cause for concern from a competition perspective, as M&As lead to a reduction in the number of players in the market and result in market concentration.

Pro-poor concerns have an ideological dimension. While the MRTP Commission has given competition law a pro-poor ethos, it is yet to be seen how the Competition Commission of India will implement the new law. Competition law needs to be flexible to meet the needs of the poorer sections of society within the larger framework of the country's goals and objectives. No one ideology or theory will be relevant in achieving this. What is needed above all is pragmatism.

NOTES

1   India adopted a strategy of planned economic development in the early 1950s. The significant developments in government policy-making that occurred over the next few decades are well documented in Bhagwati and Desai (1970), Bhagwati and Srinivasan (1975), and Ahluwalia (1991).

2   The MRTP Act drew heavily on the laws embodied in the Sherman Act and the Clayton Act of the United States; on the Monopolies and Restrictive Practices (Inquiry and Control) Act, 1948, the Resale Prices Act, 1964, and the Restrictive Trade Practices Act, 1964 of the United Kingdom; and on laws enacted in Japan, Canada, and Germany. The US Federal Trade Commission

Act, 1914 as amended in 1938 and the Combines Investigation Act, 1910 of Canada also influenced the drafting of the act.

3   The author was a member of the committee and was also subsequently involved in the preparation of the draft competition law.

4   In addition, one member of the High Level Committee expressed dissent against any competition law being drafted.

5   Based on representations received by the High Level Committee and the government, filed with the Department of Company Affairs, New Delhi.

6   The Competition Act is available at <www.competition-commission-india. nic.in/>.

7   The Supreme Court disposed of two appeals, one relating to ANSAC and the other to Float Glass, on the same day (Supreme Court 2002).

8   As noted earlier, under the new Competition Act 'combinations' includes mergers, amalgamations, acquisitions, and acquisitions of control. For the convenience of the reader, in this section the more familiar expression 'mergers' will be used.

9   See 'Good morning HP!' *SV News Services*, 10 October 2001; 'HP, Compaq merge: Competitive advantages still far off,' *Giga Information Group*, 27 September 2001; and 'Merger to create largest IT company in India,' *Dataquest*, 5 September 2001.

6

Republic of Korea

Seung Wha Chang and Youngjin Jung

1 INTRODUCTION

The Republic of Korea (Korea) is a dynamic society. The country has dealt with a series of political and socioeconomic challenges over the past several decades, and is currently trying to reach the level of economic development of an industrialized country. A useful way of showing how Korea has dealt with the many difficult economic problems it has faced is to review the development of competition law and policy to date. The globalization of the world economy will also require the country to revise its competition law and policy, in balance with related economic policies.

The aim of this chapter is to provide an overview of competition law and competition policy in Korea and analyze their relationship with other important national economic policies. Section 2 provides a historical survey of the country's competition law and policy. Section 3 examines the major components of the law and evaluates how the antitrust authority has actually enforced its provisions in practice. It also highlights elements of the law that have been tailored to Korea's unique economic circumstances. Section 4 focuses on the relationship between competition policy and related economic policies—in particular, industrial policy and trade and investment policy—and gives some case studies. Section 5 discusses Korea's recent expansion of its antitrust jurisdiction beyond its own territory. Section 6 offers some policy suggestions for other Asian developing countries based on the Korean experience with competition policy.

2   THE EVOLUTION OF COMPETITION POLICY IN KOREA

The 1960s and 1970s: The early history of competition policy

In the early 1960s, after serious political turbulence ending in a military coup, Korea's new government launched its first five-year economic development plan.[1] To promote the growth of selected labor-intensive, export-oriented industries, the government provided strong financial and tax incentives for companies engaged in export businesses while enforcing tight control of imports. By the time the second five-year economic development plan came to an end in 1971, the economy was recording annual economic growth of approximately 10 percent.

In the late 1960s, concerned about growing protectionism among major trading partners such as the United States and with the international competitiveness of Korea's labor-intensive light industries under threat from other emerging economies, the government enacted legislation to shift the focus to heavy manufacturing industries. The Industrial Machinery Promotion Act of 1967, Shipbuilding Promotion Act of 1967, Electrical Industry Promotion Act of 1969, Steel Industry Promotion Act of 1970, and Petrochemical Industry Promotion Act of 1970 demonstrated its commitment to developing the heavy manufacturing sector by providing preferential treatment to the industries covered by these laws. The heavy and chemical industry (HCI) drive was formally launched in 1973 and continued well into the late 1970s. The government directed significant financial resources and tax incentives toward this industry, marginalizing labor-intensive light manufacturing industries in the process. It encouraged a handful of companies that had performed well under the first two five-year economic development plans to enter major HCIs selected by the government.

Korea recorded annual growth of 9.6 percent throughout the 1970s, but this high rate of economic growth was attended by deepening macroeconomic imbalances and microeconomic inefficiencies. The first and second oil shocks took a heavy toll on the economy, which was very reliant on foreign raw materials. Excessive investment in equipment and facilities during the HCI drive, a construction boom in the Middle East that increased the money supply in Korea as workers repatriated their earnings, and the government's price support policy for rice led to high levels of inflation that worsened the current account balance. Excessive investment and the persistent government policy throughout the 1960s and 1970s of setting high entry and exit barriers for strategic industrial sectors solidified monopolistic and oligopolistic market structures and caused an inefficient allocation of resources. In fact, the ratio of competitive markets—markets in which the three largest companies in terms of turnover together hold less than a 60 percent share of the total market for the good or service in question—decreased from 40 percent in 1970 to 33 percent in 1981. The selective economic strategy pursued in this era also propelled the formation of the *chaebol*—Korea's family-owned industrial conglomerates, including global giants like Samsung, Hyundai, LG, and SK—further accelerating the concentration of economic power. The share of the 10 largest *chaebol* rose from about 5 percent of GDP at the beginning of the HCI drive to over 10 percent by the end (SaKong 1993: Table A.21).

Against this backdrop, the government believed that to maintain economic growth in an expanding market, it needed to create a more competitive industrial environment. Its first attempts to diffuse criticism of the country's monopolistic and oligopolistic markets were formulated during the course of rapid economic development in the 1960s (KFTC 2001a: Ch. 1). In 1963, the so-called Sambun case stirred a public outcry, leading to a public consensus on the need to contain monopolistic and oligopolistic behavior. This case involved several large corporations producing wheat flour, sugar, and cement for the domestic market who were able to charge three or four times the listed price for goods by sustaining chronic shortages of supply. Not only were they earning excessive profits, they were also practicing widespread tax evasion.

To deal with problems of this type, in 1964 the government announced a draft competition law made up of 29 articles. The law proposed the establishment of a competition law watchdog to regulate prices and contract terms. The Economic and Planning Board—the powerful bureaucratic agency in charge of economic development throughout the 1960s and 1970s—was to be in charge of the new agency. Due to strong objections from business, however, this bill failed even to be placed on the cabinet agenda—a necessary step before it could be referred to the National Assembly. In 1966 the government submitted a new bill in which the competition watchdog would play only an advisory role. As significant a setback as this was, the bill was not even considered by the National Assembly and was automatically discarded when the session ended in June 1967. The government reintroduced the bill in August 1967, but once again it failed in the face of fierce lobbying from business.

In 1968, a National Assembly investigation into the misuse of foreign capital focused public attention on another case of consumer exploitation and excessive profits. Sinjin, a monopolistic automobile manufacturer that had obtained a commercial loan from a foreign entity, was accused of selling its Korona cars in the domestic market at approximately four times the international price.[2] The government seized the opportunity to submit another competition law bill, but this was again rejected by the National Assembly in 1971. This time, business successfully argued that a competition law would be premature at a time when the goal of the Korean economy was to accumulate industrial capital and facilitate the free flow of products to the market.

The early 1970s witnessed widespread inflation caused by a worldwide oversupply of the dollar, the first oil shock, and rampant cartelization around the globe. The government tried hard to stabilize domestic prices by raising exchange rates and domestic oil prices, but this only aggravated price instability. As part of its price stabilization plan, the government once again submitted a bill to the National Assembly proposing a competition law watchdog under the Economic and Planning Board, to be composed of both government and private sector representatives. This bill failed when the president dissolved the National Assembly using his emergency powers in late 1972.

To address the issue of continuing inflation, caused in part by the previous increases in exchange rates, in late 1975 the government enacted the Price Stabilization and Fair Trade Act. Although considerable resources were expended in the former area, the act nevertheless failed to accomplish either of its putative goals of reining in prices and creating fair markets. In late 1979 a series of unprecedented political events took place in Korea, including the assassination of the incumbent president. After the military coup, the ruling elites who formed the new government wanted to project a new vision for Korean society. Bearing in mind the problems caused by the growth-first strategy of the 1960s and 1970s, the government undertook numerous social and economic reforms. These included, notably, the enactment of the Monopoly Regulation and Fair Trade Act (MRFTA) in 1980, to take effect in 1981. This was a considerable achievement considering the fierce lobbying it faced from business and the objections raised by other government agencies also charged with industrial policy. The passage of the MRFTA heralded a new phase in the regulation of monopolistic and oligopolistic behavior and represented a major step on the path to a more balanced and equitable society. The MRFTA garnered overwhelming support from the media and consumer organizations, if not from business.

The early 1980s to 1997: Regulation of economic concentration

Despite the enactment of the MRFTA, which had been intended to control mergers and regulate market-dominating behavior, the economic concentration of the *chaebol* did not abate. Rather, the market share in terms of

Table 6.1   Korea: Statistics on chaebol in the mining and manufacturing sectors, 1985

Chaebol grouping	Share of turnover (%)	Share of employment (%)	Share of value-added (%)	Share of fixed immovable assets (%)	Number of affiliated companies
Top 5	23.0	9.7	18.7	20.4	94
Top 10	30.2	11.7	24.2	27.9	147
Top 15	33.9	14.4	27.3	31.6	190
Top 20	36.4	15.5	29.5	34.4	218
Top 25	38.5	16.6	31.4	36.8	246
Top 30	40.8	17.6	33.1	39.6	270

Source: KDI (1999).

turnover of the 30 largest *chaebol* in the mining and manufacturing sectors increased from 34.1 percent in 1977 to 40.8 percent in 1985 (Table 6.1). The cross-shareholdings and cross-debt guarantees of the *chaebol* continued to expand 'like the tentacles of an octopus' (Lee 1999: 633–4).

By the early 1980s, the public's opinion of the *chaebol* was souring noticeably. The strong, growth-first strategy of the previous two decades had greatly alleviated poverty, and the general public was beginning to take more of an interest in wealth distribution and equity issues. A cross-section of society, from workers to intellectuals, now held the view that the *chaebol* had made their fortunes by virtue of cozy relations with politicians, and by exploiting the Korean people.

The then ruling Democratic Justice Party shared this negative opinion of the conglomerates. In 1987, at a public hearing on economic concentration, the party expressed its view that the *chaebol*'s tentacle-like management practices were fraught with lack of specialization and could bring about a diffusion of capital power leading to a weakening of the financial structure of the *chaebol* (Democratic Justice Party 1987). The expansion of the *chaebol* into all areas of business was hampering the sound growth of small and medium-sized enterprises (SMEs), the bedrock of the Korean economy. The overconcentration of the *chaebol* and their practice of transmitting wealth through inheritance raised questions about their legitimacy and created distrust in the economic system and in politics. Thus the issue of the *chaebol* was not confined to the economic sphere, but had political and social dimensions as well.

In the mid-1980s the Korean economy was faring well with the help of the 'three lows': low interest rates, low oil prices, and a low dollar. In this benign environment, but plagued by questions about its legitimacy, the government took the bold step of instituting a new legal system to regulate the *chaebol*. Chapter 3 of the MRFTA, created in 1986, was entitled 'Regulation of economic concentration' and contained a series of provisions to regulate 'large-scale companies.' These included a limit on holding companies, a ban on (direct) cross-shareholdings, and a ceiling on the total amount of investment that could be carried out by *chaebol*. Because the latter provision greatly restricted the *chaebol*'s entry into new areas of business, they have made unrelenting efforts ever since to have the limit eased or lifted.

These sweeping legislative changes did not alleviate economic concentration. In 1989 the number of *chaebol* with assets of more than W400 billion had risen to 43, 11 more than in 1987. Over the same two-year period the number of *chaebol*-affiliated companies increased from 509 to 673. The total amount of mutual investment among affiliates surged from W3.3 trillion to W16.97 trillion, to account for 28.1 percent of the net asset value of the 43 *chaebol* (*Chosun Daily*, 6 June 1989). The share of total turnover of the 30 largest *chaebol* in the mining and manufacturing sectors was 39.6 percent in 1994—again revealing no sign of a slowdown in economic concentration.

Until the financial crisis of 1997–98, the government continued to tighten its regulations on *chaebol* to address the problem of unrelenting economic concentration. In 1992, a provision tightening the restrictions on debt guarantees among *chaebol* affiliates was promulgated, to prevent them from excessive debt financing that might undermine their financial structure. In 1996, a new provision was added to the MRFTA to curb inside transactions among affiliated companies that were not based on arm's-length valuations. None of these attempts to stem the tide of economic concentration met with much success, however.

1997 to the present: Economic restructuring and competition policy

In the face of the intense turmoil brought about by the financial crisis of 1997–98, and under pressure from the International Monetary Fund (IMF), the government amended the MRFTA to facilitate economic and corporate restructuring. It abolished (but later reinstated) the limit on the total amount of investment, flatly prohibited debt guarantees among affiliated companies, and lifted the restriction on holding companies, though with strict conditions.

There is a strongly held view that the *chaebol* were the main cause of the financial crisis in Korea, leading to IMF supervision. The economy has rebounded nicely since 1999, but the question of how to view and deal with the *chaebol* is still clouded in controversy and awaits further research (Graham 2003). Whether or not they were the main culprit in the crisis, the *chaebol* remain at the heart of the Korean economy. The top 30 *chaebol* are engaged in businesses spread across 20 or so major industries and have more than 600 affiliates. Their total assets comprise over 45 percent of all corporate assets in Korea (Hwang and Seo 2000).

The government now appears to take the view that economic concentration is closely related to issues of corporate governance, and that regulation of economic concentration under the MRFTA should therefore give way in future to regulation under general commercial law. In early 2004 it announced an ambitious 'roadmap for market reform' under which it would lift most of the restrictions relating to economic concentration once certain conditions, such as transparency in corporate governance, were met.

3   AN OVERVIEW OF KOREA'S COMPETITION LAW[3]

Major components of competition law

The MRFTA

The MRFTA encompasses all the traditional aspects of competition policy that are the subject of competition law in other countries, such as anticompetitive mergers, cartels, resale price maintenance, monopolization, exclusion, and exclusive transactions. In addition it addresses unfair trade practices, undue subsidies, debt guarantees, and equity investment among *chaebol* affiliates.

Article 1 of the MRFTA defines its purpose as being

> to promote fair and free competition, to thereby encourage creative enterprising activities, to protect consumers, and to strive for balanced development of the national economy by preventing the abuse of market-dominating positions by enterprises and the excessive concentration of economic power, and by regulating undue collaborative acts and unfair trade practices.

Therefore, Korean competition law can be said to pursue multiple objectives in addition to the promotion of economic efficiency, which is the primary concern of US antitrust law.[4]

Certain provisions in the MRFTA can sensibly be explained only when one assumes that the act pursues diverse social goals. For instance, the Korea Fair Trade Commission (KFTC)—the government agency established under the MRFTA to enforce its provisions—has dealt with unfair trade practices in a way that protects economically weaker enterprises, indicating that maximizing economic efficiency is not its sole objective. An examination of the guidelines it has promulgated on specific sectors confirms this view. The diverse values the MRFTA embraces are also apparent in the act's exceptions and exemptions from antitrust disciplines. A clause in the cartel regulations, for example, exempts collaborative behavior designed to enhance the competitiveness of SMEs.

The most glaring example of the MRFTA's non-efficiency-oriented goals is the set of provisions on the concentration of economic power in Chapter 3 of the act. The chapter addresses the pathologies supposedly emanating from the *chaebol,* such as undue subsidies, debt guarantees, and equity investment among affiliates. The act also contains a provision to ensure arm's-length transactions among the affiliates of large business groups. In short, it can be argued that the MRFTA has broad objectives that go beyond its putative goals of promoting economic efficiency and maximizing consumer welfare.

Other legislation

Many other laws make up Korean competition law in the broader sense. For instance, both the Telecommunications Business Act and the Act on the Structural Improvement of the Financial Industry contain provisions to regulate merger and acquisition (M&A) activity in the telecommunications and financial industries. The Unfair Competition Prevention Act of 1961 regulates competition in the area of intellectual property, especially trademarks.[5] And the Consumer Protection Act of 1979 provides for a Consumer Protection Agency to enforce its provisions.

In addition to enforcing the MRFTA, the KFTC is the enforcement agency for several companion statutes governing specific areas of antitrust concern. The commission devotes significant resources to administering these laws, so it is worth looking more closely at how they are enforced.

The *Adhesion Contract Act* aims to eliminate biased contracts, written and circulated by businesses, that preclude the consumer's right to choose the terms of a transaction. It requires businesses to issue formal contracts and explain their terms to consumers, and invalidates clauses that unduly infringe on consumers' rights.

The goal of the *Fair Labeling and Advertising Act* is to ensure that consumers are given accurate information that enables them to make informed choices. It requires firms to withdraw and correct false representations and misleading advertising and to disclose all information that could be considered relevant to consumer decision-making. In addition, firms may be ordered to hand over evidential material.

The *Door-to-Door Sales Act* aims to protect consumers and secure a smooth flow of goods and services in the trouble-prone area of door-to-door sales and pyramid selling schemes. It requires pyramid businesses to purchase consumer compensation insurance or subscribe to a cooperative; to educate their sales force on illegal sales activities; and to allow buyers of their products to withdraw unconditionally from contracts within 14 days of purchase.

The *Installment Transactions Act* recognizes the consumer's right to withdraw from a contract within seven days of purchasing a product on an installment plan. It requires businesses to give consumers advance notice of 14 days or more when a contract is being terminated due to consumer default. It also invalidates contract clauses that unfairly disadvantage consumers.

The *Fair Subcontract Transactions Act* aims to establish fair subcontracting practices and create a competitive environment for small and medium-sized subcontractors. It prohibits large companies from unduly reducing payments to subcontractors, bans them from refusing to accept returned goods, and requires them to pay their subcontractors within 60 days, with interest to be paid after this set period. The act also contains other regulations to protect subcontractors from unfair actions by large companies during the transaction process.

The *Fair Franchise Transactions Act* aims to establish a fair trade system for franchise businesses and ensure the mutually beneficial and balanced development of franchisers and franchisees. The law bans various kinds of unfair transactions in franchise operations and defines the basic rules governing the relationship between franchiser and franchisee. It requires franchisers to provide up-to-date and correct information to their franchisees, bans the use of false or exaggerated information, obligates the parties to a franchise to return franchise fees under certain conditions, and sets rules for the issuance of franchise contracts.

The Omnibus Cartel Repeal Act

Drawn up to conform with the 1998 recommendations on hard-core cartels of the Organisation for Economic Co-operation and Development, the Omnibus Cartel Repeal Act was enacted in February 1999. It abolished the formation of cartels by eight categories of certified professionals, including lawyers, accountants, customs officers, patent lawyers, architects, and veterinarians. It also revised the collective optional contract system for SME products, under which collusive behavior by SMEs in government purchasing was allowed. In all, the act revised around 20 regulations that had previously been impeding market competition. The passage of the legislation indicated that the KFTC had formally begun to exercise its competition advocacy role in Korea.

A KFTC study shows that professional fees and commissions have stayed the same or decreased since the implementation of the Omnibus Cartel Repeal Act (KFTC 2001b). After the prevailing compensation standard was abrogated, price competition started to take effect and in time a new, more appropriate price level was reached in the professions. The Consumer Protection Agency has tried to ensure that consumers have access to the information they need to determine appropriate fee levels for professional services, and to select the services that best meet their needs.

The differential between professional fees for similar tasks has also lessened, with a tendency for fees to level out at the lower end of the spectrum (KFTC 2001b). Nevertheless, the differences between fees for similar tasks can be huge, with the highest price charged ranging from 3.3 to 50 times the lowest price charged. Not only has increasing price competition resulted in an overall decrease in fees, but there has been a tendency for fees to converge at the average price due to increases in the lowest fees and decreases in the highest (Table 6.2). The exception is attorneys' fees, where the prices of the most expensive services have gone up, increasing the gap between the lowest and highest fees charged for similar tasks: the highest fees were between 14.5 and 30 times the lowest fees charged in 2001.

As one might expect, professional fees for similar services differ according to location, indicating that prices are formed naturally through supply and demand. The Seoul region, where demand for professional services is greatest, records the highest prices, and this is where the most highly paid professionals are found. The difference between the highest and lowest fees charged for similar tasks is also greatest in Seoul.

Competition policy in practice

The functions of the Korea Fair Trade Commission

The KFTC is the principal government agency in charge of enforcing the MRFTA. It operates at a ministerial level under the umbrella of the Prime Minister's Office and functions as a quasi-judiciary body. The KFTC con-

Table 6.2   Korea: Fees charged by certified professionals by type of case, 1999–2001 (W10,000)

Type of case	Fee level (average)				Direction since Dec 2000
	Oct 1999	Jun 2000	Dec 2000	2001	
Lawyers					
Contract-related cases	447	429	391	387	Down
Tort cases	518	485	458	405	Down
Assault cases	462	404	387	391	Up
Traffic incidents	445	485	448	378	Down
Divorce cases	411	369	350	364	Up
CPA					
Audits of individuals' financial statements	423	404	412	385	Down
Accounting assessments & certifications	118	155	131	121	Down
Cost calculations	210	264	220	157	Down

Source: KFTC (2001b).

sists of a committee made up of nine members (the decision-making body) and a secretariat (the working body). It has more than 400 employees and a budget of over W250 billion (Table 6.3). The role of the courts in enforcing competition law in Korea is relatively limited because the system of private lawsuits does not allow for treble damages, class actions, or effective pre-trial discovery processes as in the United States. Administrative proceedings by the KFTC therefore play a central role in the enforcement of the act.

About 80–90 percent of the tasks performed by the KFTC are the traditional ones of cartel regulation, business combination reviews, regulation of abuse of market dominance, and monitoring of unfair trade practices. In addition, as mentioned earlier, the KFTC pursues policies dealing with economic concentration. The regulations set out in Chapter 3 of the MRFTA differ from traditional competition law in that they apply

Table 6.3   Korea: KFTC staffing and budget levels, 1993–2003

	Staff (no. of people)[a]	Budget (W100 million)
1993	254	64
1994	279	80
1995	341	405
1996	381	146
1997	403	184
1998	410	160
1999	402	172
2000	401	193
2001	416	220
2002	416	252
2003	416	

a   Office staff only.

Source: KFTC (2003a).

without regard to the concept of a relevant market—the cardinal element of competition policy in most jurisdictions. The philosophy that financial capital must be kept separate from industrial capital in order to prevent the *chaebol* from dominating the national economy is also reflected in the provisions of the MRFTA (Lee 2003).

Apart from its unique authority to deal with general concentration of ownership, the KFTC is endowed with the capability to conduct competition advocacy among other government agencies. As competition advocate, it seeks to prevent laws and regulations that would restrict competition from being enacted and to have existing regulations that impede competition removed. It does this by consulting with other government agencies to identify anticompetitive regulations and suggesting possible remedies to the Regulatory Reform Committee in the Prime Minister's Office. In 2000, the KFTC considered 481 cases of legislation brought to it for prior consultation. The agency is also consulted on the privatization of state-owned enterprises, where its job is to devise measures to facilitate competition during the privatization process, so that public monopolies are not simply transformed into private monopolies.

In light of the foregoing discussion, it is apparent that concerns may legitimately be raised about the conflict between the KFTC's extensive powers—over the *chaebol* in particular—and its traditional antitrust mandate, which would normally require it to pursue an efficiency maximization policy. Although there is a need to restrain the *chaebol* from abusing market-dominant positions in certain markets, it is difficult to justify a strict anti-*chaebol* policy that might decrease consumer welfare. This is even more the case in the present global economy, where the *chaebol* themselves face strong competition from foreign companies that are not bound by the same disciplines.

Enforcement of competition law

As mentioned, private lawsuits based on MRFTA provisions are rare because aggrieved individuals can file a suit before the courts only after the KFTC has been given the opportunity to take corrective action against the company concerned. Individuals could conceivably lodge a tort claim under the Civil Code, but due to the difficulty of gathering evidence this would be a rare occurrence. The prosecutor's office also plays a very limited role in enforcing the MRFTA because, in most cases, it can prosecute offenders only if the KFTC has referred the matter to it. It is therefore safe to say that the KFTC plays the dominant role in enforcing the MRFTA. In this sense, Korea's competition regime is closer to the European system than to the American system: in Europe administrative agencies play a central role in enforcement whereas in the United States multiple actors are involved in the enforcement of antitrust law. Moreover, the courts have a much greater role to play in the United States than in Korea.

To enhance the role of individuals in the enforcement of antitrust law, a new legislative bill was introduced recently to allow aggrieved individuals to file damage claims with the courts without waiting for the KFTC to finalize its proceedings. The government expects this and some other, yet to be announced, improvements to the system to spur an increase in the number of private lawsuits in Korea. On the other hand, an increasing number of enterprises have been challenging the corrective measures imposed on them by bringing administrative suits before the Seoul High Court, which exercises exclusive jurisdiction over administrative antitrust suits. About 40 such cases have been filed annually over the past several years.

A study of the KFTC's enforcement history reveals that it has tended to emphasize behavioral regulation over structural regulation. In particular, it has expended a great deal of resources on regulating unfair trade practices to correct imbalances in markets in which the parties have an unequal position. This interest of the KFTC can be attributed in part to the strong legacy of the industrial policies of the 1980s (Sung and Shin 2001). During the period 1981–2000, the KFTC issued a total of 5,521 corrective notices in connection with unfair trade practices, including cases of resale price maintenance. Most of these involved issues of vertical restraint arising from transactions between manufacturers, wholesale dealers, and retailers. Between 1981 and 1992, the KFTC issued only 94 corrective notices in connection with violations of cartel regulations. However, from 1993 to 2000 it markedly stepped up its level of enforcement, imposing as many as 238 corrective notices in connection with collusive behavior—a coveted record even compared with that of developed countries. In respect of merger controls, one of the premier structural instruments, the KFTC has only a meager record of enforcement. During the 20 years from 1981 to 2000, it issued corrective measures in only 12 cases. Despite some positive signs in recent years, out of 600 or so corporate combination filings recorded each year in 2001, 2002, and 2003, the KFTC has taken corrective action only in a very small number of cases.

Arguably the primary legal instrument to deal with Korea's entrenched monopolistic and oligopolistic market conditions is a set of MRFTA provisions on abuse of a market dominant position. Following the European model, the MRFTA does not provide for specific structural remedies with respect to enterprises that have a monopoly or near-monopoly position; it simply prohibits them from 'abusing' their market dominance. Although the KFTC can act only when individual cases of alleged abuse are filed with it, these provisions may well have played a proactive role in diffusing monopolistic and oligopolistic market tendencies. In 1996 the KFTC was given a new enforcement power that allowed it to initiate action to promote competition in markets in which monopolies or oligopolies had existed for an extended period of time. This new initiative, which has the flavor of a 'general' structural remedy, has fared well. The KFTC has conducted a series of thorough investigations into areas where an egregious monopolistic or oligopolistic market had existed for a lengthy period of time—such as automobiles, tires, steel, beer, and air-conditioners—and has taken the action necessary to repair the situation (KFTC 2001a).

Recently, the KFTC has expended greater resources on the regulation of cartels and mergers, both domestic and international. In view of the difficulty of detecting cartels and gathering evidence, the KFTC has tried to increase the effectiveness of enforcement by relying actively on a 'leniency program' under which those who report cartel-like behavior or who cooperate with official investigations are subject to lighter corrective measures. In 2002, for the first time, the KFTC applied the MRFTA extraterritorially. It imposed a $9.2 million surcharge on an international cartel in graphite electrodes, a decision that was later upheld by the Seoul High Court. Soon after, in 2003, the KFTC imposed a $3.3 million surcharge on the foreign companies involved in an international vitamin cartel. These cases are discussed in more detail in section 5 below.

The KFTC has also redoubled its efforts to strengthen its merger regulations. In 1998 it released detailed guidelines on all types of merger-related transactions—horizontal, vertical, and conglomerate—modeled on the US Horizontal Merger Guidelines. In 2000 the guidelines were applied to the case of a merger between Korea's largest mobile telecommunications company, SK Telecom, and the third-largest company, Shinsegae Telecom. The resulting behemoth would have held a 56.9 percent share of the mobile phone market. The parties to the merger argued that the takeover would improve efficiency by expediting the development of the information networking and communications industry. Based on an assessment of the proposal under the strict new guidelines, however, the KFTC ruled the merger to be anticompetitive. It nevertheless allowed the merger to proceed after ordering a corrective measure to ensure that the combined entity would have a market share of no more than 50 percent.[6] The KFTC is increasingly resorting to this technique of conditional approval—approval issued on the fulfillment of certain conditions, such as that the parties eliminate certain business divisions or operations—to 'surgically' remove the anticompetitive effects of a transaction.

Transnational M&A activities are increasingly affecting the domestic market. In recognition of this, in 2003 the KFTC announced the introduction of a notification threshold for M&As between foreign companies. One foreign company has already reportedly been fined for failing to make such a notification to the KFTC (Ahn and Jung 2004).

The KFTC has a unique set of tools to alleviate the evidentiary difficulties in enforcing the MRFTA. The three so-called statutory presumption provisions apply in the context of identifying market-dominant enterprises, determining substantial restraint of competition resulting from mergers, and identifying collusive behavior that restrains competition. A great deal of controversy has arisen over the provision on collusive behavior, in particular concerning whether it obviates the need to investigate 'plus factors' in cases of 'conscious parallelism' (Gavil, Kovacic, and Baker 2002: 255–6), that is, synchronous action that is a product of a rational, independent calculus by each member of the oligopoly, as opposed to collusion.[7] Recently the Supreme Court confirmed that it is necessary to show a plus factor in interpreting the presumption provision on collusive behavior. This could be viewed as at least a technical victory for the KFTC in cartel enforcement.[8]

Another of the extraordinary powers of the KFTC concerns the collection of evidence from financial institutions. To facilitate the investigation of internal transactions among *chaebol* affiliates with respect to funds, assets, and personnel, the KFTC has the power to ask their financial institutions to provide relevant financial information.

Finally, it would be remiss not to stress the importance of administrative surcharges in ensuring compliance with the law. Surcharges are being imposed in an increasing number of cases of anticompetitive behavior, and the ceiling on these surcharges is rising. Moreover, the KFTC is able to impose administrative surcharges without resort to the courts. This unique enforcement tool is considered very effective, mostly due to the size of the surcharges; from April 2005 companies taking part in cartels may be subject to surcharges amounting to as much as 10 percent of their total sales volume. Although strong and effective as an enforcement tool, the surcharge system also faces criticism because of the KFTC's overly wide discretion in setting the amount of the surcharges.

All countries maintain articles of law that partially or entirely exempt certain sectors from the application of competition law. Common examples are utility industries such as telecommunications and electricity, which are often government owned or regulated in the belief that they have natural monopolistic aspects. In Korea, the range of such exemptions is gradually being reduced as regulatory and technological developments in areas where corporations had previously enjoyed a monopoly position have increased the scope for competition. In recent years, the KFTC has attached special emphasis to diffusing monopolistic and oligopolistic structures in markets where public enterprises are dominant (KFTC 2001a).

Market concentration

In general, the liberalization policy undertaken since 1980 has not significantly improved Korea's market concentration ratios. In the midst of the financial crisis of 1997–98 concentration increased, but since 1999 the general, industrial, and market concentration ratios have again declined (Tables 6.4–6.6). Despite the overall fall in concentration in the mining and manufacturing sectors, which together account for about 30 percent of GDP, concentration ratios in some other leading industries and products remain very high—especially when compared with similar ratios in countries such as Japan and the United States (Table 6.7).

Table 6.4 Korea: General concentration ratio, 1981–2001 (%)[a]

Companies	1981	1990	1995	1996	1997	1998	1999	2000	2001
Production									
Top 50	36.6	30.0	33.6	34.4	37.1	38.4	38.0	38.1	36.8
Top 100	46.1	37.7	40.4	41.2	44.2	45.9	45.1	44.8	43.7
Employment									
Top 50	12.4	13.6	14.5	15.2	16.5	16.6	14.7	13.9	13.2
Top 100	19.1	18.4	18.2	18.8	20.1	20.1	18.1	17.0	16.0

a The general concentration ratio is defined as the share of total mining and manufacturing sector sales/employment accounted for by the country's 50/100 largest mining and manufacturing companies.

Source: KFTC (2003b).

Table 6.5 Korea: Three-firm industrial concentration ratio, 1980–2001[a]

	1980	1990	1995	1997	1998	1999	2000	2001
CR3 (%)								
Simple average	62.4	52.8	47.8	48.6	50.0	45.4	44.0	43.4
Weighted average	55.1	52.6	49.8	51.7	53.6	54.2	52.5	51.5
HHI								
Simple average	263.8	221.3	173.4	179.4	190.5	158.6	152.5	153.1
Weighted average	180.6	187.8	165.4	177.8	188.0	194.5	183.5	182.1

CR3 = three-firm concentration ratio; HHI = Herfindahl–Hirschman index.

a Covers companies in the five-digit Standard Industrial Classification. In 2001, there were 491 such companies.

Source: KFTC (2003b).

Table 6.6   Korea: Three-firm market concentration ratio, 1980–2001[a]

	1980	1990	1996	1998	1999	2000	2001
CR3 (%)							
Simple average	81.7	73.9	71.5	73.0	72.5	69.9	68.0
Weighted average	67.1	62.6	63.2	67.3	67.1	65.6	64.0
HHI							
Simple average	473	393	369.7	388	389	357	331
Weighted average	288	262	256.6	289	295	285	267

CR3 = three-firm concentration ratio; HHI = Herfindahl–Hirschman index.

a   Covers companies in the eight-digit Standard Industrial Classification. In 2001, there were 3,056 such companies.

Source: KFTC (2003b).

4   COMPETITION POLICY AS IT AFFECTS OTHER ECONOMIC POLICIES

Competition policy and industrial policy

Whether competition policy should prevail over industrial policy or vice versa has been a controversial question. Mainstream economic theory suggests that microeconomic industrial policies focusing on selected industries are largely ineffective; countries should therefore place more emphasis on maintaining macroeconomic stability, which will lead to virtuous circles of high rates of accumulation, efficient allocation of resources, and strong productivity growth (World Bank 1993: Ch. 3). A more recent study by Noland and Pack (2003) provides further evidence for this view.

Mainstream economic theory exhorts developing countries not to engage in the artificial allocation of resources as they carry out selective industrial policies that are likely to impede competition in a given field. A series of empirical studies on Korea's HCI drive of the 1970s, for example, concludes that the HCI policy led to distortions in the allocation of economic resources, resulting in excess capacity in favored sectors and contributing to inflation and the accumulation of foreign debt (Kim 1990; Yoo 1990). The KFTC itself appears to hold the firm belief that competi-

Table 6.7   Korea: Comparison with concentration in Japan and the United States

	Japan		Korea	
	1999	2000	1999	2000
Simple average				
CR3 (%)	71.6	72.0	72.5	69.9
HHI	264.6	269.3	389.0	357.0
	United States (1997)		Korea (2001)	
CR4 (%)	42.8		48.6	
HHI	75.8		149.3	

CR3 = three-firm concentration ratio; CR4 = four-firm concentration ratio; HHI = Herfindahl–Hirschman index.

Source: KFTC (2003b).

tion principles should be put into operation from an early stage of economic development; it has averred that industrial policies that constrain competition will lead to inefficient operations characterized by excessive investment in facilities, and to higher prices for consumers (KFTC 2001c).

Not all scholars agree with this view, however. Laffont (1998), for instance, has argued that 'it is not always the case that competition should be encouraged in developing countries.' He reasons that

> competition is an unambiguously good thing in the first-best world of economists. That world assumes large numbers of participants in all markets, no public goods, no externalities, no information asymmetries, no natural monopolies, complete markets, fully rational economic agents, a benevolent court system to enforce contracts, and a benevolent government providing lump sum transfers to achieve any desirable redistribution.

In his view, since developing countries lack most of these conditions, they may legitimately turn to industrial policies as a second-best solution.

These 'revisionist' scholars opine that 'the more competition the better' is not always an optimal policy (Telser 1987; Amsden and Singh

1994b). Singh (2003), for example, argues that higher rates of investment bring about greater *dynamic efficiency* as opposed to *static efficiency*, leading to long-term gains in growth and productivity. Governments therefore need to concentrate their efforts on creating a business environment that encourages investment. In his view, restricting competition in the market to ensure a reasonable as well as stable rate of profits is one means of making sure that firms' incentives to invest are not dampened. Referring specifically to Korea and Japan, he argues that competition law should be subordinated to the requirements of industrial policy.

Given the dearth of comprehensive empirical studies, it is difficult to determine which of these contrasting views is correct. Indeed, it may be absurd to make definitive judgments based on theory alone without looking at the specific circumstances facing individual economies. Of course, nobody knows what actually would have happened in Korea if the government had taken a different tack—for example by adopting a strong and comprehensive competition policy at an early stage of economic development. Nonetheless, one lesson we can draw from the Korean experience is that governments that adopt industrial policy tools that serve to create monopolistic market structures in the domestic market—whether intentionally or unintentionally—will most likely pay a price later on. Whether any countervailing benefits can be obtained is another question entirely, with the answer depending on many other economic variables.

Another important dimension for evaluating industrial policy in its relationship to competition policy is the surrounding environment. From the 1960s to the 1980s, when economic development in Korea was accelerating, no international disciplines existed to prevent trade or competition distortions resulting from the industrial policies of individual countries, in particular developing countries. The reality facing developing countries today is very different. The present World Trade Organization (WTO) subsidy rules have major implications for internal economic policy-making and provide standards for judging the legality of certain governmental measures, in particular industrial policy tools. Accordingly, measures that have a distortionary effect on international trade and competition are simply illegal, and may face legal challenge from other WTO members. Industrial measures that distort the domestic market (such as subsidies) may under certain circumstances also be contrary to WTO rules. Given this change in the international legal environment, countries that adopted the Korean model for economic development would very likely violate international rules.

Nevertheless, industrial policies are not illegal per se. It is possible to develop a good and effective industrial policy in harmony with competition policy, and thereby promote the national economy, without facing the risk of violating international norms. In the age of the 'new economy'—as opposed to a smoke-stack industrial economy—innovation and knowledge-based intellectual property issues come to the fore; concomitantly there is an increasing need to develop competition policy that takes greater account of the need for dynamic as well as static efficiency (Posner 2001b).[9] This allows some room for industrial policy interventions.

At least one ministry in the Korean government appears to take such a view: the Ministry of Commerce, Industry, and Energy has sought to formulate industrial policies that are in harmony with competition policy (Kim 2003). Cognizant of the limitations of the quantitative, selective industrial policies pursued during the period of rapid industrialization, the ministry is now striving to put more emphasis on qualitative, research and development (R&D)-focused industrial policies. First, as already stated, the advent of the WTO system has significantly reduced the room for industrial policy, and the provision of financial support for specific strategic industries is now very likely to violate WTO subsidy rules. Second, due to changes in the economic environment, investment-driven growth strategies are not as effective as they once were.

Economic growth rates in Korea have been declining steadily—from 7.8 percent in the 1980s to 6.6 percent in the first half of the 1990s to 6.0 percent in the latter part of the decade. In an attempt to halt this decline, the government has adopted a new strategy of innovation-driven growth. The goal is to increase total factor productivity in 10 selected new economy industries with considerable potential for growth, including digital television and broadcasting, liquid crystal displays, and artificial intelligence. To the extent that this new policy aims to build the general foundation for a competitive market environment by encouraging the R&D efforts of several industries chosen according to objective criteria, it would not necessarily conflict with competition policy or with the WTO's subsidy rules.

The case study of the broadband internet market presented in Box 6.1 shows how such a policy might work in practice. The phenomenal success of Korea's broadband internet market can be attributed to the government's skillful blend of industrial and competition policy. This case demonstrates that the two should not be viewed as being inherently in conflict—a good combination of policies can be effective in accomplishing policy goals for the national economy as a whole.

Maximizing the benefits of trade and FDI reform

As an active participant in successive General Agreement on Tariffs and Trade/WTO negotiations on trade, the Korean government has made

Box 6.1 A case study of the broadband internet market

In July 1998 Thrunet, currently the third-largest internet service provider (ISP) in terms of number of subscribers, launched Korea's first broadband internet services. It was followed by Hanaro Telecom (the second-largest ISP) in April 1999 and by KT (the largest ISP and former state enterprise) in December 1999. The ISPs offer two types of broadband internet connection: digital subscriber line—usually asynchronous digital subscriber line (ADSL)—and cable modem. ADSL uses existing copper telephone lines or optical fiber networks while cable modems employ a dedicated hybrid fiber coaxial (HFC) network.

Initially ISPs relied on HFC networks to deliver broadband internet services, and thus the overwhelming majority of subscribers were connected through cable modems. However, since KT entered the market and began competing with Hanaro Telecom for the top spot in the broadband market, ADSL use has soared. By January 2001 there were more ADSL subscribers than cable modem subscribers. As of October 2001, 56.8 percent of users were connected through ADSL, 34.9 percent through cable modems, and 7.8 percent through local area networks (LANs) (Table 6.8). This distinguishes Korea from other nations, where cable modems and HFC networks are more common.

KT provides ADSL services over existing copper telephone lines and does not own an HFC network at all. Hanaro Telecom, on the other hand, provides ADSL services over an optical fiber network that it laid itself, and cable modem services mainly through an HFC network that it leases from Powercomm. Demand from users for each type of connection is roughly

Table 6.8   Korea: Size of ISPs by connection type offered, October 2001 (no. of subscribers)

	KT	Hanaro Telecom	Thrunet	Dream-line
ADSL	3,068,511	946,871	1,558	102,244
Cable modem	–	927,487	1,215,349	77,912
LAN	487,956	6,435	–	–
B-WILL	11,532	–	–	–
Satellite	1,018	28,010	–	–
Total	3,569,017	1,908,803	1,216,907	180,156

ADSL = asynchronous digital subscriber line; LAN = local area network; B-WILL = broadband wireless local loop.

equal. Thrunet and the other ISPs mainly—or exclusively—rely on HFC networks and cable modems.

Although some ISPs own their own HFC networks, most lease them from Powercomm. It was a division of Korea Electric Power Corporation until January 2001, and originally built its HFC network for use by system operators and cable TV program providers. Approximately 60 percent of the internet services provided by Korean ISPs as of March 2002 were delivered over HFC networks leased from Powercomm (Table 6.9). Under its basic telecommunications services license, however, Powercomm itself is prevented from offering broadband internet services to end users. In addition to Powercomm, which owns about 48,000 kilometers of the country's HFC networks, another 100 or so local cable TV companies own smaller HFC networks that they sometimes lease out.

The high penetration of broadband in Korea owes much to the quality of infrastructure. The availability of HFC networks has allowed ISPs to provide broadband internet services without having to gain access to KT's telephone lines, with all the problems that would entail.

Even before the formation of a broadband internet market, the government encouraged the building of high-capacity, high-speed backbone and core networks, both within and between cities. To alleviate the cost burden, it made low-interest loans available for the two years from 1999 to 2001. It also provided R&D funding to the companies intending to build the networks; implemented a certification scheme for broadband facilities installed in apartment blocks;[10] and introduced an internet service quality evaluation system in an attempt to improve service quality and protect users.

Table 6.8 (continued)

Onse Telecom	Dacom	SK Telecom	Total (no.)	(%)
–	–	–	4,119,184	56.8
201,490	52,846	57,757	2,532,841	34.9
–	71,199	–	565,590	7.8
–	–	–	11,532	0.2
–	–	–	29,028	0.4
201,490	124,045	57,757	7,258,175	100.0

a   HFC networks are subsumed under ADSL or cable modem.

Source: Ministry of Information and Communication.

Table 6.9   Korea: ISPs' use of Powercomm's HFC network, March 2002

	Thrunet	Hanaro Telecom	Onse Telecom	Other	Total
Total number of subscribers	1,407,333	1,392,413	294,717	147,090	3,241,553
Subscribers using Powercomm's HFC network					
(no.)	672,450	956,797	286,143	25,797	1,939,044
(%)	48.0	68.7	96.3	17.5	59.8

Source: Ministry of Information and Communication.

These industrial policy measures were supported by measures to foster competition among ISPs. The government classified broadband internet services as a value-added telecommunications service under the Telecommunications Business Act, thus allowing existing providers of basic telecommunications services to offer internet services without first having to obtain an additional permit or license. New market entrants, meanwhile, only had to file a simple report with the regulators. As a result of this relaxed policy, broadband internet access became available at the competitive price of about W30,000–43,000 ($25–35) per month, encouraging dial-up users to switch to broadband.

The development strategy adopted by the government can be called 'facilities-based competition.' Unlike most other nations, where local loop unbundling has preceded retail competition in the telecommunications market, Korea encouraged the early providers, Thrunet and Hanaro Telecom, to establish their own facilities, including their own local networks. In part this was possible because Thrunet and Hanaro Telecom were able to reinvest their profits in facilities and networks and establish a presence in the broadband market before the arrival of the telecommunications heavyweight, KT.

Although facilities-based competition initially stimulated broadband penetration, it also created problems. First, basic telecommunications service providers were denied access to KT's local networks; new entrants such as Dreamline, Onse Telecom, Dacom, and SK Telecom could not use Powercomm's HFC networks either. Second, ISPs have tended to concentrate their investments in highly populated areas. When more than one ISP has invested in the same area, this has led to an unnecessary dissipation of capital. Third, some basic telecommunications service providers have run into financial difficulties because of the heavy capital requirements of network building and marketing. Fourth, although it entered the market after Thrunet and Hanaro Telecom, KT soon occupied a dominant position in the market because it could use its existing network to provide broadband internet services. Its market share was approaching 50 percent by the time local loop unbundling was implemented, a level that threatened fair competition. Finally, users in non-metropolitan areas, including small and medium-sized cities, have been disadvantaged by a lack of high-quality internet services because, under facilities-based competition, the cost to ISPs of providing such services has outweighed the benefits.

To alleviate these problems and create a fairer competitive environment, the regulators introduced local loop unbundling in April 2002.[11] However, With KT dragging its heels on providing access to its copper telephone network, this has been proceeding only slowly. In fact, on 27 February 2003 the Korea Communications Commission, a subagency of the Ministry of Information and Communication, fined KT W2 billion for refusing to give Hanaro Telecom access to its local loop, and issued a corrective order against the company.

Korea has acquired world-class broadband internet services through a successful combination of industrial and competition policy. From the start, the Ministry of Information and Communication aggressively pursued industrial policy in the sector, but without stifling competition. It fostered competition in the market by lowering entry barriers and intervening to prevent KT from gaining too much of a competitive edge. It also adopted a local loop unbundling strategy to address concerns about unfair competition. The success of the government's broadband internet strategy is apparent in the penetration ratio: according to data provided by the Ministry of Information and Communication, in June 2001 Korea had 6.5 million broadband subscribers (13.9 percent of the entire population), rising to 7.3 million (15.3 percent of the population) in October 2001.

What can we learn from this example? At an early stage of development, the government recognized the need for fundamental infrastructure. As an industrial policy measure, it required market entrants to install their own facilities while helping to create the market conditions that would make this affordable. Later, after sufficient facilities had been set up throughout Korea, the government changed tack and began to enforce an 'essential facilities' doctrine that rested on local loop unbundling. This enabled new entrants to secure a foothold in an established market on a competitive basis. This demonstrates that under certain circumstances industrial policy can function alongside competition policy to achieve an ultimate economic policy goal, without producing undesirable side effects from a competition policy perspective.

efforts to liberalize trade, especially since the 1980s. In the aftermath of the 1997–98 financial crisis, it redoubled its efforts. The simple average bound tariff rate fell from 24.4 percent in 1997 to 18.5 percent in 2000, while the applied tariff rate fell from 13.4 percent to 8.8 percent. In the context of its post-crisis agreement with the IMF and its Uruguay Round commitments, the government removed quantitative restrictions on the eight remaining items subject to balance-of-payments protection as of 1 January 2001. The import diversification system, implemented in 1978 to restrict imports from Japan (and harshly criticized as constituting an unfair trade practice), was abolished in June 1999. Export subsidies and vague import-licensing and certification procedures that were alleged to distort international trade have also been discarded (Lee, Kim, and Choi 2004).

Economic theory suggests that trade liberalization will increase national welfare in a competitive domestic market. However, there is less consensus on whether it will bring about an increase in national welfare when the domestic market is not competitive. In the case of Korea, where the domestic market is not large enough to realize economies of scale and where various trade protection measures have distorted the market and prevented domestic companies from operating in an efficient manner, research shows that trade liberalization is likely to have a 'rationalization effect' by making inefficient firms exit. The remaining firms would then be more likely to benefit from economies of scale. Trade liberalization does not automatically lead to a more competitive domestic market, however, and the best outcomes are achieved when liberalization is accompanied by measures to increase competition in the domestic market.

As with trade, the government gradually liberalized investment in services in the 1980s and early 1990s, then instituted sweeping liberalization measures in the aftermath of the financial crisis. It eliminated ceilings on foreign equity ownership in the stockmarket, relaxed the rules on cross-border M&As, and fully liberalized foreign land ownership. Foreign direct investment (FDI) increased by 69 percent between 1997 and 1998, then more than doubled to over $10 billion in 1999 (Figure 6.1). Inflows continued to increase in 2000 on a notifications basis, while decreasing slightly on an arrivals basis.

The benefits of FDI are well established in the literature on trade liberalization (Caves 1996). Not only does FDI induce stable, long-term inflows of capital, it also leads to spillovers of technology and managerial knowhow, employment creation, and regional development. According to Dunning (1993), the presence of foreign multinationals has a positive effect on labor productivity, largely through increased competition. How-

Figure 6.1　Korea: FDI flows as a share of GDP, 1980–2003 (%)

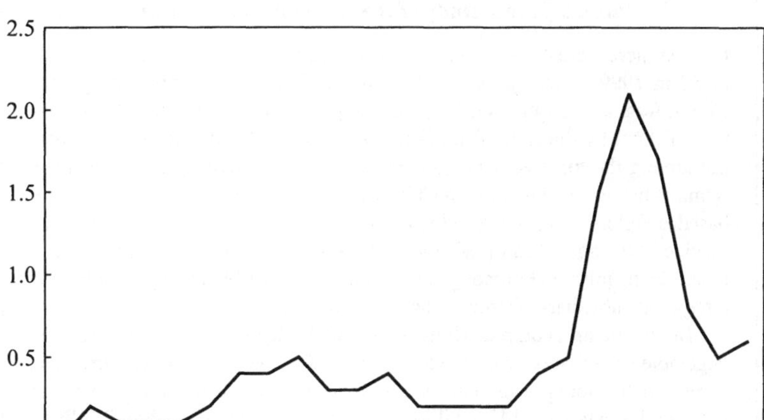

a　FDI is in US dollars. GDP is in Korean won converted to US dollars. The high
　ratio for 1999 reflects both an increase in FDI and a contraction in GDP in this
　year.

Source: FDI: UNCTAD (2004); GDP and exchange rates: IMF (2004).

ever, FDI is not necessarily conducive to market competition; big players
like the *chaebol* may hamper the development of a competitive market
economy by distorting or manipulating the course of liberalization, deregulation, and opening up (K. Lee 2002). This is yet another reason why it
is important to develop a competitive market in tandem with market liberalization.

Economic liberalization, if carried out correctly, is supposed to establish a competitive market in which financial instruments such as shares
and company bonds are transacted in an open, rules-based manner. But, in
an economy where a few players dominate such that they are able to influence the terms of transaction of corporate finance, the course that economic liberalization actually takes may differ from what its advocates had
in mind. The accompanying case studies on the vegetable seed and paper
industries demonstrate some of the effects FDI may have on domestic
competition (Boxes 6.2 and 6.3). In both cases, FDI in the form of M&As
has increased concentration, demonstrating that foreign investment does
not automatically lead to more competition in a given market.[13]

Box 6.2 A case study of the vegetable seed industry

In 1998 there were 48 major seed-producing companies in Korea, increasing to 52 in 1999. After the crisis, three of the five largest firms, Hungnong, Choon Ang, and Seoul Seed Co., were acquired by foreign multinationals—two of them by the same firm, Seminis Vegetable Seeds Inc. Another firm not among the top five, Chung-Won, was also acquired by a foreign firm. Seminis has its headquarters in California but is a subsidiary of the Mexico-based conglomerate, Savia, which holds a leadership position in financial services, packaging, and fresh foods. It established a dominant presence in Korea by acquiring Hungnong and Choong Ang in 1998 and by establishing a regional subsidiary, Seminis Asia Corporation, in 1999.

Before being acquired, Hungnong was the leading firm in the Korean vegetable seed market with a market share of 32 percent. Its main products were radish, cabbage, and chili seeds. In 1997 it was a medium-sized firm with total assets of W143.7 billion, a total sales volume of W56.7 billion, and a workforce of 387 employees. It had a very high debt-to-equity ratio of 611 percent and therefore suffered from serious financial constraints even before the post-crisis hike in interest rates. Under Seminis, Hungnong remains a separate entity, with the previous management still in full control of its operations.

Choong Ang ranked second in the domestic seed market with a market share of around 13 percent. Like Hungnong it has continued to operate as a separate establishment since being acquired. However, as Choong Ang had been Hungnong's strongest competitor, Seminis had some difficulty in co-ordinating their operations. Seminis resolved this difficulty by establishing a market-sharing mechanism under which each firm would specialize in different products. In addition, it partnered each firm with a core Seminis subsidiary—Choong Ang with Asgrow and Hungnong with Royal Sluis—under the strict principle that the two alliances would not compete with each other unless the market in question was large enough to sustain competition. Seminis also arranged to import vegetable seeds in which the Korean firms lacked competitiveness. In effect, the acquisitions have resulted in a complete restructuring of the product portfolios of the two companies.

In August 1999, Seminis invested $10 million to establish Seminis Asia Corporation. Although its primary purpose is to conduct research and retailing, it also acts as the Asian headquarters of Seminis, coordinating operations between the parent company and its Korean subsidiaries.

The competitive effect of a merger is mainly assessed in terms of changes in market share (concentration) and prices. Hungnong remains the largest firm, with almost no change in its market share since acquisition. Its 30 percent market share allows it to enjoy a dominant position in the market, while not reaching the benchmark of 50 percent used to determine a market-dominant position under the MRFTA. The combined market share of Hungnong and Choong Ang comes to around 45 percent, just short of the 50 percent benchmark. However, in reality Seminis controls both companies, even though they are nominally separate and their product portfolios have been restructured so that in effect they no longer compete with each other.

To examine whether these firms have been increasing their prices and enjoying above-normal profits since the merger, one would need detailed information on product prices and production costs. Such data are not readily available. The best readily available proxy for vegetable seed prices is vegetable prices, since the prices of vegetables and vegetable seeds are known to move together. Cabbage prices were declining until 1999 but have increased enormously since 2000. Radish prices have risen incrementally and consistently since 1998. Chili prices increased substantially in 1999 before stabilizing in 2000. Thus, it seems that prices have generally increased, although it is difficult to establish a direct connection between these increases and the merger.

One incident nevertheless leads one to suspect the increased market power of the merged entity. In July 1999, the KFTC investigated a resale price maintenance incident involving Hungnong, which had threatened to halt supplies of its products to retail outlets that sold its Hongnong brand chili seeds for less than a certain price. Hungnong told its parent company that this strategy was enabling it to maintain the price of Hongnong chili seeds, and that it had withdrawn its supplies from outlets where its policy had been violated.[12] This appears to show that although the combined market share of Seminis and its subsidiaries does not technically reach 50 percent, Seminis has established an effective dominance in the vegetable seed market, and can set prices in some lines at least. Therefore, if the relevant market were to be defined more narrowly, Seminis and its subsidiaries might breach the 50 percent threshold.

The seed industry in Korea is currently undergoing consolidation and no further new entry is expected. However, exports and imports are increasing, and so a certain amount of competition from imports can be expected. But most of these imports would be sourced from Seminis, which already has production facilities in Korea. Therefore, in the case of the vegetable seed industry, competition from abroad is unlikely to have any real pro-competitive effects.

Study of the vegetable seed industry in Korea supports the contention that investment liberalization does not guarantee increased competition in the domestic market. In practice, investment liberalization needs to be supplemented by trade liberalization (to increase imports and thereby foreign competition), and accompanied by close surveillance from the competition watchdog. This case also implies that the issue of geographical definition of a market will become critical for future competition policy, and involve a more sophisticated examination of the relationship between competition, trade, and investment policy.

Source: Yun and Lee (2001).

Box 6.3 A case study of the paper industry

The paper industry is an important part of the manufacturing sector in Korea: in 1999 it comprised almost 2 percent of total manufacturing. In the same year Korea was the 10th largest producer of paper products in the world. The industry is both energy and capital intensive; in most countries it is also highly concentrated. Until 1997 the Korean paper industry was highly oligopolistic, with just four major producers.

Procter & Gamble GmbH (P&G)—the German subsidiary of the US multinational—acquired 25 percent of Ssangyong Paper Ltd from the Ssangyong Group. It acquired another 59.4 percent through a public tender in November 1997, thus becoming a majority shareholder, and by the following month had accumulated 91.6 percent of the company. The US parent holds a 49.3 percent share of the German subsidiary. Although it already had a separate Korean subsidiary, established in 1992, the preferred strategy of the US parent was to acquire Ssangyong Paper through its German subsidiary.

Ssangyong Paper produces diapers, shampoo, soap, toothpaste, sanitary napkins, toilet paper, and packing paper for industrial use. Some of the company's diapers and sanitary napkins are supplied by Ssangyong UNI-CHARM Ltd through an exclusive contract. Ssangyong Paper holds a 45 percent share in the latter company and has the right to appoint half of its board members.

Of all the products made by P&G, the KFTC considered the merger to have anticompetitive effects only in the sanitary napkin market. At the time the diaper market was dominated by three companies: Yuhan Kimberly, Ssangyong Paper, and LG Chemicals. After acquiring Ssangyong Paper, the P&G group's combined share of the diaper market would have risen from a mere 6.6 percent to 31.5 percent. However, this still fell short of the 50 percent benchmark for market dominance, and the KFTC expected the merged entity to provide effective competition to Yuhan Kimberly, the largest holder of market share.

---

5   THE INTERNATIONAL DIMENSIONS OF COMPETITION POLICY

On 4 April 2002, the KFTC took the unprecedented step of applying Korean antitrust law extraterritorially to six foreign manufacturers of graphite electrodes. The commission imposed a total fine of $9.2 million on the manufacturers for price fixing.[14] On 29 April 2003, the KFTC concluded a sweeping investigation into an alleged international cartel by six

The sanitary napkin market was dominated by three producers—P&G Korea, Yuhan Kimberly, and Ssangyong Paper—plus a lagging fourth, Daehan Paper Co. Ltd. Following the acquisition of Ssangyong Paper, the P&G Group's combined market share increased from 47.3 percent to 63.8 percent, going over the critical 50 percent benchmark. The merger also fell foul of other 1998 merger review criteria for determining substantial suppression of competition. At the same time, the exit of Ssangyong Paper would leave the market a virtual duopoly between P&G Korea and Yuhan Kimberly, increasing the Herfindahl–Hirschman index by 1,561 from 3,158 to 4,719. The KFTC considers the paper market to have high entry barriers. New entrants need to have a high level of technology and make large capital investments. Product differentiation is a feature of the industry, with short lifecycles for each product. New entrants also come up against the incumbent companies' extensive network of patents: P&G has accumulated more than 300 patents and Kimberly Clark, the parent company of Yuhan Kimberly, possesses more than 400 patents. Because brand image is very important, incumbent firms spend a great deal on promotion: in 1996 the Korean incumbents invested about 5–12 percent of their sales revenue in advertising and marketing. Having an independent distribution network is also important; new entrants would find developing such a network extremely expensive.

The merger did not meet any of the exemption criteria set out in the pre-1998 merger rules of industry rationalization, technology development, significant quality improvement, or significant price reductions. Nevertheless, the KFTC approved the merger on a conditional basis, ordering divestiture of the sanitary napkin division and associated industrial property rights to an unrelated third party within one year. P&G was also ordered to divest itself of Ssangyong Paper's shareholding in Ssangyong UNI-CHARM within one year. The effects of this conditional approval in the market remain to be seen.

Source: Yun and Lee (2001).

foreign vitamin manufacturers, levying a total fine of $3.3 million.[15] On 26 August 2003, the High Court affirmed the KFTC's extraterritorial application of Korea's cartel regulations.[16] On 1 July 2003, the KFTC introduced a system of notification of foreign-to-foreign mergers. This series of moves to regulate behavior that has taken place outside the domestic jurisdiction reflects a growing concern about the economic impact of such behavior on the domestic market in the current age of globalization.

The six graphite electrode manufacturers investigated by the KFTC together account for about 80 percent of worldwide production. On 21 May 1992, these manufacturers met in London to settle on some basic principles that would govern their product pricing and production amounts for years to come. They agreed to raise their prices whenever any of them raised their prices in a country where there was a domestic manufacturer of graphite electrodes—the 'respect for home market' principle. They also agreed to set the prices and quantities of products to be exported to a country where there was no domestic manufacturer—the 'respect for non-home market' principle.

Graphite electrodes are an essential component in steel production. In the absence of a domestic manufacturer to supply the steel industry, Korea must import all its graphite electrodes from abroad. With 90 percent of its imports supplied by six manufacturers operating as a cartel, the KFTC recognized that Korea was suffering significant economic losses. During the period of the cartel, the six manufacturers sold about $553 million of graphite electrodes to Korean steel producers at prices that increased by approximately 48.9 percent between 1992 and 1997, from $2,255 to $3,356 per ton.

The case of the vitamin cartel investigated by the KFTC follows a similar pattern. In September 1989, six vitamin manufacturers agreed to fix their market shares at the level prevailing in 1988, both in the world market and in regional markets such as Asia. To ensure that the market share allocated to each company remained the same regardless of changes in the overall market, they regularly exchanged information on their allocated and actual sales amounts. With 'price before volume' as the guiding principle for their collective behavior, the manufacturers decided that when one of them raised its prices, the others would follow suit.

At the time only Vitamin H was produced in Korea, and the raw materials for other vitamins, such as beta carotene and vitamins A, E, and D3, were imported from abroad. During the cartel period, Korea imported approximately $185 million worth of vitamin raw materials from the six manufacturers, with prices rising during the period and declining afterwards. For example, the price of Vitamin A (0.5 miu/gm cwd) for animals rose from $26.50 per kilogram in 1989 to $31.27 per kilogram in 1998 then declined to $19.06 per kilogram in 2001 after the expiry of the cartel. Both importers and consumers clearly sustained significant economic losses due to the actions of this cartel.

The KFTC's investigation into the vitamin cartel was greatly aided by the findings of competition authorities in other countries such as the United States, Japan, and Canada. Bilateral cooperation with these countries to break the vitamin cartel helped the KFTC gain valuable experience in regulating international cartels.

On 1 July 2003, the KFTC adopted a notification requirement for foreign-to-foreign mergers. Under the revised rules, a report must be filed with the KFTC if (a) a foreign company with total assets or turnover of W100 billion or more acquires or is acquired by another company, and (b) sales in the domestic market of the acquiring or acquired company exceed W3 billion (about $2.5 million).

In the remainder of 2003, 13 such business combination notifications were filed with the KFTC, accounting for 2.2 percent of the total number of business combinations reported to it. Now that most of the restrictions that impeded M&As before the financial crisis have been removed, foreign companies are increasingly interested in entering the Korean market by way of M&As with domestic companies. In 2003 M&A activity by foreign companies increased by 14.4 percent over the previous year in terms of the number of transactions, and 169.2 percent in terms of the size of these transactions. As the previous case studies show, there is concern that the active M&A strategy being pursued by foreign companies in Korea will not necessarily lead to a pro-competitive market environment. This is especially the case when foreign companies are less interested in establishing new companies than in acquiring large, existing companies operating in monopolistic or oligopolistic markets.

6   CONCLUSION

Every country has unique political, social, economic, and cultural features, and Korea is no exception. To break the vicious circle of economic failure that existed up until the early 1960s, the Korean government aggressively pursued an intensive growth strategy throughout the 1960s and 1970s. In doing so, it relied heavily on industrial policy while virtually disregarding the implications for competition policy. This strategy was phenomenally successful economically, but came with significant political and social costs. The advent of competition law in 1981 was a manifestation of the desire to address such costs by strengthening market competition. Although Korea is often held up as a model for other developing countries, it would not be wise for them to follow its lead in every respect. In particular, to overemphasize industrial policy as Korea has done is certain to incur unnecessary costs in the end. It would be far better for developing countries to adopt a mix of industrial policy and competition policy from an early stage of economic development, possibly using Korea's approach to the development of the broadband internet market as a model.

One of the most serious problems currently facing competition policy in Korea is the excessive regulatory power of the KFTC. The KFTC exercises its authority to achieve even non-antitrust-related goals, such as lessening economic concentration in the overall economy. Regulating economic concentration—a practice that is unique to Korea (and possibly Japan)—may be inappropriate in a global economy where the *chaebol* face international competition in world markets. More fundamentally, the pursuit of non-antitrust-related goals may lead to an inefficient allocation of resources, and this would be contrary to optimal competition policy. It is therefore high time to re-examine the question of whether the KFTC should continue to regulate economic concentration. If Korea's economic circumstances and other considerations dictate a role for the KFTC in alleviating economic concentration, its mission in this area should be defined more clearly so as to minimize the negative effects of pursuing such a policy.

As globalization accelerates, economic interdependence among nations has deepened. The erosion of economic sovereignty is apparent. It is now hard to imagine a country pursuing economic policies such as competition policy without regard to international trade and investment. In an open economy, it is commonplace that one country's competition policy will affect the welfare of consumers in other countries. Against this backdrop, a great deal of attention has focused on the international implications of national competition policies. More and more countries are trying to devise policies to confront the problems emanating from international commerce. In the present age of globalization, governments need to take full account of the dynamics of competition policy on the one hand and trade and investment policy on the other. Korea seems to be on the right track in this regard, although it still needs to implement policy more effectively.

NOTES

*   The authors are indebted to Mikyung Yun and Sungmi Lee for making their case studies on the vegetable seed and paper industries available for use in this chapter.

1   The discussion in this section is based on Chang and Shin (1998), Chang (2000), and KFTC (2001a).

2   At the time, government approval was required to obtain a loan from a foreign entity. What enraged the public in this instance was that Sinjin had not only been granted the privilege of having its request for a foreign loan approved, but was also creaming off excessive profits on domestic sales of its cars.

3   This section draws on Chang (1995).

4   Areeda and Hovenkamp (2000: 4) argue as follows:

> Today it seems clear that the general goal of the antitrust law is to promote 'competition' as the economist understands that term. Thus we say that the principal objective of antitrust policy is to maximize consumer welfare by encouraging firms to behave competitively, while yet permitting them to take advantage of every available economy that comes from internal or jointly created production efficiencies, or from innovation producing new processes or new or improved products.

5   The act has been revised several times. It was renamed the Unfair Competition Prevention and Trade Secret Protection Act in 1998.

6   KFTC Decision, 16 May 2000: Case 00-76.

7   Williamson Oil Co. vs Philip Morris USA, 346 F.3d 1287, 1299 (11th Cir. 2003).

8   Supreme Court Decision, 27 August 2002: Case 00DU9779.

9   Singh (2003: note 35) criticizes competition policy in the United States and United Kingdom for placing too much emphasis on static efficiency.

10   As of June 2001, 1,147 apartment complexes had received this certification.

11   A new article on the joint utilization of subscriber lines, article 33-6, was inserted into the Telecommunications Business Act in January 2001; in April 2002 the Ministry of Information and Communication finalized its local loop unbundling guidelines.

12   KFTC Decision, September 1999: Case 9907, *kyungchok* 1010.

13   See Yun and Lee (2001) for a discussion of the effects of FDI on competition in Korea, including the case studies presented here of the vegetable seed and paper industries.

14   KFTC Decision, 4 April 2002: Case 02-77.

15   KFTC Decision, 29 April 2003: Case 03-98.

16   Seoul High Court Decision, 26 August 2003: Case 2002NU14647.

7

Malaysia

Cassey Lee

1 INTRODUCTION

The role of the private sector as an important engine of growth in Malaysia has gained increasing prominence since the early 1990s. A key policy initiative supporting this change in emphasis has been the government's privatization program, which has seen the transformation of most public utilities and other public infrastructure organizations into private entities. In addition to privatization, the government has liberalized market entry into several sectors, particularly services, to increase market competition. These changes have been accompanied by reforms to establish new regulatory institutions and mechanisms in some sectors, with some newly introduced legislation incorporating legal provisions on competition policy for the first time.

Overall, however, the regulations introduced to address competition-related issues have been limited and ineffective. Furthermore, because of the lack of a comprehensive and coherent approach to competition policy and regulation, the government has not been able to deal effectively with many of the competition-related problems that have arisen in Malaysia.

The general aim of this chapter is to discuss the existing state of competition, regulation, and competition policy in Malaysia and how these relate to some of the country's development policies and challenges. More specifically, I examine the effects of existing government policies and interventions on markets in the absence of a national competition policy. I argue that Malaysia has much to gain from the implementation of a national competition law and that, without such a law, the nation's long-term growth prospects and welfare will be compromised.

The outline for the rest of the chapter is as follows. Section 2 discusses the history of development policy in Malaysia to set the context for an evaluation of regulation and competition policy. Section 3 explores policy reforms and competition-related problems, and section 4 looks briefly at the impact of foreign competition on domestic development. Section 5 discusses the current state of competition policy advocacy and proposes one possible approach to the implementation of a national competition law.

2   THE DEVELOPMENT CONTEXT OF COMPETITION AND REGULATION IN MALAYSIA

Malaysia is a relatively small developing country with a population of about 25 million. Its nominal GDP was around $95 billion in 2002. With GDP per capita of $3,600 in that year, Malaysia is currently classified by the World Bank as a middle-income country. Historically, the country's economy has always been very open. Malaysia's trade intensity—as measured by the ratio of total exports and imports to GDP—currently stands at around 2.3. Since independence in 1957, Malaysia has relied heavily on trade as a source of economic growth and development. The pattern of trade has, however, undergone significant changes over the years. Malaysia has managed to transform itself from a major exporter of primary commodities such as tin and rubber in the 1950s to a major manufacturing exporter today. The manufacturing sector currently accounts for about 30 percent of GDP and 76 percent of exports.

Development policies and competition

Growth and equity have long been the main economic policy objectives in Malaysia. Following racial riots in 1969, the government embarked on a long-term, interventionist development policy called the New Economic Policy (NEP). The NEP, which ran from 1971 to 1990, emphasized poverty eradication and wealth redistribution among the country's different ethnic groups—with the latter goal receiving most attention in practice (Gomez and Jomo 1999: 24).[1] The NEP aimed to address the grievances of indigenous Malays (*bumiputra*) through affirmative action to increase their share of the nation's wealth. At the same time, it emphasized general economic growth as a way of mitigating the effects of discriminatory affirmative action policies on the country's non-*bumiputra* ethnic groups.

To attain the goal of wealth redistribution, the NEP set specific targets for *bumiputra* ownership in the commercial and industrial sectors. This was achieved through many means, from outright purchase of equity by trustee companies representing *bumiputra* interests to licensing, quotas, and government procurement policies that favored this group. A number of large state-owned enterprises (SOEs) and state development corporations (owned by Malaysia's state governments) were also established under the auspices of the NEP to accumulate corporate assets on behalf of the *bumiputra* community.

The two companies that have probably played the largest official role in promoting *bumiputra* interests are Perbadanan Nasional Berhad (Pernas, the National Corporation) and Permodalan Nasional Berhad (PNB, the National Equity Corporation). Pernas was set up in 1970 to acquire shares in established companies with a proven track record. PNB was set up in 1978 to establish new wholly owned and joint venture companies. Both were established as private companies owned by *bumiputra*, although they receive assistance from the government in the form of grants and government-backed commercial loans (Jesudason 1989: 85).

To accelerate *bumiputra* participation in the industrial sector, the government implemented a number of new laws and regulations. These included the Industrial Coordination Act 1975, which required manufacturing firms exceeding a given size (initially 75 or more employees or shareholder funds exceeding RM2.5 million) to apply for operating licenses from the government. The purpose of the act was to ensure that firms complied with NEP guidelines on ownership and employment. The Foreign Investment Committee, established in 1974 to monitor foreign acquisitions of Malaysian companies, was another important means to ensure that the pattern of ownership and control of private enterprises in Malaysia remained consistent with government development policy.

In the agricultural sector, the government focused its attention on the reform of distribution networks, on the basis that exploitative rural traders with monopolist–monopsonist positions in agriculture and fisheries were contributing to the persistence of rural poverty (Faaland, Parkinson, and Saniman 2003: 355–7). It set up several marketing boards to address this problem, including the Federal Agricultural Marketing Authority, the Malaysian Fish Marketing Corporation, and the National Padi and Rice Authority.[2]

The effects of the NEP on competition were mixed. During the first decade of implementation, up to around 1983, the evidence seems to indicate that, even in the presence of ethnic-based entry controls and protection in some areas of business (for example, government construction contracts), there was 'over-capacity and excessive competition' among *bumiputra* business people (Jesudason 1989: 104). In other words, too many *bumiputra* companies were competing for too few opportunities.

It appears, however, that small-scale non-*bumiputra* business people were not significantly deprived of business opportunities during this period; the practice of 'Ali-Baba'ism' flourished, particularly in heavily regulated sectors (such as public utilities) and sectors with significant levels of government procurement (such as construction of public projects).[3] The new government regulations did depress investment by the non-*bumiputra* (especially Chinese) business community (Jesudason 1989: 142–3), but there can be no doubt that this section of the business community continued to flourish. Over time, non-*bumiputra* are likely to have taken social policy constraints such as the NEP into account as simply another cost of doing business in Malaysia.

The implementation of the NEP led to a significant number of takeovers in the 1980s, mainly of foreign plantation and mining companies by PNB and Pernas. Since most of these takeovers only involved a change from non-*bumiputra* to *bumiputra* ownership, competition is unlikely to have been affected. However, Jesudason (1989: 163) noted that the NEP appeared to have reduced competition in manufacturing (where the Industrial Coordination Act 1975 effectively restricted entry into the sector) but increased competition among smaller firms (which were exempted from the provisions of the act).

In agriculture, the marketing boards set up to mitigate rural poverty had some impact on market structure and competition in the sector. In rice, for example, the National Padi and Rice Authority assumed the role of a monopoly, controlling all rice imports into the country. Other marketing boards established by the government operated in competition with existing rural traders. However, their impact on poverty eradication seems to have been compromised by their inflexibility—to be expected considering they were part of the government bureaucracy—and by their inability to provide the ancillary credit services that traditional traders were able to offer (Ishak 1994).

In the early 1980s, the government embarked on another phase of import substitution policy, this time based on the promotion of heavy industries such as cars and steel. The objective was to achieve greater economic diversification through enhanced industrial linkages in the economy. Investment in selected heavy industries was accompanied by increases in tariff and non-tariff barriers in these sectors. As a result, by 1987 the transport equipment industry (automobiles, motorcycles, and so on) and basic metal industries were reported to be among the most highly protected in Malaysia (Alavi 1996: 98).

In the mid-1980s, a severe recession brought about another major shift in government policy, this time in the form of economic liberalization and an increased emphasis on privatization.[4] The redistributive goal of the NEP remained an important element in the implementation of the privatization program; for example, the government's privatization guidelines stated that at least 30 percent of equity in privatized projects must be allocated to the *bumiputra* community.[5] Despite the extensive privatization that has taken place, regulatory reforms to ensure a level playing field between newly privatized and competing enterprises have lagged behind. To complicate matters, the government continues to be a major shareholder in many of the privatized entities through vehicles such as Khazanah Nasional (National Treasure Corporation). Khazanah Nasional, the investment holding company of the Malaysian government, is 100 percent owned by the Ministry of Finance. It was set up in 1993 as a vehicle for the government to hold equity in privatized SOEs. For example, the government continues to hold large stakes in Telekom Malaysia Berhad, the incumbent telecommunications company, and Tenaga Nasional Berhad (TNB), the country's largest energy producer and distributor.

Industry consolidation through mergers and acquisitions (M&As) has been another important feature of the economy since the financial crisis. This trend has been most evident in the financial sector, the communications and multimedia sector, and, more recently, the plantation sector. It indicates that locally owned companies are only too aware of the need to strengthen themselves in anticipation of greater competition from abroad as Malaysia implements its World Trade Organization (WTO) commitments on trade and investment liberalization.

Intuitively, it can be argued that the exclusionary nature of social policies based on affirmative action has probably reduced the degree of competition in some areas, with government procurement being one example. However, a counterfactual argument is not useful, since redistributive policies such as the NEP are considered essential for social and political stability in Malaysia. The government has long realized that the painful trade-offs that accompany redistributive policies can be softened by economic growth, such as that propelled by foreign direct investment (FDI) in the export sector. This pragmatic approach has resulted in pro-growth policies—such as market liberalization in both the tradable and non-tradable sectors—that have increased the degree of competition in affected markets. These developments are discussed in section 3.

Sectoral regulation and competition

Since independence, economic regulation in Malaysia has been instituted primarily at the sectoral level. Table 7.1 summarizes the current state of

Table 7.1   Malaysia: A summary of sectoral regulation

Sector	Regulatory agency
Distributive trade	Ministry of Domestic Trade and Consumer Affairs
Roads & road transport	Driving licenses and vehicle registry: Road Transport Department (Ministry of Transport); public and privatized roads: Malaysian Highway Authority (Ministry of Works); commercial vehicles: CVLB (Ministry of Entrepreneurial and Cooperative Development)
Railways	Railways Department (Ministry of Transport)
Ports	Corporatized ports: the respective port commissions (Johor Port Authority, Bintulu Port Authority, Klang Port Authority, Penang Port Commission); federal ports: Ministry of Transport
Airports	Civil Aviation Department (Ministry of Transport)
Communications & multimedia	Communications and Multimedia Commission
Electricity supply	Energy Commission
Water supply	Water Supply Departments (state level)

Table 7.1 (continued)

Legislation	Type of regulation
Price Control Act 1946; Supply Control Act 1961; Consumer Protection Act 1999	The Ministry of Domestic Trade and Consumer Affairs regulates the prices of essential goods. No provision has been made for competition regulation.
Road Transport Act 1987	The Ministry of Works regulates prices (tolls). The CVLB regulates entry through licensing.
Railways Act 1991; Railways (Successor Company) Act 1991	The Ministry of Transport regulates prices (fares).
Ports Authorities Act 1963; Ports Act (Privatization) 1990; various port commission acts; Merchant Shipping Ordinance	The port commissions regulate prices (fares).
Civil Aviation Act 1969; Airport and Aviation Services (Operating Company) Act 1991; Civil Aviation Regulation 1996	The Ministry of Transport regulates prices (fares).
Communications and Multimedia Act 1998; Communications and Multimedia Commission Act 1998	The Communications and Multimedia Commission advises the Ministry of Energy, Water and Communications on price and competition regulation, and regulates entry through licensing.
Electricity Supply Act 1990; Electricity Supply (Successor Company) Act 1990; Energy Commission Act 2001	Wholesale prices are regulated through agreements between independent power producers and TNB, the incumbent distributor. The Ministry of Energy, Water and Communications regulates retail energy prices.
Water Supply Act; state legislation	Privatized suppliers are regulated through concession agreements. Public suppliers are regulated by state Water Supply Departments.

sectoral regulation in the country. Economic regulation has mainly taken the form of government control over entry—through the requirement for firms to obtain licenses and permits—and, in some sectors, over prices. This sectoral approach to regulation continued even after the implementation of the major privatization program of the mid-1980s. New regulatory agencies were established in the ports, airports, electricity, and communications and multimedia sectors. While entry and prices continued to be the main focus of regulation, in a few sectors—notably the communications and multimedia sector and the electricity sector—the scope of economic regulation was expanded to include competition policy. I review economic regulation in a number of sectors, and its impact on competition, next.

The electricity sector

The electricity sector was privatized in 1990 with the corporatization and privatization of the National Electricity Board. New laws such as the Electricity Supply Act 1990 (Act 447) and the Electricity Supply (Successor Company) Act 1990 (Act 448) set out the regulatory framework for the industry. Under Act 447, the Director General of Electricity was designated the regulator of the sector, but with tariff levels requiring the approval of the Minister of Energy, Water and Communications. The legislation contained no provisions on competition policy, and at this juncture there was no autonomous regulatory agency for the sector.

Over a decade was to pass before a regulatory commission, the Energy Commission, came into being. Established under the Energy Commission Act 2001, it was a direct outcome of a study commissioned by the Asian Development Bank in 1996 on the strengthening of the regulatory framework for privatized infrastructure in Malaysia.[6] Whereas the previous regulator had been situated within the Ministry of Energy, Water and Communications, the Energy Commission was set up as an autonomous agency. Because the commission obtains its revenue directly from license holders, it is also better resourced and more self-sufficient than its predecessor.

One significant provision in the Energy Commission Act 2001 concerns the competition regulation function of the commission, namely

> to promote and safeguard competition and fair and efficient market conduct, or in the absence of a competitive market, to prevent the misuse of monopoly power or market power in respect of the generation, production, transmission, distribution and supply of electricity and the supply of gas though pipelines (Energy Commission Act 2001: 14).

This provision was included in the act in anticipation of further market liberalization of the electricity supply sector.[7] The vision was eventually to set up a scheme whereby distributors would bid on a daily spot market for electricity supplied by a pool of power producers. However, the problems of electricity deregulation in California prompted the government to back down from its plans to further deregulate the Malaysian sector. As a result—and in contrast to the situation in the communications and multimedia sector—competition regulation in the electricity sector has not advanced beyond the above broad legal provision. Now that it has no immediate impetus to implement a competition policy, the Energy Commission apparently sees no urgent need to issue guidelines on competition regulation in the energy sector.

The privatization of electricity has introduced some competition into the industry, but this is mainly confined to the electricity generation segment where independent power producers operate alongside the incumbent firm, TNB. This has enabled the Energy Commission to benchmark the incumbent's performance against that of the independent producers, thus putting pressure on it to improve its efficiency. The Energy Commission seems set to continue regulating competition in the industry through practices such as benchmarking rather than by developing and implementing a competition policy. This situation might of course change if the sector is deregulated further, but this seems unlikely in the near future.

The communications and multimedia sector

Privatization of the communications and multimedia sector began as early as 1983, when the government allowed entry into telecommunications markets (such as terminal equipment and paging services) that had hitherto been the exclusive domain of the Malaysian Telecommunications Department.[8] In 1987 the government further privatized the sector, allowing a newly established company, Syarikat Telekom Malaysia Berhad, to take over the provision of fixed line and public telephone services from the department. The Malaysian Telecommunications Department continued to regulate the industry until 1998, when a Communications and Multimedia Commission was established. The passage of the relevant acts—the Communications and Multimedia Act 1998 and the Communications and Multimedia Commission Act 1998—marked the first time law statutes containing competition-related provisions had been enacted in Malaysia.

The competition policy provisions in the Communications and Multimedia Act 1998 cover three areas: licensing of telecommunication firms, general competition practices, and access to services. The section of the act dealing with general competition practices lists types of anticompetitive conduct that are considered per se illegal. These include collusion on pricing or market share, boycotts of suppliers or other competitors, and tying arrangements between firms. The act also contains rule-of-reason provisions allowing the commission to publish guidelines on 'dominant position' and use them to identify and direct the cessation of any act that would substantially lessen competition in the communications market.[9]

Thus far, the Communications and Multimedia Commission has published three documents to explain the concepts contained in, and clarify the enforcement issues raised by, the competition-related provisions of the act. They are:

1   'Guidelines on substantial lessening of competition' (CMC 2000a). This document defines basic concepts such as 'market' and 'potential rivalry,' describes anticompetitive conduct such as predatory pricing and foreclosure, and clarifies the conditions (for example, intentionality) under which such conduct would be deemed illegal under the Communications and Multimedia Act 1998. The document also provides an analytical framework for examining cases where a substantial reduction in competition is thought to have occurred.
2   'Guidelines on dominant position in a communications market' (CMC 2000b). This document clarifies the concept of market dominance and describes the structural characteristics (large market share, high degree of vertical integration, numerous barriers to entry) and practices (anticompetitive pricing and supply behavior) that may be associated with the presence of a dominant firm. The guidelines provide an analytical framework for determining dominant position in a market.
3   'Process for assessing allegations of anticompetitive conduct: An information paper' (CMC 2000c). This paper sets out in greater detail the sequence of actions to be taken by the Communications and Multimedia Commission when investigating cases of a substantial reduction in competition or a dominant market position.

At present, the Communications and Multimedia Commission is experiencing difficulty in enforcing the competition policy provisions of the Communications and Multimedia Act 1998, for several reasons.[10] First, both the statute and guidelines lack precision because they do not include any formal threshold levels to define market dominance. Second, the commission does not have the resources to monitor and investigate conduct in the industry on a continuing basis. Although the commission has approximately 220 employees, the regulatory team responsible for competition-related matters consists of only four officers. Third, the commission has not implemented any sensor data type monitoring of the industry.[11] This is exacerbated by the fact that, under the present law, firms are obliged to provide relevant information to the commission only if they have been notified that they are under investigation for violations of the competition provisions.

There may also be some reluctance on the part of the commission to enforce competition policy more strongly owing to a perception that this could harm Malaysia's 'national champions'—government-promoted firms and industries that require some market protection to recoup the investments made in them and/or allow them to mature (the infant industry argument). One possible example of such a company is the direct-to-home satellite pay television provider, Astro. In 1996 Astro, a subsidiary of MEASAT Broadcast Network Systems (MBNS), was granted a 25-year monopoly concession to provide pay TV services via satellite transmission. The major shareholder in MBNS with a 40 percent shareholding is Usaha Tegas Entertainment Systems; it in turn is owned by T. Ananda Krishnan, reportedly a close friend of former Prime Minister Mahathir Mohamad (Gomez and Jomo 1999: 160). Other large MBNS shareholders include the investment holding company of the Malaysian government, Khazanah Nasional, which currently owns about 15 percent of the company.[12] Major competition-related concerns in the Astro case include its ability to raise prices well above those observed in other countries (such as Taipei,China), its exclusive rights to programming in Malaysia (covering 14 popular channels, including AXN, Disney, Star Movies, and ESPN), and the generous amount of spectrum awarded to the firm in its concession.[13]

Despite these observations, the Communications and Multimedia Commission has not abandoned competition regulation entirely. Complaints are received and investigated. Typically they concern licensees' access to the incumbent's network, and the commission deals with them by issuing determinations based on the relevant provisions of the act. Thus far, no competition-related complaints have proceeded beyond this stage. Hence, the overall direction of competition-related regulation in the industry is toward access regulation.

The transport sector

Competition in the transport sector is affected by regulations imposed by three ministries: the Ministry of Transport, the Ministry of Works, and the Ministry of Entrepreneurial and Cooperative Development (Table 7.1). The Ministry of Transport is the main regulator of the sector; it is responsible for transport infrastructure development and regulation (other than roads and highways). It also sets port and airport tariffs with the advice of sectoral regulatory commissions.[14] The Ministry of Works is responsible for regulating roads and highways, including those that have been privatized. The Malaysian Highway Authority in the Ministry of Works sets the tolls on privatized roads, often after consulting with cabinet and obtaining its approval. The Ministry of Entrepreneurial and Cooperative Development controls entry into the private commercial vehicle market (taxis, buses, and trucks) through its licensing arm, the Commercial Vehicle Licensing Board (CVLB).[15] The ministry itself retains responsibility for setting bus and taxi fares. The sector has been affected by a number of competition-related events in recent years. For instance, a large-scale consolidation of intracity bus services occurred in Kuala Lumpur in 1997 when the CVLB removed the numerous minibus services operating in the city, leaving behind a more concentrated market. Meanwhile, the liberalization of entry into intercity bus services resulted in excessive competition, such that established bus operators were unable to sustain the practice of cross-subsidizing profitable and unprofitable routes.[16] In general, the quality of service in both the intracity and intercity sectors has declined. Major bus operators such as Intrakota and Park May suffered financial losses (Singh 2001) and were taken over by the government in 2004.

Distributive trade

Distributive trade encompasses the domestic retail and wholesale distribution markets. The Ministry of Domestic Trade and Consumer Affairs regulates the sector based on several statutes dealing with various aspects of distributive trade. Some of the ministry's regulatory activities have had a direct impact on competition in certain markets. For example, the Price Control Act 1946 empowers the ministry to control and stabilize the prices of selected 'essential' goods, such as rice, sugar, chicken, and gasoline. Thus, the prices that traders can charge in these markets are constrained by the price ceilings set by the ministry.

The ministry also controls entry into distributive trade markets by requiring firms to obtain licenses and permits. It uses its authority in this area to achieve a variety of objectives, including wealth redistribution and the protection of domestic small firms and traders. One recent example of the latter is the restrictions placed on the issuance of hypermarket licenses in major cities such as Kuala Lumpur, Johor Bahru, and Penang, and in towns with a population of less than 350,000.[17] This policy was implemented to mitigate fears that an influx of large, foreign-owned hypermarkets in urban areas would decimate the existing small retail shops, most of them domestically owned.

The ministry has also intervened in the distributive trade sector to promote the distribution of local products. One recent example is the imposition of shelf quotas in supermarkets to ensure that locally produced goods receive adequate shelf space.[18]

M&As and competition

The number of M&As in Malaysia has fluctuated over the years depending on the state of the economy and government policy. The 1970s saw several large M&As—particularly in the plantation and mining sectors—in which foreign-owned companies were taken over by government-owned holding companies such as PNB to increase *bumiputra* participation in the economy (Jesudason 1989). In the aftermath of the banking crisis of the early 1980s (which mainly involved deposit-taking cooperatives), several large M&As took place in the financial sector mid-decade. The 1990s saw further M&As in this sector as the government sought to consolidate the industry. More recently, a significant level of M&A activity can be observed in the manufacturing sector. Table 7.2, which combines data from the Ministry of Domestic Trade and Consumer Affairs and the United Nations Conference on Trade and Development, indicates that cross-border mergers are also important in Malaysia.

The regulatory agency overseeing M&As is the Securities Commission. The legal framework for regulation is provided by two statutes, the Securities Commission Act 1993 (Part IV, Division 2) and the Malaysian Code on Takeovers and Mergers 1998. These statutes were enacted primarily to protect investors' interests; they contain no provisions to regulate the impact of M&As on competition. Another important regulatory agency in the area of M&As is the Foreign Investment Committee in the Prime Minister's Department, set up in 1974 to issue and monitor equity and ownership guidelines. Its purpose is to ensure that the pattern of ownership and control of private enterprises in Malaysia is consistent with NEP-type government development policies. M&A transactions involving foreign interests that exceed the foreign equity threshold set by the government require the approval of this committee. The government exempts export-oriented FDI from the requirement to seek approval from the Foreign Investment Committee. In the wake of the financial crisis of 1997–98, the government has also relaxed limits on foreign equity participation in Malaysian private enterprises.

Although the Foreign Investment Committee's guidelines focus mainly on distributive issues, in practice they probably do have some effect on competition: restrictions on foreign equity participation are likely to limit the amount of resources that domestic firms can obtain from foreign investors to compete in the market. Despite the existence of such

Table 7.2   Malaysia: M&A activity by sector, 1996–2002

Sector	1996	1997	1998	1999	2000	2001	2002
Domestic M&As							
RM million							
Manufacturing	355	3,339	444	690	3,338	3,232	4,091
Property	496	202	–	67	248	1,653	1,004
Distributive trade	509	4,214	7,058	398	938	6,685	1,580
Plantation	443	–	422	805	–	114	–
Mining	1,146	–	523	–	–	–	–
Finance	654	–	204	2,813	1,430	1,548	898
Construction	181	3,169	38	211	233	198	1,658
Other	–	–	–	–	290	–	–
Total	3,784	10,924	8,689	4,984	6,477	13,430	9,230
Number							
Manufacturing	33	18	6	13	39	22	28
Property	7	1	–	2	6	9	15
Distributive trade	7	7	5	4	24	8	11
Plantation	6	–	1	15	–	1	–
Mining	1	–	4	–	–	–	–
Finance	2	–	9	13	10	6	10
Construction	3	3	1	3	5	2	3
Other	–	–	–	–	1	–	–
Total	59	29	26	50	85	48	67
Cross-border M&As							
Sales							
($ million)	768	351	1,096	1,166	441	1,449	485
(RM million)[a]	2,918	1,134	4,165	4,431	1,676	5,506	1,843
Purchases							
($ million)	9,635	894	1,059	1,377	761	1,375	930
Cross-border M&As (sales in RM million as % of total M&As by size)	77.1	10.4	47.9	88.9	25.9	41.0	20.0

a   Based on an exchange rate of RM3.80/$.

Source: Ministry of Domestic Trade and Consumer Affairs; UNCTAD.

regulations, there are very few publicized cases of a proposed acquisition by a foreign interest actually being rejected. One possible case was the attempt by Singapore Telecom to acquire a RM2.2 billion stake in a major Malaysian telecommunications company, Time dotcom, in May 2002. The then Prime Minister Mahathir Mohamad is reported to have publicly rejected the proposal for 'security reasons.'[19] Judging from the press coverage of the case, however, it appears that the decision to reject the proposal was not taken by the Foreign Investment Committee.

Unfortunately, there is a severe dearth of studies on the impact of M&As and M&A-related regulations in Malaysia. At present there is no quantitative evidence on how M&As affect competition, nor are there any studies focusing on the impact of FDI regulations on M&As and competition. This implies that policy-making in these areas encounters significant challenges.

Industrial policy, privatization, and competition

The Malaysian government employs a range of industrial policy instruments to achieve its economic objectives. These include:

- trade-related instruments such as import tariffs, import licensing, and the provision of export promotion/processing zones and export-related equity/ownership incentives;
- industry promotion instruments such as investment tax allowances, research and development-related tax incentives, local content programs, and the awarding of pioneer status to certain firms;
- targeted investments in national champions such as Proton (automobiles) and Perwaja (steel);
- factor market-related instruments such as foreign labor policies, priority-sector lending guidelines, and the development of industrial estates; and
- regulatory intervention in domestic markets through licensing, price ceilings, government procurement policies, moral suasion on mergers, and market liberalization.

Table 7.3 summarizes the effects of these various instruments on competition in domestic markets. Overall, export-oriented industrial policies appear not to raise competition-related issues, probably because the goods produced are primarily exported. In contrast, import substitution strategies do raise issues related to market access, one good example being Malaysia's automotive industry. Factor market-related instruments tend to have a neutral effect on competition. In general, the impact of regulation

Table 7.3   Malaysia: Impact of industrial policies on competition in domestic markets

Type of industrial policy	Impact on competition
Export promotion (export promotion/ processing zones, export-related equity/ ownership incentives)	Neutral
Import substitution & targeted investment (national champions, import tariffs, import licensing)	Reduce competition
Factor market instruments (foreign labor policies, priority sector lending guidelines, provision of industrial areas)	Neutral
Regulation (licensing, price ceilings, government procurement policies, moral suasion on mergers, market liberalization)	Generally reduce competition (except for market liberalization)

has been to reduce competition. For example, the government's decision to take proactive measures to consolidate the financial sector in anticipation of increased competition from abroad may have reduced the level of competition in the sector. Similarly, licensing, price ceilings, and government procurement policies tend to reduce competition. On the other hand, market liberalization may increase competition. These issues are discussed further in the following section through the use of case studies.

Privatization has also had mixed effects on competition. In some sectors, such as communications and multimedia, privatization was swiftly followed by liberalization, increasing the level of competition in the industry. In the power sector, however, where only electricity generation was liberalized after the incumbent producer was privatized, competition did not increase despite the entry of new producers, because these firms secured long-term, lucrative agreements to sell their power to the incumbent. In the sewage sector, the incumbent firm operated as a private monopoly before being renationalized in 2000. The privatized incumbent in the airline industry operated as a monopoly in the domestic services sector until recently, when competition intensified with the entry of a budget carrier. Despite widespread privatization across sectors, the gov-

*Table 7.4   Malaysia: Government shareholdings in selected privatized
entities*

Company	Sector	Government share (%)
Telekom Malaysia Berhad	Communications & multimedia	34.0
Malaysia Airports Holdings Berhad	Airports	23.5
PLUS Expressways Berhad	Road transport (highways)	20.9
Projek Penyelengaraan Lebuhraya Berhad	Road transport (highways)	30.5
TNB	Power	35.6

Source: *Malaysian Business*, 16–31 January 2004.

ernment continues to hold significant shareholdings in many major privatized entities through its investment arm, Khazanah Nasional. It therefore faces a conflict of interest between its role in promoting competition through market liberalization and its desire to protect the value of its investments. Table 7.4 summarizes some of the government's existing shareholdings in privatized entities.

Supporting evidence on competition in manufacturing and services

Most of the evidence on the state of competition in Malaysia is in the form of market concentration studies in the manufacturing sector. Competition in the services sector is a neglected area, despite some anecdotal evidence, typically concerning highly visible cases that have been the subject of considerable media attention.

Quantitative evidence in the manufacturing sector

Since the early 1970s, there have been eight empirical studies of market concentration in Malaysia's manufacturing sector. In chronological order they are: Gan and Tham (1977), Gan (1978), Lall (1979), Rugayah (1993), Zainal Aznam and Phang (1993a, 1993b), Nor Ghani et al. (2000), Bhattacharya (2002), and MDTCA (2003). There are considerable differences

Table 7.5   Malaysia: A summary of market concentration studies

Study	Reference year/ period	Concentration measure used	Concentration levels published?
1 Gan & Tham (1977)	1971	CR8	No
2 Gan (1978)	1971	CR4, CR8	Yes
3 Lall (1979)	1972	CR4	Yes
4 Rugayah (1993)	1978–86	CR4, HHI	Yes
5 Zainal Aznam & Phang (1993a, 1993b)	1979, 1985, 1990	CR4 CR8	Yes
6 Nor Ghani et al. (2000)	1985–94	CR4, HHI	No
7 Bhattacharya (2002)	1986, 1996	CR4	No
8 MDTCA (2003)	1996, 1999, 2000	HHI	Yes

CR4 = four-firm concentration ratio; CR8 = eight-firm concentration ratio; HHI = Herfindahl–Hirschman index.

in the methodology adopted by these studies (Table 7.5). Different scholars have used different sets of concentration measures (CR4, CR8, HHI) over different time periods and for different sets of industries at different levels of aggregation. Some authors have published their computations of concentration measures while others have not. The two most comprehensive presentations of concentration levels are Zainal Aznam and Phang (1993a, 1993b) and MDTCA (2003). However, comparisons between the two are complicated by a revision of the statistical classification scheme in 2000 (Malaysian Department of Statistics 2000). This revision resulted in further disaggregation at a given (five-digit) classification level (see the list of new industries at the bottom of Appendix A7.1).

The studies reveal considerable differences in concentration levels between manufacturing industries. The general impression gained from them is that many of the industries in the manufacturing sector are relatively highly concentrated. Appendix A7.1, which gives a comprehensive picture of concentration levels in all sections of the manufacturing sector over the past three decades, supports this view. However, the evidence on overall trends in market concentration over the past 30 years is mixed. While Zainal Aznam and Phang [ZAP] report a general increase in concentration levels between 1979 and 2000, Nor Ghani et al. [NZAC] find a decrease in the 1985–94 period and MDTCA (2003) finds a slight increase between 1996 and 2000 (Appendix A7.1).

Most of the studies focus on testing the structure–conduct–performance hypothesis, which states that market structure (seller concentration and entry barriers) affects a firm's conduct (pricing behavior), which in turn affects its economic performance (profitability) (Scherer and Ross 1990). They test for the importance of various types of entry barriers that are related to profitability in an industry, including:

- scale economies (Gan and Tham 1977; Lall 1979; Zainal Aznam and Phang 1993a, 1993b);
- capital intensity and capital requirements (Lall 1979; Rugayah 1993; Zainal Azman and Phang 1993a, 1993b; Bhattacharya 2002; MDTCA 2003); and
- advertising and product differentiation (Gan and Tham 1977; Lall 1979; Zainal Aznam and Phang 1993a, 1993b; Bhattacharya 2002).

The evidence on the importance of entry barriers appears to be fairly conclusive (Table 7.6). This and the finding of high overall levels of concentration imply a need to monitor markets carefully to prevent anticompetitive conduct, especially within industries characterized by high levels of concentration.

A few of the studies also attempt to ascertain the influence of imports, exports, and FDI on market concentration. Generally the results are inconclusive. Rugayah (1993) found some evidence that exports and imports are related to market concentration, but this was refuted by Zainal Aznam and Phang (1993a, 1993b) and MDTCA (2003). Lall (1979) found FDI to be an important determinant of market concentration but Rugayah (1993) found to the contrary. These ambiguous empirical results on the relationship between trade and market concentration call for a more cautious approach on the part of policy-makers when linking competition to trade and FDI. Hence, the empirical support for the implementation of a competition policy may have to rest solely on the 'domestic' aspects of the economy discussed earlier.

Finally, there has been a preliminary attempt to link innovation to market structure in the manufacturing industry. Lee (2004) found innovation to be positively correlated with the level of market concentration. However, more work will need to be done, using panel data, before conclusive results can be obtained.

Table 7.6   Malaysia: Summary of results of studies testing the structure–conduct–performance hypothesis

Study	Coverage	Findings
Gan & Tham (1977)	1968–71	Barriers to entry (scale economies, advertising) have a significant influence on price–cost margins. Concentration is positively related to profitability.
Gan (1978)	1971	Concentration is positively related to profitability and this relationship is discontinuous.
Lall (1979)	1972	Barriers to entry (scale economies, capital requirements, product differentiation) are positively related to profitability. FDI is positively related to concentration, especially in non-consumer industries.
Rugayah (1993)	1978–86	Price–cost margins are positively related to seller concentration, optimal plant size, minimal capital requirements, product differentiation, competition from exports and imports, and capital intensity. FDI is not related to profitability.
Zainal Aznam & Phang (1993a, 1993b)	1979, 1985, 1990	Scale economies, capital intensity, and advertising are positively related to concentration. Foreign presence (measured by the ratio of the output of foreign-controlled firms to total industry output) has some impact on market concentration. Entry of foreign firms induces oligopolistic market structures because foreign firms are larger and have a greater degree of product differentiation than domestic firms. Import competition and export opportunities are not related to market concentration.
Nor Ghani et al. (2000)	1985–94	Using CR4 as a measure of concentration, out of 124 industries 12 showed an increase in concentration, 53 showed a decrease, and 59 did not show any significant trend.
Bhattacharya (2002)	1986, 1996	Capital intensity, advertising, and market size are positively related to market concentration.
MDTCA (2003)	1996, 1999, 2000	Efficient scale is positively related to market concentration. Firm size, capital intensity, and export competition are not significantly related to concentration.
Lee (2004)	2000–01	Propensity to innovate is positively correlated to market concentration.

Some anecdotal evidence in the services sector

There has been a dearth of studies on market concentration in the services sector. Nevertheless, it is apparent that government intervention to consolidate the financial sector did increase market concentration in this sector. Telecommunications is another non-tradable sector in which M&As have increased the level of market concentration. In Kuala Lumpur, extensive consolidation brought about by the phasing out of minibuses has resulted in monopoly or duopoly markets on some urban bus routes. This has had some impact on competition, although the situation is not well documented. The following cases highlight some of the competition-related issues in the services sector.

Market entry and competition: MAS versus AirAsia
One of the more interesting cases of competition in the services sector is that between Malaysia Airlines (MAS) and the new, no-frills, domestic carrier, AirAsia.[20] MAS was virtually a monopoly operator in the domestic airline market until 2002, when AirAsia began offering low-priced domestic flights. MAS was quick to respond by introducing a new pricing scheme under which 10 seats on every flight attracted a 50 percent discount. This was surprising since only a year earlier, in July 2001, the government had granted MAS's request to increase fares on domestic services within Peninsular Malaysia by about 52 percent. AirAsia responded to the new pricing strategy by offering even lower fares from September 2002. Despite MAS's plea for government intervention to resolve the perceived 'price war,' the government maintains that competition between the two firms is healthy. The case clearly highlights the advantages that may accrue to consumers from increased competition in the services sector.

Regulation and competition: The case of the Pangkor–Lumut ferry
Another competition-related case in the services sector that has received widespread media attention is that of the Pangkor–Lumut ferry. Ferry services between Lumut and the island of Pangkor (both in the state of Perak) are provided by two firms, Pangkor–Lumut Express Feri and Pan Silver Ferry.[21] A price war erupted between the two firms in January 2003, taking the price of an adult round-trip ticket from RM10 in December 2002 to as low as RM1 in July 2003. Ticket prices then stabilized at around RM4 until October, when they returned to RM10. There was an immediate public outcry following this price increase, but the only response of the ferry operators was to suspend the sale of monthly passes as well, thus denying frequent users of their services access to cheaper

fixed fares. The October price increase was clearly the result of collusion between the two ferry operators to avert the adverse consequences of a protracted price war; both firms claimed that they had incurred losses amounting to about RM10,000 per month during the preceding months.[22]

The government response to the problem has been haphazard. Following the public outcry in October 2003, the Perak state government tried to persuade the ferry operators to reduce their prices, with RM7 being considered reasonable. When this effort failed, the state government indicated that it would ask the Ministry of Transport to intervene by issuing more licenses on the route to create more competition. This was subsequently carried out in 2004. A major source of the current problems seems to be a legal and regulatory loophole: under the Merchant Shipping Ordinance, the tariffs charged by merchant and passenger ships of less than 40 gross registered tonnes are not regulated. The government plans to amend the law to enable it to extend its regulatory oversight to smaller vessels, but for the time being, the Ministry of Transport has had to resort to direct negotiations with the parties in an attempt to maintain reasonable fare levels.

This case clearly highlights how a lack of regulatory oversight by government can lead to anticompetitive conduct. It raises interesting questions concerning the potential links between regulation and competition. The price increase of October 2003 was clearly an outcome of the exercise of market power by two colluding firms, made possible by a lack of regulatory oversight in the sector. It could be argued that a competition law that prohibited collusion would have been able to deal with the problem. Alternatively, in the absence of a competition law, the government could have opted to regulate tariffs. But unfortunately it did not have the legal mandate to do so.[23]

Liberalization and competition: The case of the haulage industry
Developments in the haulage industry highlight some of the potential effects on competition of market liberalization.[24] The haulage industry was liberalized in 1997 to increase its efficiency. Consequently, the number of haulage firms increased from five in 1997 to about 60 in 2003. The incumbent five firms and one other firm are members of the Container Hauliers Association of Malaysia (CHAM). Most of the new entrants (about 30 firms) have joined another organization, the Association of Malaysian Hauliers (AMH).

With a large number of new entrants jostling for space in the industry, a price war broke out in 2000. By 2003, container haulage rates had fallen by 20–40 percent. In an effort to resolve the situation, the two industry associations agreed to stop giving rebates to customers with effect from 1

January 2004. This move was initiated by CHAM and supported by AMH, which issued a circular to members advising them to halt the practice of giving rebates. Thus far the CVLB, the industry regulator, has not commented on this industry initiative, even though it is the body responsible for setting price ceilings for the industry.

In the case of the haulage industry, liberalization of entry clearly precipitated a price war. The two industry associations, particularly CHAM, made a concerted effort to halt the fall in prices and increase haulage rates. Together they hold a significant market share; the share of the six CHAM members alone is about 55 percent. Nevertheless, it is still too early to tell whether their efforts will prove successful, especially given the large number of independent haulage operators who do not belong to either organization. Furthermore, the practice by some firms of renting out their haulier permits to other companies may continue to undermine the industry's resolve to coordinate prices.

This case shows how tariff regulation can compromise competition in an industry. When market conditions change such that prices fall below the regulated level, firms may collude to maintain prices at the regulated level by agreeing not to wage price wars. When this occurs, the regulated tariff acts as a focal point for a collusive price level. Moreover, as the regulated tariff level is set by the government, these explicit acts of collusion may escape any legal sanction in the absence of a competition law, even though they are clearly anticompetitive.[25] There is certainly a need to implement a competition policy to deal with such cases. But even more importantly, the government needs to recognize that regulation may need to be scaled back to allow competition to resolve such problems.

3 POLICY REFORM AND COMPETITION: SOME CASE STUDIES

Industrial policy plays an important role in economic planning and development in Malaysia. The government uses regulatory, trade, and FDI policies to support its industrial policy. The interactions between these policies often raise competition issues. This section explores these issues in greater detail through several case studies.

Industrial policy, trade liberalization, and competition: AFTA and the national car industry

The national car company, Perusahaan Otomobil Nasional (Proton), was established in the early 1980s as a key component of Malaysia's heavy industrialization program. From the start, the government tilted the playing field in the domestic car market in Proton's favor by exempting it from import duties on completely knocked down (CKD) kits. As a result, Proton was able to sell its cars at prices 20–30 percent lower than those of comparable cars produced by other car assemblers in the country (Jomo 2003). By the 1990s, Proton had become the dominant car producer in the Malaysian market.

Today, about 75 percent of passenger vehicle sales are controlled by Proton (with a share of 45 percent) and the second national car company, Perodua (30 percent). This dominant position is, however, threatened by Malaysia's commitment under the Association of Southeast Asian Nations (ASEAN) Free Trade Area (AFTA) agreement to reduce import duties to 20 percent in 2005 and to 0–5 percent in 2008.

The government is aware that the implementation of its trade liberalization commitments could seriously undermine Proton's (and Perodua's) competitiveness. Its response has been to neutralize the reduction in import duties by raising excise duties. In 2004, the import duty on CKD passenger cars from ASEAN countries was reduced from 42–80 percent to 25 percent while excise duty was increased from 55 percent to 60–100 percent. For completely built-up (CBU) units from ASEAN countries, the import duty was reduced from 140–300 percent to 70–190 percent while excise duty was increased by 60–100 percent.

Table 7.7 presents a hypothetical computation of the effect of these changes for a local car and a foreign CKD car. Table 7.8 repeats the computation, but assumes no increase in excise tax. The effect of the countervailing increase in excise tax is to increase the price of the local car while leaving that of the ASEAN car unchanged. This reduces the price competitiveness of the local car, but not to the extent that it would if the reduction in import duty had not been offset by an increase in excise tax. It is apparent from Table 7.8 that if the import duty were reduced without any increase in excise tax, consumers would pay less for foreign cars.

This example illustrates how trade liberalization (a reduction in import duty) can be neutralized by the government's use of domestic policy (an increase in excise tax) to support its industrial policy. In Malaysia's case, the increase in excise tax is probably an interim strategy aimed at buying time for the restructuring of the national car industry—possibly in the form of a future joint venture between Proton/Perodua and a major foreign producer.[26] In a signal of the government's intention to reduce the level of support for the industry, the prime minister recently stated that local automotive companies would have to depend less on government protection in the future.[27]

Table 7.7   *Malaysia: Effect of a reduction in import duty with a countervailing increase in excise tax (RM)*

	Local car	ASEAN CKD car
Pre-January 2004		
Base price	40,000	40,000
Excise tax (55%)	22,000	22,000
Excise tax rebate	−11,000	0
Import duty (50%)	0	20,000
On-the-road price	51,000	82,000
Post-January 2004		
Base price	40,000	40,000
Excise tax (80%)	32,000	32,000
Excise tax rebate	−16,000	0
Import duty (25%)	0	10,000
On-the-road price	56,000	82,000

Table 7.8   *Malaysia: Effect of a reduction in import duty with no increase in excise tax (RM)*

	Local car	ASEAN CKD car
Pre-January 2004		
Base price	40,000	40,000
Excise tax (55%)	22,000	22,000
Excise tax rebate	−11,000	0
Import duty (50%)	0	20,000
On-the-road price	51,000	82,000
No change in excise tax		
Base price	40,000	40,000
Excise tax (55%)	22,000	22,000
Excise tax rebate	−11,000	0
Import duty (25%)	0	10,000
On-the-road price	51,000	72,000

Industrial policy, market entry, and competition: EON versus Proton Edar

Industrial policy may also create problems of anticompetitive conduct, as the recent case of Edaran Otomobil Nasional (EON) versus Proton Edar illustrates.[28]

Cars produced by Proton have traditionally been distributed domestically by two firms, Proton Edar and EON. The government set up EON in 1984 as the sole distributor of the first national car, the Proton Saga. Its strategy at the time was to separate manufacturing from distribution. The dealership was privatized in 1984. Current major shareholders include the DRB-HICOM Group, Employees Provident Fund Board, the government (through Khazanah Nasional), and the Jardine Group.

Proton Edar was initially established in 1985 as a car dealership called Auto Elegance Sdn Bhd. In 1993, it evolved into Usahasama Proton DRB Sdn Bhd, a joint venture between Diversified Resources Berhad and Proton to distribute the Proton Wira. Proton Edar became a wholly owned subsidiary of Proton in 2000 and subsequently began to distribute other Proton models—the Perdana and Iswara as well as the Wira—that had previously been distributed by EON. In the same year, the 10-year distribution agreement between Proton and EON came to an end without a new dealership agreement being concluded. These changes set the stage for further intensification of the rivalry between EON and Proton Edar to distribute Proton's cars.

Problems arose following the launch of a new model, the Gen.2, on 8 February 2003. Not surprisingly, Proton chose to distribute the Gen.2 solely through its wholly owned subsidiary, Proton Edar. This put EON in the difficult position of having to obtain its supply of the Gen.2 from its competitor, Proton Edar.[29] Proton has also argued that EON should restrict itself to selling 'a single brand in a single showroom,' referring to EON's current practice of selling Audi and Chevrolet cars alongside those produced by Proton.

The dispute between EON and Proton Edar over the Gen.2 revealed a clear-cut case of anticompetitive conduct. Proton's ownership of Proton Edar constituted a severe conflict of interest. It was clearly in Proton's commercial interest to favor its own subsidiary over EON. This manifested in its decision to restrict EON's access to the Gen.2, thus restraining EON's competitiveness. Worse, EON's only source of supply of the new model was its rival, Proton Edar. Furthermore, Proton's insistence on a 'single brand' distribution policy was akin to market foreclosure to reduce competition between brands, deterring entry into the car market.

The government did not intervene during the initial stages of the dispute between EON and Proton Edar. But in February 2004, with the debate becoming more public and acrimonious, the government did finally intervene, asking each party to present its case. This led to the signing of a new five-year dealership agreement between Proton and EON on 2 March 2004.

The government's ability to mediate in the case sprang in part from its position as a major shareholder in both Proton and EON. The dealership agreement it negotiated may contain elements that require competition policy scrutiny. One such clause is the requirement that EON allocate 70 percent of its servicing capacity to Proton cars. This could be construed as the use of market power by a supplier firm (Proton) to force a buyer firm (EON) to limit the latter's ancillary services to competing suppliers. This is an important issue given the importance of ancillary services to sales of the primary product (cars).

Industrial policy to promote strong, vertically integrated structures can restrict competition. In the case of Proton, with its integration of car production and car distribution, the absence of a competition law has clearly exacerbated the problems of vertical restraint. If such a law had existed, and if Proton had been found to have acted in an anticompetitive manner, it could have been forced to divest itself of its distribution subsidiary. At present, the government 'regulates' Proton through its substantial shareholding in the firm. If the government were to divest itself of its controlling shareholding, a competition law would be needed to fill the regulatory gap.

Industrial policy, regulation, and competition: The case of the steel industry

Industrial policy can create significant problems when it fails to take into account the linkages between a targeted industry and other sectors of the economy. The steel industry in Malaysia is one such example.[30]

Along with cars, Malaysia focused on steel production as part of its heavy industrialization program in the early 1980s. The two largest steel companies in Malaysia are Perwaja, which produces billets, and Megasteel, which manufactures hot-rolled coils and cold-rolled coils. After investing more than RM10 billion in Perwaja, the government sold the then loss-making plant to the Maju Group. Megasteel, in contrast, represents an investment of about RM2.4 billion and has always been privately owned.

Both Perwaja and Megasteel are protected from foreign competition firstly by import duties and permits administered by the Ministry of International Trade and Industry, and secondly by price regulation administered by the Ministry of Domestic Trade and Consumer Affairs. Rising demand from abroad for steel scrap (the basic raw material for making steel products) in early 2003 reduced the profit margin on locally produced steel billets and bars for domestic consumption. This caused a contraction in steel production for the domestic market, and a sharp increase in prices. Domestic consumers such as the construction industry were severely affected—although both Perwaja and Megasteel experienced a significant improvement in their financial performance.

The government responded to the problem by suspending its import restrictions on steel billets and bars for six months and exempting raw materials used in the manufacture of steel from import duties. In addition, it placed restrictions on steel exports. The Ministry of Domestic Trade and Consumer Affairs was directed to prepare a new scheme to control the pricing of domestic steel billets and bars in the form of an automatic price adjustment mechanism. This new price mechanism will allow domestic steel prices to vary according to market conditions, providing an incentive for steel-makers to increase production for the domestic market.

The chain of events observed in the steel industry illustrates the complex interactions between industrial policy, competition, and trade. In this case, the implementation of industrial policy in the steel industry using trade policy (import permits and duties) and regulation (price controls) had an adverse effect on other sectors (construction and infrastructure). The temporary solution of liberalizing imports has increased competition between local and foreign steel producers, but it is unclear how industrial policy in the steel industry will evolve in the future. There is no indication that the government will ease the restrictions on steel exports until the automatic price adjustment mechanism is implemented. Neither is there any indication that the government considers industrial policy imperatives in the steel industry, in the longer run, to take precedence over the interests of other sectors.

FDI, regulation, and competition: The case of hypermarkets

FDI has been an important source of capital in Malaysia's development. It continues to be regarded in a positive light in the manufacturing sector, partly because most manufacturing FDI involves export-related activities. FDI not only provides access to capital and imported technology, it also generates employment and foreign exchange earnings. FDI in the services sector confers similar benefits, but may incur social costs in the form of the loss of small, home-grown businesses that are crowded out by foreign service suppliers. This argument is illustrated by the case of hypermarkets in Malaysia.[31]

Since the establishment of the first hypermarket, Makro, in Malaysia in 1993, the sector has grown rapidly. Today, there are about 22 hypermarkets in the urban conurbation of Klang Valley.[32] Most of them are owned by large foreign chains such as Carrefour (France), Tesco (United Kingdom), Giant (Hong Kong, China), and Makro (Netherlands). Concerned about the competitive threat that the hypermarkets pose to small neighborhood retail shops, over the past two years the government has changed its regulatory stance on FDI in the hypermarket business from an accommodating one to a hostile one. It has imposed increasingly more stringent guidelines on hypermarkets, restricting them to areas with a population of over 350,000 people, introducing shelf quotas that require hypermarkets to display a certain proportion of local products on their shelves, tightening the definition of a hypermarket to cover stores of over 5,000 square meters rather than the former 8,000 square meters, and requiring preliminary assessments of the effects of proposed hypermarkets on shops within a 3.5-kilometer radius. It has also restricted operating hours to exclude 24-hour trading. This adverse environment for FDI culminated in the decision on 20 April 2004 to place a five-year freeze on the establishment of new, foreign-owned hypermarkets in Klang Valley, Penang, and Johor Bahru. The ministry responsible, the Ministry of Domestic Trade and Consumer Affairs, has not given any reasons for this decision.

The five-year ban on the establishment of foreign-owned hypermarkets will clearly reduce the flow of FDI into the sector. This could delay the restructuring of the retail trade sector, seen as necessary to enhance local upstream–downstream linkages and improve productivity levels (Sieh 2003). The differing treatment of foreign and locally owned hypermarkets also raises issues of market access and competition in this sector, and calls into question the consistency of such policies with Malaysia's WTO and General Agreement on Trade in Services commitments.

Industrial policy, mergers, and competition: The financial sector

Countries commonly respond to the necessity to implement trade liberalization commitments by introducing industrial policy measures aimed at strengthening locally owned firms. One approach has been to encourage industry consolidation through mergers, to create large, locally owned firms that are capable of competing with foreign-owned companies. This was the approach taken in the financial sector in Malaysia.

In September 2000, Bank Negara Malaysia, the central bank, announced a consolidation of the financial sector that would reduce the number of financial institutions from 56 to just 10 'anchor banks.'[33] The decision affected 23 commercial banks, 16 merchant banks, and 17 finance companies. The main objective was to enhance the competitiveness of locally owned financial institutions in anticipation of increased competition from foreign-owned financial institutions; under its WTO commitments, Malaysia had agreed to liberalize the sector by 2003. The central bank has not publicly articulated the basis for its choice of anchor banks, but others have attempted to explain the underlying rationales. Karapayah (2002), for example, finds a bias toward size as a criterion for choosing the anchor banks, but finds no differences in financial performance between anchor and non-anchor banks.

The central bank recognizes the importance of information and competition between domestic banks for the benefits of mergers to materialize. It recently introduced a new method for determining interest rates that should help both depositors and lenders compare the cost of funds at various financial institutions, enabling consumers of bank services to make better-informed choices.

Maximizing the benefits of policy reforms

As we have seen, industrial policy, trade policy, and FDI policy are intertwined. Neglect of competition issues can substantially reduce the benefits of trade and FDI reforms that are geared toward enhancing industrial development. Lacking a coherent competition policy, the government is, in most instances, forced to rely on heavy-handed regulation delivered in an ad hoc manner to deal with any problems that arise. Its ability to adopt this regulatory role is to some extent due to its extensive ownership of shares in various large privatized companies. Clearly the Malaysian government needs to adopt a more formal and coherent approach to dealing with competition issues if it is to reap the full benefits of trade and FDI reform.

The benefits of policy reforms, be they regulatory, trade, or FDI in nature, accrue to both consumers and producers. As our earlier case studies show, Malaysian consumers stand to gain from the lower prices, higher quality, and greater variety of products that policy reforms bring about. Trade liberalization in the form of tariff reductions on passenger vehicles, for example, should lead to Malaysians paying lower prices for cars. Market liberalization in the airline sector has prompted competition between carriers, to the advantage of consumers. The same can be said of hypermarkets. However, as the cases of the Pangkor–Lumut ferry and haulage industry illustrate, the advantages of competition are quickly negated by collusion between firms to maintain high prices. And, as the case of the steel industry illustrates, policy reforms in one sector can have unintended consequences in others.

Suppliers also benefit from policy reforms in different ways depending on the type and outcome of the reform. Trade liberalization may improve market access for foreign firms into countries such as Malaysia, provided that other entry barriers (such as excise taxes on cars) are not introduced to neutralize the reduction in import tariffs. In the case of the steel industry, trade policy reforms have both increased and decreased market access—import access has improved but exports have been restrained. As the hypermarket case suggests, FDI policy reforms promise substantial long-run benefits in the form of employment generation and industry restructuring. These will only be forthcoming, however, once competition issues such as discrimination between local and foreign firms are addressed.

4   THE INTERNATIONAL DIMENSIONS OF COMPETITION POLICY AND DOMESTIC DEVELOPMENT

Because Malaysia does not have a national competition law, the government is unable to establish a permanent institution to deal with competition-related problems arising from the actions of multinationals. The little empirical evidence that exists on such problems suggests that they can be very serious. One recent example concerns the pricing of patented drugs in Malaysia. Alavi (2003) argues that there is a lack of competition in the patented drugs market in Malaysia. As a result, the prices of such drugs are not only higher than those prevailing in developed countries such as the United Kingdom, but have risen at a faster rate. Citing evidence from the mid-1990s, Alavi (2003: 189–90) finds that drug prices are from 22 percent to as much as 427 percent higher in Malaysia than in the United Kingdom. The Malaysian Auditor-General's Report for 2003 states that the government has paid up to 36 percent above market price for some medicines used in public hospitals and clinics.[34] It attributed this to the small number of *bumiputra* companies licensed to supply patented drugs on behalf of foreign pharmaceutical companies. Between 2001 and 2003, a total of 140 contracts worth RM425 million were awarded, with 83 of these (valued at RM283 million) going to one firm and the remainder being distributed among 11 other firms.

Other evidence comes from Evenett (2004), who estimated that only 0.1 percent of Malaysia's imports and 0.7 percent of its government spending needs to be affected by cartelization to justify a $10 million expenditure on competition law enforcement (based on a conservative assumption of a 15 percent rise in the prices of cartelized products). Based on Evenett's work, it is possible to make a rough estimate of the potential welfare losses from cartelization in the pharmaceutical sector. Malaysia's pharmaceutical market is currently estimated to be worth RM2.5 billion, or around $665 million (Espicom 2004). A 33 percent premium over world market prices would translate into an additional cost of RM834 million ($219 million) to consumers and the Malaysian government.

The discussion so far suggests that the implementation of a national competition policy in Malaysia can be justified on both domestic and international grounds. The implementation of such a policy would also enable the government to deal with other competition-related issues arising from international developments such as cross-border mergers. For example it would be able to take a proactive interest in cases such as the Exxon–Mobil merger, which has received close scrutiny from competition authorities in the United States and Europe.

Finally, a competition policy would help equip the government to deal with the significant developments that are occurring in international competition policy. For example, the WTO has been holding discussions at the international level on multilateral competition rules. Thus far, the stance of the Malaysian government—influenced by the lack of a national competition law in Malaysia—has been to seek deferment of this issue.

5   TOWARD THE IMPLEMENTATION OF A NATIONAL COMPETITION POLICY

The current state of competition policy advocacy

The Malaysian government has adopted a very cautious approach to the implementation of a national competition policy and law. Work in this area began as early as 1991 under the aegis of the Ministry of Domestic Trade and Consumer Affairs, but encountered political and bureaucratic resistance. In part this resistance arose from fears that a national competition policy would adversely affect the nation's export competitiveness, as well as from the belief that it would conflict with existing socioeconomic policies (such as the wealth redistribution policy) and industrial policies (such as the national champions policy). Despite these past failures, the ministry remains committed to implementing a competition law and has come up with some draft policy proposals.

The Eighth Malaysia Plan for 2001–2005, the country's most recent five-year plan, contains a specific reference to the implementation of a national competition policy and law:

> During the Plan period (2001–2005), efforts will be made to foster fair trade practices that will contribute towards greater efficiency and competitiveness of the economy. In this context, a fair trade policy and law will be formulated to prevent anti-competitive behavior such as collusion, cartel price fixing, market allocation, and the abuse of market power. The fair trade policy will, among others, prevent firms from protecting or expanding their market shares by means other than greater efficiency in producing what consumers want. In addition, a national policy and master plan on distributive trade will be formulated to facilitate an orderly and healthy development of the sector (p. 467).

This formal commitment is not the only force driving the implementation of a competition policy and law in Malaysia; FTA negotiations have provided further impetus. Even though it is far from inevitable that these talks will get off the ground, government officials are well aware of the need to implement a national competition policy and law before any such negotiations begin.

The Ministry of Domestic Trade and Consumer Affairs views competition law as supplementary to existing laws to protect consumers, such as the Trade Descriptions Act 1972, the Hire Purchase Act 1967, the Weights and Measures Act 1972, the Direct Sales Act 1993, the Money Lenders Act 1951, and the Consumer Protection Act 1999. These statutes provide protection to consumers not only by setting out consumer rights, but also by describing acts on the part of a seller that would be deemed unethical and illegal. Many of the statutes are specific to certain sectors; for example, the Trade Descriptions Act, Weights and Measures Act, and Direct Sales Act are specific to the distributive sector, and the Hire Purchase Act and Money Lenders Act are specific to the financial sector. None of these statutes deal with competition-related issues such as collusion and the abuse of market power.

The Ministry of Domestic Trade and Consumer Affairs is actively engaging other ministries in a series of dialogs to address their concerns about the proposed competition law, and build a consensus to ensure its successful implementation. It will then need to seek the endorsement of cabinet for the law. Once cabinet has given its approval, the competition law (tentatively called the Fair Trade Practices Act) will need to be drafted and eventually enacted.

In mid-2004 the Ministry of Domestic Trade and Consumer Affairs experienced a change of leadership. In a speech in July 2004, the new minister announced that the ministry intended to implement a Fair Trade Practices Act by 2005. Despite this announcement, some degree of uncertainty must remain: previously announced deadlines for the implementation of such a law have come and gone. But this should not prevent policy-makers from continuing to discuss approaches to—and challenges facing—the formulation of a competition policy for Malaysia.

Challenges in implementing a national competition policy

Several challenges lie ahead in implementing a national competition law in Malaysia. First, the government will have to reverse the devolution of competition regulation to sectoral regulators, who are likely to resist any such efforts at centralization. It will also need to convince existing national-level regulators—such as the Securities Commission, which regulates M&As of companies listed on the Kuala Lumpur Stock Exchange—of the need for a new agency to regulate competition-related issues.

Second, competition policy may come into conflict with existing industrial and socioeconomic policies, such as selective import substitution, bank consolidation, and wealth redistribution policies. Accommodating all these policies, with their varying objectives, exemptions, and authorizations, is likely to be an important element of Malaysia's proposed competition policy and law. In this regard, the government will need to be mindful that too many exemptions may weaken competition regulation and make it vulnerable to regulatory capture. When unavoidable, exemptions should be time-bound and gradually removed over time.

Third, given the extent of resistance to the implementation of a national competition policy, some compromise in the content of the policy may need to be made. One example is merger controls—and in particular whether pre-notification of proposed mergers would be necessary. India has chosen to do away with pre-merger notifications, an example that Malaysia might follow. Another way of making competition policy more palatable might be to orient it more toward conduct than market structure, as some countries in Europe have chosen to do (Haley 2002).

Fourth, a sequenced approach to the implementation of competition policy, as in India, would probably be appropriate for Malaysia. Almost all the competition-related problems discussed in this chapter were not perceived as such by the government or the public. This indicates that competition policy advocacy will remain an important area of activity for years to come.

6   CONCLUSIONS

Malaysia is a small and open economy. Its development over the past three decades has been steered by a fairly interventionist government. Informed by the need to resolve racial tensions that sparked riots in 1969, state intervention has been guided by the dual objectives of poverty eradication and wealth redistribution among the country's different ethnic groups. A major element of the government's strategy to lessen the burden of wealth redistribution has been to promote a strong private sector and export-driven economic growth.

The simultaneous implementation of privatization and selective import substitution, beginning in the early 1980s, contained contradictory elements—the former required competition to work, at least to some extent, while the latter necessitated restrictions on market access. The absence of extensive regulatory reform and the limited divestiture of government equity in privatized entities have somewhat limited the potential dividends from privatization. Clearly the country needs a national competition policy and its attendant law to address the many competition-related problems that have emerged in Malaysia.

There are, however, significant hurdles to be cleared before this can happen. These include reconciling competition policy with the country's socioeconomic objectives and ongoing industrial policies. A competition policy that is appropriate for Malaysia will be one that carefully balances the country's socioeconomic needs and that makes judicious use of exemptions.

NOTES

1   The NEP was succeeded by other long-term development policies such as the National Development Policy (1991–2000); these have continued to emphasize growth with equity. For more information on the NEP, see Faaland, Parkinson, and Saniman (2003).

2   For further details, see Wells and Fredericks (1979), Mokhtar and Meyanathan (1990), and Ishak (1994).

3   'Ali-Baba'ism' refers to the practice of subcontracting work originally obtained by *bumiputra* companies to non-*bumiputra* companies. See Bruton (1992: 295) and Jesudason (1989: 149).

4   See Naidu and Lee (1997) for a review of privatization in Malaysia up to the mid-1990s.

5   In the wake of the financial crisis of 1997–98, several projects that were privatized in the 1980s, but that subsequently experienced substantial losses, were renationalized. These included two light rail transit systems in Kuala Lumpur, the national sewage system, and the national airline, MAS.

6   The study was undertaken by the consulting firm NERA Economic Consulting. It focused on four infrastructure sectors (telecommunications, transport, water, and sewerage and waste disposal) and was completed in 1997.

7   Interview with Energy Commission officials on 1 July 2002.

8   See C. Lee (2002) for further details on telecommunications sector reforms.

9   Practices classified under rule-of-reason provisions are not per se illegal; if sufficient cause is given for the practice (such as efficiency in the case of a firm with a dominant market position), then the practice may be allowable.

10   Interview with Communications and Multimedia Commission officials, 25 June 2004.

11   Sensor data monitoring allows regulators to monitor various aspects of service provision (such as quality of service) directly through the use of sensors installed as part of telecommunications networks.

12   The source of this information is: <http://www.nttdocomo.co.jp/english/com/product/pressrelease/article/19980424-59532.html>.

13   The pricing issue is raised at <http://www.malaysia.net/dap/lks3033.htm>; the exclusive programming issue is raised at <http://www.jeffooi.com/archives/2004/06/mitv_no_threat.php>; and the spectrum issue is highlighted in ITU (2002a).

14   Privatized ports are regulated by their own port commissions. They assume an advisory capacity in relation to the Ministry of Transport on matters relating to tariffs.

15   The licensing of commercial vehicles was originally the responsibility of the Ministry of Transport. This function was transferred to the Ministry of Entrepreneurial and Cooperative Development (then called the Ministry of Public Enterprises) in the early 1970s to support NEP policies.

16   'Bus firms want CVLB to stop issuing permits,' *New Straits Times*, 4 February 2004.

17   'No hypermarkets in smaller towns,' *Star*, 17 February 2004.

18   'Govt may impose quota on goods displayed in supermarkets,' *New Straits Times*, 17 February 2004.

19   This was reported at <http://www.businessweek.com/bwdaily/dnflash/may2000/nf00515b.htm>, accessed 15 May 2000.

20   The information presented here is compiled from: 'MAS to offer cheaper fares, minus food and drink,' *Star*, 3 September 2002; 'Chan: Good to compete,' *Star*, 15 August 2003; and <http://www.malaysia.net/dap/bul1344.htm>.

21   The information presented here is compiled from: 'Fare war bleeds ferry operators,' *Star*, 25 October 2003; 'Ferry operators seek consensus,' *Star*, 3 November 2003; and 'Legal advice sought over fare dispute,' *New Straits Times*, 17 December 2003.

22   In the media the two firms were reported as having 'consolidated' their operations. The author conducted a telephone interview with the Ministry of Transport's legal advisor on 1 July 2004 to clarify the legal aspects of the case.

23 For most ports, the fares charged by private ferry operators are set by the port commissions and/or the Ministry of Transport.

24 The information presented here is compiled from: 'Call to stabilise haulage rates,' *Star*, 22 December 2003; 'Haulage groups agree to stop giving rebates,' *New Straits Times*, 19 January 2004; and 'Smaller hauliers on the road to overtaking major players,' *New Straits Times*, 4 February 2004.

25 Another important question is whether CHAM and AMH can be considered to be cartels.

26 'Proton revamp seen paving way for more foreign tie-ups,' *Business Times*, 29 May 2003.

27 'Do it on your own, says PM,' *New Straits Times*, 7 July 2004.

28 The information presented here is compiled from: 'Officials meet cabinet over distributorship,' *Star*, 12 February 2004; 'For EON, Proton Edar, it's business amid talk of rift,' *New Straits Times*, 17 February 2004; 'Proton and EON deny report on termination of distribution deal,' *Star*, 17 February 2004; 'Mahaleel: EON will have to wait for GEN.2,' *Star*, 18 February 2004; 'EON must sell Gen.2 in separate showrooms, says Proton CEO,' *New Straits Times*, 18 February 2004; and 'Proton, EON sign five-year super dealership agreement,' *New Straits Times*, 3 March 2004.

29 Commenting on EON's need to order the Gen.2 from Proton, Proton's CEO is reported to have said, 'They can order. They can wait,' and to have laughed.

30 The information presented here is compiled from: 'Steelmakers reject profiteering claims,' *Business Times*, 5 February 2004; 'Request for higher steel bar ceiling price under study,' *Business Times*, 17 February 2004; and 'Steps to increase supply of steel billets and bars,' *Business Times*, 9 April 2004.

31 The information presented here is compiled from: 'Govt may impose quota on goods displayed in supermarkets,' *New Straits Times*, 17 February 2004; 'No hypermarkets in smaller towns,' *Star*, 17 February 2004; 'Ministry orders Tesco to stop 24-hour operations,' *Business Times*, 8 April 2004; 'No more foreign-owned hypermarkets,' *Business Times*, 21 April 2004; and 'Shafie: No discrimination in decisions on hypermarkets,' *Business Times*, 22 April 2004.

32 Klang Valley covers the districts of Shah Alam, Klang, Petaling Jaya, Kuala Lumpur, Kajang, Kepong, and Puchong.

33 In an earlier announcement, in July 1999, the central bank proposed a consolidation that would have left only six anchor banks.

34 'Govt overpaid for medicines,' *Star*, 12 September 2004.

Appendix A7.1   Malaysia: Market concentration levels in manufacturing, 1971–2000[a]

Year/period Concentration measure Source	1971 CR4 GAN	1972 CR4 LALL	1979 CR4 ZAP	1985 CR4 ZAP	1990 CR4 ZAP	1978–86 CR4 RGH	1985–94 CR4 NZAC	1978–86 HHI RGH	1985–94 HHI NZAC	2000 HHI MDTCA
Manufacturing industry										
Slaughtering, meat preparation, & preserving (processing & preserving of poultry & poultry products)			0.85	0.75	0.72					0.2970
Ice cream	0.73	0.87	0.76	0.74	0.66					0.1859
Other dairy products	0.50		0.96	0.84	0.87	0.86		0.257		
Pineapple canning			1.00	1.00	1.00	1.00	+	0.347		0.6112
Other canning & preserving of fruits & vegetables	0.18	0.30	0.53	0.58	0.42	0.48		0.093		0.1871
Canning, preserving, & processing of fish, crustaceans etc.			0.26	0.62	0.38	0.39		0.089		
Coconut oil	0.31–0.73		0.27	0.45	0.48		+		+	0.2672
Palm oil		0.21	0.22	0.20	0.28	0.22		0.026		
Palm kernel oil			0.45	0.40	0.43	0.39		0.071	+	
Other vegetable & animal oils			0.87	0.84	0.85	0.92		0.355		0.2246
Large rice mills	0.16	0.16	0.13	0.15	0.15					
Flour mills			1.00	1.00	1.00					
Sago & tapioca factories	0.28	0.33	0.44	0.50	0.62					
Other grain milling (other flour/grain products)			0.87	0.98	0.98		+			0.2385
Biscuit factories	0.51	0.47	0.73	0.42	0.38		+		+	
Bakeries	0.18	0.23	0.18	0.17	0.24					
Sugar factories & refineries			0.99	0.99	0.99	0.94		0.374		0.3229
Cocoa, chocolate, & sugar confectionery (cocoa products)	0.54	0.56	0.57	0.47	0.48	0.50		0.097		0.1819

Industry								
Ice factories	0.20	0.15	0.31	0.25	0.24			
Coffee factories	0.12	0.18		0.17	0.49			0.2934
Tea factories			0.25	0.99	0.71			0.2477
Noodles & related products	0.15	0.49	0.60	0.49	0.56			
Spices & curry powder			0.55	0.36	0.42		+	+
Other food products n.e.c.			0.66	0.72	0.54	0.71	0.180	
Prepared animal feeds	0.36	0.48		0.34	0.31			
Distilling, rectifying, & blending of spirits			0.44	0.72	0.70			
Malt liquors & malt			0.77					
Soft drinks & carbonated water	0.42	0.41	0.58	0.50	0.56		+	0.1855
Tobacco manufacture	0.90	0.76	0.68	0.72	0.87			0.3551
Natural fiber spinning & weaving mills			0.65	0.48	0.51	0.54	0.130	0.2142
Dyeing, bleaching, printing, & finishing of yarns & fabric			0.54	0.77	0.81	0.65	0.335	0.2485
Handicraft spinning & weaving			0.99					0.4787
Batik making			0.46	0.50	0.45			
Synthetic textile mills (spinning & weaving of man-made fibers)			0.74	0.68	0.73			0.6714
Miscellaneous primary textiles			0.79	0.44	0.49			
Made-up textile goods			0.53	0.60	0.40			
Knitting mills			0.33	0.36	0.33			
Carpets & rugs				1.00	0.94			
Cordage, rope, & twine industries			1.00	1.00	0.85			0.3240
Textiles n.e.c.		0.25	0.63	1.00	0.98			
Clothing factories	0.35	0.36	0.38	0.33	0.19			
Miscellaneous wearing apparel n.e.c.				0.69	0.63			0.1845
Tanneries & leather finishing (tanning & dressing of leather)			1.00	0.82	0.94	0.98	0.462	0.3845

Appendix A7.1 (continued)

Year/period Concentration measure Source	1971 CR4 GAN	1972 CR4 LALL	1979 CR4 ZAP	1985 CR4 ZAP	1990 CR4 ZAP	1978–86 CR4 RGH	1985–94 CR4 NZAC	1978–86 HHI RGH	1985–94 HHI NZAC	2000 HHI MDTCA
Leather products & leather substitutes			0.43	0.52	0.51					
Footwear	0.24	0.92	0.56	0.65	0.80					
Sawmills	0.07	0.07	0.06	0.07	0.09	0.07		0.007		
Plywood, hardboard, & particle board mills	0.27		0.23	0.27	0.22	0.25		0.037		
Planning mills, window & door mills, & joinery works	0.37	0.39	0.25	0.33	0.29	0.29		0.037		
Prefabricated wooden housing				1.00	1.00	0.97		0.710		
Other wood products			0.59	0.54	0.50					
Wooden & cane containers & small caneware			0.31	0.37	0.43					
Wood & cork products				0.54	0.42					
Furniture & fixtures		0.18	0.27	0.23	0.17	0.22		0.025		
Pulp, paper, & paperboard		0.51	0.87	0.71	0.72					
Paper containers & boxes, & paperboard			0.48	0.29	0.22	0.36		0.054		
Pulp, paper, & paperboard articles n.e.c. (other paper & paperboard articles, n.e.c)			0.32	0.41	0.49					0.2319
Printing, publishing, & allied industries (publishing of newspapers, journals, & periodicals)		0.19	0.26	0.34	0.30					0.2866
Industrial gases			0.44	0.71	0.87	0.59		0.197		0.6068
Other basic industrial chemicals except fertilizers		0.52		0.46	0.41					
Fertilizers & pesticides	0.08	0.63	0.64	0.64	0.56					
Synthetic resins, plastic materials, & man-made fibers		0.18	0.97	0.79	0.56					

Paints, varnishes, & lacquers	0.72	0.57	0.66	0.78	0.67			
Drugs & medicines	0.13	0.49	0.48	0.42	0.37			
Soap & cleaning preparations	0.97	0.94	0.81	0.79	0.75			
Perfumes, cosmetics, & other toilet preparations	0.69	0.41	0.58	0.68	0.67			
Chemical products n.e.c.		0.72	0.33	0.32	0.32	0.38	0.087	
Petroleum refineries			1.00	0.87	0.88	0.98	0.489	
Miscellaneous petroleum & coal products			0.86	0.46	0.46			
Tire & tube industries			0.82	0.70	0.76	0.76	0.212	0.1742
Rubber remilling & rubber latex processing	0.11	0.11	0.17	0.18	0.14			
Rubber smokehouses	0.33	0.50	0.73	0.70	0.47	+	+	0.3928
Rubber footwear			0.65	0.75	0.76			
Other rubber products n.e.c.			0.38	0.41	0.24	0.35	0.056	
Plastic products n.e.c.			0.17	0.12	0.11	0.14	0.014	
Pottery, china, & earthenware		0.20	0.67	0.82	0.46			
Glass & glass products			0.94	0.91	0.80			0.2539
Structural clay products	0.14		0.32	0.33	0.35	0.33	0.047	
Hydraulic cement	0.99		0.97	0.82	0.72	0.93	0.248	
Lime & plaster			0.80	0.81	0.49			
Cement & concrete products	0.75	0.69	0.49	0.33	0.34			
Cut stone & stone products			0.83	0.50	0.56			
Other non-metallic mineral products n.e.c.			0.68	0.58	0.68			
Primary iron & steel basic industries	0.22	0.60	0.88	0.79	0.72	0.89	0.351	
Foundries			0.58	0.57	0.47			
Other iron & steel basic industries			0.58	0.57	0.47			
Other non-ferrous metal basic industries			0.79	0.68	0.70			
Cutlery, hand tools, & general hardware			1.00	0.44	0.51			0.2145
Furniture & fixtures primarily of metal			0.65	0.50	0.53			

Appendix A7.1 (continued)

	Year/period	Concentration measure	Source
	1971	CR4	GAN
	1972	CR4	LALL
	1979	CR4	ZAP
	1985	CR4	ZAP
	1990	CR4	ZAP
	1978–86	CR4	RGH
	1985–94	CR4	NZAC
	1978–86	HHI	RGH
	1985–94	HHI	NZAC
	2000	HHI	MDTCA

Year/period Concentration measure Source	1971 CR4 GAN	1972 CR4 LALL	1979 CR4 ZAP	1985 CR4 ZAP	1990 CR4 ZAP	1978–86 CR4 RGH	1985–94 CR4 NZAC	1978–86 HHI RGH	1985–94 HHI NZAC	2000 HHI MDTCA
Structural metal products		0.32	0.40	0.25	0.65					
Tin cans & metal boxes		0.58	0.59	0.57	0.49					
Wire & wire products		0.39	0.42	0.40	0.37					
Brass, copper, pewter, & aluminum products		0.48	0.60	0.45	0.45					
Other fabricated metal products n.e.c.		0.68	0.44	0.30	0.46					
Engines & turbines except aircraft, vehicle, & motorcycle engines		0.55	0.85	0.84						0.3000
Agricultural machinery & equipment			0.64	0.49	0.55					
Metal & woodworking machinery			0.56	0.36	0.41					
Specialized industrial machinery & equipment except metal & woodworking machinery			0.43	0.32	0.51					
Office, computing, & accounting machinery		0.28			0.90					0.3313
Refrigerating, exhaust, ventilating, & air-conditioning machinery		0.90	0.68	0.49	0.65					
Machinery & equipment n.e.c.			0.25	0.23	0.23					
Electrical industrial machinery & apparatus			0.47	0.63	0.54					
Radio & TV sets, sound reproduction & recording equipment (publishing of recorded media)			0.37	0.55	0.33					0.3344
Gramophone records & pre-recorded magnetic tapes (reproduction of recorded media)				0.98	0.66					0.2891
Semiconductors & other electronic components, & communication equipment & apparatus				0.34	0.27					

Electrical appliances & housewares	0.65	0.60	0.76				
Cables & wires	0.66	0.62	0.46				
Dry cells & storage batteries	0.79	0.65	0.61				
Electric lamps & tubes	0.82	0.99	0.85				0.1935
Miscellaneous electrical apparatus & supplies n.e.c. (domestic appliances n.e.c.)	0.44	0.45	0.45				0.2053
Shipbuilding & repairing	0.99	0.98	0.78	0.95	+	0.601		0.2379
Motor vehicle bodies	0.36	0.41	0.49	0.30		0.097		
Manufacture & assembly of motor vehicles	0.52	0.75	0.84	0.64		0.211	+	0.4831
Motor vehicle parts & accessories	0.40	0.40	0.36				
Manufacture & assembly of motorcycles & scooters	0.94	0.85	0.59					0.1882
Manufacture & assembly of bicycles (manufacture of bicycles & wheelchairs)	0.46	0.48	0.70					0.4532
Transport equipment			0.88				
Professional & scientific measuring equipment	0.90	0.94	0.92				
Photographic & optical goods		0.89	0.87					0.4043
Watches & clocks	0.88		0.83					0.2075
Jewelry & related articles		0.56	0.71				
Sporting & athletic goods		0.81	0.58				
Brooms, brushes, & mops	1.00	0.97						0.1857
Pens, pencils, office & art supplies	0.70	0.72	0.73				
Toys (games & toys)		0.89	0.83					0.2586
Umbrella making		0.73	0.62					0.2053
Other manufacturing industries	0.67	0.58	0.51				

Appendix A7.1 (continued)

| Year/period | 2000 |
| Concentration measure | HHI |
Source	MDTCA
New industries in MDTCA (2003)	
Manufacture of rigid or reinforced plastic products	0.8564
Manufacture of aircraft & spacecraft	0.8320
Building & repair of pleasure & sporting boats	0.7776
Manufacture of machinery for metallurgy	0.7072
Recycling of other metal waste & scrap	0.6050
Manufacture of musical instruments	0.5239
Manufacture of pumps, compressors, taps, & valves	0.5071
Manufacture of other transport equipment n.e.c.	0.4858
Manufacture of bearings, gears, & gearing & driving components	0.3618
Manufacture of sauces	0.3610
Retreading & rebuilding of tires	0.3597
Manufacture of toilet paper, cleansing tissue, towels, & serviettes	0.3533
Manufacture of telecommunications cables & wires	0.3429
Recycling of other non-metal waste & scrap	0.3332
Manufacture of glucose, glucose syrup, & maltose	0.5199
Sanitary towels & tampons, disposable napkins	0.3167
Weapons & ammunition	0.2763
Nuts & nut products	0.2650
Ovens, furnaces, & furnace burners	0.2648

Machinery for mining, quarrying, & construction	0.2623
Manufacture of TV & radio transmitters	0.2398
Machinery for food, beverage, & tobacco processing	0.2395
Electrical power cables & wires	0.2357
Other special purpose machinery n.e.c.	0.2234
Medical & surgical equipment & orthopedic appliances	0.2041
Production, processing, & preserving of other meat products	0.1825
Other publishing	0.1790
Production of mineral water	0.1654

CR4 = four-firm concentration ratio; HHI = Herfindahl–Hirschman index; n.e.c. = not elsewhere classified.

a   A plus sign denotes an increase in competition. New classification labels are in parentheses.

Source: GAN: Gan (1978); LALL: Lall (1979); RGH: Rugayah (1993); ZAP: Zainal Aznam and Phang (1993a, 1993b); NZAC: Nor Ghani et al. (2000); MDTCA (2003).

8

Thailand

Deunden Nikomborirak

1 INTRODUCTION

Thailand was one of the first countries in the Southeast Asian region to introduce a fully fledged competition law, in 1999. Before that, monopolistic practices were subject to the Price Control and Antimonopoly Act 1979. Despite this relatively early legal development, many restrictive practices remain unchallenged to this day. Moreover, state rules and regulations continue to pose significant barriers to competition, harboring inefficiency and rent seeking in many sectors, particularly the services sector. Study of Thailand clearly shows that simply having a competition law is not sufficient to create a more competitive and efficient market; effective law enforcement and genuine competition policy and advocacy are also required to bring this about.

This chapter is organized as follows. The next section describes the market structure of Thailand's manufacturing and service sectors in terms of market concentration. Section 3 identifies the nature of barriers to competition in markets, both public and private. Section 4 examines major government policies that affect competition in the market, namely trade policy, industrial and investment policy, and privatization policy. The following section describes the competition regime, including the legal framework, its administration, the enforcement record, and implementation problems. Section 6 examines restrictive practices originating from foreign business entities operating overseas and in Thailand. The last section contains the major findings of this chapter, lessons learned, and recommendations on how the existing competition regime could be improved.

2   MARKET STRUCTURE

The manufacturing sector

Thailand does not have a database on market shares, and data collected by the Office of Trade Competition are not available to the public. According to a survey of market structure and conduct in 12 manufacturing industries by Nikomborirak et al. (2002) and data from the Department of Internal Trade for eight other industries, many industries in Thailand are highly concentrated (Table 8.1). These are all industries that are protected by high tariffs: distilling and blending of spirits, auto tires, and motorcycle manufacturing. Others are industries that require large sunk investment costs and have high fixed costs, such as the cement, steel, and glass industries.

The services sector

Most service sectors in Thailand, bar the regulated ones, are competitive and thus are not listed in Table 8.2. Among the regulated service sectors, banking and insurance are relatively competitive, with many players in the market. So is the trucking industry, which was liberalized in 1994 when the state-owned operator lost its monopoly to handle cargo in the Bangkok port area.

The quasi-competitive services listed in Table 8.2 are those in which private operators are allowed to operate under a concession granted by either a state agency or a state enterprise. In broadcasting, for example, the Mass Communications Organization of Thailand (MCOT) operates Channel 9 but contracts out the running of another channel, Channel 3, to a private media company. The Thai military, which controls Channels 5 and 7, also contracts out most of their operations to the private sector. The Department of Public Relations operates Channel 11. The Office of the Prime Minister owns the Independent Television Channel (ITV) but has auctioned off the right to operate it to a private company.

Nearly all of these concessions involve a revenue-sharing scheme whereby the private operator has to transfer a specific revenue share to the state enterprise or agency in exchange for the right to operate. The only exception is internet services, where the Communications Authority of Thailand (CAT Telecom Ltd), the state monopoly in international communications, demands a one-third equity share in all internet service providers (ISPs). Despite the fact that these private operators have to operate under relatively unfavorable terms dictated to them by a state enterprise or agency,[1] competition is healthy in markets such as interprovincial

Table 8.1 Thailand: Market concentration in selected manufacturing industries (%)

Industry	Concentration ratio			Market share calculated by:
	CR 1	CR 2	CR 3	
1 Cement	33	59	83	Sales in 2003
2 Ceramic roof tiles	50	66	83	Sales in 2003
3 Zinc-coated steel sheets	36	59	79	Sales in 2000
4 Glass sheets	60	80	93	Sales in 2003
5 Steel				
Hot-rolled	43	67	92	Registered production capacity
Cold-rolled	55	98	100	Sales in 2000
6 Motorcycles	77	89	96	Sales in 2002
7 Auto tires	54	83	96	Sales in 2000
8 Beer	70	97	98	Sales in 2002
9 Whiskey	88	93	96	Sales in 2002
10 Instant coffee	78	83	87	Sales in 2002
11 Cellular phones	59	90	98	Number of subscribers in 2002
12 Light bulbs	40	70	78	Production volume in 2001
13 Batteries				
Alkaline	77	91	95	Sales volume in 2002
Normal	57	81	98	Sales volume in 2001
14 Modern trade	16	29	n.a.	Sales in 2001
15 Condensed milk	66	83	100	Sales in 2002
16 Liquefied petroleum gas	34	53	71	Sales in 2002
17 Plastic pellets, polyethylene	38	54	69	Sales in 2002
18 Plastic pellets, polypropylene	39	68	88	Sales in 2002
19 Plastic pellets, polyvinyl chloride	53	79	100	Sales in 2002
20 Plastic pellets, polystyrene	54	72	89	Sales in 2002

CR1 = one-firm concentration ratio; CR2 = two-firm concentration ratio; CR3 = three-firm concentration ratio; n.a. = not available.

Source: Industries 1–12: Nikomborirak et al. (2002) and Thailand Development Research Institute updates; industries 13–19: Department of Internal Trade website, <www.dit.go.th>, accessed May 2004.

Table 8.2   Thailand: Market structure in major service sectors

Industry	Firm	Market share (%)
Competitive markets		
Banking	Bangkok Bank	21.5
(share of assets	Krung Thai Bank (state)	18.3
in 2002)	Kasikornbank	13.2
	Siam Commercial Bank	11.7
	Siam City Bank	8.5
	Other eight Thai banks	26.9
Life insurance	AIA	50.9
(share of direct	Thai Life Insurance	15.9
premium life	Ayudhya CMG	7.7
insurance in 2002)	Bangkok Life Assurance	5.9
	Other 21 insurance companies	19.6
Trucking	Many operators	
Quasi-competitive markets		
Broadcasting	Channel 3 (MCOT)	25.6
(share of adver-	Channel 5 (military)	19.8
tising revenues	Channel 7 (military)	27.6
in 2002)	Channel 9 (MCOT)	11.7
	Channel 11 (Dept of Public Relations)	3.4
	ITV (Office of the Prime Minister)	11.9
Interprovincial bus	Transport Co. Ltd (state)	11.5
transport (share of no.	Cooperative bus service	88.5
of buses in 2003)		
Metropolitan bus transport	Bangkok Metropolitan Transport	47.0
(share of no. of	Authority (state)	
buses in 2003)	Private operators	53.0
Domestic voice services		
(share of number of		
subscribers in Jan 2005)		
Bangkok	TOT (state)	44.9
	Telecom Asia	55.1
Provinces	TOT (state)	62.2
	TT&T	37.8
ISPs (share of subscribers	Internet Thailand (state)	19.2
who accessed an ISP	Asia Infonet	13.0
in March 2004)	KSC	9.7
	CS Loxinfo	8.3
	Other 14 ISPs	49.8

Table 8.2 (continued)

Industry	Firm	Market share (%)
Cellular phones	AIS	59.3
(share of subscribers	DTAC	31.2
in 2002)	TA Orange	7.6
	DPC	1.7
	TOT (state)	0.1
	CAT Telecom (state)	0.0
Monopolies		
Cable television (private)	United Broadcasting Corporation	100.0
Rail transport (state)	State Railways of Thailand	100.0
International voice services (state)	CAT Telecom	100.0
Satellite (private)	Shinsat	100.0
Electricity purchase & sale (state)	EGAT	100.0
Electricity transmission (state)	EGAT	100.0
Electricity distribution in metropolitan areas (state)	Metropolitan Electricity Authority	100.0
Electricity distribution in rural areas (state)	Provincial Electricity Authority	100.0
Gas purchase & sale (state)	Petroleum Authority of Thailand	100.0
Gas distribution (state)	Petroleum Authority of Thailand	100.0
Water production & distribution in metropolitan areas (state)	Metropolitan Water Authority	100.0
Water production & distribution in rural areas (state)	Provincial Water Authority	100.0
Dominant market		
Electricity generation	EGAT	80.0
(share of production capacity)	Independent power producers	20.0

Source: Nikomborirak (2001); BMTA Annual Report (2002).

bus transport and internet services. In other markets, such as metropolitan bus services, state enterprises continue to dominate the industry.

Many regulated service sectors continue to be state monopolies (Table 8.2). The two exceptions are cable television and satellite services, where private monopolists operate under concession. In other market segments where the state enterprise is not a monopoly, it nevertheless retains its dominant position owing to rules and regulations that help to preserve its position in the market. For example, in air transport, until recently private operators were not allowed to offer direct flights on routes already serviced by Thai Airways. This meant that Bangkok Airways had to make a stopover at Sukhothai when flying from the capital to the country's second largest city, Chiang Mai. Price floors were also imposed to ensure that private operators did not undercut Thai Airways' prices. It was not until early 2004 that such rules were abolished upon the entry of Air Asia, a low-cost airline in which the prime minister and his family hold an equity stake.

Electricity generation has been open to private participation since the early 1990s, and Thailand now has several independent power producers. However, the country continues to use the 'single buyer' model whereby the Electricity Generating Authority of Thailand (EGAT) is the sole purchaser of all electricity generated. It then sells this electricity to another state monopoly in distribution. Competition in the generation market is limited by the requirement to sell to the dominant producer: a new operator cannot enter the market without first securing a contract to sell electricity to EGAT.

To conclude, there can be no doubt that government rules and regulations serve to protect the monopoly or dominant position of state-owned enterprises (SOEs) in many regulated services, resulting in a relatively high market concentration in these industries.

Trends in market concentration

With Thailand's economy still reeling from the financial crisis that broke out in 1997, further consolidation in many industries—in particular those with very low capacity utilization rates, such as cement and steel—will be necessary. While market consolidation may lead to better capacity allocation and lower per unit production costs, it may also result in more concentrated markets that would hamper the competitive process. As we shall see in section 4 below, the competition authority has already received complaints about excessive pricing for hot-rolled steel and price fixing for cement.

At the same time, many industries—in particular telecommunications, banking, and retailing—have witnessed major mergers and acquisitions (M&As) involving foreign investors (Table 8.3). Although market concentration in these industries may not have changed in the absence of greenfield investment, competitive pressures brought on by the entry of highly competitive multinational enterprises (MNEs) have helped to shake up these formerly cozy markets. In many cases, foreign investors have acquired smaller players in markets where firms were experiencing financial difficulties (banking, cellular phones, cement, beer) in order to establish a competitive foothold in the market with the hope of gaining market share from the dominant incumbent later on.

More recently, there has been a rise in the number of M&As among Thai enterprises, especially in the services sector where the threat of competition from American providers after the bilateral free trade agreement (FTA) with the United States comes into effect has promoted market consolidation. For example, in May 2004 the government merged three small banks, two of them owned by the state (Thai Military Bank and Industrial Finance Corporation of Thailand) and one of them foreign owned (DBS Thai Danu Bank). There have also been reports of possible mergers in the cell phone and cinema industries. In light of the trend, one can expect markets to become more concentrated in the future, unless the government opens up service markets that are at present still beyond the reach of foreign players.

To conclude, many industries are highly concentrated, in particular in services where SOEs still dominate the landscape. It should also be noted that because of the country's relatively well-developed transportation network, the relevant geographical market for any particular product sold in Thailand is likely to be the national market. Thus, the number of players in any particular product market would tend to be small compared with countries that are archipelagos or in which there are other geographical separations of markets such as an underdeveloped transportation network. One should therefore take care when making cross-country comparisons of market concentration figures.

High market concentration, in particular in industries with large sunk investments, is common among small economies where the size of the market is limited. But in many industries, market concentration results not from the the size of the operations but rather from barriers to competition constructed by the state, such as tariffs, restrictive foreign investment rules, or stringent licensing conditions. The following section examines the nature of the barriers to competition, both public and private, that shape market structure.

Table 8.3   Thailand: Trends in market concentration in selected industries, 1997–2004

Industry	Acquisition, merger, or new entry
1 Cement	In 1997 Holcim (Switzerland) acquired 33.7% of the second-largest producer, Siam City Cement In 2001 Cemex (Mexico) acquired 99% of the seventh-largest producer, Saraburi Cement In 1998 Cement Française (France) acquired 37% of Jalaprathan Cement, the fourth-largest producer TPI Polene, the third-largest producer, is currently undergoing debt restructuring. Siam City Cement has placed a bid to acquire 75% of the company
2 Ceramic roof tiles	None
3 Zinc-coated steel sheets	None
4 Glass sheets	None
5 Steel	In July 2002 NTS Steel Group, Siam Construction Steel, and Siam Iron Steel merged to form Millenium Steel
6 Motorcycles	None
7 Auto tires	None
8 Beer	In 2004 San Miguel (Philippines) acquired Amarit, the fourth-largest producer with a market share of less than 2%
9 Whiskey	In January 2003 the government liberalized liquor distillation, leading to the entry of new small-scale producers

10	Instant coffee	None
11	Cellular phones	In 1998 Singtel (Singapore) acquired 20% of AIS, the market leader with a market share of 60% In 1998 Telkom Malaysia (Malaysia) acquired a minority share in DPC In 2001 a major new entrant, Wireless Communications Service, acquired a minority share in TA Orange, the third-largest operator with a market share of 7.6% In 2001 AIS, the largest cellular operator, acquired 97.5% of DPC, the fourth-largest provider with a market share of 7.6%
12	Light bulbs	None
13	Batteries	
	Alkaline	None
	Normal	None
14	Modern trade	Foreign retailers such as Auchon, Carrefour, and the Casino Group (Big C) (France), Makro (Netherlands), Royal Ahold (Netherlands), and Tesco (United Kingdom) have conducted takeovers of domestic modern trade
15	Banking	Foreign banks—United Overseas Bank (Singapore), Standard Chartered Bank (United Kingdom), and ABN Amro (Netherlands, exited 2004)—conducted takeovers of three ailing domestic banks, none ranked in the top five In May 2004 the government merged the Industrial Finance Corporation of Thailand and the Thai Military Bank with a private bank, DBS Thai Danu Bank (Singapore)

Source: Cement: Wu (2002); cellular phones, banking, and modern trade: Nikomborirak (2000a); all others: Nikomborirak et al. (2002) and Thailand Development Research Institute updates.

3   BARRIERS TO COMPETITION IN THE THAI ECONOMY

Barriers to competition from imports

Thailand is an open economy, with the value of trade (exports plus imports) representing approximately 108 percent of its GDP in 2001. However, Thailand still maintains high tariffs compared with other members of the Association of Southeast Asian Nations (ASEAN). The country's average applied tariff rate is 38.2 percent for agricultural products and 13.9 percent for manufactured goods. Table 8.4 shows average tariff rates for three-digit International Standard Industrial Classification industries. Most rates range between 10 and 50 percent, with peaks in the beverages industry (46.7 percent) and the clothing industry (33.6 percent).

Thailand's tariff regime remains complex, with 46 rates. It is also distortionary in that, in some cases, tariffs on raw materials or intermediate goods are significantly higher than those on the final product. Products that are protected by high tariffs include agricultural products, import-competing goods—in particular autos and auto parts—fabrics and apparel, beverages, certain electrical appliances, and luxury goods such as wine and spirits, tobacco, and wool carpets. For example, the tariff on completely knocked down auto kits is 33 percent, and that on luxury passenger cars and sport utility vehicles is as high as 80 percent. Current tariffs on parts and components range from 40 to 60 percent. The applied tariff rate on fabrics is 40 percent, and 45 percent for apparel. Tariff rates on agricultural products are high across the board even in the absence of domestic production. For example, duties on ready-to-eat food products range from 40 to 50 percent, the highest in ASEAN. Those on meat, fresh fruit, and vegetables are similarly high. These are often bound rates under the World Trade Organization (WTO).

Under the Common Effective Preferential Tariff Scheme (CEPT)—the mechanism by which the ASEAN Free Trade Area (AFTA) was established—tariff rates are significantly lower. On 1 January 2003, tariffs on all products were lowered to 0–5 percent, with the exception of those placed on the CEPT's temporary exclusion list, sensitive list (mainly agricultural products), and general exceptions list (mainly products relating to national security, culture, and health). Thailand appears to have the smallest number of items on these lists, as can be seen in Table 8.5. It should also be noted that AFTA has a very liberal rule-of-origin regime: to be eligible for preferential tariff rates, products need to contain only 40 percent local content. This threshold applies to all products. In effect, this means that many Thai industries are now facing increasingly strong competitive pressures from neighboring countries.

Table 8.4   Thailand: Average tariff rates for selected manufacturing industries, 2003 (%)

ISIC code	Description	Average tariff
311	Food products	27.6
313	Beverages	46.7
321	Textiles	26.3
322	Clothing	33.6
332	Furniture except metal	20.0
341	Paper products	24.7
342	Printing & publishing	15.9
351	Industrial chemicals	7.8
352	Other chemicals	10.8
371	Iron & steel products	20.0
381	Metal products	19.1
383	Electrical machinery	12.8
384	Transport equipment	26.4

Source: WTO (2003).

The contribution of imports to competition is evident in a study of trade practices in 12 manufacturing industries by Nikomborirak et al. (2002). The authors found that two product markets that were subject to low import tariffs—batteries and light bulbs—did not experience any restrictive business practices even when the market was highly concentrated. In contrast, markets that were protected by high tariffs, such as alcoholic beverages (whiskey and beer) and motorcycles, and those in which goods are not easily traded, such as cement and cellular phone services, did have competition problems.

As well as being a member of AFTA, Thailand is engaged in the negotiation of bilateral FTAs with several countries. It has signed Trade and Investment Framework Agreements with Bahrain, the People's Republic of China (PRC), and India, as well as with developed countries such as the United States, Japan, and Australia (Appendix A8.1). The country is beginning to feel the impact of these FTAs; the first 'early harvest' provisions under the agreement with the PRC became effective in late 2003.

Table 8.5   Thailand: Products listed under CEPT, 2002 (no.)

Country	Inclusion list	Temporary exclusion list[a]	Sensitive list[b]	General exceptions list[c]	Total
Brunei Darussalam	6,276	0	14	202	6,492
Indonesia	7,213	0	4	68	7,285
Malaysia	10,039	218	83	53	10,393
Philippines	5,571	6	46	16	5,639
Singapore	5,859	0	0	0	5,859
Thailand	9,104	0	7	0	9,111
Viet Nam	5,505	696	51	139	6,391
Lao PDR	2,098	1,291	88	74	3,551
Myanmar	3,580	1,823	21	48	5,472
Cambodia	3,115	3,523	50	134	6,822
ASEAN-10	58,360	7,557	364	734	67,015
(% of all products)	87.1	11.3	0.5	1.1	100.0

a The temporary exclusion list comprises products that are subject to delayed reductions in tariffs. These exclusions expired on 1 January 2003, when all products on the list had to be transferred to the inclusion list, where bound tariff rates must not exceed 5 percent.

b The sensitive list comprises products whose tariffs will decline gradually to less than 5 percent by 2010. Certain products, in particular rice, are classified as 'highly sensitive.' Tariff rates for these products may exceed the 5 percent threshold even after 2010.

c The general exceptions list comprises products that are sensitive to national security, culture, and similar concerns. They may never be included in the tariff reduction scheme.

Source: Ministry of Foreign Affairs website, <www.mfa.go.th/asean/asean_web/docs/economic_afta.doc>.

These required tariffs on most fruits and vegetables to be eliminated by 1 October 2003, leading to an instantaneous influx of fresh food products from the PRC into Thailand. Thailand's FTA with Australia was signed on 5 July 2004. It is expected to expose the local automobile market to stiff competition from Australia—a production base for large cars—starting from its January 2005 effectivity.

The services sector appears to be elusive to trade liberalization at the bilateral level. Except for the bilateral agreement with the United States, which is expected to cover services, there is no clear indication that FTAs will lead to a progressive opening up of the services sector to competition.

Barriers to competition from foreign suppliers

The most important law governing foreign-controlled businesses is the Foreign Business Act 1999, which replaced the former Alien Business Law (National Executive Council Announcement No. 281) of 1972. Before the introduction of the Alien Business Law, foreigners were generally permitted to do business in Thailand freely, with few restrictions. The 1972 law classified businesses into three main categories, each with different foreign ownership restrictions. It applied to all businesses except those that were subject to *sui generis* laws, such as public utilities, finance, and the media.

The Foreign Business Act 1999 guarantees most favored nation (MFN) treatment for all except American investors, who are already covered by the 1968 Treaty of Amity and Economic Relations between the Kingdom of Thailand and the United States of America. It retains the three business categories of the law it replaced, although the list of businesses in each category has changed. (A complete list of businesses in each category is given in Appendix A8.2.) Businesses listed in category 1 are absolutely prohibited to foreigners unless an exception is made under a special law or treaty.[2] They include mass media, rice, animal husbandry, and other resource-based businesses. Businesses that appear in the second category involve national security or safety; art, culture, and handicrafts; or natural resources and the environment. Foreigners are not permitted to start new businesses listed in this category without special permission from the Minister of Commerce with cabinet approval. The third category consists of businesses that the government believes are particularly vulnerable to foreign competition. They include mining, salt farming, forestry, fishery, professional services, and all other services unless specified in the ministerial regulations. As with the previous category, foreigners may apply for permission to operate businesses listed in this category. The only difference is that the power to grant permission is vested in the Director General of the Department of Business Promotion, Ministry of Commerce, and the Foreign Business Committee established under the Foreign Business Act. To obtain a license, applicants must be able to convince the relevant local authorities that the particular investment project could not be conducted competently by a local firm.

From the list of businesses prohibited to foreigners (Appendix A8.2), it would appear that the manufacturing sector is very much open to foreign investment, except for a few businesses that concern national security and the environment. The services sector, however, remains relatively closed. Although the new investment law appears to be more liberal in that it takes a 'negative list' approach to defining the sectors that are subject to investment restrictions, a 'positive list' approach still applies in practice in the services sector. This is because the third category includes 'other categories of service business except those prescribed in the ministerial regulations.' Moreover, sector-specific law may impose even more stringent conditions on foreign participation. For example, the Telecommunications Act 2001 caps the foreign equity share of a facilities-based operator at only 25 percent. The relatively closed services sector contributes to inefficiencies, which in turn impose costs on the manufacturing sector.

Barriers to competition due to state rules and regulations

Many domestic laws and regulations pose barriers to entry. As can be seen in Table 8.6, many of the manufacturing industries that display high market concentration receive various forms of state protection, such as high tariffs or surcharges imposed on competing imported products, stringent licensing conditions that make new entry difficult, and changes in the excise tax regime that benefit the incumbent monopoly.[3]

Certain laws or cabinet decisions also grant exclusive rights to SOEs to provide services to the public. For example, until 2001 the law granted a statutory monopoly in the ownership and operation of all telecommunications services to two state enterprises, the Telephone Organization of Thailand (TOT) and CAT Telecom. Private participation in the industry was subject to build–transfer–operate (BTO) agreements whereby the private operator built the network and then transferred ownership of it to TOT or CAT Telecom in exchange for the exclusive right to operate the network for a specified period of time. The private concessionaire thus lost the right to claim ownership of any assets and was subject to the operating conditions set by the state enterprise, some of which restricted competition. Fortunately, with the enactment of the Telecommunications Act in 2001, this statutory monopoly is now void. However, the terms and conditions of the concessions remain intact despite the passage of the new law, and despite the corporatization of TOT and CAT Telecom.

Similarly, the state-owned metropolitan and interprovincial bus operators hold an exclusive right to provide services on main routes. But unlike the case of telecommunications, the bus monopolies are granted by exec-

Table 8.6   Thailand: Barriers to competition in selected markets

Industry	State restrictions	Private restrictions
Manufacturing		
1 Cement	None	Restrictions on output; exclusive dealing; exclusive distribution
2 Ceramic roof tiles	None	Exclusive dealing
3 Zinc-coated steel sheets	None	None
4 Glass sheets	None	Exclusive dealing; exclusive distribution
5 Steel		
Hot-rolled	None	Exclusive dealing
Cold-rolled	Antidumping surcharges	Exclusive dealing
6 Motorcycles	Restrictions on new investment; high import duties	Exclusive dealing
7 Auto tires	None	International monopsony
8 Beer	Stringent licensing conditions; excise tax	Tied sales; exclusive dealing; predatory pricing
9 Whiskey	Stringent licensing conditions (until 2002); excise tax	Predatory pricing; foreclosure on supply of essential inputs
10 Instant coffee	Tariffs	None
11 Light bulbs	None	None
12 Batteries		
Alkaline	None	None
Normal	None	None
Services		
13 Cellular phones	Exclusive concessions; excise tax	Bundling (service & handsets)
14 Cable television	State approval of merger to form a monopoly	Bundling (channels); excessive pricing

Source: Steel: Department of Internal Trade website, <www.dit.go.th>, accessed May 2004; cable television: Subcommittee Report (2000); all others: Nikombori-rak et al. (2002).

utive power—that is, through a cabinet decision—rather than through legislation. Again, private operators can only operate under concessions from the state enterprise for which they pay a 'royalty' in the form of a fixed fee or a share of the profits.

Barriers to competition from private anticompetitive practices

The competition cases discussed earlier show that private restrictive practices occur in a few concentrated markets. Nikomborirak et al. (2002) reveal the various types of private anticompetitive practices that occur in certain markets, including price fixing, tied sales, predatory pricing, exclusive dealing, and monopolization of inputs (Table 8.6). Exclusive dealing stands out as the most widespread form of abuse of dominance. However, this practice can be difficult to identify, as distributors are rarely prohibited outright from selling a competitor's products. Rather, they are presented with various options that encourage them to enter into exclusive contracts, with the more attractive deals involving an exclusive distribution agreement in exchange for financial and marketing support from the manufacturer.

Interestingly, the survey found few complaints of monopoly pricing, with the exception of cement, where quantity fixing was reported, and steel, where antidumping surcharges had fed directly into high domestic prices. This seems to suggest that the anticompetitive practice of exclusive dealing has not had much of an impact on consumer welfare. Possibly this is because the production sector in Thailand is relatively open in the absence of licensing requirements or limits on foreign equity ownership; only a few industries, such as the distillation of alcoholic beverages, have *sui generis* laws that impose lower ceilings on foreign ownership. The only major barrier to competition in the manufacturing sector, apart from technology that gives rise to scale economies, appears to be import tariffs. It should be noted, however, that many of the complaints filed with the Trade Competition Commission do involve alleged monopoly pricing and price fixing, as will be shown in section 4 of this chapter. Gypsum board, lysine, television receivers, and container haulage have all been the subject of complaints. This indicates that there are cases where private restrictive practices have led to a reduction in consumer welfare.

Another interesting finding of the survey by Nikomborirak et al. (2002) is that exclusive dealing is practiced only when a particular firm is the clear market leader with a market share exceeding 40 percent, and the second-ranking firm in the market is far behind. Oligopolistic markets, in which a few players each have a market share of 20–40 percent, do not practice exclusive dealing. This seems to suggest that the market share threshold for market dominance hovers around that figure.

But market share is not the only determinant of market power. The survey found that in the case of instant coffee, where one brand had an 88 percent share of the market, exclusive dealing did not occur. This was simply because the manufacturer was faced with a group of even stronger distributors in the form of the large foreign supermarket chains: Carrefour, Tesco, Makro, and the Casino Group (Big C). Similarly, in markets where competition from imports is high owing to low tariff protection, market share does not necessarily indicate market power, as discussed earlier.

In the services sector, both cellular phones and cable television services, where private operation prevails, have been the subject of complaints about excessive pricing (Table 8.6). Interestingly, the survey found that state regulations were often the source of price collusion. In the case of cellular phones, the terms of concessions inhibit private concessionaires' ability to make price adjustments, contributing to price rigidity. Similarly, in the case of the cement market, tacit price collusion is facilitated by the state's price control regime, whereby producers have to obtain permission from the Department of Internal Trade for any price increase. In other utility service markets such as electricity, water, and transport, where state enterprises remain a monopoly or the dominant player in the market, complaints are rare because these enterprises are not profit seeking.

Missing from the survey are anticompetitive practices undertaken by state enterprises, which are exempt from competition law. As mentioned earlier, many government-owned enterprises in Thailand hold de facto regulatory power derived from their ability to place conditions on the operations of private concessionaires. The absence of sector-specific regulatory agencies—in telecommunications, water, electricity, and transportation—allows SOEs to wield the regulatory authority in their possession in ways that reduce competition in the market.

For example, in the 1990s TOT, the state-owned domestic telephone service provider, handed out several long-term BTO telecommunications concessions to private companies. Since TOT and CAT Telecom held a statutory monopoly in both infrastructure and services, they were able to impose conditions on private concessionaires that limited their ability to compete with TOT. Concessionaires, for their part, were willing to accept these conditions because they were eager to enter a lucrative industry. The terms and conditions set out in the concessions covered such matters as tariff schedules, tariff adjustments, the technical specifications of telecommunications equipment, the introduction of new services, and the location of new fixed lines. Private concessionaires had to obtain prior approval from TOT before acting on any of these matters. In other words, TOT has acted as the regulator for the private companies to whom it has given concessions.

TT&T, a private company, has held a concession to install and provide 1.5 million fixed line telephone services in provincial areas since 1992. The company complained that TOT had refused to approve its request to provide low-priced, domestic long-distance services based on the internet protocol (IP). This request was made in response to TOT's own introduction of such a service in 2000. The inability of the two parties to agree on an appropriate revenue share (including interconnection charge) to be paid to TOT for the 'new service' caused TT&T to lose a significant portion of its market share to the state operator before a compromise was finally reached in 2003. The private fixed line operator servicing the Bangkok area, Telecom Asia, decided that the 30 percent revenue share demanded by TOT was unacceptable. It opted to build its own IP network rather than lease one from TOT.[4]

Such practices are clearly anticompetitive and unfair, but there is little that a private concessionaire can do because, as an SOE, TOT is exempt from the provisions of the Trade Competition Act. Several attempts have been made to negotiate the removal of anticompetitive clauses in telecommunications concessions, but without success (TDRI 2001a).

In cases where state enterprises do not compete with private concessionaires, they may collude with the concessionaires to maintain high prices. For example, although state telecommunications operators are not involved in the provision of mobile services, they collect sizeable revenue shares from the private firms operating under their statutory monopoly rights and thus have an interest in ensuring that the concessionaires show a healthy bottom line.[5] As a result, monthly subscription fees remained relatively high despite consumer complaints until the entry of a major third player, TA Orange, in 2001 (Nikomborirak et al. 2002). Similarly, MCOT, the broadcasting regulator, receives a 6 percent share of the private cable television monopoly's revenue. It is therefore not surprising that it has done little to address consumers' complaints about hikes in monthly subscription fees.

Summary

State rules and regulations pose a major barrier to competition in the Thai economy, in particular in utility industries where new entry is restricted due to exclusivity granted to SOEs, and where foreign participation is severely limited. Such exclusivity encourages anticompetitive practices on the part of state enterprises, as can be seen from the case of domestic telephone services.

In manufacturing, anticompetitive practices such as exclusive dealing and price fixing prevail in a few industries that are highly concentrated, such as motorcycles, cement, ceramic roof tiles, glass, and steel. Most of these products are either bulky or fragile, or are not easily traded, and are therefore less subject to competition from imports. For those that are easily traded, such as steel and motorcycles, tariff protection allows local producers to wield market power. The anticompetitive practices found in the alcoholic beverages industry are directly attributable to state restriction of competition. The case of whiskey illustrates clearly that state-sponsored monopolies can have damaging spillover effects on competitive markets. The removal of such state rules would easily solve the problem.

State-constructed barriers to competition are shaped by the various economic policies that have a bearing on the degree of competition in the domestic market. These include trade, investment, industrial, and privatization policies. To understand why these barriers are present and how they may change in the future requires an understanding of the underlying policies. This is the focus of the next section.

4 THE EFFECTS OF TRADE, INDUSTRIAL, INVESTMENT, AND PRIVATIZATION POLICIES ON COMPETITION

First of all, it should be noted that Thailand has never had a competition policy as such. That is, there has never been a requirement to justify the various laws, policies, and measures that were implemented in terms of their implications for a competitive environment in the market or the economy as a whole. It is therefore impossible to assess the implications of competition policy on the trade and investment regime. However, one can instead examine how trade, investment, and other economic policies have affected the intensity of competition in the market.

Trade policy

As discussed earlier, the current government has focused on establishing bilateral FTAs with major trading partners such as the United States and Japan in the expectation that these will stimulate competition in the domestic market (Appendix A8.1). It has already concluded agreements with Australia, Bahrain, India, and the PRC and is negotiating with Japan, Peru, and the United States.[6]

There are concerns, however, that selective trade liberalization, particularly in certain service sectors, will lead to higher market concentration.

Under the proposed FTA with the United States, the entry of large US multinationals may lead, in the longer run, to American domination of Thai markets in the absence of competition from other, non-American, multinational operators. For example, if Thailand accedes to the US request to open up the express delivery market to American companies only, global operators like TNT and DHL will not be allowed to compete, and the domestic market may end up being dominated by a few large American operators, such as Federal Express and Courier. Unless Thailand considers opening up the market on an MFN basis, the threat of market dominance is real. Thailand has not liberalized any of its service markets in the absence of commitments in its bilateral and multilateral agreements to do so, and so empirical evidence on the impact of service liberalization is lacking. Nevertheless, a study by Nikomborirak (2004a) indicates that the entry of foreign banks such as ABN Amro, United Overseas Bank, United Bank of Singapore, and Standard Chartered Bank since the crisis through acquisitions of ailing Thai banks appears to have broken the domestic banking cartel, bringing about a remarkable improvement in service. Customers now enjoy longer banking hours, more diversified financial services as a result of customer segmentation, and credit card services that are free of annual fees (TFRC 2003).

Bilateral FTAs that involve a developed country must contain competition policy provisions, under the General Agreement on Tariffs and Trade (GATT) requirement that such agreements cover 'substantially all trade' (article XXIV).[7] So far, Australia is the only developed country to sign an FTA with Thailand. The competition policy provisions in the agreement are relatively weak in that they focus mainly on voluntary cooperation between the competition authorities of the two countries.

The FTA between Thailand and the United States, which will be based on the existing agreement between Singapore and the United States, is likely to contain more advanced commitments on the implementation of domestic competition law. In a nutshell, the competition policy chapter in the Singapore–US FTA requires each party to (a) maintain measures to proscribe anticompetitive conduct; (b) prohibit SOEs from engaging in restrictive trade practices or abusing their monopoly position unless granted an exception on efficiency grounds; and (c) ensure that SOEs act solely in accordance with commercial considerations in the sale and purchase of goods or services.[8]

The first element would require Thailand's Trade Competition Commission to urgently settle the threshold for dominant market share to ensure that competition law is effective in proscribing anticompetitive acts. This would benefit both Thai consumers and Thai businesses. The second element would require amendment of the Trade Competition Act 1999 to remove the current exemptions provided to SOEs. The author believes that a blanket exemption for state enterprises is unjustified, but that exceptions made on a case-by-case basis can be justified on public interest grounds. The final element requiring state enterprises to operate on a commercial basis seems to go beyond the normal scope of competition law and encroaches on government procurement rights. There is no clear reason why one would need to monitor the manner in which SOEs operate, unless such practices were unfairly restricting competition in the market.

In short, FTAs may help pressure the Thai government to make the current competition law enforceable. At the same time, however, certain sections of some of the proposed agreements represent an unjustified invasion of the sovereign right to operate state enterprises.

Industrial and investment policy

Thailand has never really had 'target industries' and does not have a policy of promoting domestic companies to become 'national champions.' Industrial policy has focused instead on supporting companies that employ advanced technology, invest in research and development, provide training programs, utilize available domestic resources (including labor), and promote industrial linkages. Firms with such qualifications are likely to receive investment incentives from the Board of Investment (BOI) regardless of the type of industry they may be in. In general, then, industrial and investment policy does not support restriction of competition in the manufacturing industry, possibly with the following exception.

Investment law empowers the BOI to impose import surcharges in order to protect the financial interests of promoted companies (Nikomborirak 2004a). In the past the BOI has used this power sparingly. Steel products were the only ones to benefit greatly from import surcharges. When these were outlawed by the WTO, they were replaced by antidumping measures: 23 of the 24 antidumping cases investigated by Thailand since the promulgation of the antidumping law in 1999 involve steel products (Nikomborirak and Naewmalee 2004). The market protection afforded by the imposition of antidumping surcharges has allowed steelmakers to maintain high prices, causing complaints of excessive pricing to be filed with the Trade Competition Commission (Table 8.7). However, complaints about the other products and services shown in Table 8.7 cannot be traced back to market protection afforded by the investment promotion regime.

Table 8.7   Thailand: Cases before or awaiting submission to the Trade Competition Commission

Practice	Product/service	Decision of the commission
Submitted		
1 Refusal to supply (1)	Video movies	Private sector agreed to cease the behavior.
2 Tied sales	Whiskey & beer	Abuse of dominance found, but section on abuse of dominance was not yet functioning.
3 Monopoly pricing	Cable TV services	Case was handed over to MCOT, the sector regulator.
4 Refusal to supply (2)	Video movies	
5 Predatory pricing	Eggs	
6 Tied sales (product & spare parts)	Electricity generators	
7 Tied sales	Whiskey & bottled water	
8 Restriction of competition (details not available)	All-purpose cleaning sponges	
9 Unfair pricing	International shipping services	The Office of Trade Competition asked international shippers to give domestic shippers 90 days' notice of any future rate adjustment.
10 Exclusive dealing	Motorcycles	An unfair trade practice was found under section 29. The commission is in the process of gathering evidence for a court case.
11 Monopoly pricing	Ferry service between Samui & Don Sak	
12 Minimum sales requirement	Computer games	
13 Restriction of competition	Printing & writing paper	A 1987 cabinet decision required all government departments to procure their printing & writing paper from a designated private supplier. This decision has been repealed.

14	Tied sales	Motorcycle accessories
15	Predatory pricing	Fertilizer
16	Refusal to supply	Petroleum
17	Monopoly pricing	Corn seed (animal feed)
18	Merger	Paper

Under investigation

1	Predatory pricing	Plastic straws attached to UHT cartons
2	Monopoly pricing	Hot-rolled steel
3	Price fixing	Gypsum board
4	Price fixing	Container haulage
5	Product hoarding	Lysine
6	Bid rigging	Gasoline
7	Price fixing	Purchase of turtles for export to PRC by large traders

Awaiting submission

1	Unfair trade practice	Discount stores
2	Price fixing	Cement
3	Unfair trade practice	Department stores
4	Price fixing	Plastic resins
5	Price fixing	Movie theaters
6	Excessive pricing	Parking cards (with magnetic strip)
7	Price fixing	Television receivers
8	Price fixing (international buyers)	Rubber

Source: Department of Internal Trade, <www.dit.go.th>, accessed May 2004.

Privatization policy

Privatization has been on every government's agenda for the last two decades, but the policy seems to change with each change of government. Thus, there is no coherent privatization policy in Thailand to indicate a general trend on this issue.

However, since the early 1990s there has been a clear policy to promote private sector participation in the provision of basic services such as telecommunications, energy, and transport. SOEs in the telecommunications sector were restrained from expanding their existing networks or becoming involved in new services such as paging and mobile telephones. Instead, concessions were handed out to private operators in segments such as the installation and operation of mobile phone and fixed line telephone services in Bangkok and the provinces, as well as satellite, broadband, public telephone, and ISP services. In exchange for exclusive operating rights, private concessionaires handed over large shares of their revenue to state enterprises.[9] The concessions contributed to the rapid expansion of the telecommunications market and helped sow the seeds of competition in the sector, despite the restrictions placed on the private concessionaires. The number of fixed line and mobile telephones has grown rapidly since 1992 when private participation began (Figures 8.1 and 8.2).

Over the same period, a similar move toward partial privatization has been evident in the power sector as well. Many independent and small private companies have been issued licenses to generate electricity. However, EGAT remains the dominant player in the electricity generation market and is the single buyer of all electricity. As long as the private sector is denied access to the transmission network, industrial and large users will be deprived of the freedom to buy electricity directly from source.

More recently, the government has turned to selling equity stakes in state enterprises to private investors rather than introducing private competition into the market (Nikomborirak 2004c). In 2002 it sold a 30 percent equity share in the Petroleum Authority of Thailand, the sole buyer of natural gas and the owner of the gas pipeline network. In 2004 it sold a 30 percent stake in the Airport Authority of Thailand, which operates five international airports in Thailand including Bangkok International Airport. Most recently, in April 2004, the government tried to sell a 30 percent equity share in EGAT but faced strong opposition from the electricity union. Academics have also voiced their concerns about the sale of equity shares in state enterprises that still hold monopoly and regulatory power. Consumers too are worried about the absence of a regulatory framework and independent regulatory body to protect their interests.

Figure 8.1   Thailand: Number of fixed line telephone connections, 1990–2003 (million)

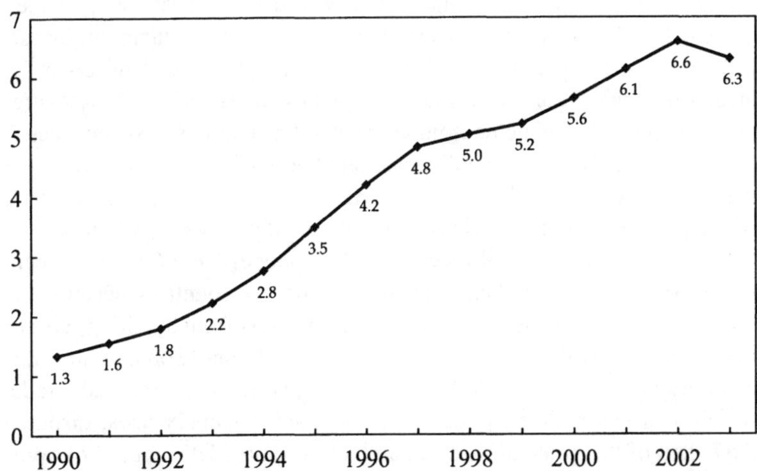

Source: TOT Annual Report (1992–99); TT&T Annual Report (2003).

Figure 8.2   Thailand: Number of cellular phones, 1990–2003 (million)

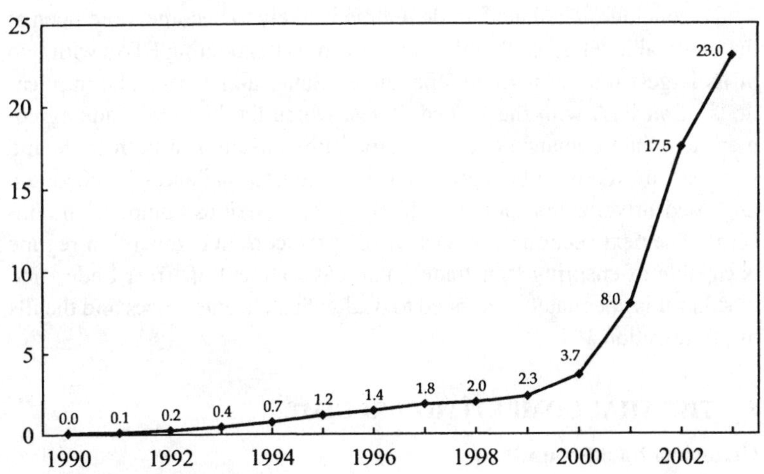

Source: 1990–99: ITU (2002b); 2000–03: TT&T Annual Report (2003).

These partially privatized state monopolies are likely to pose competition problems. Not only do they hold a dominant position in the market but they are also exempt from competition law, as discussed earlier. Once they become listed companies with shareholders who expect maximum investment returns, the pressure on them to generate profits will no doubt be greater than when they were wholly owned by the state. The drive to create a healthy bottom line does not bode well for their business practices.

Unfortunately for the public, past regulatory experience suggests that the government is unable or unwilling to protect consumers' interests when private companies abuse their monopoly power (Nikomborirak 2004c). For example, until recently mobile phones were 60–300 percent more expensive in Thailand than in neighboring countries because the government failed to stop private cellular operators from bundling sales of mobile phones with subscriptions for mobile services (Somkiat and Rattanarumitrsorn 2002: 33, Table 5). The Department of Internal Trade, which oversees both the price control and antimonopoly laws, disputed the extent of this price differential and allowed the blatant abuse of dominance to continue until a new entrant, TA Orange, entered the market in 2001. At this point the incumbent succumbed to competitive pressure and abandoned its expensive bundled service voluntarily. In light of the government's limited ability to regulate private operators, the transfer of ownership of state monopolies from the state to private investors does not bode well for fair competition.

To conclude, Thailand's trade regime is likely to become more open at the bilateral level given that the government is negotiating FTAs with two of its largest trading partners, the United States and Japan. The implications of an FTA with the United States, where the bilateral trade agreement template demands deep and broad liberalization in both trade and services, are likely to be significant. In contrast, Thailand's botched and unguided privatization policy is likely to pose serious competition concerns. The next section examines whether the current competition regime is capable of ensuring 'fair trade' in an environment of 'freer trade,' and whether it is adequately equipped to deal with state enterprises and the ills of privatization.

5   THE THAI COMPETITION REGIME

Historical background

Thailand first adopted a competition law in 1979: the Price Control and Antimonopoly Act 1979, which has since been replaced by two new laws (see below). The objective of the law was to protect consumers from inflationary pressures and from widespread collusive practices among businesses that had led to excessive pricing. The provisions on anticompetitive practices were incomplete and did not cover many types of vertical restraint or M&As. While the price control mechanism was implemented and worked well, the antimonopoly provisions proved harder to enforce. This was because a business accused of anticompetitive practices had to be officially declared a 'controlled business' by the competition authority—that is, the Department of Internal Trade—before the law could be enforced. Since there were no clear rules to define a monopolistic business, only one business, ice manufacturing, was declared a controlled business during the two decades in which the law was in effect.

Under the Anand administration (1990–91), the government strongly promoted competition in the marketplace and removed many of the government measures that had been distorting the market. For example, it lowered tariff peaks in the automobile industry, removed licensing requirements in the cement industry, and abolished price controls on gasoline (Supanit 2002). At the same time, the government encouraged private participation in the provision of infrastructure services, in particular in the telecommunications and electricity generation sectors, issuing concessions and contracts to many private operators.

This pro-competition policy was possible only because the Anand government was not an elected one. The military appointed Anand, a highly respected diplomat-turned-businessman, as the new prime minister in the midst of political chaos in order to appease the public. He staffed his cabinet with technocrats and law academics rather than professional politicians. His government was therefore free from the money politics that normally plague the political process. Because the government was not indebted to any particular business group, it was able to launch a series of economic reforms despite their possibly adverse effect on vested interests.

In keeping with its policy to promote the market mechanism, the government recognized the need to safeguard fair competition. In 1991 it set up a commission to reform antitrust law in Thailand. The commission recommended that a new competition law be drafted, and in 1992 the draft legislation was submitted to parliament after being approved by cabinet. However, parliament was dissolved before the law could be passed.

It was not until 1999, two years after the economic crisis, that parliament finally passed the Trade Competition Act under the Chuan government. Unlike in Indonesia, in Thailand the passage of a competition law was not a condition imposed by the International Monetary Fund (IMF), and it was not mentioned in any of the eight Letters of Intent that the Ministry of Finance and Bank of Thailand submitted to the IMF between 1997 and September 1999.[10]

According to Supanit (2002), the new constitution passed in October 1997, which clearly advocates free and fair competition, smoothed the way for the passage of the Trade Competition Act.[11] Article 87 states that:

> The State shall encourage a free economic system through market force, ensure and supervise fair competition, protect consumers, and prevent direct and indirect monopolies, repeal and refrain from enacting laws and regulations controlling businesses which do not correspond with the economic necessity, and shall not engage in an enterprise in competition with the private sector unless it is necessary for the purpose of maintaining the security of the State, preserving the common interest, or providing public utilities.

The constitution also guarantees the right of Thai nationals to engage in business activities under free and fair competition. Article 50 stipulates that a person shall enjoy the liberty to engage in an enterprise or occupation, and to undertake fair and free competition. Private operators have resorted to this section in demanding fair trade in markets where state enterprises operate under certain privileges. Thus, the promulgation of a competition law can be viewed as a necessary tool to fulfill the spirit of the constitution.

The legal framework

In 1999, the Price Control and Antimonopoly Act 1979 was replaced by two laws: the Trade Competition Act 1999 and the Goods and Services Price Control Act 1999. Thus in effect the price control provisions were separated from the antimonopoly provisions. Two commissions were formed: the Goods and Services Price Control Commission, which is responsible for price controls, and the Trade Competition Commission, which is responsible for safeguarding fair competition in the markets. The secretariats of both commissions reside within the Department of Internal Trade in the Ministry of Commerce.

The Trade Competition Act applies to all enterprises and business activities except (a) state enterprises; (b) cooperatives and agricultural cooperatives; and (c) central and regional government agencies and other businesses as prescribed by the ministerial regulations. To date, no business has been granted an exemption by means of the ministerial regulations.

Although the competition regime contains very few de jure exemptions, it has plenty of de facto exemptions as a result of the administrative body's failure to pass the requisite implementing rules and regulations, as will be elaborated in greater detail below. For example, after five years the Trade Competition Commission has yet to pass the threshold market shares that would (a) define a 'dominant' business for the section on abuse of dominance, and (b) determine the post-merger level of market concentration that would trigger a mandatory pre-merger notification. In effect, all business practices that constitute an abuse of dominance and all mergers that may foreclose future competition are effectively exempted at present. Moreover, all the provisions on restrictive practices in the Trade Competition Act are subject to a rule-of-reason approach that permits reasonable exceptions to the law. While there is nothing wrong with an approach that allows flexibility in the implementation of the law, the absence of implementing regulations and guidelines implies that exceptions may be arbitrary, discriminatory, and unpredictable.[12]

The main substantive provisions of the law concern abuse of dominance (section 25), merger controls (section 26), and collusive practices (section 27). The act also specifies the types of abuse of dominance and collusive practices that may constitute a violation of the law. A few horizontal restrictions, such as price fixing, quantity fixing, and bid rigging, are governed by a per se rule, but most practices are governed by a rule of reason.[13]

Section 29 of the law deals with unfair trade practices. It prohibits any act contrary to free and fair competition that obstructs, damages, or restricts other business operations. The scope of application of this section is unclear because it is overly broad and vaguely worded, leaving too much discretion to the administrator of the law. Businesses have questioned its 'catch-all' provisions and are pressuring the competition authority to pass implementing regulations that specify the types of behavior that would be prohibited under this section.

The administrative body

The Office of Trade Competition (the secretariat to the Trade Competition Commission) resides within the Department of Internal Trade, Ministry of Commerce. The Trade Competition Commission consists of the Minister of Commerce as chair, the Permanent Secretary for Commerce as vice-chair, the Director General of the Department of Internal Trade as secretary, the Permanent Secretary for Finance, and from eight to twelve experts from various disciplines who are nominated by the Minister of Commerce and appointed by cabinet. Strangely, the law stipulates that at least one-half of the experts must be private sector representatives; the current practice is to have three commissioners from the Federation of

---

Box 8.1 The cable television monopoly

United Broadcasting Corporation (UBC), the nationwide cable television service, became a monopoly in February 1998 following the merger of the two incumbent operators, International Broadcasting Corporation and United Television Network. This merger was not subject to state regulation because the Trade Competition Act of 1999 had not yet been passed. Although public sentiment was against the merger, it was approved by MCOT, the government organization authorized to issue broadcasting licenses. The main justification given for the merger was that prices had increased steeply since the onset of the financial crisis and sharp depreciation of the baht in 1997. The 'efficiency defense' was that with a single operator, movie licenses could be procured at a lower cost since competition between the two operators would be eliminated.

A little over a year after the merger, UBC raised the monthly subscription fee for its 'gold' package—the package with the greatest number of channels—by a whopping 22.5 percent, from B890 ($22.25 at an assumed exchange rate of B40/$) to B1,090 ($27.25) in May 1999 (Nikomborirak 2000b). The company argued that this increase was justified because it was still recording losses each year and had added new channels that had increased consumers' choice. However, a consumer group filed a complaint to the competition authority alleging that the cable operator was abusing its monopoly position by charging excessive prices.

The expert subcommittee assigned to investigate the case found that the merger had ended the fierce price and non-price competition between the

---

Thai Industries and another three from the Chamber of Commerce. Each appointed commissioner has a two-year term. Terms are not staggered, so a change in government can mean a change in the entire composition of the commission when commissioners' terms expire. The commission is therefore very vulnerable to political influence.

Past performance

The performance of the Trade Competition Commission has been dismal. According to the Department of Internal Trade's own website, the Trade Competition Office has handled 18 competition cases since its establishment in 1999 (Table 8.7). Seven cases are reportedly currently under investigation and eight more are awaiting submission. No details are given concerning the nature of the alleged anticompetitive practices, the results of investigations, or the commission's decisions and the remedies taken.

two incumbents (Subcommittee Report 2000). However, it was not able to establish whether UBC's pricing was excessive, since that would have involved a complex cost assessment exercise that would need to be carried out by the sector-specific regulator. Nevertheless, the subcommittee found that UBC had abused its dominant position by limiting consumer choice: by failing to offer a lower-priced 'silver' package with fewer channels, UBC had forced customers to subscribe to its 'gold' package, which included many expensive sport and movie channels. This was a clear violation of its licensing conditions.

The Trade Competition Commission agreed that the cable operator was a monopoly, and therefore potentially subject to the antimonopoly provisions of the law, but decided to refer the case to MCOT as the government agency responsible for monitoring compliance with licensing agreements and approving tariffs. Although UBC's charges were not revised, public pressure constrained further price increases for several months. Subscribers are presently given the choice of subscribing to a less expensive 'silver' package. However, consumers still do not have a real choice as this package does not include any licensed channels (such as CNN and Discovery) and the remaining channels show only in-house productions.

Licensing authority is currently being transferred to an independent sector-specific regulatory agency, the National Broadcasting Commission. It is hoped that once this regulatory agency is established, consumers will be better protected against such abuses of market power.

Four cases have been the subject of so much public attention that the Trade Competition Commission had to provide some solution. Nevertheless, it has managed not to declare an official decision on any of them. These cases involved excessive pricing by the cable television monopoly; tied sales of whiskey and beer by a near-monopoly whiskey producer; unfair trade practices in retail trade; and exclusive dealing in the motorcycle market. No charges were brought in the first two cases. In the case of the cable monopoly, the commission decided to ask MCOT to review the charges (Box 8.1). In the tied sales case, the commission did find evidence of abuse of dominance but could not enforce section 25 of the law because 'dominance' is not defined in the implementing regulations (Box 8.2). The case has therefore been temporarily suspended until a formal definition of dominance is officially declared.

The third case concerns unfair trade practices in retail industry (Box 8.3). The economic crisis of 1997 created widespread distress in the indus-

---

Box 8.2 Tied sales of whiskey and beer

Before being liberalized on 1 January 2000, liquor production was rigidly regulated by the government. All production took place under concession from the government, which owned all 13 of the country's liquor production facilities. In 2000 the government decided to sell off its aging factories, which were in dire need of major overhaul or replacement. Through the bidding process, all of the factories were sold to members of the Sura Maharas/Sura Thip group (later known as the Sang Som group). It had held a monopoly in the domestic liquor industry since 1986 when Sura Thip merged with Sura Maharas, its only competitor. Although the whiskey market was supposedly fully liberalized, the stringency of the licensing conditions—including requirements governing minimum capacity, minimum registered capital, land, and distance from natural waterways—foreclosed any potential entry. Hence, the monopoly has continued.

Competition problems first appeared in 1994, when the liquor monopoly entered the beer market, which at the time was dominated by Singha brand beer. In an attempt to take market share away from Singha, the liquor monopoly employed various anticompetitive practices. In particular, it tied sales of its Chang brand beer to sales of its white liquor, which was in great demand. Retailers were often forced to sell the excess supply of beer at below cost, while raising the price of liquor to cover the revenue shortfall. This tactic brought instant results in terms of market share: Chang's share of the beer market rose from zero in 1994 to 75 percent in 2004.

In 2002, the Trade Competition Commission conducted an investigation into Sang Som's tactic of tying sales of whiskey and beer. It concluded that there had been an infraction of the law but that because section 25 on abuse of dominance was not enforceable, nothing could be done. The liquor monopoly later employed the same tying and dumping tactic to expand into the bottled water market as well, this time forcing many small local manufacturers out of business. It is unfortunate that the Trade Competition Commission has not taken any action to stop such blatantly anticompetitive practices.

Source: Islam (2001); Nikomborirak et al. (2002b).

---

try. In response to these difficulties, parliament passed the Foreign Business Act 1999, which allowed wholly foreign-owned retail stores that met a total minimum capital requirement of B100 million to operate in Thailand. As a result, most discount stores in Thailand are now owned by foreign MNEs. While these foreign retail companies compete vigorously among themselves and with Thai department stores, which no doubt benefits consumers, their extremely aggressive business culture has caused tremendous friction with suppliers, both large and small. Some of their business practices, such as mandatory enrollment of suppliers in price promotion schemes, preferential treatment for house brand products, and the collection of various service fees, were alleged to be unfair. In response to suppliers' complaints, the Trade Competition Commission published a Retail Industry Code of Ethics, but did not declare an official decision. The code is unlikely to give small suppliers effective protection against unfair trade practices.

The fourth case of exclusive dealing constituted a landmark in that it was the first case in which the Trade Competition Commission found an infraction of the law and decided to take legal action against the defendant. Retailers complained that Honda, the motorcycle manufacturer, had threatened to cease supplying its products to them, and to open competing stores nearby, should they refuse to become an exclusive agent. Honda is a very popular brand, with approximately 80 percent of the motorcycle market. Interestingly, the company was found to have violated section 29 of the law on unfair trade practices rather than section 25 on abuse of dominance, despite the fact that exclusive dealing clearly constitutes an abuse of dominance rather than an unfair trade practice. Although the commission's decision can be explained by the fact that section 25 is still unenforceable, its failure to take the same action in the tied sales case referred to earlier raises suspicions that enforcement is selective and discriminatory.

To sum up, the competition regime in Thailand barely functions, as is evident from the Trade Competition Commission's performance record. This is not surprising given that the commission has met only eight times in the five years since its inauguration in 1999.[14] This poor track record can be attributed to many factors, including political intervention, lobbying by interest groups, legal loopholes, and lack of transparency in administration. With so few cases having been dealt with, it is clear that the majority of anticompetitive practices go unchallenged.

But more worrying is the fact that the law is apparently being applied on a discriminatory basis due to the absence of clear rules and regulations and a lack of transparency in the administration of the law. For example, it has never been clear why the Trade Competition Commission would decide to invoke section 29 and take legal action against Honda for exclusive dealing, but not do so in the tied sales case. The seemingly discriminatory treatment is glaring when both cases represent an abuse of dominance through vertical restrictions.

Box 8.3 Large foreign retail stores

The financial crisis that broke out in 1997 forced many large domestic retail suppliers to sell out to a foreign partner or new foreign investor as domestic consumption plunged. The sudden emergence of large foreign retail chains such as Tesco of the United Kingdom, Carrefour and Casino of France, and Royal Ahold of the Netherlands faced strong protests from local suppliers, local department stores, and the public. (Royal Ahold has since sold its share of the Tops supermarket chain back to the Thai partner.)

In 2001, at the height of the controversy over the rapid expansion of foreign retail stores, the Thai Research Fund commissioned the Thailand Development Research Institute to conduct a study into the impact of large-scale multinational retailers on the Thai economy, in particular on consumers, small-scale corner stores, wholesalers, and suppliers (Poapongsakorn et al. 2001). The study found that of 145 items surveyed, the prices of all except fresh food products were lower in the large retail stores than in the traditional small-scale retail stores (Table 8.8). Apart from lower prices, large discount stores offered the convenience of 24-hour shopping, a greater variety of products, and more sanitary food preparation techniques.

A study by ACNielsen cited in Poapongsakorn et al. (2001) indicates that the number of small traditional retailers fell by 2–5 percent per year during 1997–2001, but does not isolate the impact of the entry of foreign discount stores from other factors such as the economic crisis. Poapongsakorn et al. (2001), who interviewed 97 small traditional store owners nationwide, found that the presence of large foreign stores had contributed

Table 8.8   Thailand: Index of prices in large and traditional retail stores[a]

Type of product	Large distributors	Traditional retailers	Fresh food markets
Dry food	108.0	120.8	
Fresh food	117.2		106.5
Household goods	105.1	118.0	
Apparel & other body care products	106.4	118.6	

a   Prices are presented as indices based on the lowest price of the particular product found in any discount store.

Source: Poapongsakorn et al. (2001: 105, Table 4.5).

to a 7 percent reduction in traditional retailers' sales. Some small stores complained about predatory pricing associated with the 'loss leader' strategy adopted by large retailers. This is the practice whereby a certain product is sold at below cost in order to attract customers into the store. It should be noted, however, that small stores benefit from being able to buy products from the large discount stores at lower prices than they would be able to obtain from wholesalers. One-quarter of the sales of the discount stores are made to small traditional retailers.

Wholesalers were the group most adversely affected by the entry of foreign discount chains, although no data are available on the number that have had to exit the market. As mentioned earlier, many small retailers now procure their products directly from discount stores, bypassing the wholesalers altogether.

Suppliers were the most vocal in protesting about the practices of foreign discount stores. This is understandable given that the discount stores wield their considerable negotiating power to secure large discounts from suppliers (Table 8.9). In addition to the squeeze on their margins, suppliers complained about such unfair trade practices as payments associated with slotting allowances and advertising, excessive rebates on large-volume sales, and discriminatory treatment of their products versus house brand products. Poapongsakorn et al. (2001) found no evidence that the presence of large retailers had led to lower prices for agricultural products. This is because large retailers have to compete with fresh food markets, which have ready access to cheap supplies of fresh food products.

Poapongsakorn et al. (2001) found no evidence of anticompetitive practices among large foreign retailers. Due to fierce competition in the market, the rents that large discount stores were able to extract from suppliers were passed on to consumers in the form of lower prices. The authors therefore felt that the government should not impose a ban on permits for new stores, because this might serve to limit competition in the market.

Table 8.9   Thailand: Discount obtained from suppliers by large discount stores, wholesalers, and retailers (%)

Trading partner	Discount (min–max)	Average
Large discount stores	5–10	6.25
Wholesalers	3–5	4.0
Retailers	0–2	0.2

Source: Poapongsakorn et al. (2001: vii, Table 1).

Implementation problems

Lack of independence of politics and big business

Much of the dismal performance of the Trade Competition Commission can be attributed to political intervention and lobbying by business. This is no surprise given that the Minister of Commerce is the commission's chairperson and many representatives from the private sector are members. According to Poapongsakorn (2002), political intervention and lobbying have occurred throughout investigations, both explicitly and behind the scenes.

Perhaps the most blatant and damaging instance of lobbying concerns the promulgation of a dominance threshold to make the provisions on abuse of dominance enforceable. In June 2000, the Trade Competition Commission proposed a threshold for dominance of 33.33 percent in market share and B1 billion in sales revenue in the relevant market. It was hoped that the threshold would be passed quickly, ensuring that the relevant provisions could be applied to the cases being investigated at the time. But after intense lobbying from business, cabinet approval of the proposed threshold was delayed until after the decisions on these cases had been handed down. A few months later, the Federation of Thai Industries publicly opposed the proposed definition of market dominance (*Bangkok Post*, 2 October 2000). With lobbying intensifying after the election in January 2001, the new government decided to return the proposed dominance threshold to the Trade Competition Office for review. Business groups have proposed a 50 percent market share threshold, but such a high threshold would severely circumscribe the scope of application of the law, as under it only a handful of companies would be large enough to be classified as dominant. Even so, the revised dominance threshold has not made it through cabinet to date, rendering the provisions on abuse of dominance and mergers ineffective.

Another event that has raised suspicions of regulatory capture is the case involving tied sales of whiskey and beer. The Trade Competition Commission concluded that the tied sales and cross-subsidization of whiskey and beer constituted a clear breach of section 25 of the Trade Competition Act. Unable to act under this section, the commission did not resort instead to section 29, as it did in the case of exclusive dealing practiced by Honda. According to Takasila and Chitmunchaitham (2002), the fact that one of the commissioners is a director on the board of a company affiliated with the powerful whiskey conglomerate may have been a factor in this seemingly discriminatory treatment between the two abuse of dominance cases. The conglomerate is known to be one of the largest contributors to political parties, charities, and sports events, and it is staffed with high-ranking retired bureaucrats.

Lack of implementing rules and regulation

Thailand's laws often give broad discretionary power to the administrative body. This goes for the Trade Competition Act as well. As a result, the administration and enforcement of the law can be arbitrary and discriminatory, in particular when there are no implementing rules or guidelines.

Moreover, the law contains vague terminology that leaves considerable scope for interpretation on the part of the administration. Section 25, for example, stipulates that a business operator with a market-dominating position shall not:

1 *unreasonably* fix or maintain the purchasing or selling prices of goods or services;
2 *unreasonably* impose compulsory conditions, directly or indirectly, on other businesses that restrict their operations;
3 suspend, reduce, or restrict services, production, purchasing, distribution, deliveries, or importation *without justifiable reasons* ...; or
4 intervene in the operation of another person's business *without justifiable reasons* [author's emphasis].

Words like 'unreasonably' and 'without justifiable reasons' provide the basis for a rule-of-reason approach in assessing cases of abuse of dominance. While there is nothing wrong with administrative discretion, the absence of implementing guidelines to expand on vague terms like these makes law enforcement uncertain and subjective.

Section 26, which deals with M&As, is similarly vague. It contains no mention of the types of defense that may be admissible for mergers, such as an 'efficiency defense' or a 'failing firm defense.'

Section 27 describes 10 different types of agreement, four of which are prohibited on a per se basis. These are price fixing, quantity fixing, bid rigging, and entering into an agreement to have market domination or control. The last of these is somewhat vaguely worded. It seems to refer to an 'ex ante intention' rather than an actual business practice, and thus would involve a subjective judgment. Firms have to obtain permission from the Trade Competition Commission to enter into any of the six other types of agreement described in section 27. The law states that permission may be granted if it is 'commercially necessary' to undertake such an agreement, but there are no implementing regulations to elaborate on what this term actually means.

Finally, section 29 is a catch-all section focusing on unfair trade practices. Unfair trade practices do not necessarily have anticompetitive effects. They occur when there is an imbalance in the bargaining position of two businesses that leads one party to take advantage of the other by prescribing unfair conditions for trade. The key feature that distinguishes section 29 from previous sections is that, under its provisions, the impact of the alleged unfair trade practice must be assessed. But again, there are no implementing regulations or guidelines to define what constitutes an unfair trade practice or how its consequences should be assessed. The business community understandably feels uneasy about the extremely broad scope of section 29.

In 2000, the World Bank provided experts to help draft the implementing regulations and guidelines for the key substantive provisions on abuse of dominance, collusive practices, mergers, and unfair trade practices (World Bank 2000a, 2000b). The proposed implementing regulations clarified the definition of a relevant market, the threshold market share and annual sales figure for dominance, the definition of market power, the types of pricing that would be considered 'unfair,' the criteria for merger approvals, and the circumstances in which collusive practices would be permitted. The proposed guidelines set out the concrete steps that would be taken to assess an alleged restrictive business practice, providing clarity for the law administrator as well as businesses.

The proposed implementing regulations and guidelines would have helped make the administration of the Trade Competition Act more transparent and predictable. However, the Trade Competition Commission did not even set up a subcommittee to examine the proposal. It is true that the commission has been preoccupied with cases that have captured public and media attention, such as the threshold market share for dominance and unfair trade practices in the retail industry. But its lack of interest in establishing implementing rules and regulations may also be a sign of its unwillingness to give up any of its discretionary power.

Inappropriate legal sanctions

Thailand's competition law is unique in that violations of any section of the law are subject to criminal penalties. However, the burden of proving allegations of restrictive practices 'beyond reasonable doubt' is a major obstacle to the enforcement of competition law, particularly in cases of collusive practices where hard evidence is difficult to obtain. As a result, the Office of Trade Competition has resorted instead to administrative sanctions such as the imposition of fines. While such sanctions can be both time and cost saving, they are not transparent, as the details of the settlement are not placed in the public domain. Hence, the competition regime is open to accusations of arbitrary and discriminatory behavior.

Lack of transparency in administration

The investigations of the Trade Competition Commission are conducted in secrecy. In the last two competition cases it considered (the cable television monopoly and the tied sales of whiskey and beer), neither a finding-of-fact report[15] nor a formal written decision was made available to the public.[16] It is not clear how the commission arrived at its decisions or whether there were differing views among commissioners. Details have merged only in occasional newspaper interviews given by the commission's secretary and in a competition policy paper Thailand submitted to the WTO Working Group on Interaction between Trade and Competition in April 2002.[17]

In each case, the lack of a formal written decision by the commission indicates that a legitimate decision—that is, actual discussion followed by the taking of votes—may not have occurred. In the cable television case, a formal written decision would have bound the Trade Competition Commission to its decision to transfer the case to the relevant state regulator, thus creating a precedent in terms of its legal jurisdiction. In the tied sales case, where the commission did find evidence of abuse of dominance, a formal written decision to subject the alleged violation to section 25 of the act (which remains ineffective in the absence of a dominance threshold) might have set a precedent for other alleged abuse of dominance cases, such as the Honda case that followed.

Human resource and capacity constraints

The objective of a competition law is to protect the competitive process and foster competition by prohibiting anticompetitive practices. But distinguishing anticompetitive from pro-competitive business practices is no easy task. For example, is price undercutting a sign of predation aimed at destroying a competitor or is it a sign of healthy price competition? Does exclusive distribution promote competition between brands or does it restrict price competition among distributors? Sorting out these different effects requires a thorough understanding of the law, economics, the market, and market dynamics, as well as of the business of the private company in question.

In this regard, the institutional design of the Trade Competition Commission and the Office of Trade Competition does not attract qualified persons. To begin with, commissioners are engaged only on a part-time basis. They all hold full-time jobs elsewhere, so the amount of time they can allocate to the consideration of competition cases is likely to be minimal. The only compensation commissioners are entitled to is a meeting fee of B250 (about $6.25 at B40/$). With such paltry pay, the job has to be considered mere charity. In addition, when the minister who chairs the commission is not particularly interested in enforcing the law, as is the case at present, meetings may be infrequent.

For several years, the Office of Trade Competition also faced a severe shortage of skilled personnel in terms of both technical knowledge and practical knowhow. When it was first established, the office was staffed by personnel from the former price control regime whose job it had been to monitor product pricing. Their new area of work, the study of production costs, took them into the unfamiliar territory of monitoring private company behavior. Fortunately, over the years this group of staff has acquired advanced analytical skills through domestic training programs and through bilateral and international technical assistance. However, the office still faces a severe shortage of legal experts in the area of competition law and policy. It currently has only one employee whose profession is law.

Lack of funding

As a small office in the Department of Internal Trade, which in turn is part of the Ministry of Commerce, the Office of Trade Competition is overshadowed in importance by other areas that command large budgets to carry out more visible, sensitive, and controversial programs, such as the price support policy for agricultural products. Moreover, when politics is closely tied to big business, the development of competition law and policy is unlikely to attract much support. In 2003, the total budget allocated to the office was a mere B2.5 million ($62,500), doubling to B5.4 million in the following year. With such limited funding, it is extremely difficult for the Office of Trade Competition to conduct thorough investigations into the restrictive practices reported to it.

Lack of protection of confidential information

The enforcement of competition law is complaint driven; that is, an investigation is launched when the competition authority receives a complaint from an affected party. Most complainants are small businesses and consumers. Often their complaints concern a large business that is in a position to affect their well-being. Small suppliers that file a complaint against a large retailer may have their contracts terminated; dealers that complain about a manufacturer risk having their supplies cut off. Thus, to encourage cooperation before and during investigations, there needs to be an effective program to protect complainants and informants from possible retaliation. Strict protection of confidential information for all parties is equally important for effective enforcement of the law. If confidential information is leaked, then the private sector will lose its trust in the competition authority. The authority would then face great difficulty in gathering information during future investigations.

Lack of public awareness and support

Competition law and policy is not just about implementation of the law; it is also about building a culture of competition across the nation. In Thailand, such a culture has not yet been established. In policy-making, producers' interests often take precedence over those of consumers—the business community is extremely tight-knit and well connected compared with Thailand's dispersed and unorganized consumers. While consumer organizations and civil society are slowly gaining strength and visibility, the scope of their activities is severely limited by human and financial constraints. Non-government organizations (NGOs) in Thailand tend to focus mainly on health and environmental issues, where the effects on the public are immediate and obvious. They often perceive competition law as being about 'business disputes' that do not concern them, or as being linked to capitalism and free trade, which they may be opposed to on principle.

Consumer groups are most interested in competition cases where these involve excessive price increases. For example, the country's automatic electricity tariff adjustment mechanism has been the subject of persistent scrutiny from consumer groups, who view it as a convenient way of passing on the inefficiencies of the state enterprise to consumers in the form of high costs. The series of post-merger price increases by the cable television monopoly prompted a similar public outcry. In most cases the public calls for price controls—a remedy it is familiar with—without realizing that, if not well implemented, these can give rise to all sorts of market distortions that, in the end, may not benefit consumers at all. Obviously, educating the public to understand how competition serves to protect consumers' interests is a challenging task facing the competition authority and the country.

It should be noted that in an environment where the competition authority is inherently vulnerable to political intervention and lobbying from big business, there is little hope for effective implementation of the law. In such an environment, public pressure from the non-government sector—from NGOs, civil society groups, academics, and the media—is vital.

Lessons learned

Thailand's experience shows clearly that simply having a competition law is not sufficient in the absence of the political will to see that it is properly enforced. The promulgation of the law in order to fulfill the spirit of the constitution did not bode well for its enforcement. This stands in stark contrast to the situation in the Republic of Korea, where a competition law was passed and amended several times with the specific objective of battling the rising concentration of economic power in the hands of the *chaebol*.

Political intervention, opposition from big business, and institutional limitations have proved to be major hurdles in law enforcement, paralyzing the competition agency. Pressure for change thus needs to come from outside the government. Building public awareness of competition law and policy is a prerequisite for effective implementation. This process will take much longer if unsupported by the domestic political, legal, institutional, and social environment.

That said, having a competition law is still better than not having one. Despite the lack of effective enforcement of the Trade Competition Act 1999, the mere existence of the law has helped restrain anticompetitive practices that were once carried out unchallenged. Politicians have been held accountable for the lack of enforcement of the law. Small enterprises are beginning to understand that they have a right to complain to the Office of Trade Competition and to demand protection, and they are beginning to exert pressure on the government to make the law effective. Most importantly, an Office of Trade Competition has been created, and its staff have received extensive training.

There are also positive signs that a competition culture is beginning to take root in Thailand. A government policy to remove the concession fees imposed on incumbent telecommunications operators and replace them with an equivalent excise tax on telecommunications services faced strong opposition from consumer groups on the basis that it would serve only to preserve the incumbents' market dominance by raising the costs for new entrants. Such opposition would have been unimaginable in the past, when the public would have been concerned only about issues that affected them directly, such as the actual prices they had to pay for services. Although the proposed telecommunications policy would not have led to an immediate change in prices, the public nevertheless realized that barriers to entry would eventually lead to less choice, poorer service, and higher prices. It is fair to say, then, that there has been a slow but sustainable building of competition culture and the rule of law since the passage of the competition law.

The author believes that competition law and competition institutions are important to economic development, especially in developing countries. This law in particular serves to dissipate rents; these tend to accumulate in developing economies where the small size of the market may lead to market failure, and where proper regulatory oversight to restrain rent-seeking business practices is often absent.

The problem is likely to intensify where money politics exists. Monopolistic rents lead to the concentration of wealth among a few privileged persons or families, who can then finance their entry into politics and secure the power to design policies that further entrench their monopolistic positions. If a developing country happens to fall into this particular trap, the chances of competition being introduced in the domestic market are slim. It is therefore of utmost urgency that a developing country equips itself with a competition regime that can counter the formidable (financial and political) strength of incumbent suppliers and operators who would like to fend off competition in order to secure their own private interests.

Passing and implementing a competition law will always be an uphill battle. Not only does such a law run counter to the interests of large and powerful businesses, it is also often associated with western capitalism or free market propaganda. Thus, it can easily fall prey to nationalistic fervor that in some cases is drummed up by the local monopolists themselves. Thus, competition policy advocacy is as important, if not more important, than competition adjudication. A country needs to build a wide competition constituency among academics, civil society, and the media. This is indeed a herculean task, but one that is well worth undertaking.

6   FOREIGN ANTICOMPETITIVE PRACTICES

Foreign trade and investment—and thus foreign suppliers and service providers—have played a major role in the development of Thailand's small open economy. This section examines whether foreign companies operating in or outside Thailand have engaged in restrictive practices that have affected Thai consumers or producers. Indeed, cross-border restrictive practices, in particular cartels, were one of the major issues discussed by the WTO before competition policy was finally dropped from the list of new issues to be negotiated in the Doha Round of talks.

Antirestrictive practices undertaken by foreign companies may take place within or outside the domestic territory. In the first case, such practices are within the reach of the national competition law since the alleged violator is operating within national boundaries. The opposite is true for the second case. Although most competition laws adopt an 'effects doctrine' whereby the law applies to all persons and entities whose practices have an effect on the domestic economy, in practice it is not usually possible for the national competition authority to investigate or impose sanctions on persons and entities that do not reside within the national territory. Thus, in the absence of mutual legal assistance agreements and due cooperation from foreign competition authorities, it is almost impossible for small countries like Thailand to enforce the law extraterritorially. Large countries may be able to do so, however, as their market size lends them superior bargaining power against certain MNEs. For example, the European Union was able to enforce its antitrust law against Microsoft.

Restrictive practices of foreign companies operating in Thailand

While the entry of foreign companies has generally promoted competition and benefited consumers, in a few cases it has had the opposite effect. The cement industry is one such instance. Cement was one of the industries worst hit by the financial crisis that broke out in July 1997. The local construction industry came to a halt with the collapse of the finance and real estate markets, and several firms were taken over by foreign suppliers. In 2001 Siam Cement, the second-largest player in the market and already majority owned by a foreign cement supplier, made a bid for the third-largest company, TPI Polene, a locally owned firm that was in the middle of a debt-restructuring process. There is no clear indication as yet as to who will eventually own this company, as the founder refuses to relinquish control under the proposed restructuring plan. However, an executive of the foreign company involved in the takeover announced that he expected to see a doubling in the price of cement in the domestic market once the takeover goes through. The merger appears invincible since the merger provisions in the Trade Competition Act of 1999 were not (and still are not) effective in the absence of a threshold post-merger market share that would trigger a mandatory pre-merger notification. According to the analysis of many security houses, the merger is likely to lead to collusion and, hence, an increase in the price of cement.

Cross-border restrictive practices

In theory, Thailand's competition law applies extraterritorially to all restrictive practices that have an effect on the domestic market regardless of where they took place. In practice, however, it is almost impossible to investigate restrictive practices that take place outside the national boundary without due cooperation from the competition authorities in the countries in which the MNEs are registered. The fact that most competition regimes provide an exemption for cartels that do not have an effect on their own domestic markets allows these collusive practices to remain in no-man's land.

As a small, open economy, Thailand relies extensively on imports. This renders it vulnerable to price-fixing and market-sharing agreements undertaken by international cartels. According to a number of studies, Thailand has been affected by international cartels in vitamins, heavy electrical equipment, steel, and cigarettes, to name a few.[18] In the case of the vitamin cartel, Evenett (2003) estimated the size of the loss to amount to $78.5 million in overcharges out of a total import value of $271.6 million for the period 1990–99 during which the cartel operated. Unfortunately, similar cost estimates are not available for other cartels.

Thailand is also affected by shipping cartels that are beyond the reach of the domestic competition law. Like export cartels, liner shipping is often exempted from antitrust provisions in the industrialized countries that have national shipping lines. This exemption has allowed shipping operators to allocate markets among themselves and set freight tariffs. Thai exporters complain that they are often burdened with ancillary charges such as terminal handling charges and adjustments for fuel and currency fluctuations. This is consistent with the finding of a report by the Organisation for Economic Co-operation and Development on the liner shipping industry that ancillary charges constitute a method by which the industry passes on its most significant variable costs to shippers (OECD 2002). The report also questions whether these charges are made on a cost recovery basis, given the lack of transparency in how rates are determined. As a result, Thailand's small shippers, who lack the bargaining power to negotiate more favorable rates, have had to shoulder high costs that further disadvantage them in terms of cost competitiveness.

Fink, Mattoo, and Neagu (2001) point out that small countries are unlikely to be able to challenge such anticompetitive practices. They suggest that article IX of the General Agreement on Trade in Services, which addresses private anticompetitive practices, be strengthened. They propose the abolition of exemptions for liner shipping cartels and recommend that foreign consumers be given the ability to challenge questionable practices in the national courts of countries whose citizens own or control the liners.

The Thai experience shows that something can be done. As reported in Nikomborirak (2002a), the Thai Frozen Food Association was able to obtain preferential freight rates from the liner operators and persuade them to waive their terminal handling charges. Unfortunately, it is the only trade association that has been able to do so. Other attempts to repeat its success have failed, mainly because large players in other industries are unwilling to sacrifice their competitive edge by uniting with smaller players that have less bargaining strength and thus face higher freight rates. The liner operators offer attractive rebates to large shippers, who are content with the deal they have secured and thus unwilling to help smaller competitors in the same industry. Without the support of the large shippers, smaller shippers can never hope to exert enough bargaining power to counter the market power of the liner operators.

To better balance the negotiating power of domestic shippers and international shipping companies, the government considered passing domestic regulations that would require the latter to consult the domestic shippers' association, the National Council of Thai Shippers, before any price increase was enacted. A draft maritime bill stipulates that adequate notice of a rate increase must be given to the local regulatory agency—the Office of Maritime Promotion Commission—and that shipping liners must negotiate with shippers before any increase. Liners intending to increase their freight rates are required to give 90 days' notice to the office and outline the reasons for the increase (TDRI 2001b). If the office does not lodge an objection within 15 days, the new rates will come into force. But if an objection is lodged and the two parties fail to reach agreement, an impartial committee whose decision is final will arbitrate the case.

The new government that came into power in 2001 has not pushed for promulgation of the proposed law. In response to a complaint from the National Council of Thai Shippers, however, the Trade Competition Commission has requested the liner operators to provide 90 days' notice of any rate changes. It remains to be seen whether the liners will comply with this request.

7   CONCLUSION

In Thailand's case, many of the barriers to competition can be traced back to state rules and regulations. In the manufacturing sector, the state imposes high tariffs to protect domestic industries, in particular heavy industries such as steel and automobile and motorcycle assembly. In both cases, state protection combined with inherent scale economies in production have given rise to concentrated markets and abuse of market power. The state decision to grant exclusive concessions to a private enterprise in the case of liquor distillation has spawned a very powerful conglomerate that has begun to exert its monopoly power in the formerly competitive beer and bottled water markets.

In the services sector, SOEs and other state agencies compete in handing out concessions that give private companies the right to exploit a monopoly in exchange for a share of the revenue thus generated. Their attempt to preserve monopoly rents, mostly in infrastructure services, has contributed to monopolies and highly concentrated markets in services such as telecommunications, transportation, and energy. The current government policy of privatizing state monopolies without introducing competition does not bode well for competition. In the absence of independent regulatory bodies that can act in the public interest, consumers are likely to be the losers from private or joint state–private ventures that aim to secure monopoly rents.

Thailand's experience shows that simply having a competition law is not enough to solve competition-related problems. Political intervention, opposition from big business, and institutional limitations have proved to be major hurdles to law enforcement, and have paralyzed the competition agency. Bilateral and regional FTAs can, however, be a very effective safeguard against anticompetitive practices. Thailand is already experiencing a marked increase in competition in certain product markets following the introduction of trade liberalization measures under AFTA and the bilateral agreement with the PRC. The simple conclusion from the Thai case is that, where state supervision fails, one needs to rely on market forces to discipline undesirable restrictive trade practices.

All that being said, perhaps one should not despair given that governments come and go. Should Thailand ever have a government that is less influenced by the interests of big business, much may be done to improve the current regime. The most urgent task is to make the administration and enforcement of the law as transparent as possible. Full disclosure of information can go a long way in shielding an agency against undesirable influences, even if it is lacking in structural and financial independence from the government of the day.

The tasks that lie ahead include the following. Detailed implementing guidelines must be formally established to provide the business sector with clear rules on what practices are and are not allowable. Clear internal procedures covering all areas from the handling of complaints through to protection of confidential information, witness protection, and prosecution must be set up and made public. Clear rules on conflict of interest among commissioners must be established. All non-confidential information should be disclosed on websites, in particular details of Trade Competition Commission meetings and decisions, the reasons for decisions, and the minority views of commissioners.

Another urgent task is to pass the threshold market shares for dominance and pre-merger notifications, so that sections 25 and 26 of the law become enforceable. Much of the back-up technical work for this has already been done. The Office of Trade Competition needs to be better funded, and it needs to recruit more legal personnel to ensure that the law is enforced effectively.

NOTES

1   The terms and conditions of concessions often contain clauses that restrict private concessionaires' ability to compete with the state enterprise. For example, private operators may be required to obtain approval from the state enterprise for any price adjustment, expansion of services, or introduction of new programs or services.

2   A 'foreigner' refers to a natural person who is not of Thai nationality, or a juristic entity (1) that is established under foreign law; (2) in which half or more of the capital is owned by foreigners, even if the company is incorporated under Thai law; or (3) in which half or more of the value of the total capital is invested by foreigners, even if more than half the capital is owned by Thai nationals. (The third requirement is effectively a bar on the use of Thai nationals as nominees.)

3   For example, when informed of a pending increase in the excise tax on alcoholic beverages, the incumbent whiskey monopoly built up a large inventory of whiskey equivalent to three years' supply. This allowed it to gain a price advantage over newcomers, who were subject to the higher excise tax.

4   'Cell phones: TA hangs up on Y-Tel 1234 plan for cheap calls,' *The Nation*, 11 August 2003.

5   For example, according to its annual report for 2003, TOT earned $400 million from revenue-sharing agreements with private telecommunications concession holders in 2003. The other state-owned operator, CAT Telecom, earned approximately $50–67 million according to *Telecom Journal* No. 515 [in Thai]. MCOT's annual report for 2003 shows that it collected $12 million from the private cable television operator and the private operator of Channel 3 free-to-air television.

6   The agreements with India, PRC, and Bahrain contain early harvest provisions whereby tariffs on selected goods are eliminated or substantially reduced immediately after the agreement is signed. Liberalization of services and investment is to be negotiated at a later date. The FTA with Australia is comprehensive in that it covers trade in goods, services, and investment. However, the extent of liberalization in services and investment is limited.

7   GATT allows developing countries that sign a bilateral agreement with another developing country to be selective in terms of the scope of liberaliza-

tion by means of an 'enabling clause' that allows them greater flexibility in forming FTAs.

8   For more detailed analysis of the competition chapter in the Thai–US FTA, see TDRI (2004).

9   For more detail on the role of the private sector in the development of the telecommunications industry in Thailand, see Cairns and Nikomborirak (1998).

10 The Letters of Intent can be found on the Bank of Thailand website at <www.bot.or.th>.

11 The Constitution of the Kingdom of Thailand 1997 [in English] can be found at <www.krisdika.go.th>.

12 For more details on exceptions and exemptions to the competition law, see Nikomborirak (2004b).

13 In the case of abuse of dominance, words such as 'unreasonably' and 'without justifiable reasons' provide the basis for a rule-of-reason approach, as discussed later in the text. In the case of mergers and certain collusive practices, a notification requirement gives the administrative authority the discretionary power to assess the merits of each case individually.

14 This information is given on the Department of Internal Trade's website. Most of these meetings took place under the Chuan government, which ended in February 2001.

15 The subcommittee responsible for examining the cable television case in fact submitted a relatively comprehensive report to the Trade Competition Commission, but the commission failed to inform the public about its existence. The report is currently available by contacting the Thailand Development Research Institute at <www.info.tdri.or.th/>.

16 This can be verified by visiting the Department of Internal Trade's website at <www.dit.go.th>. It provides no information on past decisions, let alone investigatory reports.

17 The paper can be found at the WTO website under the code WT/WGTCP/W/188.

18 See, for example, 'The price is not quite right,' *Economist*, 5 July 2001 on cigarettes. Several major multinational tobacco companies lobbied the Thai government for import liberalization, knowing that they would be able to raise the price of cigarettes sold in Thailand after import liberalization. They actively sought to reassure the government that the threat from foreign tobacco imports was not real. At the same time, the companies reportedly agreed to supply the illegal market in order to convince the local authorities that high excise taxes would only lead to more smuggling.

Appendix A8.1   Thailand: Free trade agreements with other countries[a]

Bahrain (2010)

- A Trade and Investment Framework Agreement became effective on 29 December 2002.
- Under early harvest provisions, tariffs on 626 products were reduced immediately to 3 percent, and to zero on 1 January 2005. Early harvest products include seafood, fruit, vegetables, textiles, chemical products, cement, natural gas, and jewelry.
- Thailand has offered to categorize the remaining 5,000 products into three groups: fast-tracked products (40 percent) on which tariffs would be reduced to zero by 1 January 2005; normally tracked products (40 percent) on which tariffs would be reduced to zero by 1 January 2007; and other products (20 percent) on which tariffs would be reduced to zero by 1 January 2010.

People's Republic of China

- A Trade and Investment Framework Agreement was signed on 18 June 2003.
- Tariffs on early harvest fruits and vegetables in tariff classifications 07–08 were reduced to zero on 1 October 2003. Early harvest products comprise fresh fruit and vegetables such as potatoes, tomatoes, beans, coconuts, cabbages, carrots, lettuces, pineapples, plums, and apricots.

India (2010)

- A Trade and Investment Framework Agreement was signed on 9 October 2003.
- Tariffs on 84 early harvest products were halved in March 2004, were halved again in March 2005, and will fall to zero in March 2006. Early harvest products include fruits, prepared and preserved seafood, precious stones, forms and plastic, machinery, electronic parts, and electrical appliances.

United States

- A Trade and Investment Framework Agreement was signed in October 2002.
- FTA negotiations are expected to begin in April 2005, but the United States wants Thailand to solve intellectual property rights and customs valuation problems before negotiations start.

Australia (2005)

- An FTA was signed on 5 July 2004 and is expected to become effective on 1 January 2005.
- Thailand has offered to reduce tariffs on 5,505 products, 2,934 of which would have their rates cut to zero.
- Australia has offered to reduce tariffs on 6,108 products, 5,123 of which would have their rates cut to zero.
- Both countries have agreed to negotiate further liberalization, in particular of services and investment, every three years.

Japan

- A Trade and Investment Framework Agreement was signed in late 2002.
- Three rounds of working-level negotiations have taken place to establish a bilateral FTA.
- The parties have been unable to reach a consensus on tariff reduction measures for industrial and agricultural goods.

Peru

- The parties have agreed to establish a Trade and Investment Framework Agreement that will cover transport and tourism; it will eliminate tariffs and reduce the number of non-tariff barriers by 2015.
- Negotiations for an FTA started in January 2004 and are expected to finish by the end of 2005.

---

a   Anticipated year of completion is in brackets after the country name.

Source: Department of Trade Negotiations, Ministry of Commerce, August 2003.

Appendix A8.2   Thailand: Businesses listed under the Foreign Business Act of 1999

List 1

1   Newspaper, radio, and television businesses
2   Rice farming, farming, and gardening
3   Animal husbandry
4   Forestry and wood fabrication
5   Fishery for marine animals in Thai waters and within specified economic zones
6   Extraction of Thai herbs
7   Trade in Thai antiques or national historical objects
8   Production of Buddha images and alms bowls
9   Land trading

Nature of any exception
• Foreign equity participation must comprise less than half of the registered capital.

List 2

Group 1: National safety/security-related businesses
1   Production, sale, repair, and maintenance of
   a   Firearms, ammunition, gun powder, explosives
   b   Accessories for firearms, ammunition, and explosives
   c   Armaments, ships, aircraft, and military vehicles
   d   Equipment or components, all categories of war materials
2   Domestic land, water, or air transportation, including domestic airline businesses

Group 2: Businesses affecting art, culture, and handicrafts
1   Trade in antiques or Thai arts and handicrafts
2   Production of carved wood
3   Silkworm farming and the production, weaving, and printing of Thai silk
4   Production of Thai musical instruments
5   Production of goldware, silverware, nielloware, bronzeware, and lacquerware
6   Production of traditional Thai crockery

Group 3: Businesses affecting natural resources and the environment
1   Manufacture of sugar from sugarcane
2   Salt farming, including of underground salt

3   Rock salt mining
4   Mining, including blasting or crushing
5   Wood fabrication for furniture and utensil production

Nature of any exception

- Foreign equity participation must comprise less than half of the registered capital, unless special permission is granted by the Minister of Commerce with cabinet approval.
- Foreigners operating businesses in this category must meet two conditions:

  1   At least 40 percent of all shares must be held by Thai persons or juristic persons (given reasonable cause, the minister may lower this to 25 percent with cabinet approval)
  2   The number of Thai directors shall not be less than two-fifths of the total number of directors

List 3

1   Rice milling, and flour production from rice and other types of grain
2   Fishery, specifically marine animal culture
3   Forestry from forestry plantations
4   Production of plywood, veneer board, chipboard, or hardboard
5   Production of lime
6   Accounting services
7   Legal services
8   Architectural services
9   Engineering services
10 Construction, except:

   a   Construction that renders a basic service to the public in public utilities or transport, that requires special tools, machinery, technology, or construction expertise, and in which the foreign firm invests minimum capital of B500 million
   b   Other categories of construction as prescribed by the ministerial regulations

11 Brokerages or agency business, unless in connection with:

   a   The underwriting of securities or services connected with future trading of commodities, financial instruments, or securities
   b   Trade in or procurement of goods and services necessary for production, or for use among affiliated enterprises
   c   Trade, purchase, or distribution, or seeking both domestic and foreign markets for the sale of domestically manufactured or imported goods in the manner of international business operations, in which the foreign firm invests minimum capital of B100 million
   d   Any other category as prescribed by the ministerial regulations

12 Auctions, except:

   a Auctions by international bidders that do not involve the sale of Thai antiques, historical artifacts, handicrafts, or works of art

   b Any other category as prescribed by the ministerial regulations

13 Internal trade connected with native products or produce not yet prohibited by law

14 Retailing of all categories of goods for which the total minimum capital is less than B100 million, or less than B20 million per shop

15 Wholesaling of all categories of goods for which the total minimum capital per shop is less than B100 million

16 Advertising

17 Hotels, except hotel management

18 Guided tours

19 Sale of food or beverages

20 Plant cultivation or propagation

21 Other categories of service business except as prescribed in the ministerial regulations

Nature of any exception

• Foreign equity participation must comprise less than half of the registered capital, unless special permission is granted by the Director General of the Department of Internal Trade in the Ministry of Commerce with the approval of the Foreign Business Committee.

Source: APEC, <http://www1.apecsec.org.sg/download/ieg/invst4-thai.pdf>, accessed September 2004.

9

Viet Nam

Vu Quoc Huy

1   INTRODUCTION

Viet Nam is a country in economic transition. Its legal framework is underdeveloped and law enforcement is weak. Moreover, the country continues to experience the legacy of a centrally planned economy where the government took control of the 'commanding heights' and deliberately assigned markets to particular firms or groups of firms with a view to avoiding duplication of activities and establishing strong business groups. Competition in this context was nonexistent by default.

The situation has changed dramatically since 1986, when Viet Nam embarked on the process of renovation and reform known as *doi moi*. The monopoly of the state over the economy has gradually been eroded, paving the way for a more competitive business environment, greater private sector development, and increased foreign investment. Foreign direct investment (FDI) has grown rapidly and there has been a dramatic surge in private sector activity. The government has recently introduced significant policy changes, with more to come. The country has signed a historic bilateral trade agreement (BTA) with the United States that commits the Vietnamese government to far-reaching policy changes. The ongoing negotiations on accession to the World Trade Organization (WTO) will add to the policy agenda. The country is heading in the direction of establishing more market-based institutions that protect property rights, enforce contracts, and provide a level playing field for business.

Competition policy emerges against this background as a new challenge facing Viet Nam as it attempts to maintain the momentum for reform while ensuring sustainable development. This chapter addresses some of the issues related to this new challenge using scarce evidence that is available in Viet Nam. The chapter is organized as follows. Section 2 describes developments in Viet Nam under *doi moi*, highlighting major achievements and challenges and their implications for competition policy. Section 3 reviews the current legal framework and its relation to competition policy. It discusses a number of existing legal documents that address competition-related issues, focusing on lessons learned during implementation of their provisions. Section 4 summarizes the major policy instruments, both explicit and implicit, that have been implemented in the pursuit of industrial policy. It examines the effects of these industrialization policies on competition and their implications for the future. Section 5 tests links between competition and economic development using evidence from industrial data. Finally, the chapter provides some recommendations for drafting and implementing a new competition law.

2   DEVELOPMENT BACKGROUND

The last two decades have been an extraordinary period for the people of Viet Nam. The country has undergone a dramatic transformation sparked by *doi moi*, a series of comprehensive reforms that have transformed the country from a centrally planned economy to a modern, socialist-oriented market economy ruled by law. By unleashing choice and opportunity for millions of ordinary people, the reforms initiated in the 1980s resulted in remarkable achievements and improved all aspects of economic and social life.

Rapid economic growth combined with steady poverty reduction

By unleashing the physical and creative potential of the Vietnamese people and strengthening incentives to work and generate income, *doi moi* has resulted in rapid economic growth for nearly two decades. Since 1986, the economy has managed to maintain a remarkable annual growth rate of 6.3 percent. Even considering the low base from which Viet Nam started—namely per capita GDP of around $1,000 in purchasing power parity terms in the mid-1980s—this growth rate was remarkable, especially given the rather gloomy records of other developing countries during that period.

Growth has essentially been positive and high in all key sectors. Even during the Asian economic crisis, when many countries in the region suffered serious setbacks, Viet Nam successfully managed to maintain a relatively high growth rate of 5 percent, the highest in the region after the

People's Republic of China (PRC). Industry and services have enjoyed the fastest growth while agricultural growth has been lower than the national average at approximately 3–4 percent per annum. Nevertheless, this is a very high rate by international standards. The rapid growth of the industrial and service sectors has seen their share of the economy increase, while the importance of agriculture for the economy as a whole has gradually diminished. The share of agriculture has dropped from over one-third in 1986 to less than one-quarter at present. The share of industry, meanwhile, has increased from about 27 percent in 1987 to around 39 percent today.

Despite rapid growth in the industrial sector, the pace of urbanization has been relatively slow. The majority of the population (78 percent of the total population), including most of the country's poor, still live in rural areas, relying heavily on agriculture-based income-generating activities. The slow rate of urbanization and high proportion of the population living in rural areas have differing implications for future development and economic growth and for continuing poverty reduction (NCSSH 2001; SRV 2002). The past two decades have been a period of extensive and concentrated development when investment was directed into capital-intensive industries and infrastructure in and around large growth centers. While this did help to increase labor productivity and establish a modern industrial base for the country, it also raised some concerns about the sustainability of the economy. The capital-intensive industrialization strategy aggravated the existing development gap between regions, as well as between rural and urban areas. This in turn intensified rural–urban migration. Since job creation was not enough to absorb the labor surplus in rural areas, many rural dwellers moved to urban centers in search of employment and income-generating opportunities.

At the same time, it should be noted that rapid growth and the way reforms have been initiated and implemented in Viet Nam have resulted in significant reductions in poverty by any standard or measure.[1] Based on an internationally comparable poverty line, poverty declined from 57 percent in 1993 to 37 percent in 1998 and further to 29 percent in 2002 (Table 9.1). Poverty as measured by the national poverty line also dropped significantly and steadily during the period. What is remarkable is that this poverty reduction took place in all regions of Viet Nam, albeit at different rates, reflecting the broad-based and relatively pro-poor nature of growth. One of the factors explaining the nexus between positive growth and poverty reduction in Viet Nam was the decision to start the reform process by targeting the agricultural sector. The government began by giving land use rights to farmers, most of them poor. This created a strong supply

Table 9.1   Viet Nam: Poverty incidence, 1993–2002 (%)[a]

	1993	1998	2002
Northern Uplands	79	59	43
Red River Delta	63	29	22
North Central	75	48	42
Central Coast	50	35	24
Central Highlands	70	52	51
Southeast	33	8	10
Mekong Delta	47	37	22
All Viet Nam	57	37	29

a   Based on an internationally comparable poverty line.
Source: GSO (1999, 2003).

response that helped farmers increase their production and income. If poverty continues to fall at this rate, Viet Nam will meet its Millennium Development Goals for poverty well ahead of schedule.[2]

Very rapid growth in FDI and international trade

The open door policy resulted in very rapid growth in FDI and international trade, at a pace rarely seen in other countries. Strong economic growth led to significant increases in the production of many commodities. From a country that had suffered chronic shortages of goods, Viet Nam became a net exporter of a range of commodities. Demand for production and consumption also increased, fueling demand for imported goods and services.

Viet Nam has recorded very high rates of growth in international trade since *doi moi* got under way. Both exports and imports grew at an annual rate of 22 percent in the period 1990–2001. The ratio of total external trade to GDP stood at 94 percent in 2001, one of the higher ratios in the world (World Bank 2003b). Viet Nam's major trading partners have traditionally been members of the Association of Southeast Asian Nations (ASEAN, accounting for about one-fifth of exports and more than one-quarter of imports), the European Union, Japan, and the Republic of Korea (Korea). External trade with the PRC and the United States has experienced rapid growth in recent years, although the level of trade is still relatively low. A positive change in the composition of trade has seen a rise in the share of manufactured goods in total exports, reducing the country's reliance on primary commodity exports and accompanying volatility. Viet Nam now has a greater diversity of trading partners, with the share of European and US markets increasing and reliance on Asian markets decreasing.

The promise of continued strong growth, combined with a more open trade and investment regime, has made Viet Nam an attractive destination for FDI. During the past decade Viet Nam has succeeded in attracting FDI worth $38 billion. The 3,818 foreign investment projects currently active in Viet Nam, most of them in the areas of industrial production, tourism, construction, and food processing, contribute about 30 percent of industrial output and account for nearly one-third of total exports. FDI in the information and communication technology sector makes a significant contribution to the economy not only in terms of production and services, but more importantly in terms of the knowledge and technology transfer that is crucial for the sector's development.

Adoption of a market economy leading to significant structural change

The development of a market economy combined with proactive economic integration has resulted in significant structural change in the Vietnamese economy. While agriculture remains the main source of income for the majority of the population, the importance of the industrial and service sectors has progressively increased. The labor force has also experienced major changes. As one would expect, employment in traditional sectors of the economy has fallen and the share of new, modern sectors has increased. The share of the labor force employed in the agricultural sector dropped from 72 percent in 1990 to 66 percent in 2000, while the share employed in the services sector during this period increased gradually from 17 percent to almost 22 percent. Overall, the labor force has grown at a steady rate of 2.2 percent annually, but employment creation during the reform period has been modest compared with the high growth rate of output.

There are many explanations for this modest employment creation record, some of them controversial. One explanation links it to the continuing role of state-owned enterprises (SOEs) and its crowding out effect on private sector development (World Bank 2001; NCSSH 2001). Another sees it as a natural outcome of the deepening integration of the Vietnamese economy, a process characterized by increases in productivity but diminishing demand for labor as the competitiveness of the economy improves (Jenkins 2002). Viet Nam also has a poor record in off-farm employment, a crucial factor in rural development and sustainable poverty reduction. Underemployment in rural areas remains high—at 25 percent as of July 2002—and has shown virtually no improvement for years (GSO 2003). One reason given for the slow growth in off-farm employment is the poor quality of the rural labor force. Another is lack of information on jobs and market opportunities. Farmers fail to diversify their production or take advantage of market opportunities because they lack information on the current market climate for their products. The private sector is expected to be the most important source of employment in the future.

Changes in the composition of ownership

Significant changes have taken place in the composition of ownership in the economy. Once dominated by the state sector, the economy now accommodates FDI and a thriving private sector. Over 88,264 newly established enterprises were registered between January 2000 and the end of February 2004. The number of joint stock companies registered during that period was 10 times the number registered during the previous nine years. These enterprises created 1.6–2 million new jobs, or 90 percent of all newly created employment, and injected more than $10 billion into the economy (GSO 2004).

The government's crowded policy agenda includes significant commitments contained in the historic BTA signed with the United States. The ongoing negotiations on WTO accession will add to the policy agenda. The common feature of all these developments is that the country is committed to establishing market-based institutions; granting equal rights to all stakeholders; establishing institutions that protect legal rights, private property rights, and contract enforcement; and providing a level playing field for business. Competition policy emerges against this development background as a new challenge facing Viet Nam as it continues to implement reform while attempting to ensure sustainable development.

3   THE LEGAL FRAMEWORK FOR COMPETITION POLICY

The transition from central planning to a market economy was accompanied by the development of a legal framework to support this process and help market forces operate. Much remains to be done, however, before a well-functioning legal framework can be established. The current legal framework in Viet Nam is characterized by incompleteness, frequent changes, and inconsistencies. The process of formulating, adopting, and implementing laws is not at all clear and the effectiveness of law enforcement is doubtful.

Some argue that the government has focused too much on passing laws at the expense of effective implementation of laws (UNDP and CIEM 2001). Many basic laws are not well designed, providing only general principles and directions that must then be interpreted by supporting decrees, ordinances, laws, and instructions. In many cases this has led to inappropriate interpretations of the law and inconsistencies between the various supporting pieces of legislation: nearly 10,000 legal documents issued by ministries and local governments in the period 1992–97 were found to be inconsistent with various laws (Doan 2002). Other supporting legislation has been drafted without sufficient regard for the existing and evolving institutional environment and the conditions for subsequent implementation and enforcement, and so has quickly become irrelevant. An instruction issued by the Customs Office, for example (Instruction N45/2000/TTLT-BTC-TCHQ) was revoked because it imposed unrealistic customs fees that were impossible to comply with, ending its short-lived 55-day existence (UNDP and CIEM 2001).

Lack of public awareness of legal rights and obligations, limited information about the current legal system, and suspicion about the effectiveness of the judicial system in helping to settle legal disputes are some of the reasons explaining the current situation in the legal system in Viet Nam (Thanh 2001; Kokko 2004).[3] Uncertainty about outcomes and the relatively high cost of pursuing legal action also discourage people from having recourse to the courts. For their part, the enforcement authorities suffer from a serious lack of financial and human resources (Dung 2002; Long 2003).

Viet Nam's laws, particularly its economic regulations, tend to be vague owing to the preference of most government agencies for consensus law-making, and to be temporal due to the ever-changing policy environment of a fast-paced, developing economy (Day 2004). Competition regulations are no exception in this regard. Competition is governed by a number of legal documents, decrees, ordinances, laws, and instructions, most of them focused on price controls, quantitative controls on production, and licensing. Little attention has been paid to identifying and dealing with what is known in international experience as 'anticompetitive behavior' (Huan 2003). For instance, Viet Nam has had a Decree on Price Management since 1992, but no case of price mismanagement has ever been brought before the courts despite numerous anecdotal allegations.

The government worked on the final draft of a competition law that was recently adopted by the National Assembly. This was a welcome step, but the question of effective implementation remains open. Other major laws and regulations that have a bearing on competition-related issues are summarized below.

The Commercial Law (1997)

The Commercial Law (1997) is the only single law to contain an explicit 'provision on competition.' Article 8 prohibits the following types of anti-competitive behavior: speculation; predatory pricing; dissemination of false information with the purpose of damaging the trade reputation of a competitor; hampering, attracting, bribing or threatening a competitor's employees or customers; and violating a competitor's trademark or intellectual property rights.

Article 192 of the Commercial Law prohibits advertising that would harm the interest of the state or other traders, as well as advertising that makes direct comparisons between the firm's own products and a competitor's products or that imitates a competitor's advertisements. Government Decree No. 44/2000/ND-CP on Pricing (2000), which is based on the Commercial Law, stipulates that a promotional price should not be less than 70 percent of the price before the promotion, and that the value of a promotional gift in the form of a good or service should not exceed 30 percent of the unit price of the good or service before the promotion (article 13). The Commercial Law was approved unanimously by the National Assembly. Its implementation, on the other hand, has been subject to many qualifications. It is important to note that at the time the law was drafted and approved, the government retained a strong central planning mentality, and this was clearly reflected in the text and spirit of the law. Thus section 2 contains separate articles setting out the government's 'guiding principles' for each sector (by ownership) in commercial activities. Article 10, for example, explicitly states that

> the government invests in financial, human, and infrastructure resources to develop the state sector, trading in key commodities to ensure the 'leading role' of the government in commercial activities by managing supply and demand and by stabilizing prices.

While the law stipulates that the government will 'ensure equal treatment for all sectors before the law as far as commercial activities are concerned' (article 7) and 'protect the property rights and other legal rights of persons engaged in trade in the private sector' (article 12), it encourages them at the same time to 'cooperate and form joint ventures with state trading companies' (article 12). Article 16 unambiguously states that [the Vietnamese government] 'restricts imports of those commodities that are produced domestically and in which domestic demand can be met.' The government will also 'protect domestic production in a rational manner.' There is obviously a strong inclination for the law to support state trading companies in commercial activities.

How the Commercial Law has been implemented is hard to fathom. Since the law is so broad, covering so many activities and requiring the involvement of so many government bodies, no special government agency could be assigned to enforce its implementation. Article 264 specified that the government would provide detailed instructions on the implementation of the law. Later on, as has been the case with most legislation in Viet Nam, the government issued a number of supporting legal documents (ordinances, decrees, and instructions) interpreting the provisions of the law and providing instructions on how it should be implemented. Some legal terms that were very broadly defined in the law, such us 'illegal competitive behavior,' required further elaboration, but this process has never been adequately completed. Of the 14 decrees that were supposed to be developed to ensure the law's proper implementation, only two had been produced by 2001, one on external trade and the other on advertising (UNDP and CIEM 2001). To the best of the author's knowledge, no published statistics are available to help assess how widely or effectively the law has been implemented. Despite some anecdotal evidence concerning violations of the law, no official lawsuit has followed.

It has become obvious that many of the provisions in the Commercial Law are now obsolete because of the rapid changes experienced since the law was passed in 1997. With the enactment of the new Law on Enterprises in 2000, the signing of the BTA with the United States in 2001, and the implementation of reforms to meet WTO accession conditions, some of its provisions are now out of alignment with reality. Thus, where the BTA with the United States requires Viet Nam to provide trading rights to all economic entities without discrimination, article 33 of the Commercial Law states that

> business entities may carry out commercial activities with foreign countries only upon satisfaction of all conditions stipulated by the government and upon carrying out registration with the competent state body.

Many of the law's provisions do not comply with the national treatment and most favored nation (MFN) principles that underline most of the country's trade agreements and WTO commitments. There is therefore an urgent need for change in the regulatory framework. Clearly this has been a major driving force behind the drafting of the new competition law that will be submitted to the National Assembly for approval in 2004.

The Price Decision (1992) and Price Ordinance (2002)

One of the most visible and frequently mentioned tools for competition management in Viet Nam is the regulation of behavior with respect to prices, retail price maintenance, discriminatory pricing, and so forth (Cuthbertson, Nguyen, and Thai 1999). The Price Decision issued by cabinet in 1992 provided for very direct and heavy government control over the prices of a number of commodities. The decree specified that the government had the authority and responsibility to set prices for electricity, posts and telecommunications, water supply services provided by government-funded projects, government-owned houses, land, and natural resources. In addition the government was charged with setting price thresholds for a number of key commodities, including refined oil, metal, cement, rail and maritime services, fertilizers, rice, and some imported goods. The Ministry of Finance, the Pricing Committee,[4] and provincial governments were assigned responsibility for implementation and enforcement of the Price Decision. These government agencies investigated suspected violations of price controls and imposed administrative fines and remedies in cases of confirmed violations. Official data on the number of cases and their seriousness are not available, however.

On the face of it, some of these price control measures may look similar to those used to counter uncompetitive and unfair behavior as specified in a competition regime. However, at the time the Price Decision was promulgated it was not intended to form part of a competition policy. State control of production and trading was taken for granted and a private sector had yet to emerge. The purpose of the price controls in this context was to ensure price stability and protect consumers.

As with the Commercial Law, it became clear that many of the provisions in the Price Decision were no longer consistent with the rapidly evolving institutional and policy environment. The government's commitments under ASEAN Free Trade Area and other trade agreements with regard to customs valuations, the removal of quantitative controls on imports and exports, and other matters required it to eliminate many of the decree's price control mechanisms. Deregulation in some sectors with wider participation of the private sector also called for a new approach to price management.

In this context, the new Price Ordinance approved in 2002 set a new framework for government control over prices. It addressed the issues of monopolistic pricing and collusion for the first time in Viet Nam. A monopolistic price is defined as the price for goods and services set by the sole trader in a market, or the price fixed by a monopolistic group of businesses colluding to dominate market prices. Collusion for monopolistic price fixing is defined as an agreement between organizations and/or individual producers or traders to fix prices, and in this way dominate the market and harm the legal interests of other producers and traders, consumers, or the state (Law on Prices (2002), article 4(4–5)).

According to the Price Ordinance, when indications of monopolistic pricing or collusion for monopolistic price fixing are found, the government may take remedial measures that include requesting the colluding parties to (a) stop using the monopolistic price in all their transactions, and (b) apply the price used before the collusion began (article 19). An implementing decree states that enterprises engaged in monopolistic pricing or collusion for monopolistic price fixing may face administrative punishment, a requirement to compensate victims for their losses, and court action.[5]

The Price Ordinance also gives a definition for predatory pricing, again for the first time in Viet Nam. Predatory pricing occurs when there is

> a sale of a good or service in the Vietnamese market at a price that is lower than usual for the purpose of winning market share, restraining legal competition, or harming the legal interests of other organizations, individual producers and traders, or the state.

The remedies for predatory pricing include fixing minimum prices, administrative fines, compensation for competitors' losses, and other relevant penalties (article 26).

Despite these innovative provisions, the ordinance still preserves a strong role for the state in controlling the prices of a number of commodities, as with the previous Price Decision. The central government will continue to set the prices of refined oil; rail, maritime, and air services; water; telecommunications services; and 'other services important to the nation's and people's well-being.'[6] The government will also continue to apply measures, both at the central and the local level, to stabilize the prices of key commodities such as refined oil, cement, steel, fertilizers, rice, coffee, cotton seed, sugar cane, and some medicines.

Laws governing enterprises

Reflecting the continuing legacy of central planning even as market forces have taken hold, enterprises in Viet Nam are subject to four different laws according to their ownership. These are the Law on State-owned Enterprises (1995), which accommodates all state-funded economic establishments; the Law on Foreign Investment (1996), which covers enterprises and economic activities having foreign-invested capital; the Law on Cooperatives (1997), which regulates establishments governed by Cooperative Standard Rules and Regulations; and the Law on Enterprises (2000), which regulates Vietnamese joint stock and private businesses.

This complex legal setting means, among other things, that the legal norms established for the proposed competition act may differ depending on the ownership of the enterprises in question. Rather than facilitating healthy rivalry, such a legal environment is likely to encourage abuse of position to win market share or enjoy government protection. In particular, SOEs and foreign-invested firms, which already receive preferential treatment under the law, may find it more lucrative to continue to seek government protection and preferential treatment rather than invest in advanced technology or cut costs to improve their competitiveness.

Underlying the different legal provisions applying to the four economic sectors are the government's view on the role of each sector, especially the role of the state sector in the economy. The objective of the Law on State-owned Enterprises, for example, is 'to develop the key role of the state economic sector in a multisectoral market economy.' The law consistently stipulates that 'SOEs are entitled to preferential investment and the re-investment facilities of the state' (Introduction and article 8(e)). As long as the state controls the country's major financial and banking facilities, SOEs will continue to receive preferential allocation of resources, thus curtailing development opportunities for new private initiatives and significantly reducing rivalry as well as growth.

As mentioned earlier, most Vietnamese laws provide only a general legal framework, leaving the formulation and promulgation of more concrete regulations to the administrative bodies in charge of each sector— usually the ministries. Thus implementation depends very much on the way the ministries in particular interpret the law.[7] But as well as being charged with state management of the sector, the ministries are the authorized owners of the lower-ranking SOEs and hence have an institutional interest in protecting or at least favoring their 'own' SOEs. The latter motivation often takes precedence in the formulation, interpretation, and implementation of laws and policies. The lack of a clear distinction and separation between the regulator (government agency) and operator (business) is often blamed for the inability of the regulator to promote competition (Doanh 2004).

Cuthbertson, Nguyen, and Thai (1999: 10) argue that in Viet Nam the application of western antimonopoly law aimed at either preventing the creation of market power or regulating its exercise once created, would come up against some policies aimed at deliberately consolidating and creating market power for certain SOEs and general corporations.

In this context, government policies on the powerful business conglomerates known as general corporations have very important implications for competition policy in Viet Nam, as discussed in more detail later in the chapter.

While the new Law on Enterprises does not address the issue of competition directly, its approval and implementation provides many interesting implications and lessons for the development and implementation of a competition policy in Viet Nam. The law is rigorous in giving all citizens the freedom to engage in business activities. It replaces the previous requirement to obtain 'authorization' from the chair of a Provincial People's Committee with automatic business registration. It clearly identifies all the documents required to register a business and prohibits the registrar from requesting any additional material. This is the first time this has been done in Viet Nam, and marks a tremendous step forward in terms of reducing the time and cost of market entry. The Law on Enterprises also restricts the power of the ministries and Provincial People's Committees to issue licenses and permits and gives state agencies responsibility for organizing post-registration monitoring. These provisions promote the fundamental competition principle of free entrepreneurship.

In an unprecedented step, the prime minister established a task force to oversee the implementation of the Law on Enterprises. It identified 180 unlawful or unnecessary licenses and permits and recommended their cancellation or replacement (Doanh 2004). The task force turned out to be instrumental in ensuring effective implementation of the law, in avoiding sectoral and local resistance to change, and in achieving coordinated supervision and monitoring of the new law.

State sector restructuring and the creation of general corporations

The possibility that dominant companies may exercise their market power was not entertained by the legislators of the Law on Enterprises. In the current version of the law, mergers and acquisitions (M&As) are considered an internal decision of the corporation and are therefore subject solely to the arrangement of the companies concerned (articles 107–108). Article 114 on state management of enterprises does not consider an enterprise's behavior toward other enterprises. Article 7(d) of the Law on State-owned Enterprises, which gives SOEs the right to participate in state general corporations, also disregards the market power of SOEs.

The policy to restructure and improve the effectiveness of the state sector by grouping SOEs in the same sector under state general corporations has been in operation since 1994. As expressed in a prime ministerial decision,[8] the general corporations were established to

1 strengthen the accumulation of state capital and increase competitiveness;
2 abolish the administrative dependence of SOEs on sectoral ministries and local administrative authorities;
3 level the playing field for central and local SOEs; and
4 strengthen the management of the state over enterprises regardless of ownership.

Clearly, the coexistence of a comprehensive competition policy dealing with such issues as M&As and abuse of dominance alongside policies to promote a powerful set of state-owned business groups raises questions about the consistency of competition policy. The impending application of national treatment and MFN clauses following Viet Nam's accession to the WTO also calls for serious consideration of the potentially conflicting objectives of competition policy and other government policies. The next section examines the major instruments the government has used to pursue its industrialization objectives, and their implications for competition policy.

4   MAJOR INSTRUMENTS OF INDUSTRIAL POLICY AND THEIR IMPLICATIONS FOR COMPETITION POLICY

There are two competing views on the priorities for dealing with competition issues in Viet Nam. The first can be labeled the 'pro-government' standard, and is shared by many government establishments as well as the domestic business community. In essence, it argues that domestic firms are increasingly being subjected to unfair competition on their own soil from strong multinational enterprises with an overwhelming advantage in financial resources and market position. There is thus a need to design a workable framework that would help address this emerging issue. The second view is that competition in Viet Nam is limited because SOEs still play a leading or dominant role in the economy while the private sector faces enormous constraints to development. The focus of competition policy should therefore be on abolishing state monopolies and promoting a level playing field. The truth probably lies somewhere between these two extremes.

As quoted above, Cuthbertson, Nguyen, and Thai (1999) identify the potential conflict between competition law aimed at preventing or regulating market power and policies aimed at consolidating and creating market power for certain SOEs and general corporations. It is therefore important to examine the nature of the set of government policies, both explicit and implicit, and their implications for the development and implementation of competition policy. Industrialization policies have an important role to play in this respect and therefore demand special attention.

Industrialization and modernization have been a strategic development objective of Viet Nam for a long time. The 10-year socioeconomic development strategy for 2001–10 adopted by the ninth Party Congress re-emphasized their importance for the country's development. While there has been a significant shift in development priorities at the central level toward the creation of a freer market economy, in practice there is also a strong emphasis on traditional, government-led industrialization policies similar to those applied so successfully in the past by Korea and Japan. Preference in the form of protective and promotional measures has been given to specific sectors of the economy. This has important implications for competition policy in Viet Nam.

The major instruments used by developing countries in pursuit of their industrial policy objectives are external, product, and factor market interventions (Pangestu 2002). These measures have also been applied in Viet Nam from time to time. In addition, because Viet Nam is a country in transition from a centrally planned economy to a market economy, direct government interventions in markets are still visible.

External market interventions

External market interventions are clearly reflected in Viet Nam's current trade policy. Over the past two decades the government has made significant policy improvements, giving the country a more open, transparent, and enabling trade policy regime. The right to trade has been expanded to cover virtually every sector of the economy regardless of ownership. But looking back, other, less attractive, characteristics of the trade regime are also apparent (Vu 2001).

The motivations for protection have not always been clear. Price and quantitative controls were placed even on imported goods and commodities not produced in Viet Nam at the time, such as refined oils, fertilizers, some kinds of steel, cement, and even paper. Quantitative restrictions now apply only to petroleum and sugar, but five years ago they were placed on over a dozen commodities (Table 9.2). Petroleum is still on the list

*Table 9.2   Viet Nam: Products subject to quantitative restrictions,
1999–2003*

1999	2000	2001	2002	2003
Petroleum	Petroleum	Petroleum	Petroleum	Petroleum
Sugar	Sugar	Sugar	Sugar	Sugar
Fertilizer	Steel	Steel	Cement	
Steel	Cement/ clinker	Cement/ clinker	Motorcycles	
Cement/ clinker	Glass	Motorcycles		
Glass	Motorcycles	Cars		
Motorcycles	Cars	Vegetable oil		
Cars	Paper			
Paper	Vegetable oil			
Electric fans				
Ceramic tiles				
Porcelain				
Caustic soda				
Bicycles				
Vegetable oil				
Plastics				
Plastic packaging				

Source: Athukorala (2004).

because the government considers it to be a strategic commodity that
needs to be supplied smoothly and monopolistically by the government
(Price Ordinance (2002)). Sugar is on the list because of a government
program initiated in 1994 to build a sugar industry capable of ensuring
self-sufficiency in supply. The program was a great failure owing to the
inefficiency of the sugar mills (Dapice 2003). Nevertheless, the government retained quantitative quotas on sugar imports in order to protect the
mills from foreign competition and support farmers who relied on the
mills to take their sugar cane. Motorcycles and cement were on the list
until recently because the government wanted to support these infant
industries.

The incidence of protection across industries is mixed but its impact on competition is clear: most protectionist measures have created barriers to entry and led to high concentration in the affected sectors. Domestic prices for commodities in protected sectors are generally higher than those in international markets as well as in neighboring countries. For example, in 1999 one ton of cement cost $29 in Korea, $39 in Singapore, and $46 in Thailand, but $73 in Viet Nam (CIE 1999). Firms operating in protected industries tend to earn huge profits, but their capacity to meet the challenges of deepening integration and increasing competition is in doubt. Honda, for example, reportedly accrued large profits even during the Asian crisis because of its protected position in the market. Most heavily protected industries, such as cement and motorcycles, appear to be uncompetitive (CIEM 2002). The overall level of protection has been declining gradually but steadily, but the consequences of protection are still visible.

Import tariffs are perhaps the most common tool governments of developing countries use to protect domestic industries and limit competition from outside. Viet Nam is no exception in this regard. The average tariff rate seems moderate, but dispersion remains high, suggesting that the distortionary impact of tariffs is not small. The average import-weighted tariff for all traded commodities was 21.0 percent in 1997, falling slightly to 19.6 percent in 2003 (Table 9.3). However dispersion as measured by the coefficient of variation was as high as 130.7 percent in 2003. Manufacturing remains the most protected sector in the economy even though the effective rate of protection fell significantly from 121.5 percent in 1997 to 46.3 percent in 2003 (Athukorala 2004).

Aware of the negative effects that import substitution and protection policies may have on other sections of the economy, especially exporters, the government has often introduced counter or neutralizing measures in the form of export promotion measures, duty drawbacks, exemptions from some domestic taxes and fees, preferential credit, and, recently, a performance-based rewards system. In 2001, for example, with exports slowing due to weaker demand in the international market, the government adopted a series of export promotion measures aimed at encouraging firms to expand their exports and find new partners and markets. A value-added tax rebate and exemption scheme for exporters and a program of awards for improved export performance were implemented during that time. Before the export quota on rice was abolished in 1997, a special fund was set up to support those who bought and exported rice under government orders. A study of the textile and garments sector shows that although the official tariffs on textiles and wearing apparel are quite high

Table 9.3   Viet Nam: Nominal and effective rates of protection, 1997 and 2003

	1997		2003	
	Nominal	Effective	Nominal	Effective
Weighted average				
Agriculture	8.1	7.7	12.7	14.7
Mining	9.4	6.1	3.6	0.0
Manufacturing	30.6	121.5	30.3	46.3
All traded goods sectors	21.0	72.2	19.6	27.1
Simple average	23.3	59.5	20.3	26.4
Coefficient of variation	133.8	156.0	102.5	130.7

Source: Athukorala (2004); Technical Group (1999).

(at 31 percent in 1997 and 28 percent in 2002 for textiles and 42 percent in 1997 and 49 percent in 2002 for wearing apparel), most companies in the sector are exempt from import duties.[9] This dual policy stance in the trade regime makes Viet Nam an interesting case: an economy that has achieved outstanding export performance despite having a highly protected trade regime. In fact the trade to GDP ratio in Viet Nam is around 100 percent, one of the highest in the world, and export growth has been spectacular at around 20 percent per annum for the past decade.

To what extent have these external market interventions affected competition in Viet Nam? One thing is clear: they have reduced *foreign competition* in the domestic market. What is less clear is their impact on *domestic competition*. In some cases the removal of protection has led to significant improvements in competition, evidenced by an increase in new entry and a fall in prices and marginal profits. The easing and subsequent abolition of the quota on rice exports in 1997 and the decision to allow private firms to export rice in 1998, for example, led to the emergence of numerous small private rice traders who bought paddy from farmers and sold processed rice to exporting companies. Competition in the rice market may have been very tough for these rice traders, but growers obtained better prices. The difference between the export price of rice in Viet Nam and Thailand narrowed significantly due to these measures (Vu 2001). But in other cases the impact is not so clear. There is a danger that some monopolies will simply change from being government owned to being privately owned or having mixed ownership. Most quotas were removed in 2000, but competition in some sectors shows little sign of change if one looks at the number of firms or price indicators.

Factor market interventions

Factor market interventions include policies to regulate foreign investment so that the host country realizes a net benefit from FDI. While Viet Nam's policy toward FDI has become more liberal and open, the government continues to place restrictions on foreign investment that effectively limit competition and have profound implications for competition. On the surface these measures seem to be aimed at limiting foreign competition only, but in many cases they protect all the sector's incumbents, both foreign and domestic. The main restrictions on FDI are summarized below.

Restricted areas and forms of operation

At present FDI is not allowed at all in some areas, or is subject to tight restrictions. In telecommunications and the media, for example, the government permits foreign participation only through business cooperation contracts. In some sectors, such as oil and gas, air transportation and airport construction, forestation, and tourism, foreign firms must form joint ventures with at least one Vietnamese partner (Decree 24/2000/ND-CP). Foreign firms were not allowed to hold equity in listed companies, and joint ventures were not permitted to go public, until 2004.

Performance-based requirements

FDI is subject to a number of performance-based requirements. These include local content requirements, export-sharing arrangements, and legal capital requirements. The regulations covering local content are perhaps the most complicated, because of the way local content is defined and because of the tax rate applying to each case. Guidelines issued by the Ministry of Planning and Investment in 1994 stipulate that foreign firms involved in motorcycle manufacturing should achieve a local content ratio of 5–10 percent in the second year of operation, rising to 60 percent in five to six years. A regulation on FDI issued in 2000 requires the foreign partner to a joint venture to contribute at least 30 percent of total capital (Decree 24/2000/ND-CP).

Although export performance requirements have been removed for many products, 14 products remain on the list of approved performance-based requirements (Decision 718/2001/QD-BKH). These products include motorcycles, cars, diesel engines, and ships under 30,000 deadweight tons. Enforcement, however, seems to be lax. A survey conducted recently by the US–Viet Nam Trade Council shows that

> while most companies interviewed continue to have such provisions in their investment contracts, all have said that the governing authorities do not in practice seek to enforce them, and have in general not experienced problems in this area (US–Viet Nam Trade Council 2004: 47).

Regulations governing financial and land markets

Foreign firms in the financial market may be in a better position than their domestic counterparts, but this is not the case as far as the land market is concerned. Due to complex and restrictive regulations applying to land, foreign firms are denied the right to own land and are given only limited access to land. There has, however, been some progress in this area. Recently the government extended land use rights to overseas Vietnamese, many of whom are foreign investors.[10] The government is also currently considering legislation that would enable land use rights to be used as collateral for mortgages with offshore banks.

The government used to provide some financial intervention and support for selected industries and SOEs, but the number of such measures has dropped off significantly since it decided to reform the state sector. As a consequence, bank loans to SOEs have fallen as a share of total lending (World Bank 2002). Credit growth in 2003, for example, was estimated to reach approximately 28 percent, of which credit for SOEs increased by around 16 percent but loans to the private sector rose by 31 percent. Nevertheless, small and medium-sized enterprises (SMEs) and the private sector still have limited access to credit compared with large SOEs and foreign firms, due to complicated collateral requirements.

The government recently set up a Special Development Assistance Fund with total assets of around D5,000 billion ($300 million) to provide subsidized credit to certain industries and regions under criteria set by the government. There is concern about the effectiveness and sustainability of this fund, but whether it will have any impact on competition is harder to assess.

Special programs to establish powerful conglomerates

The idea that the country should be self-sufficient and self-reliant still prevails in Viet Nam. This has entailed the promotion of key industries, with the state sector taking a leading role. In the early 1990s, faced with increased competition in international markets, as well as from foreign companies within Viet Nam, the government saw the establishment of large, state-sponsored business groups—or general corporations as they are known—as one possible response.

Two types of general corporation, GC90 and GC91, are now operating in Viet Nam. The former were established by Government Decree 90/1994 and are under the ministries. The latter were established by Decree 91/1994 and are under the central government; that is, they are formed by a prime ministerial decision. At present there are 17 central government GC91s with 450 firm-members and 71 ministerial GC90s with 1,057 firm-members. In addition, seven GC90s have been established by local governments. These general corporations together account for 27 percent of the total number of SOEs and 77 percent of all assets possessed by SOEs (CIEM 2002). According to their charters and related regulations, general corporations can transfer the capital they receive from the government to firm-members, and the latter have full autonomy to use these resources for their business activities as they see fit. General corporations can, however, adjust or reallocate resources as necessary to ensure the smooth operation of the group as a whole. It is the general corporation that determines the *market division* among firm-members and universally imposes ceiling prices on imports and floor prices on exports for all firm-members. This internal market arrangement effectively limits competition from non-members.

After 10 years of operation, the performance of the general corporations is mixed, as are their implications for competition. Some general corporations, such as Vietnam Airlines and Vietnam Posts and Telecommunications, are monopolies. Based on profit-based performance indicators such as profit to capital, profit to revenue, or profit to labor ratios, these general corporations are performing very well. Telecommunications, for example, has experienced exceptionally high growth rates and undergone rapid modernization in recent years. Between 1990 and 2000, the industry's output grew by nine times, recording the second highest rate of growth in the world after the PRC. During the period 1995–2002, the sector had the highest rate of growth in the Asian region (Doanh 2004). The net profit ratio of Vietnam Posts and Telecommunications in 2002–03 was as high as 40 percent (Vinh 2004). Protection and the monopolistic position enjoyed by these enterprises in the domestic market are the main reasons for their exceptional performance.

On the other hand, some general corporations have performed well with less direct support and protection from the government. Vietnam National Textile and Garment Corporation (VINATEX), a general corpo-

Table 9.4   Viet Nam: Financial performance of selected firms in general corporations by industry group (%)

Industry	Gross profit margin	Return on assets	Return on equity
Paper	13.2	1.8	3.5
Steel	7.1	3.1	6.0
Cement	27.4	13.9	22.5
Food	11.3	4.0	14.3
Rubber	29.0	8.3	9.9
Sugar	1.5	−2.6	−17.5
Seafood	3.4	1.4	7.4
Textiles	10.3	4.0	5.7
Ports (maritime services)	23.2	4.3	5.8

Source: Packard (2004).

ration in the textile and garments sector, is one example. Although the profit margin in the sector is low, VINATEX has notched up an impressive employment record and export performance. The number of employees in the sector as a whole increased from 232,000 in 2000 to 356,000 in 2002, an increase of 54 percent in two years. Total exports of garments increased from $1.5 billion in 1997 to $2.4 billion in 2003 (STARS 2004).

Table 9.4 shows financial performance indicators for selected firms belonging to general corporations. This information needs careful interpretation because it does not tell us anything about non-state firms operating in similar fields of business. It is therefore hard to draw any sensible conclusions about the efficiency of state versus non-state firms from these data. Nevertheless, this limited information does provide some insight into the relative degree of protection and competition accorded different sectors in Viet Nam. The cement industry, for example—dominated by the Vietnam Cement Corporation—has a very high profit margin ratio, reflecting limited competition, difficult exit and entry, and rigid price controls in the sector. The troubled sugar industry, on the other hand, has experienced negative returns on assets and equity despite operating under a similar price control and management scheme. The seafood and textile industries both have a very high degree of openness (ratio of exports to total output) and face a high level of competition. There is virtually no government support, subsidies, or administrative intervention for their business activities.

Mergers, acquisitions, and liquidations, if these terms can be applied to general corporations, have mostly been done in an administrative manner following a government or ministry decision. Seven mergers have been completed to date, including two in construction, one in food processing, and one in mineral exploration (SOE Reform Committee 2004). In early 2004, the government was considering a plan to put general corporations under privatization schemes. Deregulation measures like those implemented in the telecommunications sector in 2004—the opening of the market to the private sector and the relaxation of price controls—may change the situation and could lead to significant changes in the competition landscape of the economy as a whole.

To sum up, so far the government of Viet Nam has pursued a classical industrialization policy of supporting the establishment of a 'national industrial base' for modernization. In doing so it has employed a number of classical instruments of 'industrial promotion,' some of which have led to more competition whereas others have led to significantly less competition. In some cases the outcome has been to enhance domestic competition but to restrict foreign competition in the domestic market. It is therefore impossible to generalize as to whether this industrialization policy has led to more or less competition. Both ownership and openness have a role to play in determining the competition landscape of a particular sector, but the final outcome seems to depend on other factors as well. Conduct matters more than just ownership and openness.

This is the case for two reasons. First, under pressure from various sectors of the economy and faced with the need to make policy trade-offs, the government introduced offsetting measures to neutralize the initial impact of some of its industrialization promotion measures. To take trade policy as an example, the government adopted measures to protect certain sectors and industries using infant industry, price stabilization, and other rationales, while at the same time adopting a set of neutralizing measures (export promotion schemes, duty drawbacks) to avoid undermining the development of other sectors as well as its own objectives in other areas. Such sectors would then operate with minimum distortion and hence competition would be established.

Second, due to weak enforcement and a lack of appropriate institutions to support smooth and effective implementation, many of the desired effects of industrialization policy measures have never been realized.

Local content and export requirements are a good illustration of this. As mentioned earlier, although export requirements are officially considered a prerequisite for obtaining a license for a new joint venture in some areas, in most cases firms do not see this requirement as binding. The extent to which a sector or industry is operating in a more or less competitive environment is therefore best judged from the actual operation of the firms in that sector. The next section provides information on indicators that help to reveal the degree of competition prevailing in a particular sector, based on data from the Industrial Survey for 2001 carried out by the General Statistics Office.

5   THE LINKS BETWEEN COMPETITION AND ECONOMIC DEVELOPMENT: EVIDENCE FROM INDUSTRIAL DATA

Common measures of competition include concentration ratios (the share of the three, five, and 10 largest firms in an industry's total output) and the Herfindahl–Hirschman index.[11] Appendix A9.1 calculates the Herfindahl–Hirschman index for all sectors covered by the Industrial Survey for 2001, based on firms' total assets, labor, fixed assets, and revenue. Appendix A9.2 summarizes five performance indicators for a similar set of sectors over the three-year period from 2000 to 2002. These are the ratios of total capital to labor, fixed assets to labor, revenue to labor (labor productivity as measured by the revenue generated by one unit of labor), profit to capital, and profit to revenue. Appendix A9.3 shows the concentration ratios for the top three firms in each industry in terms of revenue. It also shows the number of SOEs, foreign-invested firms, and private firms among the top three firms in each sector. Finally, Appendix A9.4 gives a summary of nominal and effective rates of protection by manufacturing sector.

This information should be interpreted with care. The quality of data has always been a problem in Viet Nam, with the classification and even the method of collecting data varying greatly across sectors and localities. In addition, the various indicators contain their own measurement problems. Nevertheless, the results obtained from this dataset should shed light on the nature of the linkages between competition and economic development in Viet Nam.

First, it was found that the ranking of sectors by degree of concentration changed depending on which variable—labor, revenue, or capital— was used, even when the same measure of concentration ratio—for example, the Herfindahl–Hirschman index—was applied. Thus, whereas the concentration ratios for posts and telecommunications were similar regardless of the variable used, wide differences were found in other sectors such as textiles, food and beverages, and wearing apparel. Inflexibility of capital and labor in some sectors may explain this difference.

Second, there is a quite strong and positive relationship between the profitability and sales concentration ratios—the correlation ratio between the variables given in Appendix A9.2 is 0.41. This result is not surprising but it does confirm the assertion in the previous section that restrictions and barriers to entry are good for incumbents. The case of cement again can be seen as a good example.

Third, the state sector retains its dominant position in some sectors, but foreign-invested and private sectors have taken the lead in others (Appendix A9.3). This reflects the significant changes that have taken place in the economy in recent years as the government has sought to promote the market mechanism and encourage wider private sector participation in economic activity. While SOEs remain at the top of many traditional sectors, such as mining, tobacco production, and electricity, the private sector and FDI have a dominant position in sectors such as basic metals, electronics, telecommunications equipment, and motor vehicles. What is important here is that the latter sectors tend to be more high-tech and export-oriented than the former. The role of the emerging private sector and FDI in introducing new technology and expanding Viet Nam's trading relationship with the rest of the world cannot be underestimated.

However, the relationship between protection and competition turns out to be weak. The correlation between the degree of competition (measured by the Herfindahl–Hirschman index in Appendix A9.3) and the degree of protection (given in Appendix A9.4) is negative but statistically not significant. This is a little surprising since there is a view that trade liberalization can complement and even substitute for domestic competition, at least in the case of traded goods. Some in Viet Nam hold high hopes that deepening economic integration, in particular the implementation of the BTA with the United States and compliance with WTO accession conditions, will promote competition and stimulate further domestic reform. Perhaps both measures—the effective rate of protection and the concentration ratio—need further elaboration and revision.

At the sectoral level, micro observations seem to provide different results. The cases of rice production and garment exports tend to support the contention that the removal of trade barriers has significantly increased performance in these sectors by promoting competition. Sectors that have been shielded from foreign competition and that have faced limited domestic rivalry, meanwhile, tend to be ineffective and unable to adjust to the new environment. Clearly more evidence on this subject is needed before any definite assertions can be made.

6   CONCLUSIONS AND RECOMMENDATIONS

Viet Nam is a country in transition with further rapid changes likely to lie ahead. Despite the absence of a formalized competition policy, the basic elements of a competition regime are embodied in existing legal documents, ordinances, and instructions. What is missing is a comprehensive framework and efficient institution to put competition policy principles into practice in a way that supports the country's development. Potentially conflicting objectives and policies in a number of areas will make the successful implementation of even a well-designed competition regime difficult. Current industrialization policies, whether stated explicitly or implicit in the measures that are actually implemented, are in serious conflict with the government's future reform agenda and commitments toward economic integration.

A new competition law will be approved by the National Assembly in December 2004. Given Viet Nam's current institutional settings, legal framework, and level of development, it is essential that the new legislation incorporates the valuable experience acquired over the past 20 years of reform in Viet Nam, that it reflects international experience, and that it is forward looking.

1   It is important to review possible areas of inconsistency between the proposed competition policy and current policies to ensure that the competition framework is not in conflict with the country's development agenda. Experience with trade negotiations show that the two processes—negotiation and implementation—often become disconnected due to institutional segmentation, causing many problems during the implementation phase. Moreover, openness and the equitization of SOEs alone cannot ensure a better competitive environment. Existing regulations that are not consistent with competition principles as embodied in the draft competition law will need to be abolished gradually. In this sense it will be important to carry out a legal review of all relevant regulations and their implications for the new competition regime. The government should undertake this exercise in consultation with stakeholders, especially the business community.

2   The new competition regime should be forward looking in the sense that it should take account of the country's rapidly evolving institutional environment. Although Viet Nam has been engaging more deeply in international economic integration and accelerating the *doi moi* process, many policy decisions have failed to consider this evolving environment and have therefore been short-lived. The draft competition law is supposed to serve the country's long-term development

objectives, ensure fair competition, and protect the national interest. It should therefore take into account not only the current level of development in Viet Nam, but also the future development landscape and the profound institutional and policy changes yet to come. M&As are almost nonexistent at present, but they will begin to occur in the near future. The financial market will most likely be opened to competition from both domestic and foreign companies. New types of business activities will emerge, putting other competition-related issues on the agenda. The proposed competition law needs to capture all these dynamics and translate them into the text of the law, and into implementation modalities. In this regard, international experience in formulating, enacting, and implementing competition law should prove very useful for Viet Nam. As it implements its BTA, WTO, and other international commitments, Viet Nam is likely to confront issues similar to those already faced by many other countries. Learning how countries such as India have equipped their competition policy to cope with the new economic environment could yield dividends for Viet Nam.

3 Implementation will be crucial for effective and credible realization of the law's major provisions. In this context, the government should consider using the Law on Enterprises as a model. A highly competent and powerful implementation agency is a prerequisite for successful and credible implementation of the law. This agency should be equipped with highly motivated and competent staff and should be protected from interference from ministerial and sectoral interests.

4 Since Viet Nam has not previously had a competition regime, it will need to carry out wide-ranging advocacy activities, especially in the early stages of implementation of the law. Study of cases that have competition implications will be important not only for advocacy, but to help identify the capacity and institutions needed to deal effectively with competition abuses.

To summarize, the competition-related problems that have emerged in Viet Nam in recent years reflect a serious institutional vacuum in identifying and dealing effectively with such cases. The demand for a comprehensive but highly relevant and effective competition law is therefore understandable and justified. What the country does *not* need is a law that fails to address the potential conflicts between competition policy and other government policies, and that lacks an effective institution to properly implement its ideas. Viet Nam is in a position to turn its proposed competition law into another success story like the Law on Enterprises or—and this is more likely—to translate it into 'just another law' that has little impact on the economy.

POSTSCRIPT

After more than three years of consultation and 15 drafts, Viet Nam's first Competition Law was officially approved by the National Assembly on 4 December 2004. The law contains six chapters and 123 articles and will take effect from 1 July 2005 (Phillips Fox 2004).

Chapter 1 provides general provisions that define the scope of application of the law. Two broad sets of competitive practices are regulated by the new Competition Law: practices in restraint of competition and unhealthy competitive practices. The former include (a) agreements in restraint of competition; (b) abuse of a dominant market position or a monopoly position; and (c) economic concentration. The latter are defined as any conduct by an enterprise that is against the norms of business ethics or that causes loss or damage to the lawful rights, or harms the interests, of another enterprise or consumers. Unhealthy competitive practices include the provision of misleading information to customers, coercion of customers, misleading and deceptive advertising and promotions, multi-level selling, infringement of business secrets, defamation or coercion of another enterprise, disruption of business activities of another enterprise, and discrimination by industry associations. These practices are prohibited and are not subject to any exemptions.

Chapter 2 of the Competition Law regulates restraint of competition and Chapter 3 regulates unhealthy competition. Chapter 4 concerns the State Competition Authority and Competition Council. Chapter 5 sets out procedures for complaints and investigations of anticompetitive practices. The major provisions of the law are as follows.

Restraint of competition

The law lists eight broad categories of agreements that would be considered to restrain competition. However, only three of these categories are prohibited strictly and unconditionally: agreements that prevent or impede other enterprises from participating in the market or developing a business; agreements to exclude from the market enterprises that are not parties to the agreement; and tender collusion. The other five categories—price-fixing agreements; market-sharing agreements; agreements to restrict sale and production; agreements to restrict technology development, or investment; and agreements to fix trading conditions—are prohibited only where the participating parties have a combined market share of 30 percent or more of the relevant market. However, the Minister of Trade, upon recommendation from the State Competition Authority, may grant exemptions if certain criteria (such as an increase in the competitiveness of SMEs or the promotion of technical or technological progress) are met.

Abuse of dominant market position or monopoly position

The law has a special section dealing with abuse of a dominant market position or monopoly position. Market dominance and monopolies are not prohibited as such; it is the abuse of such a position that is deemed unlawful. An individual enterprise will be deemed to hold a dominant market position if it has a market share of at least 30 percent of the relevant market or has the ability to impose 'substantial restraint of competition.' An individual enterprise will be deemed to be in a monopolistic position if no other firm can compete in the relevant market. The law uses market share alone to determine whether a group of enterprises holds a dominant market position. The following groups will be deemed to hold a dominant market position if they act in concert to restrain competition:

- two enterprises with a market share of 50 percent or more in the relevant market;
- three enterprises with a market share of 65 percent or more in the relevant market; or
- four enterprises with a market share of 75 percent or more in the relevant market.

Behavior that is considered abuse of a dominant market position under the new law includes predatory pricing, minimum resale-price fixing, restrictions on production or distribution, restrictions on market or technological developments, discrimination in trading conditions, and product tying or bundling. In addition to these practices, behavior that is considered abuse of a monopoly position includes imposing disadvantageous conditions on customers and unilaterally changing or rescinding a contract without a legitimate reason.

Economic concentration

The new Competition Law regulates mergers, consolidations, acquisitions, joint ventures, and other (undefined) forms of economic concentration. The regulations apply to existing foreign-invested enterprises, but not to M&As and joint ventures involving new foreign investors in Viet Nam, or if the economic concentration would result in an SME. An SME is defined as an enterprise with a registered capital of at most D10 billion or employing at most 300 people in a given year. Any economic concentration in which the participating parties have a combined market share above 50 percent is prohibited unless the economic concentration results in an SME or an exemption is granted. Exemptions are available where one or more of the participating parties is at risk of being dissolved or becoming insolvent (as decided by the Minister of Trade) or where the economic concentration enhances exports, socioeconomic development, or technical progress (as decided by the prime minister).

Any economic concentration where the participating parties have a combined market share of 30–50 percent must be notified to the State Competition Authority, unless the economic concentration results in an SME. The commission must confirm in writing whether the proposed economic concentration can proceed without exemption or requires prior exemption. At this notification stage, the commission is not entitled to exercise any discretion—its role is simply to confirm how the proposed economic concentration may proceed under the Competition Law.

The State Competition Authority and the Competition Council

The regulatory role of the government in implementing the Competition Law is assigned to two states bodies: the State Competition Authority and the Competition Council. The law provides a detailed description of the roles and responsibilities of each of these two regulatory bodies. The State Competition Authority will be established under the Ministry of Trade to receive, evaluate, and make recommendations on applications for exemptions from the Competition Law; to investigate competitive practices; and to penalize unhealthy competitive practices. The head of the commission will be appointed by the prime minister on the recommendation of the Minister of Trade. The Competition Council will hear and deal with competition cases concerning practices in restraint of competition. It will consist of 11–15 members appointed by the prime minister on the recommendation of the Minister of Trade. A panel of at least five members of the council will sit on investigative hearings into competition cases.

Complaints and investigations of anticompetitive practices

The Competition Law sets out the steps for dealing with any alleged breach of its provisions, including legal proceedings. Cases may be investigated by the Competition Authority on its own initiative or upon receipt of a complaint. Any organization or individual believing their rights or interests to have been infringed has the right to lodge a complaint with the Competition Authority. The limit on the commencement of legal proceedings is two years from the date on which the alleged breach of the law occurred. Where a preliminary investigation indicates the existence of an offense, an official investigation will be conducted. During the investigative stage, administrative preventive measures may be imposed on the firm upon request from the complainant. The law also sets out a maximum timeframe during which competition cases must be resolved. In the case of unhealthy competition practices, the timeframe is 90 days. In the case of economic concentration, abuse of market dominance and/or monopoly, and restraint of competition, the timeframe for resolving complaints is 180 days. Up to two extensions are allowed, each of no more than 60 days.

Confirmed breaches of the law attract a range of remedies. These include warnings; fines of up to 10 percent of the firm's total turnover in the financial year preceding that in which the anticompetitive conduct took place; revocations of business registration certificates and practitioner certificates; and confiscation of the facilities used in breach of the law. The law also provides for compulsory measures such as restructuring of an enterprise that abuses its dominant market position; division or separation of enterprises that merge or consolidate; compulsory resale of that part of an enterprise that was acquired; public correction of false information; and removal of illegal terms and conditions from a contract or business transaction.

NOTES

1   Several different poverty measures are in use in Viet Nam, although all are based on income. The poverty measure developed by the Ministry of Labor, Invalids, and Social Affairs is used in all official government documents related to poverty reduction programs down to the grassroots level. The internationally comparable poverty measure used by both the World Bank and the General Statistics Office is based on the Viet Nam Living Standards Survey.

2   The Millennium Development Goals for poverty are to reduce by half the proportion of people living on less than a dollar a day, and to reduce by half the proportion of people who suffer from hunger, by 2015 (UNDP 2003).

3   A survey by a group of researchers at the Ministry of Labor, Invalids, and Social Affairs attempted to gauge the familiarity of SMEs with recent institutional changes and legislation. The results were quite striking: on a scale of 1 to 4, where 1 indicated good knowledge of the law in question and 4 indicated no knowledge, the average score was between 2 and 3. Insurance, land, and environmental laws were among the least well understood (Kokko 2004).

4   The Pricing Committee was a separate government body under the prime minister. It is now called the Department for Price Management and is under the Ministry of Finance.

5   Government Decree No. 170/2003/ND-CP on Implementation of the Price Ordinance (2003).

6   Government Decree No. 170/2003/ND-CP on Implementation of the Price Ordinance (2003).

7   For example, the Commercial Law states that 'the Ministry of Trade is responsible for the implementation of state management in trade' (article 246). In a decision related to the import and export activities of enterprises in industrial parks and export-processing enterprises, the ministry interpreted this to mean that 'the Ministry of Trade maintains the balance of the national economy by regulating a number of goods and inputs' (Decision of the Minister of Trade No. 0908/TM-XNK dated 28 October 1997).

8   Decision No. 91/TTG of the Prime Minister in 1994 on Piloting the Establishment of Business Groups.

9   A survey of 150 textile and garment enterprises conducted by the Institute of Economics in 2000 shows that although the sector relies heavily on imported inputs, its import tax commitments are very low (Institute of Economics 2000). In 1999, imported materials accounted for 66 percent of total materials purchased. By 2000 this share had increased to 77 percent. However, 58 percent of these imports were totally exempt from tax in 1999, and the rest were subject to low tax commitments. As a whole, the tax rate for the sample was barely 1 percent.

10   Decision 79/2001/QD-CP and Decree 81/2001/ND-CP.

11   The Herfindahl–Hirschman index is the sum of the squares of the percentage market shares held by the firms in a market. If there is a monopoly, or one firm with all sales, the Herfindahl–Hirschman index will be 10,000. If there

is perfect competition, with an infinite number of firms with near-zero market share each, the index will be approximately zero. Most industry structures will have a Herfindahl–Hirschman index of between zero and 10,000.

Appendix A9.1   Viet Nam: Herfindahl–Hirschman index by sector

Sector	Total assets	Labor	Fixed assets	Revenue
Agriculture, hunting, & related service activities	121	166	782	251
Forestry, logging, & related service activities	243	186	1,217	242
Fishing, operation of fish hatcheries & fish farms, & related service activities	219	96	725	578
Mining of coal & lignite; extraction of peat	588	500	1,606	623
Mining of metal ores	1,129	1,374	3,013	1,754
Other mining & quarrying	367	184	6,240	273
Manufacture of food products & beverages	169	42	2,816	108
Manufacture of tobacco products	1,076	995	2,070	1,276
Manufacture of textiles	373	161	3,533	275
Manufacture of wearing apparel; dressing & dyeing of fur	168	68	2,722	181
Tanning & dressing of leather; manufacture of luggage, handbags, & saddlery	586	175	6,536	420
Manufacture of wood & products of wood & cork, except furniture	180	133	1,964	233
Manufacture of paper & paper products	635	234	2,094	872
Publishing, printing, & reproduction of recorded media	409	106	866	285
Manufacture of coke, refined petroleum products, & nuclear fuel	3,403	1,568	5,934	2,204
Manufacture of chemicals & chemical products	181	165	1,648	279
Manufacture of rubber & plastics products	208	166	4,353	169
Manufacture of other non-metallic mineral products	596	58	4,269	301
Manufacture of basic metals	829	1,905	2,355	840
Manufacture of fabricated metal products, except machinery & equipment	223	90	2,255	154
Manufacture of machinery & equipment n.e.c.	636	210	4,224	639
Manufacture of office, accounting, & computing machinery	9,434	8,628	9,951	9,952
Manufacture of electrical machinery & apparatus n.e.c.	394	476	2,911	395
Manufacture of radio, television, & communication equipment & apparatus	873	291	8,318	688
Manufacture of medical, precision, & optical instruments, watches, & clocks	1,441	1,059	3,064	1,444

Manufacture of motor vehicles, trailers, & semi-trailers	896	246	3,077	1,194
Manufacture of other transport equipment	853	172	7,712	1,162
Manufacture of furniture; manufacturing n.e.c.	178	151	1,377	225
Recycling	5,397	6,298	10,000	6,231
Electricity, gas, steam, & hot water supply	4,706	4,862	4,925	4,454
Collection, purification, & distribution of water	1,001	466	3,610	1,367
Construction	35	16	1,223	24
Sale, maintenance, & repair of motor vehicles & motorcycles	210	163	645	255
Wholesale trade & commission trade, except of motor vehicles & motorcycles	95	44	723	85
Retail trade, except of motor vehicles & motorcycles	148	63	4,518	145
Hotels & restaurants	359	147	1,216	332
Land transport; transport via pipelines	669	285	8,092	399
Water transport	658	177	5,956	720
Air transport	5,368	3,883	9,705	4,665
Supporting & auxiliary transport activities; activities of travel agencies	512	431	2,955	341
Posts & telecommunications	4,485	4,542	4,975	4,287
Financial intermediation, except insurance & pension funding	445	303	1,822	377
Insurance & pension funding, except compulsory social security	3,509	2,892	9,877	3,623
Activities auxiliary to financial intermediation	2,665	1,396	2,098	3,749
Renting of machinery & equipment without operator	330	285	661	284
Computer & related activities	6,860	4,707	9,557	4,945
Research & development	91,314	1,281	9,705	1,747
Other business activities	5,339	104	9,975	2,930
Education	2,027	861	4,215	3,887
Health & social work	3,503	1,078	9,045	2,916
Sewage & refuse disposal, sanitation, & similar activities	939	320	4,435	449
Recreational, cultural, & sporting activities	693	641	2,697	815

n.e.c. = not elsewhere classified.

Source: Author's calculations, based on data from the Industrial Survey for 2001.

Appendix A9.2   Viet Nam: Main performance indicators by sector (ratio)[a]

Sector	Capital to labor	Fixed assets to labor	Revenue to labor	Profit to capital	Profit to revenue
Agriculture, hunting, & related service activities	40.7	101.7	40.7	1.0	3.2
Forestry, logging, & related service activities	9.7	43.7	34.0	1.6	5.1
Mining of coal & lignite; extraction of peat	89.3	29.0	78.3	0.9	0.4
Extraction of crude petroleum & natural gas	14,936.7	3,303.7	5,096.3	52.8	52.6
Mining of metal ores	10.0	24.7	69.0	10.5	7.8
Other mining & quarrying	6.7	34.0	57.7	5.0	5.6
Manufacture of food products & beverages	15.7	95.7	274.0	3.7	2.6
Manufacture of tobacco products	130.7	67.3	482.3	10.8	5.6
Manufacture of textiles	44.0	95.0	112.0	0.6	0.9
Manufacture of wearing apparel; dressing & dyeing of fur	16.7	23.7	49.7	2.1	2.0
Tanning & dressing of leather	51.0	27.7	48.0	1.0	0.9
Manufacture of wood & wood products	5.3	27.0	74.0	2.2	1.9
Manufacture of paper & paper products	17.0	100.7	189.7	2.1	1.8
Publishing, printing, & reproduction of recorded media	12.3	73.7	196.0	7.0	6.7
Manufacture of coke, refined petroleum products, & nuclear fuel	94.0	587.3	1,435.7	7.0	5.9
Manufacture of chemicals & chemical products	33.3	92.3	316.7	5.9	4.6
Manufacture of rubber & plastics products	19.7	106.0	194.7	1.0	0.9
Manufacture of other non-metallic mineral products	36.7	208.3	183.0	2.1	3.4
Manufacture of basic metals	50.3	129.3	362.3	4.7	3.5
Manufacture of fabricated metal products	13.0	101.3	164.3	0.6	0.5
Manufacture of machinery & equipment n.e.c.	20.7	76.7	148.0	2.0	2.3
Manufacture of office, accounting, & computing machinery	507.3	459.0	2,133.3	−2.9	−2.2
Manufacture of electrical machinery & apparatus n.e.c.	52.0	111.3	239.0	5.4	5.2

Manufacture of radio, television, & communication equipment & apparatus	76.7	234.7	516.7	6.2	5.6
Manufacture of medical, precision, & optical instruments	39.3	141.0	155.3	1.5	2.2
Manufacture of motor vehicles, trailers, & semi-trailers	42.7	203.7	474.7	9.8	9.0
Manufacture of other transport equipment	49.0	144.3	340.3	6.2	5.7
Manufacture of furniture; manufacturing n.e.c.	10.0	35.0	81.0	3.1	3.1
Recycling	1.3	24.0	86.0	2.4	1.2
Electricity, gas, steam, & hot water supply	5,039.0	821.7	317.0	2.6	9.3
Collection, purification, & distribution of water	57.0	282.7	111.3	2.6	9.8
Sale, maintenance, & repair of motor vehicles & motorcycles	3.3	56.3	1,026.3	1.9	0.4
Wholesale trade & commission trade, except of motor vehicles	11.7	62.3	1,099.3	1.4	0.5
Retail trade, except of motor vehicles & motorcycles	15.3	186.7	653.3	−0.9	−1.9
Land transport; transport via pipelines	7.7	47.3	65.3	3.2	3.3
Water transport	20.3	120.0	170.0	2.9	3.1
Air transport	2,208.0	252.3	725.3	10.0	7.3
Supporting & auxiliary transport activities	16.7	103.0	148.3	8.9	10.9
Posts & telecommunications	2,844.7	182.0	173.7	16.6	34.7
Financial intermediation, except insurance & pension funding	593.0	989.3	489.3	0.8	8.6
Insurance & pension funding	903.0	379.7	612.7	1.0	1.8
Activities auxiliary to financial intermediation	42.7	446.0	156.0	1.7	21.9
Real estate activities	102.7	1,607.0	350.3	0.0	−4.3
Renting of machinery & equipment	2.7	83.0	185.0	−5.7	−5.7
Computer & related activities	3.3	30.0	139.7	−7.3	−6.7
Other business activities	14.0	140.0	116.0	5.7	17.6
Other community, social, & personal service activities	19.3	64.7	44.7	3.0	6.5
Other service activities	1.3	30.0	46.7	1.0	1.1

n.e.c. = not elsewhere classified.

a   Average for the three years from 2000 to 2002.

Source: Author's calculations, based on data from the Industrial Surveys for 2000–03.

Appendix A9.3   Viet Nam: Concentration ratio for the top three firms in each industry and breakdown by ownership

Sector	Share of total revenue (%)	Number of firms in top three		
		State	Foreign-invested	Private
Agriculture, hunting, & related service activities	20.6	2	0	1
Forestry, logging, & related service activities	20.1	3	0	0
Fishing, operation of fish hatcheries & fish farms, & related service activities	30.5	3	0	0
Mining of coal & lignite; extraction of peat	31.1	3	0	0
Mining of metal ores	58.0	2	0	1
Other mining & quarrying	22.0	3	0	0
Manufacture of food products & beverages	10.7	1	2	0
Manufacture of tobacco products	53.2	3	0	0
Manufacture of textiles	20.7	1	2	0
Manufacture of wearing apparel; dressing & dyeing of fur	17.7	2	1	0
Tanning & dressing of leather; manufacture of luggage, handbags, & saddlery	28.2	0	3	0
Manufacture of wood & products made of wood & cork, except furniture	18.7	1	2	0
Manufacture of paper & paper products	43.4	3	0	0
Publishing, printing, & reproduction of recorded media	21.7	3	0	0
Manufacture of coke, refined petroleum products, & nuclear fuel	77.4	0	3	0
Manufacture of chemicals & chemical products	23.6	2	1	0
Manufacture of rubber & plastics products	13.0	2	0	1
Manufacture of other non-metallic mineral products	21.3	2	1	0
Manufacture of basic metals	41.1	1	2	0
Manufacture of fabricated metal products, except machinery & equipment	12.5	1	2	0
Manufacture of machinery & equipment n.e.c.	38.5	1	2	0
Manufacture of office, accounting, & computing machinery	100.0	0	2	1
Manufacture of electrical machinery & apparatus n.e.c.	26.8	0	3	0
Manufacture of radio, television, & communication equipment & apparatus	35.6	0	3	0

Manufacture of medical, precision, & optical instruments, watches, & clocks	57.1	0	3	0
Manufacture of motor vehicles, trailers, & semi-trailers	45.9	0	3	0
Manufacture of other transport equipment	48.4	0	3	0
Manufacture of furniture; manufacturing n.e.c.	18.6	0	3	0
Recycling	100.0	0	0	3
Electricity, gas, steam, & hot water supply	98.4	2	1	0
Collection, purification, & distribution of water	50.0	2	1	0
Construction	3.8	3	0	0
Sale, maintenance, & repair of motor vehicles & motorcycles	19.3	2	0	1
Wholesale trade & commission trade, except of motor vehicles & motorcycles	12.1	3	0	0
Retail trade, except of motor vehicles & motorcycles	15.6	1	0	2
Hotels & restaurants	23.6	3	0	0
Land transport; transport via pipelines	30.4	2	0	1
Water transport	38.4	1	2	0
Air transport	100.0	2	0	1
Supporting & auxiliary transport activities; activities of travel agencies	21.8	3	0	0
Posts & telecommunications	96.3	3	0	0
Financial intermediation, except insurance & pension funding	20.4	3	0	0
Insurance & pension funding, except compulsory social security	96.1	1	2	0
Activities auxiliary to financial intermediation	96.7	3	0	0
Real estate activities	21.1	0	2	1
Renting of machinery & equipment without operator	100.0	2	1	0
Computer & related activities	67.2	1	2	0
Other business activities	57.4	2	0	1
Education	78.9	0	1	2
Health & social work	77.1	0	3	0
Recreational, cultural, & sporting activities	24.9	2	1	0
Sewage & refuse disposal, sanitation, & similar activities	42.3	3	0	0

n.e.c. = not elsewhere classified.
Source: Author's calculations, based on data from the Industrial Survey for 2001.

Appendix A9.4   Viet Nam: Nominal and effective rates of protection by manufacturing sector (%)

Sector	Nominal rate of protection	Effective rate of protection
Processed & preserved meat & by-products	10.14	18.28
Processed vegetable & animal oils & fats	15.53	29.15
Milk, butter, & other dairy products	23.20	25.35
Cakes, jams, candy, cocoa, & chocolate products	44.60	57.54
Processed & preserved fruits & vegetables	34.30	49.87
Liquor (excluding beer)	99.52	146.44
Beer	100.00	146.71
Non-alcoholic beverages	50.00	86.65
Sugar of all kinds	18.65	33.66
Coffee, processed	43.62	53.88
Tea, processed	50.00	52.13
Cigarettes & other tobacco products	34.94	55.24
Processed seafood & by-products	30.89	37.55
Rice, processed	40.63	170.45
Other food manufactures	15.53	24.44
Glass & glass products	25.36	31.38
Ceramics & by products	24.47	43.17
Bricks & tiles	48.99	70.22
Cement	37.95	46.32
Concrete, mortar, & other cement products	25.20	31.58
Other building materials	7.51	−1.02
Paper pulp, paper products & by-products	16.72	18.29
Processed wood & wood products	4.18	0.36
Basic organic chemicals	2.86	−6.12
Basic inorganic chemicals	2.21	−0.32
Chemical fertilizers	0.35	−2.75
Other fertilizers (non–chemical)	0.00	−3.47
Pesticides	3.81	0.85
Veterinary drugs	0.00	−3.06
Medicines	5.34	4.53
Processed rubber & by-products	10.01	11.28
Soap & detergents	19.61	46.12
Perfumes & other toiletry preparations	16.41	29.11
Plastic, original & semi-processed	1.04	−2.36

Appendix A9.4 (continued)

Sector	Nominal rate of protection	Effective rate of protection
Plastic products	30.42	57.18
Paints	3.89	1.81
Ink, varnish, & other painting materials	5.26	2.07
Other chemical products	5.66	3.25
Medical instruments & apparatus	0.11	−4.91
Precision & optical equipment	6.84	3.48
Home appliances & parts	33.31	49.11
Motorcycles & accessories	100.00	148.69
Bicycles & accessories	34.34	43.85
Machine tools	10.00	4.93
Other general purpose machinery	5.49	2.46
Special purpose machinery	2.72	−20.66
Passenger motor vehicles	58.85	66.74
Other transport equipment	12.11	9.83
Transformers	11.80	12.64
Other electrical machinery & equipment	7.60	0.96
Broadcasting, television, & communication machinery	13.38	10.13
Non-ferrous metals & products (except machinery equipment)	6.61	1.95
Ferrous metals & products (except machinery equipment)	5.74	−31.38
Textiles	38.37	70.01
Fibers & thread (all kinds)	4.94	0.99
Clothing	49.50	76.90
Carpets & tapestry textiles	40.00	67.72
Weaving & embroidery of textiles (except carpets)	31.25	37.09
Leather (products of tanneries)	20.96	23.69
Leather goods	26.16	30.81
Animal feeds	9.30	−5.89
Products of printing industry	10.95	−3.70
Publishing	4.77	−0.78
Unclassified products	31.40	23.71
Gasoline & lubricants (refined)	2.65	−0.66

Source: Athukorala (2004).

10

Lessons from the six country analyses

Simon J. Evenett

1 INTRODUCTION

The purpose of this concluding chapter is two-fold: to draw out several themes that recur in the six chapters describing country experiences with competition laws and proposals to enact such statutes, and to identify a number of lessons for policy-makers in the coming years. It is hoped that these observations will be of interest to government officials in the Asia-Pacific region, to scholars of that region and of competition law and its enforcement in developing countries, and to officials from international organizations and civil society. To sharpen the discussion, the remarks in this chapter concerning competition law and its implementation are organized around the following four questions:

1   Is competition law a threat to development?
2   Is the Asia-Pacific region different?
3   Is competition law inherently anti-big business?
4   Is effective implementation possible?

A few caveats and preliminary comments are also in order. First, although these four questions cover many of the important matters relating to competition law in the Asia-Pacific region, the reader should not conclude that these are the only issues of significance. Second, even though the comments presented here draw extensively on the country analyses, these concluding remarks are mine and do not necessarily represent the views of the authors of the country studies. The latter, after all, have had the opportunity to present their own policy recommendations and findings in earlier chapters. My intention here is to look across chapters, to identify common themes and findings, and to draw from the experiences of other developing countries where that is relevant.

The six country analyses in this volume highlight many of the nuances associated with competition law and its enforcement. These nuances often make competition law seem an alien and complex beast to those used to analyzing relatively more straightforward policy instruments, such as ad valorem tariffs. Such complexity does not mean competition law is unnecessarily burdensome or bad; instead it points to the fact that a number of interrelated factors influence the effectiveness of its enforcement. Indeed, the country analyses demonstrate the importance of administrative, judicial, and political-economy factors as well as economic considerations in the design and use of competition law. In this respect competition law is similar to sectoral regulation, which experience has shown can vary markedly in its effectiveness. Given that many developing countries in the Asia-Pacific region have turned to competition laws in the wake of perceived failings of apparently more straightforward reforms (such as trade reforms, investment liberalization, and privatization or corporatization), it would seem that policy-makers appreciate the limits of some of the relatively clear-cut advice given to them in the 1990s.

In the remainder of this chapter I discuss each of the four questions posed above and make a number of policy recommendations. I then tie together a number of the themes raised in this volume in some final remarks.

2   IS COMPETITION LAW A THREAT TO DEVELOPMENT?

It is striking reading the country analyses just how many times policy-makers in the Asia-Pacific region have turned to competition law when prominent liberalizing reforms have not had the desired effect. That is not to say that these reforms have retarded development, but rather that they have often produced unintended side effects, such as enabling incumbent firms to exploit market power to the detriment of purchasers and often of the economy as a whole. Given that few business interests have actively supported the enactment and enforcement of competition laws, the recent interest in these statutes by Asian policy-makers almost certainly does not reflect a desire to promote narrow commercial interests. Instead, by their own actions Asian policy-makers appear to have accepted that competition laws have a role to play, possibly even a pro-development one. Of course, enactment does not necessarily lead to effective implementation, nor does it mean that influential commercial and bureaucratic interests have been completely overridden. Even so, it would seem that the debate over competition law in the Asia-Pacific region has shifted from the black-and-white question of whether competition laws are good or bad to a discussion of what types of competition law best promote the standard of living and how best to implement and enforce such laws.[1]

There are certain similarities in the rationales for the heightened recent interest in competition laws by policy-makers in the six Asian nations studied here. In the Republic of Korea (Korea), India, Malaysia, and Thailand, tackling anticompetitive practices rose up the policy agenda after measures to promote private sector development were seen as generating unfortunate by-products. In Korea this is putting the matter mildly, as curbing the power of the *chaebol* became a significant policy imperative after the 1997–98 financial crisis—a crisis that many Korean observers thought was brought on by the actions of the large conglomerates themselves. Proposals to adopt more stringent competition legislation in Viet Nam and the PRC had similar motives: first, as a constructive step toward the development of a market economy, and second, as a defensive measure to 'level the playing field' (increasingly in the PRC's case between domestic firms on the one hand and foreign firms and joint ventures involving foreign firms on the other).

There are also similarities in the considerations that these nations took on board when drafting their competition laws. The desire, for better or for worse, to preserve national industrial policies was a prominent concern in drafting India's and Viet Nam's recent competition laws. Such concerns would echo those in Beijing and Kuala Lumpur as to the appropriate provisions of these nations' proposed competition legislation. Quite distinctly, there are parallels between India's and Malaysia's concerns about the impact of a competition law on the well-being of certain favored societal groups. (Indeed, it appears that Malaysian academics and policy-makers have examined India's, and for that matter South Africa's, experiences in this regard.) The interest in the late 1990s in Korea and Thailand in more vigorous competition laws was due to yet another factor: the perception that incumbent firms have taken too much advantage of their substantial market positions with little or no offsetting benefits for the rest of the economy.

These findings have a number of policy implications. First, while country circumstances inevitably differ, a small number of factors have been important in nations with similar levels of development. Now that approximately 100 nations have adopted some form of competition law, this suggests that on certain matters there is plenty of room for cross-country learning and the sharing of experiences by policy-makers. International and regional development agencies can play an important role in fostering this international exchange of experience and associated expertise.

The second implication for policy-making is that competition legislation is adaptable enough to take account of a wide variety of initial conditions and societal objectives. Transition economies have tailored competition laws to their own circumstances, reconciling industrial and social policy objectives with the broader goals of competition statutes. Such reconciliations have used exemptions, exceptions, and exclusions from the reach of competition law, along with injunctions to consider factors other than consumer welfare and economic efficiency when implementing these laws. Of course, the fact that such reconciliations are feasible does not make any one set of associated compromises and trade-offs desirable.

Ideally, policy-makers would consider whether fostering or (explicitly or tacitly) allowing anticompetitive practices is the most effective way to attain a nation's social or industrial policy goals. Generally, constraining competition between firms is a suboptimal means to promote developmental ends. Indeed, one might have thought that one side benefit of debates over the merits of enacting and enforcing competition laws is that questions are raised as to the efficacy of existing measures that effectively constrain competition in the pursuit of some 'developmental' goal. However, the typical reaction to proposals for competition laws that might infringe on these measures is initially defensive, with the affected commercial and social interests, and the government agencies and ministries that 'oversee' such interests, seeking to preserve the status quo, often by opposing the enactment of competition laws. It is an open question as to whether the passage of time will undermine these favored groups' knee-jerk reactions against competition legislation.

Another interesting feature of the country studies is that, even though competition laws in the Asia-Pacific region tend to have a higher priority attached to them than previously, the contributors to this volume do not see competition law as a panacea. If this view is shared by policy-makers in the region, then it may well indicate a very healthy state of affairs as competition law may be asked to bear an appropriate load—misplaced expectations in the past having essentially damned many potentially useful liberalizing measures. This modest view of the prospects of competition law in the Asia-Pacific region may well reflect these laws' relative youth. Moreover, the fact that the country analyses in this book have identified few robust linkages between competition law enforcement and poverty reduction is probably a reflection of the limited experience with the former.

The contributors to this volume are also careful to stress that greater attention to competition law should not come at the expense of measures to remove inappropriate state impediments to domestic and international competition, a proposition with which I entirely agree. It should be noted, however, that measures to tackle private anticompetitive practices can complement, or even reinforce, measures to rationalize state intervention in national markets. In fact, measures to expand the scope for interfirm rivalry and private sector ownership (by, say, deregulation in the case of the former and privatization in the case of the latter) can be consistent with steps to ensure that such rivalry is preserved (by enacting and appropriately enforcing competition legislation).[2] Even though these measures can be implemented together, the enactment and enforcement of competition laws can and often does proceed without any connection to attempts to free markets from state intervention.

3   IS THE ASIA-PACIFIC REGION DIFFERENT?

It is all too common in discussions of development policy to hear arguments to the effect that a given region is 'different' and therefore needs a new recipe for growth, poverty alleviation, and so on. These arguments are often advanced to explicitly or implicitly reject the approaches taken in other parts of the world, typically the industrialized world. A number of discussions in recent years in international fora on the relationship between competition law and economic development have had this flavor. It is therefore appropriate to ask, on the basis of the country studies in this volume and what is known about other developing countries and their competition laws, just how similar or different the Asia-Pacific region actually is.

In the previous section I identified four principal considerations raised in the six country studies in connection with the adoption of competition laws: development of a market economy; the need to tackle anticompetitive practices and the desire on the part of some to curb the powers of large firms; the relationship between competition law and industrial policy; and the relationship between competition law and social policy objectives, such as favoring certain societal groups. These considerations resonate with those of other developing countries at comparable stages of development. The use of competition law as one instrument in effecting the social and economic transformation of South Africa has parallels with the experiences of Korea and Malaysia as described in this volume. The transition economies of Eastern Europe and the countries comprising the former Soviet Union faced many of the same challenges identified in the

PRC and Viet Nam country studies, although naturally their experiences are not identical. Moreover, concern about the anticompetitive conduct of large firms after a decade of reform and liberalization is an important impetus behind the renewed interest in competition law in Latin America. These similarities imply that the Asia-Pacific region is not alone in wanting to tackle the harm created by anticompetitive practices and that countries in the region should take advantage of opportunities for learning from the experiences of peers.

When one considers the range of anticompetitive practices experienced in the Asia-Pacific, which the country analyses have identified in the relevant enforcement records of active competition agencies and in numerous case studies, it is apparent that these find counterparts in other parts of the developing world. Cartelization, anticompetitive mergers and acquisitions (M&As), abuse of a dominant position and the like can be found in these country analyses, just as they can in countries at all levels of development. It is difficult to assess accurately the relative importance of different types of anticompetitive practices across countries and regions, not least because researchers typically can only rely on those practices that are the subject of complaint or enforcement action, which may well generate a biased sample of cases. Even so, certain Asian nations appear to place greater priority on taking action against predatory pricing by firms than do the larger industrialized jurisdictions. In this respect the experience in the Asia-Pacific may be similar to that in Africa, where a recent study found quite a few alleged instances of predatory pricing (Evenett and Jenny 2004). Given the considerable skepticism among scholars and practitioners of competition law in industrialized countries as to the viability of predatory pricing by firms, it may be worth examining whether the pre-conditions for such a commercial strategy are more likely to be found in the Asia-Pacific region. If so, then different circumstances may legitimately call for different enforcement priorities.

The Asia-Pacific region is similar to many other developing countries in another important respect, namely the tendency to omit M&A provisions from national competition legislation. This omission is said to reflect the political strength of corporate interests and, separately, the power of ministries that wish to promote large firms. It is worth noting here that there are a number of different types of merger review regimes and that developing countries need not immediately adopt the one with the most rigorous oversight of M&As. Moreover, the absence of a merger review regime can place a greater burden on the abuse of dominance provisions in a national competition law, as anticompetitive acts by a merged or acquired entity can be tackled ex post. Worse still, the absence of a merger review law will, in the presence of tough anticartel provisions, provide a strong incentive to firms who might otherwise cartelize a market to merge with one another. This consideration suggests that policy-makers should consider the full set of anticompetitive strategies available to firms when deciding which provisions to enact and enforce.

To summarize, even though the economies of the Asia-Pacific region differ from one another and from those outside the region, when it comes to the motivations and challenges faced when designing and enacting competition laws, there are plenty of commonalities with other developing countries. Participation in international fora such as the International Competition Network and the Inter-Governmental Group of Experts of the United Nations Conference on Trade and Development, as well as bilateral technical assistance and capacity-building programs, can strengthen the design and the enforcement of competition law in the Asia-Pacific region.

4   IS COMPETITION LAW INHERENTLY ANTI-BIG BUSINESS?

No reader of the country analyses in this volume can avoid noticing the widespread emphasis by policy-makers in the Asia-Pacific region on promoting large firms, except possibly in Korea in recent experience. The motives for the promotion of large firms, however, appear to differ, from a generalized desire to be self-reliant to equating national economic prowess with export competitiveness or the performance of so-called national champions in international markets. The country analyses strongly suggest that opposition to the enactment and enforcement of competition laws—in particular to laws establishing powers to review proposed M&As—has often centered on the perception that such laws are inherently anti-big business. Perhaps it cannot be stressed enough that properly enforced competition law does not target firm size but rather threats to, and actual distortions of, the competitive process and resource allocation. A merger between two domestic firms that offered the prospect of reducing incremental production costs (by allowing the execution of larger production runs, for example) need not fall foul of a properly enforced competition law. Now, if this merged entity decided to raise prices to domestic consumers, then a competition enforcement agency might raise objections. However, without such harm to domestic purchasers, and in the absence of some other concerns (such as the buying power of the combined entity), the size of the merged entity ought not be an independent concern of the officials tasked with enforcing the competition law. Similarly, mergers that help lower costs and promote export performance should under a broad set of circumstances be approved by competition agencies.

The points made in the last paragraph are hardly novel, nor are they particularly subtle, which makes one wonder whether there could be other explanations that account for the repetition of the size-based argument against the adoption of competition law. First, there could be a concern that the officials responsible for implementing competition law will not have the necessary skills or experience to assess whether or not a merger is pro-competitive, and therefore that errors of diagnosis and prescription could be made. If this really is a concern, then the solution is to ensure adequate training for enforcement officials, even if this means delaying the full implementation of the merger review law until the necessary expertise is in place, or phasing it in.

A second underlying concern could be that the officials enforcing the competition law may be motivated by considerations other than those stated in the competition law. Private firms may fear that political interference from a minister could influence the outcome of an official merger review. While this logical possibility cannot be ruled out, especially when the competition agency is not independent of elected officials or their appointees, not enacting a merger review law on these grounds seems far too sweeping a solution. Mechanisms that would increase the autonomy of competition enforcement officials and make political leaders pay a higher 'price' for interfering in the merger review process may well be preferable alternatives. These last two arguments highlight the importance of implementation-related matters, to which I now turn.

5   IS EFFECTIVE IMPLEMENTATION POSSIBLE?

It is a straightforward and inconvenient fact that policy-makers cannot legislate anticompetitive practices out of existence. Firms, being rational decision-makers, will trade off the benefits of engaging in anticompetitive acts against the likelihood of enforcement action and any resulting punishments, be they fines or otherwise. The deterrent effect of a competition law therefore depends on firms' perceptions of the effectiveness of the implementation of competition law. Enactment of such laws is not enough; what matters is judicious and efficient implementation.

The country analyses in this volume provide plenty of evidence of the challenges faced when implementing competition laws. In fact, I know of no more comprehensive account of the failings of a competition law enforcement agency in a developing country than can be found in this volume's chapter on Thai experience. As was noted there, the noble intentions of policy-makers in enacting the 1999 competition law have been undermined by a combination of the following six factors: interference from government ministers, officials, and other politicians; lobbying by interest groups; legal loopholes; a lack of transparency in decision-making; lack of human capacity; and, relatedly, a lack of funding. Moreover, a standard prescription for policy-makers concerning the implementation of competition laws, namely that competition agencies should be functionally independent of government ministries, seems less relevant in the Thai case. As I understand it, in Thailand the creation of an independent regulatory agency requires a change in that country's constitution. Such a change is most unlikely, as it would be in many jurisdictions—including many of those in the industrialized world. The imperative, then, is to find other measures that secure some if not all of the benefits of independence.

One option worth exploring would be to give representatives of purchasers and those potentially harmed by anticompetitive practices a say in decision-making at competition agencies.[3] Moreover, 'sunshine'—that is, attention from the media and others—on the plight of the victims of anticompetitive practices may offset some of the disadvantages of the lack of independence of the competition agency from government ministries and their interlocutors.

Policy-makers in developing countries will also find the Korean experience, described in considerable detail in this volume, instructive in this regard. To bolster the prestige and credibility of the competition enforcement agencies in Korea, its government decided to endow the Korea Fair Trade Commission (KFTC) with significant powers to force the economic restructuring of large business groups and tackle anticompetitive practices. In addition the chairman of the KFTC sits in the cabinet of the national government and is directly responsible to the prime minister. In principle this set of institutional arrangements provides the chairman of the KFTC with the mandate as well as the means to present pro-competitive recommendations on a wide range of economic matters to influential policy-makers. It appears, however, that this combination is not necessarily an unalloyed good. In the view of some observers, the mandate of economic restructuring has dominated the KFTC's decision-making, sometimes to the detriment of economic efficiency and the goals of competition law. If this analysis is correct, the greater stature given to the agency responsible for implementing Korean competition law has come at the expense of the effectiveness of that law.

The Thai and Korean examples highlight the difficulties faced in designing an effective system to implement national competition law.

Given these difficulties, some might erroneously conclude that competition law should not be enacted at all. In the absence of any effective alternatives for tackling anticompetitive practices, this conclusion would be tantamount to throwing the baby out with the bathwater. Alternatively put, and at the risk of mixing metaphors, there is a serious risk here of policymakers and analysts making the perfect the enemy of the good. The same type of commercial and other pressures faced by competition enforcement agencies also confront the regulators of banks, utilities, and other sensitive sectors. Seen in this light, the challenges faced in effectively implementing competition law are not unique to this form of economic legislation. Indeed, former officials from established competition agencies in countries with political representatives that are especially sensitive to corporate interests and support recount (off the record) just how much time they spent countering the attempts of commercial interests to water down powers to enforce competition laws.

Although this is difficult terrain, readers should not be unduly pessimistic. Opportunities do arise that can be exploited to raise the stature and credibility of competition enforcement agencies. A judicious choice of cases is one factor that is often credited with raising the credibility of a competition agency. Knowing what cases to fight, and when, can be particularly important for nascent competition agencies in industrialized as well as developing countries. The inclusion of commitments in bilateral and regional trade agreements to properly enforce competition laws can help the relevant enforcement agencies secure more funding from national legislatures. Given the resurgence of interest in regionalism in the last 10 years, which shows little sign of abating, the latter point may be of particular interest. Finally, in the aftermath of corporate scandals concerning 'rip-offs' and the like, resourceful leaders of competition enforcement agencies and government ministries can further strengthen their positions. Of course, bureaucratic imperatives need not always lead to greater welfare for purchasers and a better allocation of national resources (two prominent goals of competition law), but this does not mean that every opportunity for such entrepreneurship should not be seized.

In sum, much more is known about the principles of competition law and competitive markets than about the minutiae of the effective implementation of these laws in the Asia-Pacific region and elsewhere. This state of affairs is not surprising given the fact that interest in such laws has only picked up in the last 10 years. While the challenge is clear, a reliable set of adaptable solutions is not so readily identified. Documentation and analysis of implementation experience, and the sharing of such evidence, will help in this regard, just as it does in pretty much every other significant area of economic regulation requiring substantial post-legislative enforcement action.

6 CONCLUDING REMARKS

As the backlash against the Washington Consensus, and against the often simplistic mantras of the 1990s, continues, policy-makers in developing countries often have a clearer sense of the problems that their nations face than the effective solutions available to them. The side effects—or in some cases, unintended consequences—of certain liberalizing reforms in the 1990s have helped propel dealing with anticompetitive practices up the policy agenda. Officials and analysts in developing countries, including in the Asia-Pacific region, have rightly given greater attention to competition law and its associated principles. However, enactment does not guarantee effective enforcement. The imperative in the coming years is therefore to design implementing practices and institutions that are robust, judicious, and transparent in societies in which there is a legacy of tight business–state relations (not least because in some Asian nations the state used to own many important companies). This is as much a political and legal challenge as an economic one. Moreover, given that some commercial interests will always have an incentive to weaken the enforcement of competition law, this challenge will endure—just as it has in jurisdictions with well-established competition law enforcement regimes. Supporters of equitable economic development, where both purchasers—including the poor—and producers reap the benefits of progress, will recognize the importance of this challenge, which amounts to nothing less than making sure that market forces work for the good of all.

NOTES

1   I return to this matter when addressing the fourth major question posed in this chapter.
2   Having said that, there is one well-known trade-off between the promotion of interfirm rivalry and privatization, namely that which occurs when competition is deliberately frustrated so as to enhance the value of a firm that is being privatized by a government. Here the interests of purchasers—who need not just be consumers—are sacrificed to those of the national treasury and, in principle, the nation's taxpayers.
3   The obvious caveat here is that purchasers and other parties with a direct interest in a specific case or enforcement action should be recused.

References

Abid Hussain Committee Report (1997), *Report of the Expert Committee on Small Enterprises*, New Delhi: Ministry of Industry, Government of India.

ADB (Asian Development Bank) (2004), 'Foreign direct investment in developing Asia,' Part 3 of *Asian Development Outlook 2004,* Hong Kong, China: Oxford University Press.

Agarwal, M. (2002), 'Analyses of mergers in India,' M.Phil dissertation, Delhi: Delhi School of Economics, University of Delhi.

Aghion, P., and P. Howitt (1996), 'A model of growth through creative destruction,' *Econometrica*, 60: 323–51.

Aghion, P., M. Dewatripont, and P. Rey (1999), 'Competition, financial discipline and growth,' *Review of Economic Studies*, 66: 825–52.

Aharoni, Y. (1986), *The Evolution and Management of State Owned Enterprises*, Cambridge MA: Harper and Row, Ballinger.

Ahluwalia, I.J. (1991), *Productivity and Growth in Indian Manufacturing*, Delhi: Oxford University Press.

Ahn, S. (2002), 'Competition, innovation and productivity growth: A review of theory and evidence,' *Economics Department Working Papers No. 37, ECO/WKP(2002)3*, Paris: OECD, 17 January.

Ahn, Y.S., and Y. Jung (2004), 'Merger control in Korea,' *2004 Asia Pacific Antitrust Review*, Global Competition Review. Available at http://www.global competitionreview.com/apar/kor_merger_control.cfm.

Alavi, R. (1996), *Industrialisation in Malaysia: Import Substitution and Infant Industry Performance*, London: Routledge.

Alavi, R. (2003), 'Patent protection and its impact on drug prices in Malaysia,' in M.H. Shah, K.S. Jomo, and P.K. Lit (eds), *New Perspectives in Malaysian Studies*, Kuala Lumpur: Malaysian Social Science Association.

American Bar Association (2002), 'The economics of innovation: A survey,' Comments on the Section of Antitrust Law, American Bar Association, July.

American Bar Association (2003), 'Report on antitrust policy objectives,' American Bar Association Antitrust Law Section, 12 February. Available at <http://www.abanet.org/antitrust/policyobjectives.doc>.

Amsden, A.H. (1989), *Asia's Next Giant: South Korea and Late Industrialization*, Oxford: Oxford University Press.

Amsden, A.H. (2001), *The Rise of the Rest: Challenges to the West from Late-Industrializing Economies*, New York: Oxford University Press.

Amsden, A.H., and A. Singh (1994a), 'The optimal degree of competition and dynamic efficiency in Japan and Korea,' *European Economic Review*, 38: 941–51.

Amsden, A.H., and A. Singh (1994b), 'Growth in developing countries: Lessons from East Asian countries,' *European Economic Review*, 38: 941–51.

An, T., and Y. Yang (2002), 'Characteristics of industries prone to price competition and firm strategy' [in Chinese], *Economic Research Journal*, June: 46–54.

Anderson, R.D., and N.T. Gallini (eds) (1998), *Competition Policy and Intellectual Property Rights in the Knowledge-based Economy*, Georgetown, Ontario: University of Calgary Press.

Anderson, R.D., and F. Jenny (2002), 'Competition policy as an underpinning of development and trade liberalization: Its relationship to economic restructuring and regulatory reform,' paper prepared for presentation at the Seoul Competition Forum, Seoul, 6–8 November.

Anderson, R.D., and S.D. Khosla (1995), 'Competition policy as a dimension of economic policy: A comparative perspective,' *Industry Canada Occasional Paper*, May.

APEC (Asia-Pacific Economic Cooperation) (1995), 'The Osaka Action Agenda: Implementation of the Bogor Declaration.' Available at <http://www.apec.org/apec/about_apec/how_apec_operates/action_plans_.downloadlinks.0002.LinkURL.Download.ver5.1.9>.

APEC (1999), *Competition Law for Developing Economies*, Singapore: APEC Trade and Investment Committee.

Areeda, P.E., and H. Hovenkamp (2000), *Antitrust Law*, Vol. 1, 2nd edition, Boston MA: Little, Brown & Co.

Athukorala, P. (2004), *Trade Policy Reforms and the Structure of Protection in Vietnam*, paper prepared for the Asian Development Bank and the Vietnamese Ministry of Finance, Ha Noi, March.

Audretsch, D.B., W.J. Baumol, and A.E. Burke (2001), 'Competition policy in dynamic markets,' *International Journal of Industrial Organization*, 19: 613–34.

Bai, C., Y. Du, Z. Tao, and S. Tong (2005), 'Local protectionism and regional specialization: Evidence from China's industries,' *Journal of International Economics*, forthcoming.

Baker, J. (1999), 'Developments in antitrust economics,' Policy Watch Paper, *Journal of Economic Perspectives*, 13(1): 181–94.

Basant, R. (2000), 'Corporate response to economic reforms in India,' *Economic and Political Weekly*, 35(10): 813–22.

Baumol, W.J. (2001), 'When is inter-firm coordination beneficial? The case of innovation,' *International Journal of Industrial Organization*, 19: 727–37.

Becker, G.S. (1968), 'Crime and punishment: An economic analysis,' *Journal of Political Economy*, 76: 169–217.

Beena, P.L. (1998), 'Mergers and amalgamations: An analysis of the changing structure of Indian oligopoly,' PhD dissertation, New Delhi: Centre for Economic Studies and Planning, Jawaharlal Nehru University.

Bhagwati, J.N., and P. Desai (1970), *Planning for Industrialisation and Trade Policies since 1951*, Delhi: Oxford University Press.

Bhagwati, J.N., and T.N. Srinivasan (1975), *Foreign Trade Regimes and Economic Development: India*, Special Conference Series on Foreign Trade Regimes and Economic Development, New York: National Bureau of Economic Research.

Bhattacharya, M. (2002), 'Industrial concentration and competition in Malaysian manufacturing,' *Applied Economics*, 34: 2,127–34.

Bora, B., P.J. Lloyd, and M. Pangestu (1999), 'Industrial policy and the WTO,' *Policy Issues in International Trade and Commodities, Study Series No. 6*, Geneva: United Nations Conference on Trade and Development.

Brooks, D.H., and H. Hill (2004), *Managing FDI in a Globalizing Economy: Asian Experiences*. London: Palgrave Macmillan.

Brooks, D.H., E.X. Fan, and L.R. Sumulong (2004), 'Foreign direct investment: Recent trends and the policy context,' in D.H. Brooks and H. Hill (eds), *Managing FDI in a Globalizing Economy: Asian Experiences*, London: Palgrave Macmillan, pp. 1–27.

Bruton, H.J. (1992), *The Political Economy of Poverty, Equity, and Growth*, New York: Oxford University Press for the World Bank.

Burgess, R., and A.J. Venables (2004), 'Toward a microeconomics of growth,' *Policy Research Working Paper 3257*, Washington DC: World Bank.

Cairns, R., and D. Nikomborirak (1998), 'An assessment of Thailand's new telecommunications plan,' *Telecommunications Policy*, 22(2): 145–55.

Carlin, W., S. Fries, M. Schaffer, and P. Seabright (2001), 'Competition and enterprise performance in transition economies: Evidence for a cross-country survey,' *Working Paper No. 376*, William Davidson Institute at the University of Michigan, May.

Carlton, D.W., and J.M. Perloff (1994), *Modern Industrial Organization*, 2nd edition, New York: HarperCollins.

Caves, R.E. (1996), *Multinational Enterprise and Economic Analysis*, 2nd edition, Cambridge: Cambridge University Press.

Centre for Monitoring Indian Economy (various issues), *Monthly Review of the Indian Economy*, Mumbai: Economic Intelligence Service, Centre for Monitoring Indian Economy.

Chakravarthy, S. (2004), 'India's new Competition Act 2002: A work still in progress,' *Business Law International*, 5(2): 240–93.

Chang, S.W. (1995), 'Korea,' in J. Garrett (ed.), *World Antitrust Laws and Practices*, Boston MA: Little, Brown & Co.

Chang, S.W. (2000), 'The role of law in economic development and adjustment process: The case of Korea,' *International Law*, 34(1): 267–87.

Chang, S.W., and K.S. Shin (1998), 'The role of law and legal institutions in Asian economic development: The case of Korea,' *Development Discussion Paper No. 661*, Cambridge MA: Harvard Institute for International Development, Harvard University, November.

Chen, K.Y.E., and P. Lin (2002), 'Competition policy under laissez-faireism: Market power and its treatment in Hong Kong,' *Review of Industrial Organization*, 21: 145–66.

China Statistics Press (1997), *China Large and Medium-sized Enterprises Yearbook 1996*, Beijing.

China Statistics Press (2002), *China Large Enterprise Groups Yearbook 2001*, Beijing.

Church, J., and R. Ware (1998), 'Network industries, intellectual property rights and competition policy,' in R.D. Anderson and N.T. Gallini (eds), *Competition Policy and Intellectual Property Rights in the Knowledge-based Economy*, Georgetown, Ontario: University of Calgary Press, Chapter 8.

CIE (Centre for International Economics) (1999), *Vietnam's Trade Policies*, Canberra and Sydney: CIE, December.

CIEM (Central Institute for Economic Management) (2002), *Viet Nam's Economic Report*, Ha Noi.

CMC (Communications and Multimedia Commission) (2000a), 'Guidelines on substantial lessening of competition,' *Discussion Paper No. RG/SLC/1/00(1)*, Kuala Lumpur.

CMC (2000b), 'Guidelines on dominant position in a communications market,' *Discussion Paper No. RG/DP/1/00(1)*, Kuala Lumpur.

CMC (2000c), 'Process for assessing allegations of anti-competitive conduct: An information paper,' *Information Paper No. IP/Competition/1/00(1)*, Kuala Lumpur.

Cuthbertson, A.G., T.H. Nguyen, and D.T. Thai (1999), *Competition Policy in Viet Nam*, Canberra and Sydney: Centre for International Economics, October.

Dapice, D. (2003), *Vietnam's Economy: Success Story or Weird Dualism? A SWOT Analysis*, Cambridge MA: Centre for Business and Government, Harvard University.

Day, A. (2004), 'Legal reform and economic development in Vietnam and China: A comparative analysis,' MA in Law and Diplomacy thesis, Medford MA: Fletcher School, Tufts University.

De Soto, H. (2000), *The Mystery of Capital: Why Capitalism Triumphs in the West and Fails Everywhere Else*, New York: Basic Books.

Democratic Justice Party (1987), *Public Hearing on Issues of Economic Concentration* [in Korean], Seoul, 16 September.

Dervis, K., and J.M. Page (1984), 'Industrial policy in developing countries,' *Journal of Comparative Economics*, 8: 436–51.

Djankov, S., and P. Murrell (2002), 'Enterprise restructuring in transition: A quantitative survey,' *Journal of Economic Literature*, 40(3): 739–92.

Djankov, S., R. La Porta, F. Lopez-de-Silanes, and A. Schliefer (2002), 'The regulation of entry,' *Quarterly Journal of Economics*, 117(1): 1–37.

Doan, N.M. (2002), *Law Effectiveness: Theory and Evidence in Viet Nam*, Ha Noi: Political Publishing House.

Doanh, L.D. (2004), 'Enterprise law,' paper presented at a Conference on Transitional Economies, Ha Noi, June.

Dung, N.V. (2002), 'Theoretical foundation for legal measures to establish and enhance legal awareness in Viet Nam,' *Journal of Democracy and Law*, 3: 4–6.

Dunning, J. (1993), *Multinational Enterprises and the Global Economy*, Wokingham: Addison-Wesley.

EIS (Economic Intelligence Service) (1999), *Industry: Market Size and Shares*, Mumbai: Centre for Monitoring Indian Economy, August.

Espicom (2004), 'Market intelligence report: Malaysia,' Chichester: Espicom Business Intelligence, July. Available at <http://www.espicom.com/web.nsf/structure/TocsWPM02/$File/Malaysia.PDF>.

Evenett, S.J. (2003), 'Study on issues relating to a possible multilateral framework on competition policy,' paper distributed at the Working Group on Interaction between Trade and Competition Policy, Geneva: World Trade Organization.

Evenett, S.J. (2004), 'Competition, competition law and development in the Asia-Pacific,' Manila: Asian Development Bank, mimeo.

Evenett, S.J. and F. Jenny (2004), 'An inventory of allegations of anti-competitive practices in Sub-Saharan Africa,' Oxford: University of Oxford, mimeo.

Evenett, S.J., M.C. Levenstein, and V.Y. Suslow (2001), 'International cartel enforcement: Lessons from the 1990s,' *World Economy*, 24: 1,221–45.

Expert Group (1999), *Report of the Expert Group on Interaction between Trade and Competition Policy*, New Delhi: Ministry of Commerce, Government of India, January.

Faaland, J., J. Parkinson, and R. Saniman (2003), *Growth and Ethnic Inequality: Malaysia's New Economic Policy*, Kuala Lumpur: Utusan Malaysia.

Fair Trade Commission of Japan (2004), 'Main features of the proposal to amend the Anti-monopoly Act,' press release, 1 April.

Fels, A. (2001), *Competition Policy: Governance Issues: What Are the Alternative Structures?* Canberra: Australian Competition and Consumer Commission.

Fink, C., A. Mattoo, and I.C. Neagu (2001), *Trade in International Maritime Services: How Much Does Policy Matter?* Washington DC: World Bank.

Gallini, N.T., and M.J. Trebilcock (1998), 'Intellectual property rights and competition policy: A framework for the analysis of economic and legal issues,' in R.D. Anderson and N.T. Gallini (eds), *Competition Policy and Intellectual Property Rights in the Knowledge-based Economy*, Georgetown, Ontario: University of Calgary Press, Chapter 2.

Gan, G. (2003), 'Creating an environment for fair competition,' speech given at the Forum Celebrating the Ten-year Anniversary of the Introduction of the Anti Unfair Competition Law, Beijing.

Gan, W.B. (1978), 'The relationship between market concentration and profitability in Malaysian manufacturing,' *Malaysian Economic Review*, 23(1): 1–13.

Gan, W.B., and S.Y. Tham (1977), 'Market structure and price–cost margins in Malaysian manufacturing industries,' *Developing Economies*, 15(3): 280–92.

Gavil, A.I., W.E. Kovacic, and J.B. Baker (2002), *Antitrust Law in Perspective: Cases, Concepts and Problems in Competition Policy*, Thomson/West.

Geroski, P.A. (1990), 'Innovation, technological opportunity, and market structure,' *Oxford Economic Papers*, 43(2): 586–602.

Gilbert, R., and S. Sunshine (1995), 'Incorporating dynamic efficiency into merger analysis: The use of innovation markets,' *Antitrust Law Journal*, 63(2): 569–601.

Gilbert, R., and W.K. Tom (2001), 'Is innovation king at the antitrust agencies? The intellectual property guidelines five years later,' *Working Paper CPC01-020*, Berkeley CA: Institute of Business and Economic Research, Competition Policy Center, University of California.

Glen, J., K. Lee, and A. Singh (2001), 'Persistence of profitability and competition in emerging markets,' *Economic Letters*, 72: 247–53.

Glen, J., K. Lee, and A. Singh (2002), 'Competition, corporate governance and financing of corporate growth in emerging markets,' *Accounting and Finance Discussion Papers No. 00-af46*, Cambridge: Department of Applied Economics, University of Cambridge.

Global M&A Research Center (2003), *China Mergers and Acquisitions Yearbook, 2003*, Beijing.

Gomez, E.T., and K.S. Jomo (1999), *Malaysia's Political Economy: Politics, Patronage and Profits*, 2nd edition, Cambridge: Cambridge University Press.

Government of India (2000), *Report of the High Level Committee on Competition Policy and Law*. Available at <http://www.dca.nic.in/comp/mainfile.htm>.

Graham, E. (2003), *Reforming Korea's Industrial Conglomerates*, Washington DC: Institute for International Economics.

Graham, E., and J.D. Richardson (eds) (1997), *Global Competition Policy*, Washington DC: Institute for International Economics, Chapter 1.

Grossman, G.M., and E.L.-C. Lai (2004), 'International protection of intellectual property,' *American Economic Review*, 94(5): 1,635–53.

GSO (General Statistics Office) (1999), *Results of Viet Nam Living Standards Survey 1997–1998*, Ha Noi: Statistical Publishing House.

GSO (2003), *Bi-annual Statistical Report*, Ha Noi: Statistical Publishing House.

GSO (2004), *Results of Industrial Surveys*, Ha Noi: Statistical Publishing House.

Haley, J. (2002), 'Competition law for the Asia-Pacific Economic Cooperation community: Designing shoes for many sizes,' *Washington University Global Studies Law Review*, 1(1–2): 1–3.

Hazari Committee Report (1955), *Hazari Committee Report on Industrial Licensing Procedures*, New Delhi: Ministry of Industry, Government of India.

Henderson, J.V., and A. Kuncoro (1996), 'Industrial centralization in Indonesia,' *World Bank Economic Review*, 10(3): 513–40.

Henderson, J.V., T. Lee, and Y.-J. Lee (2001), 'Scale economies in Korea,' *Journal of Urban Economics*, 49(3): 479–504.

High Level Committee (2000), *Report of the High Level Committee on Competition Policy and Law*, New Delhi: Department of Company Affairs, Government of India.

Hill, H. (2004), 'Six Asian economies: Issues and lessons,' in D.H. Brooks and H. Hill (eds), *Managing FDI in a Globalizing Economy: Asian Experiences*, London: Palgrave Macmillan, pp. 29–77.

Hobday, M. (1995), *Innovation in East Asia: The Challenge to Japan*, Aldershot: Edward Elgar.

Hoekman, B., and P. Holmes (1999), 'Competition policy, developing countries and the WTO,' *World Economy*, 22(6): 875–93.

Huan, D.V. (2003), 'Relationships between competition law and other specific laws in legal regulations in Viet Nam,' *Journal of Democracy and Law*, 8: 13–17.

Hwang, I., and J.-H. Seo (2000), '*Chaebol* governance and reform in Korea,' unpublished paper, on file with *Law and Policy in International Business*, Georgetown Law Center, August.

ICN (International Competition Network) (2002), 'Report prepared by the Advocacy Working Group,' International Competition Network, <www.international competitionnetwork.org>.

IMF (International Monetary Fund) (2004), *International Financial Statistics Online Database*. Available at <http://ifs.apdi.net/imf/ifsbrowser.aspx?branch =ROOT>.

IMF (2005), World Economic Outlook Online Database. Available at <http:// www.imf.org/external/pubs/ft/weo/2005/01/data/index.htm>.

Industrial Policy (1991), 'Industrial Policy Statement', Ministry of Industrial Development, Government of India, New Delhi, 24 July.

Institute of Economics (2000), *Competitiveness in the Textile and Garment Sector in Viet Nam*, Ha Noi.

Ishak, H.O. (1994), *Market Power, Vertical Linkages and Government Policy: The Fishery Industry in Peninsular Malaysia*, Kuala Lumpur: Oxford University Press.

Islam, M. (2001), 'Competition in the Thai liquor market,' in Thailand Development Research Institute (TDRI) (ed.), *Competition Survey Report*, paper prepared for the Canadian International Development Agency, Bangkok: TDRI.

ITU (International Telecommunication Union) (2002a), 'Multimedia Malaysia: An internet case study,' Geneva, March. Available at <http://www.itu.int/itu-doc/gs/promo/bdt/cast_int/80898.html>, accessed December 2004.

ITU (2002b), *ITU World Telecommunication Indicators*, Geneva.

Jenkins, R. (2002), 'Globalisation and employment in Viet Nam,' revised version of a paper presented at the DFID Workshop on Globalization and Poverty in Vietnam, Ha Noi, 23–24 September.

Jesudason, J. (1989), *Ethnicity and the Economy: The State, Chinese Business, and Multinationals in Malaysia*, Singapore: Oxford University Press.

Jiang, X. (1996), *Industrial Policy in the Transition Period: An Analysis of the Chinese Experience* [in Chinese], Shanghai: Shanghai People's Publisher.

Jiang, X. (2002a), 'Promoting competition and maintaining monopoly: Dual functions of Chinese industrial policies during economic transition,' *Washington University Global Studies Law Review, Symposium on APEC Competition Policy and Economic Development*, 1: 49–69. Available at <www.law.wustl.edu/Publications/WUGSLR/volume_1.html>.

Jiang, X. (2002b), 'FDI, market structure, and competition behavior of foreign firms' [in Chinese], *Economic Research Journal*, September: 31–8.

Jomo, K.S. (2003), *M Way: Mahathir's Economic Legacy*, Kuala Lumpur: Forum.

Jones, P.L., P. Tandon, and I. Vogelsang (1990), *Selling Public Enterprises: A Cost–Benefit Methodology*, Cambridge MA: MIT Press.

Jung, Y., and Q. Hao (2003), 'The new economic constitution in China: A third way for competition regime?' *Northwestern Journal of International Law and Business*, 24: 107–72.

Karapayah, T. (2002), 'Bank consolidation as a strategic response to the banking crisis: An analysis of the choice of anchor banks,' M.Ec. research paper, Kuala Lumpur: University of Malaya.

KDI (Korea Development Institute) (1999), 'Analysis of monopolistic and oligopolistic market structures' [in Korean], Seoul, December.

KFTC (Korea Fair Trade Commission) (2001a), *History of the Development of a Market-oriented Economy: A 20-Year History of the Korea Fair Trade Commission* [in Korean], Seoul.

KFTC (2001b), 'Investigation results on fees of 8 licensed professionals including lawyers and accountants,' press release, Seoul.

KFTC (2001c), 'The relationship between growth-centered industrial policy and competition policy.' Available at <http://ftc.go.kr/data/hwp/wto200103.htm>, accessed 13 July 2004.

KFTC (2003a), *White Paper on Fair Trade*, Seoul.

KFTC (2003b), 'Survey of market structure in 2001' [in Korean], Seoul, 9 December.

Kim, J.H. (1990), 'Korean industrial policy in the 1970s: The heavy and chemical industry drive,' *KDI Working Paper 9015*, Seoul: Korea Development Institute.

Kim, J.-K. (2003), 'Korea's industrial policy,' paper presented at the International Trade Law and Policy Program, Seoul: College of Law, Seoul National University.

Kokko, A. (2004), 'The internationalisation of small and medium enterprises in Viet Nam,' paper presented to the Asian Economic Forum Conference, Hong Kong, China, 14 March.

Kolasky, W., and A. Dick (2002), 'The merger guidelines and the integration of efficiencies into antitrust review of horizontal mergers,' paper presented at a celebration to mark the 20th Anniversary of the 1982 Merger Guidelines: The Contribution of the Merger Guidelines to the Evolution of Antitrust Doctrine, 10 June.

Kong, X. (2001), *Interpretation and Application of the Antimonopoly Laws in China* [in Chinese], Beijing: Publishing House of the People's Court.

Kumar, N. (1998), 'Liberalisation and changing patterns of foreign direct investments: Has India's relative attractiveness as a host of FDI Improved?' *Economic and Political Weekly*, 33(22): 1,321–9.

Kumar, N. (2000a), *Globalisation and the Quality of Foreign Direct Investment: An Empirical Analysis of the Role of Multinationals in Industrialisation, Export-expansion and Innovation in Host Countries*, London and New York: Routledge and UNU Press.

Kumar, N. (2000b), 'Mergers and acquisitions by MNEs: Patterns and implications,' *Economic and Political Weekly*, 5 August, pp. 2,851–8.

Kumar, N. (2003), 'Liberalisation, foreign direct investment flows and economic development: The Indian experience in the 1990s,' *Discussion Paper RIS-DP 65/2003*, New Delhi: Research and Information System for the Non-Aligned and Other Developing Countries.

Kumar, N. (2004), 'India,' in D.H. Brooks and H. Hill (eds), *Managing FDI in a Globalizing Economy: Asian Experiences*, London: Palgrave Macmillan, pp. 119–52.

Laffont, J. (1998), 'Competition, information, and development,' paper prepared for the Annual World Bank Conference on Development Economics, Washington DC, 20–21 April.

Laffont, J., and J. Tirole (2000), *Competition in Telecommunications*, Cambridge MA: MIT Press.

Lall, S. (1979), 'Multinationals and market structure in an open developing economy: The case of Malaysia,' *Westwirtschafthiches Archiv*, 115(2): 325–50.

Lall, S. (2004), 'Reinventing industrial strategy: The role of government policy in building industrial competitiveness,' *G-24 Discussion Paper Series*, Geneva: United Nations Conference on Trade and Development, April.

Lardy, N. (1998), *China's Unfinished Economic Revolution*, Washington DC: Brookings Institution.

Lau, L.J. (1996), 'The role of government in economic development: Some observations from the experience of China, Hong Kong, and Taiwan,' in M. Aoki, H. Kim, and M. Okuno-Fujiwara (eds), *The Role of Government in East Asian Economic Development*, Oxford: Clarendon Press, pp. 41–73.

Lee, C. (2002), 'Telecommunications reforms in Malaysia,' *Annals of Public and Cooperative Economics*, 73(4): 521–40.

Lee, C. (2004), 'Determinants of innovation in the Malaysian manufacturing sector: An econometric analysis at the firm level,' Kuala Lumpur: University of Malaya, mimeo.

Lee, H.-G. (1999), *History of the Formation of the Korean Chaebol* [in Korean], Seoul: Dae-Myeong Publishing Co.

Lee, K. (2002), 'Business groups as an organizational device for economic catch-up,' unpublished paper, Seoul: School of Economics, Seoul National University, 15 July.

Lee, K.U. (2003), 'Economic development and competition policy in Korea,' *Washington University Global Studies Law Review*, 67, Winter/Summer.

Lee, P., and T. Chan (2002), *Mega Competition among Chinese Enterprises*, Taipei: Xianye Business Management Consulting Ltd.

Lee, S.-B., J.-D. Kim, and N.-G. Choi (2004), 'Korea,' in D.H. Brooks and H. Hill (eds), *Managing FDI in a Globalizing Economy: Asian Experiences*, London: Palgrave Macmillan, pp. 153–88.

Leibenstein, H. (1966), 'Allocative efficiency versus "X-efficiency",' *American Economic Review*, 56(3): 392–415.

Leibenstein, H. (1978), 'X-inefficiency Xists: Reply to an Xorcist,' *American Economic Review*, 68(1): 203–11.

Li, C., and H. Ma (2002), 'Antimonopoly legislation should be delayed,' *Fazhi Ribao* [*Legal Daily*], 6 March.

Lin, P. (2001), 'Intellectual property right protection in China,' in Y.Y. Kueh and W. Zheng (eds), *Globalisation and the Sino–US Economic and Trade Relationship*, Beijing: China's Social Sciences Press, pp. 372–97.

Lin, P. (2004), 'Merger control in China,' Hong Kong, China: Lingnan University, mimeo.

Lin, P. (2005), 'The evolution of competition law in East Asia,' in E. Medalla (ed.), *Competition Policy in East Asia*, London: RoutledgeCurzon.

Litan, R.E., and C. Shapiro (2001), 'Antitrust policy during the Clinton administration,' *Working Paper CPC01-22*, Berkeley CA: Institute of Business and Economic Research, Competition Policy Center, University of California, July.

Lloyd, P.J. (2001), 'A competition policy for Malaysia,' *Malaysian Journal of Economic Studies*, 38(1&2): 81–90.

Long, N.C. (2003), 'Some issues on implementing decisions on enterprises' bankruptcy,' *Journal of Democracy and Law*, 3: 27–9.

Mahalonobis Committee Report (1964), *Mahalonobis Committee Report on Distribution and Levels of Income*, New Delhi: Government of India.

Majumder, S. (2004), 'Why selective FDI makes no sense,' *Hindu Business Line*, Chennai, 29 June.

Malaysian Department of Statistics (2000), *Malaysia Standard Industrial Classification 2000*, Kuala Lumpur.

MDTCA (Ministry of Domestic Trade and Consumer Affairs) (2003), 'Study of restrictive business practices and their effects on Malaysia's competitive dynamics,' Kuala Lumpur.

Mehta, R. (2003), *Indian Industrial Tariffs: Towards WTO Development Round Negotiations*, New Delhi: Research and Information System for the Non-Aligned and other Developing Countries.

Melo, A. (2001), 'Industrial policy in Latin America and the Caribbean at the turn of the century,' *Research Department Working Paper No. 459*, Inter-American Development Bank, August.

Mittal, D.P. (2003), *Taxmann's Competition Law*, New Delhi: Taxmann Allied Services (P) Ltd.

MOFTEC (Ministry of Foreign Trade and Economic Cooperation) (2003), *Catalog Guiding Foreign Investment in Industry*, Beijing.

Mokhtar, T., and S. Meyanathan (1990), 'Rice market intervention system in Malaysia: Scope, effects and the need for reform,' in *Issues and Challenges for National Development*, Kuala Lumpur: Faculty of Economics and Administration, University of Malaya.

Monopolies Inquiry Commission (1965), *Monopolies Inquiry Commission Report*, New Delhi: Government of India.

Moran, T.H. (2002), *Strategy and Tactics for the Doha Round: Capturing the Benefits of Foreign Direct Investment*, Manila: Asian Development Bank.

MRTP Commission (Monopolies and Restrictive Trade Practices Commission) (1975), *RRTA vs. Bata India Limited*, RTPE No. 3/1974–46 Company Cases 679, New Delhi.

MRTP Commission (1996), *Decision of the Monopolies and Restrictive Trade Practices Commission in Modern Food Industries Ltd. Case*, 1996 3 Comp LJ 154, New Delhi.

MRTP Commission (1997), *Alkali Manufacturers Association of India vs. American Natural Soda Ash Corporation (ANSAC) and Others*, 1997 (5) CTJ, 288, New Delhi.

Naidu, G., and C. Lee (1997), 'The transition to privatization: Malaysia,' in A. Mody (ed.), *Infrastructure Strategies in East Asia: The Untold Story*, Washington DC: World Bank.

Naughton, B. (1995), *The China Circle: Economics and Technology in the PRC, Taiwan and Hong Kong*, Washington DC: Brookings Institution Press.

Naughton, B. (1999), 'How much can regional integration do to unify China's market?' San Diego: University of California, mimeo.

NCSSH (National Center for Social Sciences and Humanities) (2001), *Viet Nam Human Development Report*, Ha Noi: Political Publishing House.

Neumann, P., and J. Guo (2003), 'The slow boat to antitrust law in China,' Shanghai: Faegre & Benson LLP. Available at <www.faegre.com/articles/article_print.aspx?id=1200>.

Nikomborirak, D. (2000a), 'Mergers and acquisitions in Thailand,' paper presented at a seminar on foreign direct investment in ASEAN organized by the ASEAN Secretariat and the UNDP, Kuala Lumpur, 9–10 October.

Nikomborirak, D. (2000b), 'Case discussion on the cable television monopoly in Thailand,' paper presented at the World Bank Course on Competition Law and Policy, Singapore, 14–21 May.

Nikomborirak, D. (2001), 'State-owned enterprises: The last bastion of monopoly and the greatest challenge to competition authority,' paper presented at the Fifth APEC/PFP Course on Competition Policy, Bangkok, 13–15 March.

Nikomborirak, D. (2002a), 'Shipping cartels: What can we do about them?' *TDRI Quarterly Review*, March 2004. Reprint of paper presented at the PAFTAD Seminar on Competition Policy, Manila, 16–18 September 2002.

Nikomborirak, D. (2002b), 'Thailand: Competition law and policy,' paper submitted to the World Bank Building a Constituency in Thailand project, Bangkok: Thailand Development Research Institute.

Nikomborirak, D. (2004a), 'An assessment of the investment regime: Country report: Thailand,' paper presented to the 'Investment: The Southern Agenda' conference organized by the International Institute for Sustainable Development, Bangkok, 21–22 May.

Nikomborirak, D. (2004b), 'Exemptions and exceptions: Implications for economic performance: The case of Thailand,' in P. Brusick, A.M. Alvarez, L. Cernat, and P. Holmes (eds), *Competition, Competitiveness and Development Lessons from Developing Countries*, Geneva: United Nations Conference on Trade and Development, pp. 91–109.

Nikomborirak, D. (2004c), 'Privatization: Does the public benefit?' [in Thai], in J. Pinthong (ed.), *Roo Than Thaksin Vol. 2* [Catching up with Thaksin Vol. 2], Bangkok: Ko Kid Duay Khon Printing House.

Nikomborirak, D., and K. Naewmalee (2004), 'Negotiations on improving anti-dumping rules' [in Thai], in *Progress Report 1: Project on Preparing Guidelines and Strategies for the Doha Round of WTO Negotiations*, report submitted to the Office of Industrial Promotion, Ministry of Industry, Bangkok.

Nikomborirak, D., S. Cheevasittiyanond, R. Chitmunchaitham, and W. Paiboonchit-aree (2002), *A Survey of Trade Practices in 12 Industries* [in Thai], Bangkok: Thailand Development Research Institute. Available at <www.info.tdri.or.th>.

Nolan, P. (2001), *China and the Global Economy: National Champions, Industrial Policy and the Big Business Revolution*, New York: Palgrave.

Noland, M., and H. Pack (2003), *Industrial Policy in an Era of Globalization: Lessons from Asia*, Washington DC: Institute of International Economics.

Nor Ghani, M.N., Z. Osman, A.Z. Abdullah, and C.Y. Jun (2000), 'Trends in the Malaysian industrial market structure,' *Jurnal Ekonomi Malaysia*, 34: 3–20.

OECD (Organisation for Economic Co-operation and Development) (2002), 'Competition policy in liner shipping: Final report,' *DSTI/DOT(2002)2*, Paris.

OECD (2003a), 'Issues for trade and competition in the global context: A synthesis,' *CCNM/GF/COMP/TR(2003)3*, Paris.

OECD (2003b), *Hard Core Cartels: Recent Progress and Challenges Ahead*, Paris.

OECD (2003c), 'The objectives of competition law and policy and the optimal design of a competition agency,' submission by the Republic of Ireland to the OECD Global Forum on Competition, *CCNM/GF/COMP/WD(2003)17*, Paris, 15 January.

OECD (2003d), 'Coverage of competition law: Illustrative examples of exclusions,' *Document CCNM/GF/COMP/TR(2003)17*, Paris.

Okimoto, D.I. (1990), *Between the MITI and the Market*, Stanford CA: Stanford University Press.

Packard, L.A.T. (2004), *Report on Diagnostic Auditing of State-owned Enterprises: Policy Implications*, Ha Noi.

Pangestu, M. (2002), 'Industrial policy and developing countries,' in B. Hoekman, A. Matoo, and P. English (eds), *Development, Trade and the WTO: A Handbook*, Washington DC: World Bank.

Park, S.-R., and J.K. Kwon (1995), 'Rapid economic growth with increasing returns to scale and little or no productivity growth,' *Review of Economics and Statistics*, 77(2): 332–51.

Perkins, D. (2001), 'Industrial policy and financial policy in China and Vietnam: A new model or a replay of the East Asian experience?' in J. Stiglitz and S. Yusuf (eds), *Rethinking the East Asian Miracle*, New York: Oxford University Press and World Bank.

Phillips Fox (2004), 'Competition law update.' Available at <http://www.usvtc. org/Documents/Vietnam%20Laws/CompetitionLawUpdateDec2004.pdf>, accessed January 2005.

Poapongsakorn, N. (2002), 'The new competition law in Thailand: Lessons for institution building,' *Review of Industrial Organization*, 2: 185–204.

Poapongsakorn, N., A. Siamwalla, M. Phongpraphaphan, P. Supying, and S. Mathrsurarak, (2001), 'The retail business in Thailand: Impact of large-scale multinational corporation retailers' [in Thai], Bangkok: Thailand Development Research Institute.

Porter, M. (1990), *The Competitive Advantage of Nations*, London: Macmillan Press.

Porter, M., M. Sakakibara, and H. Takeuchi (2000), *Can Japan Compete?* New York: Basic Books.

Posner, R. (1976), *Antitrust Law: An Economic Perspective*, Chicago IL: University of Chicago Press.

Posner, R. (1977), *Economic Analysis of Law*, Boston MA: Little, Brown & Co.

Posner, R. (2001a), 'Antitrust in the new economy,' *Antitrust Law Journal*, 68(3): 925–44.

Posner, R. (2001b), *Antitrust Law*, 2nd edition, Chicago: University of Chicago Press.

Primeaux, W. (1977), 'An assessment of X-efficiency gained through competition,' *Review of Economics and Statistics*, 59(1): 105–8.

Pugel, T. (1984), 'Japan's industrial policy: Instruments, trends, and effects,' *Journal of Comparative Economics*, 8(4), 420–35.

Ramachandram, V. (1993), 'Technology transfer, firm ownership, and investment in human capital,' *Review of Economics and Statistics*, 75(4): 664–70.

Rao, S.L. (1998), 'Towards a national competition policy for India,' *Economic and Political Weekly*, 33(9), Mumbai, 28 February–6 March.

Reserve Bank of India (various issues), *Reserve Bank of India Bulletin*, Mumbai.

Roberts, M.J., and J.R. Tybout (1997), 'The decision to export in Colombia: An empirical model of entry with sunk costs,' *American Economic Review*, 87(4): 545–64.

Rodriguez-Clare, A. (2004), 'Microeconomic interventions after the Washington Consensus,' Research Department, Inter-American Development Bank, August.

Rodrik, D. (1995), 'Trade and industrial policy reform,' in J. Behrman and T.N. Srinivasan (eds), *Handbook of Development Economics*, Vol. 3B, Amsterdam: Elsevier Science Publishers, pp. 2,925–82.

Rodrik, D. (2004), 'Industrial policy for the twenty-first century,' Cambridge MA: JFK School of Government, Harvard University, mimeo.

Rugayah, M. (1993), 'The market structure of selected Malaysian manufacturing industries,' *Economic Bulletin for Asia and Pacific*, 44(1): 17–29.

Sachar Report (1978), *Report of the High-powered Expert Committee on Companies and MRTP Act*, New Delhi: Ministry of Law, Justice and Company Affairs, Government of India, August.

Sachs, J., and A. Warner (1995), 'Economic reform and the process of global integration,' *Brookings Papers on Economic Activity*, 1(1): 1–118.

SAIC (State Administration for Industry and Commerce) (2002), *China Industry and Commerce Management Yearbook 2002*, Beijing.

SAIC (2004), *The Competition-restricting Behavior of Multinational Companies in China and Countermeasures*, Beijing.

Sakakibara, M., and M. Porter (2001), 'Competing at home to win abroad: Evidence from Japanese industry,' *Review of Economics and Statistics*, 83(3): 310–22.

SaKong, I. (1993), *Korea in the World Economy*, Washington DC: Institute for International Economics.

Sanekata, S., and K. Wilks (1996), 'The Fair Trade Commission and the enforcement of competition policy in Japan,' in G.B. Doern and K. Wilks (eds), *Comparative Competition Policy*, Oxford: Clarendon Press.

Scherer, F.M. (1992), 'Schumpeter and plausible capitalism,' *Journal of Economic Literature*, 30: 1,416–33.

Scherer, F.M., and D. Ross (1990), *Industrial Market Structure and Economic Performance*, Boston: Houghton Mifflin.

Schumpeter, J.A. (1942), *Capitalism, Socialism and Democracy*, New York: Harper and Row.

Sheng, H., and W. Zhang (2000), 'Antimonopoly in China: The case of telecommunications,' [in Chinese], in Ji Xiaonan (ed.), *On Antimonopoly Law in China*, Beijing: Publishing House of the People's Court, pp. 454–71.

Sieh, M.-L. (2003), 'Is WTO a boon or a bane for shoppers and retailers in Malaysia?' inaugural lecture, Kuala Lumpur: University of Malaya.

Singh, A. (1999), 'Competition policy, development and developing countries,' Geneva: United Nations, 26 November, mimeo.

Singh, A. (2002), 'Competition and competition policy in emerging markets: International and development dimensions,' *G-24 Discussion Paper Series No. 18*, Geneva: United Nations, 18 September.

Singh, A. (2003), 'Multilateral competition policy and economic development: A developing country perspective on the European Community proposals,' paper presented at the fifth session of the Intergovernmental Group of Experts on Competition Law and Policy, Geneva, 2–4 July.

Singh, G. (2001), 'Better urban transport,' *SPENA Newsletter*, 3(1): 1–3, June.

Smarzynska, B.K. (2002), 'Composition of foreign direct investment and protection of intellectual property rights: Evidence from transition economies,' *Policy Research Working Paper No. 2786*, Washington DC: World Bank.

Smith, H. (2000), *Industry Policy in Taiwan and Korea in the 1980s: Winning the Market*, Cheltenham: Edward Elgar.

SOE Reform Committee (2004), *Review of SOE Reform Program*, Ha Noi.

Somkiat, T., and T. Rattanarumitrsorn (2002), 'The global telecommunications market and the Thai market' [in Thai], report submitted to the Thai Research Foundation, Bangkok: Thailand Development Research Institute.

Sridhar, V. (2003), 'Cementing a monopoly,' *Frontline*, 20(17), 16–29 August. Available at <http://www.frontlineonnet.com/fl2017/stories/20030829004009700.htm>.

SRV (Socialist Republic of Viet Nam) (2002), *Comprehensive Poverty Reduction and Growth Strategy (CPRGS)*, Ha Noi, May.

STARS (Support for Trade Acceleration Project) (2004), *An Assessment of the Economic Impact of the United States–Viet Nam Bilateral Trade Agreement*, Ha Noi: National Political Publishing House.

State Statistics Bureau (various years), *China Statistical Yearbook*, Beijing: China Statistics Publishing House.

Steinfeld, E.S. (1998), *Forging Reform in China: The Fate of State-owned Industry*, Cambridge: Cambridge University Press.

Stigler, G. (1976), 'The Xistence of X-efficiency,' *American Economic Review*, 66(1): 213–16.

Subcommittee Report (2000), 'Report on the investigation of a complaint against the cable television service' [in Thai], report prepared for the Trade Competition Commission, Bangkok.

Sung, S.-M., and K.S. Shin (2001), *Twenty Years of Competition Policy* [in Korean], Seoul: Korea Development Institute.

Supanit, S. (2002), 'Thailand report on competition law and policy.' Available at <http://www2.jftc.go.jp/eacpf/02/thailand_r.pdf>.

Supreme Court (2002), *Haridas Exports vs. All India Float Glass Manufacturers Association*, 6 SCC 600, New Delhi.

Takasila, S., and R. Chitmunchaitham (2002), 'Monopolies and politics' [in Thai], unpublished paper in 'Building a Constituency for Competition Policy and Competition Law,' Bangkok: Thailand Development Research Institute.

TDRI (Thailand Development Research Institute) (2001a), 'Telecom concessions conversion' [in Thai], report submitted to the Ministry of Transport and Communications, Bangkok.

TDRI (2001b), 'Role of government in promoting multimodal transport' [in Thai], in TDRI (ed.), *A Study on Multimodal Transport Development in Thailand*, report submitted to the Ministry of Transport and Communications, Bangkok, Chapter 5.

TDRI (2004), 'An assessment of the Thai–US free trade agreement,' paper submitted to the American Chamber of Commerce and the Thai–US Business Council, Bangkok. Available at <www.tusbc.org>, accessed November 2004.

Technical Group (1999), *Trade Policy in Viet Nam*, Ha Noi: Institute of Economics.

Telser, L.G. (1987), *A Theory of Efficient Cooperation and Competition*, Cambridge: Cambridge University Press.

TFRC (Thai Farmers Research Centre) (2003), 'Special services for customers … A major overhaul of banking services' [in Thai], *Current Views*, 9(1,376).

Thanh, B.V. (2001), 'Unfair competition in Viet Nam: Issues and legal aspects,' PhD thesis, Ho Chi Minh: Ho Chi Minh City Law School.

Tilton, M. (1996), *Restrained Trade: Cartels in Japan's Basic Materials Industries*, Ithaca NY: Cornell University Press.

UNCTAD (United Nations Conference on Trade and Development) (1997), *World Investment Report 1997: Transnational Corporations, Market Structure and Competition Policy*, New York and Geneva: United Nations.

UNCTAD (2002), 'Closer multilateral cooperation on competition policy: The development dimension,' consolidated report on issues discussed during the Panama, Tunis, Hong Kong, and Odessa regional post-Doha seminars on competition policy held between 21 March and 26 April 2002, 15 May.

UNCTAD (2004), *Foreign Direct Investment Database*, Available at <http://stats. unctad.org/fdi/eng/ReportFolders/Rfview/explorerp.asp?IF_Mode=0&IF_ ViewShared=1&IF_Embedded=1>.

UNDP (United Nations Development Programme) (2003), *Human Development Report 2003. Millennium Development Goals: A Compact among Nations to End Human Poverty*, New York: Oxford University Press.

UNDP and CIEM (United Nations Development Programme and Central Institute for Economic Management) (2001), *Issues of Competition in Viet Nam*, Ha Noi: Statistical Publishing House.

US Department of Justice and Federal Trade Commission (1997), *Horizontal Merger Guidelines*, Washington DC, April.

US–China Business Council (2003), 'Foreign investment in China, 2003.' Available at <www.uschina.org/statistics/2003foreigninvestment.html>.

US–Viet Nam Trade Council (2004), *The U.S.–Vietnam Bilateral Trade Agreement: A Survey of U.S. Companies on Implementation Issues*, Ha Noi.

Vickers, J. (2003), 'Competition economics,' annual public lecture to the Royal Economic Society, London, 4 December.

Vinh, L.D. (2004), 'Making the competition environment healthy,' *Viet Nam Economic Times,* 51, March.

Vu, Q.H. (2001), 'Trade liberalisation and poverty,' background paper for the United Nations Development Programme's Pro-poor Macro Policy Project, mimeo.

Wade, R. (1990), *Governing the Market: Economic Theory and the Role of Government in East Asian Industrialization*, Princeton NJ: Princeton University Press.

Wang, X.Y. (2002), 'The prospect of antimonopoly legislation in China,' *Washington University Global Studies Law Review*, 1(1): 201–31.

Wang, X.Y. (2004), 'Issues surrounding the drafting of China's anti-monopoly law,' *Washington University Global Studies Law Review*, 3(2): 285–96.

Wang, X.Z. (2001), 'Competition law and policy in China,' paper presented to the OECD Global Forum on Competition, Paris: OECD.

Watson, A., C. Findlay, and Y. Du (1989), 'Who won the "wool war"? A case study of rural product marketing in China,' *China Quarterly*, 118: 213–41.

Weinstein, D. (1995), 'Evaluating administrative guidance and cartels in Japan (1957–1988),' *Journal of the Japanese and International Economics*, 9(2): 200–23.

Wells, R.J.G., and L.J. Fredericks (1979), 'Food policies in Malaysia with particular reference to self-sufficiency and poverty reduction goals,' *Kajian Ekonomi Malaysia*, 16(1&2): 44–71.

White, L. (2001), 'Network economics and public policy: A primer,' *Milken Institute Review,* Second Quarter: 38–46.

Winston, C. (1998), 'U.S. industry adjustment to economic deregulation,' *Journal of Economic Perspectives*, 12(3): 89–110.

World Bank (1993), *The East Asian Miracle: Economic Growth and Public Policy*, New York: Oxford University Press.

World Bank (2000a), 'Draft implementing regulations for sections 25, 26, 27 and 29 of the Trade Competition Act,' unpublished report prepared for the Office of Trade Competition, Ministry of Commerce, Bangkok.

World Bank (2000b), 'Draft guidelines for sections 25, 26, 27 and 29 of the Trade Competition Act,' unpublished report prepared for the Office of Trade Competition, Ministry of Commerce, Bangkok.

World Bank (2001), *Viet Nam Development Report 2002*, Ha Noi.

World Bank (2002), *Viet Nam Development Report 2003*, Ha Noi.

World Bank (2003a), *Innovative East Asia: Future of Growth*, Washington DC.

World Bank (2003b), *Viet Nam Development Report 2004*, Ha Noi.

World Bank and OECD (1997), *A Framework for the Design and Implementation of Competition Law and Policy*, Paris.

WTO (World Trade Organization) (1997), 'Special study on trade and competition policy,' in *Annual Report of the World Trade Organization*, Geneva, Chapter 4.

WTO (1998), 'Synthesis paper on the relationship of trade and competition policy to development and economic growth,' *WT/WGTCP/W/80*, 18 September.

WTO (2001), 'Communication from Korea to the Working Group on the Interaction between Trade and Competition Policy,' Geneva.

WTO (2003), *Trade Policy Review: Thailand*, Geneva.

Wu, J.C. (2002), 'The mineral industry of Thailand,' in *US Geological Survey Minerals Yearbook 2002*. Available at <http://minerals.usgs.gov/minerals/pubs/country/2002/thmyb02.pdf>.

Xie, W. (2001), *Catching Up and Price Wars: Analyses of the Color TV and Automotive Sectors in China* [in Chinese], Beijing: Economic Management Press.

Yamamura, K. (1988), 'Caveat emptor: The industrial policy of Japan,' in P. Krugman (ed.), *Strategic Trade Policy and the New International Economics*, Cambridge MA: MIT Press.

Yang, J. (2002), 'Market power in China: Manifestations, effects and legislation,' *Review of Industrial Organization*, 21: 167–83.

Yoo, J.-H. (1990), 'The industrial policy of the 1970s and the evolution of the manufacturing sector,' *KDI Working Paper 9017*, Seoul: Korea Development Institute.

Young, A. (2000), 'The razor's edge: Distortions and incremental reform in the People's Republic of China,' *Quarterly Journal of Economics*, 115: 1,091–135.

Yun, M., and S. Lee (2001), 'Impact of FDI on competition: The Korean experience,' *Working Paper 01-04*, Seoul: Korea Institute for International Economic Policy.

Zainal Aznam, Y., and H.E. Phang (1993a), 'Industrial market structure in Malaysia, 1979–1990,' *Working Paper No. 21*, Kuala Lumpur: Bank Negara Malaysia.

Zainal Aznam, Y., and H.E. Phang (1993b), 'Determinants of industrial market structure in Malaysia, 1979–1990,' *Working Paper No. 22*, Kuala Lumpur: Bank Negara Malaysia.

Author index

Subject index

travel agencies' pricing, 79
WTO accession, 90, 92, 98, 102n
Yangtze River Delta, 89
China Unicom, 82
Choon Ang, 188
closed economies/sectors, 32, 256
Coca-Cola, 150
Commonwealth of Independent States (CIS), 19–20
Compaq, 147
competition
    advocacy, 6–7, 29, 41, 76, 79
    see also China, People's Republic of; India; Korea, Republic of; Malaysia; Thailand; Viet Nam
competition law, 1–26, 34–5, 339–49
    definition/description, 7
    and development, 340–3
    enforcement, 9–23, 24, 30–1, 32, 34–5, 45, 47–70, 76–8, 346–9
        effect on economic perform-ance, 19–23
    exemptions, 8
    and industrial policy, 64–7
    instruments, 6–8
    objectives, 4–6, 13, 18, 25n
    penalties, 75, 81–2
    see also China, People's Republic of; India; Korea, Republic of; Malaysia; Thailand; Viet Nam
competition policy
    efficiency, 2–4, 5, 12
    and government policy interface, 129–56
    instruments, 2, 6–8
    objectives, 2, 4–6, 11
    overview, xiii–xiv
    principal goal, 64–5
    see also China, People's Republic of; India; Korea, Republic of; Malaysia; Thailand; Viet Nam
concentration ratios, 54, 58, 62, 86, 88–9, 146–52, 176–8, 191, 320–1, 328–9n, 334–5

consumer welfare, 4, 10, 14, 17, 29–30, 65, 66, 168, 173, 194, 195n, 227, 258, 342
Container Hauliers Association of Malaysia (CHAM), 218–19, 233n
Coty Inc., 95
Courier, 262
cross–border trade, 27, 128, 285, 286–8
currencies, x

D

Dacom, 183, 184
Daephan Paper Co. Ltd., 191
DBS Thai Danu Bank, 249, 251
DELL, 147
Deng Xiaoping, 90
DHL, 262
domestic markets, 13–14, 20, 29–31, 34, 39, 40, 44–5, 52, 54, 63–4, 68, 70, 80, 90, 93–5, 103n, 117, 163, 175, 180, 186, 189, 191, 193, 211–12, 224, 261–2, 285, 287, 314, 317, 319
Dreamline, 182, 184

E

Eastern Europe, 343
Eastman Kodak, 96
economic
    growth, 2, 10, 14, 25n, 38, 45, 50, 53–4, 56, 59, 61, 157, 181, 198
    performance, 1, 6, 9–24, 25n, 30–1, 51, 53, 56, 65, 215
    reform, 83–4
    theory, xiii, 2, 24, 29, 178–80, 186
        structure–conduct–performance hypothesis, 215–16
    transition, 42–3
    see also China, People's Republic of; India; Korea, Republic of; Malaysia; Thailand; Viet Nam
economic crisis
    see financial crisis, Asian